Other titles in this
series include:

Globalization: A Reader for Writers
Maria Jerskey
(ISBN: 9780199947522)

Language: A Reader for Writers
Gita DasBender
(ISBN: 9780199947485)

Sustainability: A Reader for Writers
Carl Herndl
(ISBN: 9780199947508)

Identity: A Reader for Writers
John Scenters-Zapico
(ISBN: 9780199947461)

culture

A READER *for* WRITERS

John Mauk
Miami University of Ohio

New York   Oxford
Oxford University Press

Oxford University Press publishes works that further Oxford University's
objective of excellence in research, scholarship, and education.

Oxford   New York

Auckland   Cape Town   Dar es Salaam   Hong Kong   Karachi
Kuala Lumpur   Madrid   Melbourne   Mexico City   Nairobi
New Delhi   Shanghai   Taipei   Toronto

With offices in

Argentina   Austria   Brazil   Chile   Czech Republic   France   Greece
Guatemala   Hungary   Italy   Japan   Poland   Portugal   Singapore
South Korea   Switzerland   Thailand   Turkey   Ukraine   Vietnam

Published by Oxford University Press.
198 Madison Avenue, New York, New York 10016
http://www.oup.com

Oxford is a registered trademark of Oxford University Press

Library of Congress Cataloging-in-Publication Data
Mauk, John.
    Culture : a reader for writers / John Mauk, Northwestern Michigan College.
        pages cm
    Includes bibliographical references and index.
    ISBN 978-0-19-994722-5 (pbk.)
        1. College readers. 2. English language--Rhetoric--Handbooks, manuals, etc.
3. English language--Grammar--Handbooks, manuals, etc. 4. Report writing--
    Handbooks, manuals, etc. 5. Culture in literature. I. Title.
    PE1417.M45655   2014
    808'.0427--dc23
                                                                2013037247

Printing number: 9 8 7
Printed in the United States of America
on acid-free paper

brief table of contents

contents

"For all the elegance implied with 'fine,' the word can also reek of 'She thinks she's all that.'"

"The notion that policies should focus almost exclusively on preventing the next attack has also masked an ideological battle within homeland-security policy circles between 'never again' and its antithesis, commonly referred to as 'shit happens' . . ."

"Ultimately, there's nothing wrong with acronyms. They may be a quintessentially modern annoyance, fooling us into thinking we have a greater grip on life's complexities than we really do."

"Art and religion both struggle toward what can't be said. They use symbols and they stretch their words as far into wordlessness as possible."

"One of the most exciting developments that technological advances have facilitated is the breaking down of the hierarchy of ideas, allowing great ideas to bubble to the surface from virtually anywhere."

"Is this new wave of Internet interaction, social media, ironically making us more apart, lonely, or unproductive? There's been a fair amount of research on these questions and the results are often surprising and contradictory."

"Anonymity affords virtual partners certain protections and perks, but it also makes it exceedingly easy to lie."

"The first thing I didn't write about quitting Facebook was a status update to my friends saying, I'm quitting Facebook."

Photo Gallery I

"On Twitter, the home of microbloggers, the octothorpe has a new career, reborn as the 'hashtag.'"

"What we are witnessing is a change in the attention that mediates and gives rise to friendship."

"Most of the biosphere cannot see the infosphere; it is invisible, a parallel universe humming with ghostly inhabitants. But they are not ghosts to us—not anymore."

"As much as I am worried about my two young boys being bombarded by superhero-slacker images, I am even more worried about the jobs that might not be available to them when they hit adulthood."

"A hundred years ago, you wouldn't have been in this position, shopping for a bathing suit, because there was no such thing."

"As a nation we have only begun to reconsider language that respects an individual's humanity when speaking about the lives of people in immigrant communities."

"It is becoming ever more clear to educators that students learn best when they engage with a wide spectrum of individuals, both like and unlike themselves—that is, if they are part of a campus community that resembles our diverse society and multicultural world."

"In the most religiously diverse nation in human history and the most religiously devout nation in the West at a time of global religious conflict, how people from different faith backgrounds get along and what they do together is a crucial question."

"Perhaps the post-9/11 atmosphere in the West, which led to intense criticism of Islam and its views of women, spurred Muslim Americans into corrective action."

"Today the illusion of community is everywhere, but the late night show is the one place where it does not unfurl in a sidebar of piecemeal commentary but in the midst of the action, in a way that allows the host to participate and respond."

"Sure, *The Five-Year Engagement* may have been a flop, but that doesn't mean it didn't imperil thousands of Americans with unrealistic romantic expectations, and, further, continue a long tradition of movies cementing bad habits and relationship turmoil."

"One of the most unfortunate (and surprising) side-effects of the triumph of computer-generated animation was the death of the female protagonist in children's movies."

"For all its faults, *Brave* is shockingly radical for a mainstream movie. As with *Wall-E* before it, *Brave* is an example of what happens when Pixar gets political."

"Hip hop's rise has been, at root, a straightforward process of free-market enterprise: an excellent product has been pushed with great skill and new markets opened up with real dynamism and flair."

7   Nature: How We Share the Planet   251

"If you appreciate a good campfire—better yet, if you appreciate the difference between a good campfire and a great campfire—you're probably a connoisseur of wood and a fastidious builder of woodpiles."

"Wildness tells us that everything is hitched to everything else. But the extinction crisis is rapidly uncoupling myriad vital relationships and fraying the fabric of life on earth."

"This is the bedbug paradox. For most individuals their bites have only nuisance value. Yet they arouse much more disgust than many other insects whose bites transmit potentially lethal infections."

"Even as progressive men renounce the traditional notion of subordinated femininity, many still harbor conflicted notions about manhood. They want to feel individually reckless, but not socially irresponsible."

"Although we have seen houseflies for millennia, complained about them in a thousand languages using a hundred thousand adjectives, in some ways they are still among the least known guests at the table."

"As beautiful as it is bountiful and awe-inspiring, life proceeds via the taking of life, and is therefore no less likely to be ugly, amoral, and awful. And we are stuck in it, up to our necks . . . and more."

"Any proposal to fix environmental problems by turning away from technology risks worsening them, by attempting to deny the ongoing coevolution of humans and nature."

8   Politics: How We Govern   299

"The Occupy movement is not unlikely to last forever, nor would it be a good thing if it did. It could be forgotten like so many movements of the past. But it instead it could be remembered as the progenitor of the 99 Percent Movement."

"Why has the public for so long tolerated Wall Street's reckless abuses of power and accepted the resulting devastation? The answer lies in a cultural trance induced by deceptive language and misleading indicators backed by flawed economic theory and accounting sleight-of-hand."

"We gave billions to the banks (including foreign-owned banks), which they used to increase their own bonuses. What if that money went into infrastructure development, hiring people to build bridges, sewer systems, roads?"

"No one gets through life unscathed, and in the end we die. If we truly accept death as part of life, with its attendant break-downs of the body and the many sorts of mischance that befall us along the way, then we do well to offer one another solidarity and succor."

"If you are talking about the death penalty now, you are talking about closing the barn door after the mare is a mile down the road, and if you are talking about gun control, you're bringing a knife to a gun fight."

"The real challenges at hand are about violent crime, huge taxpayer burdens, the rule of law, and ensuring that our southern border does not become an open door for radical terrorists."

"The United States upholds the strictest of immigration policies in order to keep the country safe, yet it allows thousands of relatively unchecked, unfiltered, potentially dangerous people into the country each year with the childlike belief that it creates diversity."

9   War: How We Fight   339

"When the oil spill in Michigan began, I heard about a memorial service for Paul Miller, a 22-year-old Marine corporal from the nearby village of Lake Ann, who was killed on July 19 in Afghanistan."

"In many ways our ethical stability is preserved by our sense of community, security, and home. War takes all of those elements away, immerses the military in danger, and makes its members vulnerable to an involuntary loss of self-control."

"When the occupiers ran out of the buildings where they had been sheltering to grab the supplies, agents opened fire on them. The first member of the occupation to die, a Cherokee, was shot by a bullet that flew through the wall of a church."

"Forget full-scale invasions and large-footprint occupations on the Eurasian mainland; instead, think: special operations forces working on their own but also training or fighting beside allied militaries (if not outright proxy armies) in hot spots around the world."

Photo Gallery II

"I stayed up late on the night of May 1 to hear President Obama's stunning announcement: A special-forces mission, which could have gone humiliatingly wrong, had instead succeeded in killing Osama bin Laden, the man behind the worst terrorist attack on American soil."

"The allure of combat is a trap, a ploy, an old, dirty game of deception in which the powerful, who do not go to war, promise a mirage to those who do."

"A short time ago, just a small band of brave witches and wizards at Hogwarts School stood between the dark forces and their ascension to power. Now their evil leader is dead, his armies are scattered, and the wizarding world can begin to recover from the terror they inflicted."

rhetorical contents

argument (evaluation)

causal analysis

definition and classification

profile and ethnography

rhetorical analysis

reflection and revelation

preface

If we look to the past, we can see the remnants of other cultures. We can look at an ancient Roman statue and understand something about the people and their civilization. We can read Shakespeare's *Romeo and Juliet* and understand something about sixteenth-century England. Or we can watch a movie such as *Gone with the Wind* or *The Wizard of Oz* and understand something of twentieth-century America. But we don't necessarily have to study the past to understand culture. We can feel it churning around and within us. We can hear it clamoring on YouTube and spilling out of cable television. We can see it dramatized in the video games, advertisements, literature, and reflexes of everyday life.

In other words, culture is not dead. It is happening right now. It is an action—an ongoing process through which things become normal. Sometimes, that process is smooth. People accept a tool or practice into their lives without much wrangling or suspicion. They wake up, for instance, to their neighbors selling off horses for a new mode of transportation or getting rid of their landlines for cell phones. Other times, the process is noisy and grating. People complain, rally, and even protest against change. Defenders of the old bring out their cultural shields. Champions of the new come with megaphones, essays, and t-shirts. They write, sing, and spray paint the unfamiliar into existence. The more they say, the more they create familiarity. And regardless of anyone's particular likes or dislikes, the entire process *is* culture.

Culture: A Reader for Writers presents a broad spectrum of writers who are dealing with change, who are contesting and grappling with the trends around them. Some defend the status quo, some wonder what to make of new gadgets, some embrace uncertainty, and others celebrate whatever feels new and different. Each chapter takes on a particularly urgent subject of contemporary conversation: work, consumerism, language, social media, identity, entertainment, nature, politics, and war. The articles within each chapter embody a range of responses—from wonder to fear, from hope to grave concern. They also demonstrate different writing styles, political leanings, spelling, and usage conventions from publications outside of the United States. In other words, the chapters themselves show culture at work. They show how many people, voices, interests, and nationalities convene around, but speak differently about, shared issues. And the photo galleries, nestled between chapters, give shape and imagery to the subjects.

Culture: A Reader for Writers is part of a series of brief single-topic readers from Oxford University Press designed for today's college writing courses. Each reader in this series approaches a topic of contemporary conversation from multiple perspectives:

- **Timely** Most selections were originally published in 2010 or later.
- **Global** Sources and voices from around the world are included.
- **Diverse** Selections come from a range of nontraditional and alternate print and online media, as well as representative mainstream sources.

In addition to the rich array of perspectives on topical (even urgent) issues addressed in each reader, each volume features an abundance of different genres and styles. Useful but nonintrusive pedagogy includes:

- **Chapter introductions** that provide a brief overview of the chapter's theme and a sense of how the chapter's selections relate both to the overarching theme and to each other.
- **Headnotes** introduce each reading by providing concise information about its original publication.
- **"Analyze" and "Explore" questions** after each reading scaffold and support student reading for comprehension as well as rhetorical considerations, providing prompts for reflection, classroom discussion, and brief writing assignments.
- **"Forging Connections" and "Looking Further" prompts** after each chapter encourage critical thinking by asking students to compare perspectives and strategies among readings both within the chapter and with readings in other chapters, suggesting writing assignments

(many of which are multimodal) that engage students with larger conversations in the academy, the community, and the media.

- **An appendix on "Researching and Writing About Culture"** guides student inquiry and research in a digital environment. Co-authored by a research librarian and a writing program director, this appendix provides real-world, transferable strategies for locating, assessing, synthesizing, and citing sources in support of an argument.

about the author

John Mauk has a PhD in rhetoric from Bowling Green State University and a master's degree in language and literature from the University of Toledo. He has taught first-year college courses for fifteen years and has published several successful writing guides. He is a practicing and published fiction writer as well as an avid student of philosophy. He currently teaches at Miami University of Ohio. (For more information, please see www.johnmauk.com)

acknowledgments

A reader is nothing without a list of committed writers. I salute the contributors in these chapters—people far and wide, from a range of intellectual places and academic disciplines. Thank you for giving voice to a living culture. I am especially humbled by and grateful for my writerly comrades—Fleda Brown, Steven Krause, and Patricia Ann McNair—who wrote for this project, and to my recent students—Sharon Angel, Douglas LaForest, Kat Langdale, and Jason Storms—whose work appears in these chapters. Thanks also to Benjamin Busch for sharing his vibrant photography and adding an important dimension to this project. And thanks much to the savvy team at Oxford. I assumed that working with you would be a distinct pleasure, but I was surprised, amazed really, at each turn. Specifically, thank you to Meg Botteon for so much heavy lifting throughout this project—from inception to production—and to my longtime friend Carrie Brandon for her vision and prowess. Thanks also to Talia Benamy for assisting and facilitating the whole process. Finally and always, thanks to Karen for helping with this and everything else.

And while everyone above made the project speak, look, and work in various ways, our reviewers helped us to stay on the right track. Thanks to the following important teachers and scholars: Eric Abbey, Oakland Community College; Mathew J. Bartkowiak, University of Wisconsin–Marshfield/Wood County; Carlton Clark, Collin College; Joy Clark, Yakima Valley Community College; Jacqueline DiChiara, Bergen Community College; Sharynn Owen Etheridge, Claflin University; Cheryl Finley, University of California–Merced; Christopher Gerben, Stanford University; Nora Gold, Baruch College; Malvina King, Hillsborough Community College.

1 Work: What We Do

There are countless songs, television shows, novels, poems, and films dedicated to work—or more specifically to how much people hate their jobs. If there's one prevailing statement about Americans and work, it's that we desperately need more and that we hate it when it finally comes along. In short, Americans have a tangled relationship with work. The typical professional, across many fields, has among the world's smallest allotted vacation time, the least amount of sick leave, and the longest work week. We yearn to get free for a weekend and then take the overtime if it's available. But we also resist some of the worst jobs—those that have been shipped to countries with fewer labor, safety, and exploitation laws. We're gluttons for hard work, but for a particular kind.

Despite the conditions, there is another prevailing truth: The nature of work is changing. In his article "Of Apprentices and Interns," Ross Perlin says that work is "a shifting, uneven landscape, fought over and redefined in every culture and in every age." Whatever we mean by "a good job" will likely change as new tools replace old ones, as another generation moves into full-time employment, and as the economy accommodates global interconnectivity. When the markets shift, when a company gets downsized, when consumption in Europe or Asia slows even slightly, millions of jobs are affected. They get temporarily frozen, redefined, or obliterated. In this sense, work actually represents culture. It shows the perpetual state of movement—the collisions created by competing values, economic tremors, and personal hopes.

The readings in this chapter all focus on work: how to get a job, how to succeed in a particular work environment, how to make sense of employment trends, and even how to manage the hollow weirdness of white-collar professionalism. Amy Reiter and Julie Hanus deal with the complex politics of office life. Elizabeth Dwoskin and Mike Rose explore the issue of socioeconomic class that is often eclipsed by other, more visible, issues. Patricia Ann McNair dramatizes a unique class of workers—those fortunate enough to carry their jobs in their minds and through the streets of foreign cities. Finally, Christian Williams and Jason Storms connect work to broader economic worries.

Amy Reiter
Why Being a Jerk at Work Pays

Amy Reiter writes about pop culture and women's issues for such publications as *The Daily Beast*, *Glamour*, the *Huffington Post*, the *Los Angeles Times*, the *New York Times*, *Salon*, and the *Washington Post*. In the following *Daily Beast* article, Reiter considers the payoff of certain workplace behaviors.

For years, I tried to be a very nice person at work—a dream colleague, a team player, the sort of woman who gave women a good name in the workplace. I thanked people. I apologized. I expressed concern. I took responsibility for making things right, even when I wasn't the one who had made them go wrong.

Then one day I looked up from my under-challenging, midlevel job and noticed that my boss, who was generally regarded as kind of a jerk, but a smart and talented one, never, ever thanked people. He never apologized. And he didn't appear to give a rip about what was going on in the lives of anyone around him. He never took responsibility when things went wrong, preferring instead to label someone else the culprit and chew them out.

It suddenly occurred to me: he had gained responsibility, power and a big, cushy salary not despite the fact that he was a jerk, but because of it. Maybe no one liked him, but everyone respected him. Whereas I, arguably no less competent, but assuredly a whole lot more pleasant and agreeable, was drifting along in a rudderless career—pal to all, boss to none.

I'm not alone in my thinking: A recent study examining the relationship between agreeableness, income, and gender, published in *Journal of Personality and Social Psychology,* found that the workplace does tend to reward disagreeable behavior. Disagreeable men tend to earn more than agreeable men, and disagreeable women, though they earn less than both nice and not-nice guys, earn more than agreeable women, researchers found.

The study, entitled "Do Nice Guys—and Gals—Really Finish Last?"   5 (conducted by Timothy A. Judge of the University of Notre Dame's Mendoza College of Business, Beth A. Livingston of Cornell University's School of Industrial and Labor Relations, and Charlice Hurst of University of Western Ontario's Richard Ivey School of Business), provided an analysis of the data from three separate surveys conducted over the past two decades including responses from thousands of workers of various ages, salary levels, and professions. The authors also conducted a survey of their own, asking 460 business students to weigh in on hypothetical personnel decisions.

"'Niceness'—in the form of the trait of agreeableness—does not appear to pay," the authors concluded.

Although I could never pull off my boss's level of rudeness (nor would I have wanted to), I nevertheless decided to shed just a bit of my workaday warmth by making two seemingly small changes: to stop saying "thank you" or "I'm sorry." Straightaway. Cold turkey. Just to see what would happen.

I started with e-mail, where I had often signed off with a chipper "thanks!" or apologized for inconveniencing someone with a request or for taking a while to reply. I was no longer sorry it took so long to get back to anyone. Neither did I feel either regretful about asking them to do something or grateful to them in advance for doing it.

I painstakingly reread every message to make sure neither polite phrase had sneaked through. And after I'd carefully excised each self-effacing slip, I hit send with a new set to my jaw, a hard glimmer in my eyes.

10   The effect was immediate: Colleagues began to treat me with more respect. Celebrity publicists—a notably power-aware lot whom I often contacted in my job—were more responsive. Even interns (those pecking-order experts) seemed to regard me with a new sort of awe.

> "The effect was immediate: Colleagues began to treat me with more respect."

Emboldened, I sought to eliminate "sorry" and "thank you" from my spoken workplace interactions as well, sometimes literally covering my mouth (passing it off as a "thoughtful" pose) during meetings to keep from uttering them. I found myself smiling less and bargaining harder.

My new confidence gave me the inner wherewithal to launch a freelance business (I'm now my own boss). My career—and my income—lurched upward.

At first, my new sense of power and its rewards felt thrilling. I learned to bargain firmly and unapologetically and was paid fairly—and it seemed to me that, when people paid more for my work, they tended to value it (and me) more highly, further increasing my own sense of worth. But there were also times I pushed too hard and lost assignments. And I began to worry about my reputation. Had my new self-assurance made me overly demanding? Were people starting to think of me as a diva?

My concerns may have been valid. The recent study also found that the rewards of disagreeableness for women are limited—far more so than for men. What's more, if women push their disagreeable behavior in the workplace too far, they risk a major backlash.

15   "People attribute disagreeable—i.e., self-interested, tough, argumentative—behavior in men and women differently," study coauthor Judge told me. "If a man is disagreeable, he is thought to be tough and leader-like. If a woman is disagreeable, the 'b-word' is applied to her."

I had found myself bumping against these very boundaries: placing a higher value on respect and remuneration than likeability, I had advanced, but I feared I was becoming unlikable. Had I become, as Judge politely put it, a "b-word"?

This past summer, I had a breakthrough. It happened when I wrote an essay that was included in a collection of works by "mommy bloggers." An e-mail group was formed so that those of us who were involved could introduce ourselves to each other. Every single person, in their initial e-mails, included a sort of apology ("I've never been included in something like this before!") and an expression of thanks ("I'm so honored").

Reading through the e-mail chain, I saw these expressions not as displays of powerlessness, but of kindness, openheartedness and candor, a desire for connection and support. We were thankful. We were sorry. We were also in it together. I added my own expressions of modesty and gratitude to the highly agreeable chain, and felt the camaraderie surround me like a warm blanket.

In the intervening months, I've sought to find a middle ground. I will now allow the occasional "thank you" to pass, and I will apologize if I feel it is justified, though I still try not to do either reflexively.

That's the sort of balanced approach Judge, the study coauthor, recommends. "I tell women there is a difference between disagreeing and being disagreeable," he says. "Be firm, logical, assertive, and persistent—but do not ever show hostility, anger, or other negative emotions."

We women are held to different standards of agreeability than men, Judge cautions, adding, "This of course is not fair—but fair does not always describe the world in which we live."

Sorry to break the news. And thanks!

Analyze

1. What is the difference between self-assured and demanding behavior? Why is the distinction important to Reiter's argument?
2. Given Reiter's descriptions of coworkers, how might she define a jerk? What behaviors make someone a jerk?
3. In your own words, describe Reiter's middle ground in communication—and how that constitutes a "breakthrough."
4. When describing a coworker, Reiter explains, "It suddenly occurred to me: he had gained responsibility, power and a big, cushy salary not despite the fact that he was a jerk, but because of it." Why is this statement especially important to her argument about work behavior and success?
5. What does Reiter's argument say about American culture?

Explore

1. In your experience, do nice people finish last? Why or why not?
2. Why do you think niceness might garner less respect than assertiveness?
3. Do you value likability over respect—or vice versa? What specific daily behaviors get you liked? What behaviors garner respect?
4. In your experience, are women "held to different standards of agreeability than men"? Give specific examples to support your answer.
5. Explain how Reiter's thinking about women might relate to Elizabeth Dwoskin's thoughts on "dirty" jobs.

Elizabeth Dwoskin
Why Americans Won't Do Dirty Jobs

A staff writer for *Bloomberg Businessweek*, Elizabeth Dwoskin writes on a range of issues related to politics, immigration, education, and health care. In the following article, Dwoskin examines the problems inherent in the immigrant labor subculture of the United States.

Skinning, gutting, and cutting up catfish is not easy or pleasant work. No one knows this better than Randy Rhodes, president of Harvest Select, which has a processing plant in impoverished Uniontown, Ala. For years, Rhodes has had trouble finding Americans willing to grab a knife and stand 10 or more hours a day in a cold, wet room for minimum wage and skimpy benefits.

Most of his employees are Guatemalan. Or they were, until Alabama enacted an immigration law in September that requires police to question people they suspect might be in the U.S. illegally and punish businesses that hire them. The law, known as HB56, is intended to scare off undocumented workers, and in that regard it's been a success. It's also driven away legal immigrants who feared being harassed.

Rhodes arrived at work on Sept. 29, the day the law went into effect, to discover many of his employees missing. Panicked, he drove an hour and a half north to Tuscaloosa, where many of the immigrants who worked for him lived. Rhodes, who doesn't speak Spanish, struggled to get across how much he needed them. He urged his workers to come back. Only a handful did. "We couldn't explain to them that some of the things they were scared of weren't going to happen," Rhodes says. "I wanted them to see that I was their friend, and that we were trying to do the right thing."

His ex-employees joined an exodus of thousands of immigrant field hands, hotel housekeepers, dishwashers, chicken plant employees, and construction workers who have fled Alabama for other states. Like Rhodes, many employers who lost workers followed federal requirements—some even used the E-Verify system—and only found out their workers were illegal when they disappeared.

In their wake are thousands of vacant positions and hundreds of angry   5 business owners staring at unpicked tomatoes, uncleaned fish, and unmade beds. "Somebody has to figure this out. The immigrants aren't coming back to Alabama—they're gone," Rhodes says. "I have 158 jobs, and I need to give them to somebody."

There's no shortage of people he could give those jobs to. In Alabama, some 211,000 people are out of work. In rural Perry County, where Harvest Select is located, the unemployment rate is 18.2 percent, twice the national average. One of the big selling points of the immigration law was that it would free up jobs that Republican Governor Robert Bentley said immigrants had stolen from recession-battered Americans. Yet native Alabamians have not come running to fill these newly liberated positions. Many employers think the law is ludicrous and fought to stop it. Immigrants aren't stealing anything from anyone, they say. Businesses turned to foreign labor only because they couldn't find enough Americans to take the work they were offering.

At a moment when the country is relentlessly focused on unemployment, there are still jobs that often go unfilled. These are difficult, dirty, exhausting jobs that, for previous generations, were the first rickety step on the ladder to prosperity. They still are—just not for Americans.

For decades many of Alabama's industries have benefited from a compliant foreign workforce and a state government that largely looked the other way on wages, working conditions, and immigration status. With so many foreign workers now effectively banished from the work pool and jobs sitting empty, businesses must contend with American workers who have higher expectations for themselves and their employers—even in a terrible economy where work is hard to find. "I don't consider this a labor shortage," says Tom Surtees, Alabama's director of industrial relations, himself the possessor of a job few would want: calming business owners who have seen their employees vanish. "We're transitioning from a business model. Whether an employer in agriculture used migrant workers, or whether it's another industry that used illegal immigrants, they had a business model and that business model is going to have to change."

On a sunny October afternoon, Juan Castro leans over the back of a pickup truck parked in the middle of a field at Ellen Jenkins's farm in northern Alabama. He sorts tomatoes rapidly into buckets by color and ripeness. Behind him his crew—his father, his cousin, and some friends—move expertly through the rows of plants that stretch out for acres in all directions, barely looking up as they pull the last tomatoes of the season off the tangled vines and place them in baskets. Since heading into the fields at 7 a.m., they haven't stopped for more than the few seconds it takes to swig some water. They'll work until 6 p.m., earning $2 for each 25-pound basket they fill. The men figure they'll take home around $60 apiece.

10   Castro, 34, says he crossed the border on foot illegally 19 years ago and has three American-born children. He describes the mood in the fields since the law passed as tense and fearful. Gesturing around him, Castro says that not long ago the fields were filled with Hispanic laborers. Now he and his crew are the only ones left. "Many of our friends left us or got deported," he says. "The only reason that we can stand it is for our children."

He wipes sweat from beneath his fluorescent orange baseball cap, given to him by a timber company in Mississippi, where he works part of the year cutting pine. Castro says picking tomatoes in the Alabama heat isn't easy, but he counts himself lucky. He has never passed out on the job, as many others have, though he does have a chronic pinched nerve in his neck from bending over for hours on end. The experiment taking place in Alabama makes no sense to him. Why try to make Americans do this work when they clearly don't want it? "They come one day, and don't show up the next," Castro says.

It's a common complaint in this part of Alabama. A few miles down the road, Chad Smith and a few other farmers sit on chairs outside J&J Farms, venting about their changed fortunes. Smith, 22, says his 85 acres of tomatoes are only partly picked because 30 of the 35 migrant workers who had been with him for years left when the law went into effect. The state's efforts to help him and other farmers attract Americans are a joke, as far as he is concerned. "Oh, I tried to hire them," Smith says. "I put a radio ad out—out of Birmingham. About 15 to 20 people showed up, and most of them quit. They couldn't work fast enough to make the money they thought they could make, so they just quit."

Joey Bearden, who owns a 30-acre farm nearby, waits for his turn to speak. "The governor stepped in and started this bill because he wants to put people back to work—they're not coming!" says Bearden. "I've been farming 25 years, and I can count on my hand the number of Americans that stuck."

It's a hard-to-resist syllogism: Dirty jobs are available; Americans won't fill them; thus, Americans are too soft for dirty jobs. Why else would so many unemployed people turn down the opportunity to work during a recession? Of course, there's an equally compelling obverse. Why should farmers and plant owners expect people to take a back-breaking seasonal job with low pay and no benefits just because they happen to be offering it? If no one wants an available job—especially in extreme times—maybe the fault doesn't rest entirely with the people turning it down. Maybe the market is inefficient.

Tom Surtees is tired of hearing employers grouse about their lazy countrymen. "Don't tell me an Alabamian can't work out in the field picking produce because it's hot and labor intensive," he says. "Go into a steel mill. Go into a foundry. Go into numerous other occupations and tell them Alabamians don't like this work because it's hot and it requires manual labor." The difference being, jobs in Alabama's foundries and steel mills pay better wages—with benefits. "If you're trying to justify paying someone below whatever an appropriate wage level is so you can bring your product, I don't think that's a valid argument," Surtees says.

In the weeks since the immigration law took hold, several hundred Americans have answered farmers' ads for tomato pickers. A field over from where Juan Castro and his friends muse about the sorry state of the U.S. workforce, 34-year-old Jesse Durr stands among the vines. An aspiring rapper from inner-city Birmingham, he wears big jeans and a do-rag to shield his head from the sun. He had lost his job prepping food at Applebee's, and after spending a few months looking for work a friend told him about a Facebook posting for farm labor.

The money isn't good—$2 per basket, plus $600 to clear the three acres when the vines were picked clean—but he figures it's better than sitting around. Plus, the transportation is free, provided by Jerry Spencer, who runs a community-supported agriculture program in Birmingham. That helps, because the farm is an hour north of Birmingham and the gas money adds up.

Durr thinks of himself as fit—he's all chiseled muscle—but he is surprised at how hard the work is. "Not everyone is used to this. I ain't used to it," he says while taking a break in front of his truck. "But I'm getting used to it."

Yet after three weeks in the fields, he is frustrated. His crew of seven has dropped down to two. "A lot of people look at this as slave work. I say, you do what you have to do," Durr says. "My mission is to finish these acres. As long as I'm here, I'm striving for something." In a neighboring field, Cedric Rayford is working a row. The 28-year-old came up with two friends from Gadsden, Ala., after hearing on the radio that farmers were hiring. The work is halfway complete when one member of their crew decides to quit. Rayford and crewmate Marvin Turner try to persuade their friend to stay and finish the job. Otherwise, no one will get paid. Turner even offers $20 out of his own pocket as a sweetener to no effect. "When a man's mind is made up, there's about nothing you can do," he says.

20   The men lean against the car, smoking cigarettes and trying to figure out how to finish the job before day's end. "They gotta come up with a better pay system," says Rayford. "This ain't no easy work. If you need somebody to do this type of work, you gotta be payin.' If they was paying by the hour, motherf—s would work overtime, so you'd know what you're working for." He starts to pace around the car. "I could just work at McDonald's (MCD)," he says.

Turner, who usually works as a landscaper, agrees the pay is too low. At $75 in gas for the three days, he figures he won't even break even. The men finish their cigarettes. Turner glances up the hill at Castro's work crew. "Look," he says. "You got immigrants doing more than what blacks or whites will. Look at them, they just work and work all day. They don't look at it like it's a hard job. They don't take breaks!"

The notion of jobs in fields and food plants as "immigrant work" is relatively new. As late as the 1940s, most farm labor in Alabama and elsewhere was done by Americans. During World War II the U.S. signed an agreement with Mexico to import temporary workers to ease labor shortages. Four and a half million Mexican guest workers crossed the border. At first most went to farms and orchards in California; by the program's completion in 1964 they were working in almost every state. Many *braceros*—the term translates to "strong-arm," as in someone who works with his arms—were granted green cards, became permanent residents, and continued to work in agriculture. Native-born Americans never returned to the fields. "Agricultural labor is basically 100 percent an immigrant job category," says Princeton University sociologist Doug Massey, who studies population migration. "Once an occupational category becomes dominated by immigrants, it becomes very difficult to erase the stigma."

Massey says Americans didn't turn away from the work merely because it was hard or because of the pay but because they had come to think of it as beneath them. "It doesn't have anything to do with the job itself," he says. In other countries, citizens refuse to take jobs that Americans compete for. In Europe, Massey says, "auto manufacturing is an immigrant job category. Whereas in the States, it's a native category."

In Alabama, the transition to immigrant labor happened slowly. Although migrant workers have picked fruit and processed food in Alabama for four decades, in 1990 only 1.1 percent of the state's total population was foreign-born. That year the U.S. Census put the combined Latin American and North American foreign-born population at 8,072 people. By 2000 there were 75,830 Hispanics recorded on the Census; by 2010 that number had more than doubled, and Hispanics are now nearly 4 percent of the population.

That first rush of Hispanic immigrants was initiated by the state's 25 $2.4 billion poultry and egg industry. Alabama's largest agricultural export commodity went through a major expansion in the mid-'90s, thanks in part to new markets in the former Soviet Union. Companies such as Tyson Foods (TSN) found the state's climate, plentiful water supply, light regulation, and anti-union policies to be ideal. At the time, better-educated American workers in cities such as Decatur and Athens were either moving into the state's burgeoning aerospace and service industries or following the trend of leaving Alabama and heading north or west, where they found office jobs or work in manufacturing with set hours, higher pay, and safer conditions—things most Americans take for granted. In just over a decade, school districts in once-white towns such as Albertville, in the northeastern corner of the state, became 34 percent Hispanic. By the 2000s, Hispanic immigrants had moved across the state, following the construction boom in the cities, in the growing plant nurseries in the south, and on the catfish farms west of Montgomery. It wasn't until anti-immigration sentiment spread across the country, as the recession took hold and didn't let go, that the Republican legislators who run Alabama began to regard the immigrants they once courted as the enemy.

A large white banner hangs on the chain-link fence outside the Harvest Select plant: "Now Hiring: Filleters/Trimmers. Stop Here To Apply." Randy Rhodes unfurled it the day after the law took effect. "We're getting applications, but you have to weed through those three and four times," says Amy Hart, the company's human resources manager. A job fair she held attracted 50 people, and Hart offered positions to 13 of them. Two failed the drug test. One applicant asked her out on a date during the interview. "People reapply who have been terminated for stealing, for fighting, for drugs," she says. "Nope, not that desperate yet!"

Rhodes says he understands why Americans aren't jumping at the chance to slice up catfish for minimum wage. He just doesn't know what he can do about it. "I'm sorry, but I can't pay those kids $13 an hour," he says. Although the Uniontown plant, which processes about 850,000 pounds of fish a week, is the largest in Alabama and sells to big supermarket chains including Food Lion, Harris Teeter, and Sam's Club (WMT), Rhodes says overseas competitors, which pay employees even lower wages, are squeezing the industry.

When the immigration law passed in late September, John McMillan's phone lines were deluged. People wanted McMillan, the state's agriculture commissioner, to tell them whether they'd be in business next year. "Like, what are we going to do? Do we need to be ordering strawberry plants for next season? Do we need to be ordering fertilizer?" McMillan recalls. "And of course, we don't have the answers, either."

His buddy Tom Surtees, the industrial relations director, faces the same problem on a larger scale. Where McMillan only has to worry about agriculture, other industries, from construction to hospitality, are reporting worker shortages. His ultimate responsibility is to generate the results that Governor Bentley has claimed the legislation will produce—lots of jobs for Alabamians. That means he cannot allow for the possibility that the law will fail.

30   "If those Alabamians on unemployment continue to not apply for jobs in construction and poultry, then [Republican politicians] are going to have to help us continue to find immigrant workers," says Jay Reed, who heads the Alabama Associated Builders & Contractors. "And those immigrant workers are gone."

Business owners are furious not only that they have lost so many workers but that everyone in the state seemed to see it coming except Bentley, who failed to heed warnings from leaders in neighboring Georgia who said they had experienced a similar flight of immigrants after passing their own immigration law. Bentley declined to be interviewed for this story.

McMillan and Surtees spend their days playing matchmaker with anxious employers, urging them to post job openings on the state's employment website so they can hook up with unemployed Alabamians. McMillan is asking Baptist ministers to tell their flocks that jobs are available. He wants businesses to rethink the way they run their operations to make them more attractive. On a road trip through the state, he met an apple farmer who told him he had started paying workers by the hour instead of by how much they picked. The apples get bruised and damaged when people are picking for speed. "Our farmers are very innovative and are used to dealing with challenges," McMillan says. "You know, they can come up with all kinds of things. Something I've thought about is, maybe we should go to four-hour shifts instead of eight-hour shifts. Or maybe two six-hour shifts."

McMillan acknowledges that even if some of these efforts are successful, they are unlikely to fill the labor void left by the immigrants' disappearance. Some growers, he says, might have to go back to traditional mechanized row crops such as corn and soybeans. The smaller farmers might have to decrease volumes to the point where they are no longer commercially viable. "I don't know," says McMillan. "I just don't know, but we've got to try to think of everything we possibly can."

Since late September, McMillan's staff has been attending meetings with farmers throughout the state. They are supposed to be Q&A sessions about how to comply with the new law. Some have devolved into shouting matches about how much they hate the statute. A few weeks ago, Smith, the tomato farmer whose workers fled Alabama, confronted state Senator Scott Beason, the Republican who introduced the immigration law. Beason had come out to talk to farmers, and Smith shoved an empty tomato bucket into his chest. "You pick!" he told him. "He didn't even put his hands on the bucket," Smith recalls. "He didn't even try." Says Beason: "My picking tomatoes would not change or prove anything."

While the politicians and business owners argue, others see opportunity. Michael Maldonado, 19, wakes up at 4:30 each morning in a trailer in Tuscaloosa, about an hour from Harvest Select, where he works as a fish processor. Maldonado, who grew up in an earthen-floor shack in Guatemala, says he likes working at the plant. "One hundred dollars here is 35

700 quetzals," he says. "The managers say I am a good worker." After three years, though, the long hours and scant pay are starting to wear on him. With the business in desperate need of every available hand, it's not a bad time to test just how much the bosses value his labor. Next week he plans to ask his supervisor for a raise. "I will say to them, 'If you pay me a little more—just a little more—I will stay working here,'" he says. "Otherwise, I will leave. I will go to work in another state."

Analyze

1. Select one of Dwoskin's sentences that best captures the complexity of the immigrant/labor problem.
2. Beneath the obvious tension between the law and the need for labor, what does this article suggest about American workers and consumers?
3. Consider the historical information in paragraph 22. How does it change or affect Dwoskin's portrayal of the current problem?
4. Where do you think Dwoskin comes down on this issue? Is she for or against the immigration law in Alabama? Point to specific statements that support your understanding.
5. Consider the way Dwoskin uses quotations from laborers and employers. How do the specific quotations help to characterize the situation? How they portray both groups: workers and laborers?

Explore

1. Have you ever worked as a farm laborer or in a food processing plant? How does your answer (*yes* or *no*) influence your thinking on the immigrant labor issue?
2. Should U.S. law allow for migrant workers to enter the country? Why or why not?
3. If undocumented workers had to leave the United States suddenly and by the tens of thousands, what do you imagine would happen? What would be the most immediate result? What would be the long-term results?
4. What does Dwoskin's article suggest about a global economy?
5. What would you do if your company suddenly lost its workforce? What if you couldn't attract enough workers to process your stock?

Julie Hanus
White Collared: When Did Our Jobs Turn into a Joke?

Julie Hanus writes and blogs for *Utne Reader,* which describes itself as an enclave "of independent ideas and alternative culture." In her work, Hanus explores a range of topics such as the politics of food, digital culture, spirituality, the environment, and the arts. In the following article, Hanus analyzes the culture of white-collar work.

Remember *Laverne & Shirley?* Archie Bunker? Louie De Palma on *Taxi?* Norm and Cliff on *Cheers?* As these working-class characters live on in late-night reruns, a very different sort of everyperson is dominating the airwaves: the charmingly disengaged, sometimes bungling, always put-upon white-collar worker.

It's a logical trend. Since 1984, the number of U.S. workers has increased by more than 30 million, and 90 percent of that growth has been in the white-collar and service sectors. More citizens work at non-manual labor than ever before, and as technology, outsourcing, and offshoring continue to eliminate blue-collar jobs, pop culture has turned its attention to the office dweller.

The most popular and pointed TV treatment of this phenomenon is a biting satire more or less hijacked from Britain. In *The Office,* the interactions between big boss Michael Scott, played by comedian Steve Carell, and his underlings at Dunder Mifflin are governed by a rubric under which each character is reduced to his or her fundamental office identity. Dwight, assistant (to the) regional manager, is the guy guzzling the Kool-Aid. Sales rep Jim is smart, but often slacking. Pam, meekly poised behind the front desk, hopes to become an illustrator someday, because "no little girl ever dreams about becoming a receptionist."

The show's lead characters cleave into two groups: those who "get it" and those who don't. The latter class is represented by the clownish, not-so-lovable nerd Dwight who gullibly fawns over his foolish manager and mercilessly pursues advancement. He and his kind are the show's jesters. The better half, employees in the know, are its heroes.

5   They immediately spot the stupidity in empty managerial parables, sigh
as they play along (for now, of course), and fend off lunacy by playing mostly
harmless tricks on their naive officemates. They also demonstrate their
superior grasp of the situation by casting incredulous glances at the camera,
pained conspiratorial gazes that say: *Can you even believe this? You see that
this is all B.S., right?*

For NBC, the formula has proven to be comedic gold. Lurking just
below the public's laughter, though, is a grim reminder of what it means to
be a modern-day worker bee.

The white-collar workspace hasn't always conjured up visions of monkey-
like morons shuffling papers and wasting time on the Internet. When the
United States began shifting to a postindustrial society in the aftermath of
World War II, writes Nikil Saval in the Winter 2008 issue of the culture
journal *n + 1,* corporations like General Electric and IBM offered a new breed
of white-collar workers highly secure, salaried work, along with decent benefits and abundant vacation time. What's more, working *meant* something.

By the 1980s, however, economic instability had prompted companies
to spread resources thin—to cut pay, slash benefits, and eliminate good jobs
in favor of low-pay positions—in order to beef up profit margins. Swaths of
Generation X watched their boomer parents get dropkicked in return for
decades of good, hard work. Perhaps most notably, those who were affected
responded by doing very little to protest—and white-collar workers have
been rolling over ever since.

"Young technical and professional workers are as bewildered by the 'new
economy' as manufacturing workers have been for a generation," labor activist Jim Grossfeld writes in the January 2007 issue of the online political
journal the *Democratic Strategist.* However, in "White Collar Perspectives
on Workplace Issues," Grossfeld's study for the Center for American
Progress, an important difference between the two groups is revealed.
Whereas blue-collar laborers organized to protest workplace issues such as
unsatisfactory wages and benefits, white-collar workers have gone on the defensive with a disillusioned attitude. Believing instability and declining workplace conditions are "unavoidable in today's economy," and that corporations
are too formidable, they've concluded that nothing can be done but to lower
expectations and dodge disappointment. Reject loyalty and avoid betrayal.

10   The standards slid, unchecked. These days, U.S. workers put in longer
hours than workers in any other developed country and take the least
vacation. If they're actually insured, the benefits are often astronomically

expensive. There's no stability, either; white-collar workers hold an average of nine jobs before the age of 35. Instead of getting angry, they turn a scorned cheek to their employers, defiantly laughing along with *The Office* heroes at the absurdity of it all.

Assistant (to the) regional manager Dwight isn't mocked because he's an insufferable suck-up; he's ridiculed because he fails to recognize that it's all a waste of energy.

When the cartoon strip *Dilbert* first appeared in 1989, it depicted employees who knew better than their buzzword-slinging managers. In that two-dimensional universe, the people making things inefficient were the ones who were portrayed as fools; the evolving workplace was problematic, but the work had potential for value. Now the work itself is what's mocked, which, given the fact that most people spend a bulk of their lives at work, can't help but threaten the collective psyche and further damage the domestic workplace.

White-collar workers already report more occupational stress than their blue-collar counterparts and suffer twice as much from severe depression. Job satisfaction is falling, dropping from 60 percent in the mid-'90s to about 50 percent in 2005, according to a report from the Conference Board, a business-research organization. Forty percent of workers feel disconnected from their employers, and a quarter admit to showing up just to collect a check. In other words, some 35 million workers are either content to not care or have bought into the idea that there's no reason to. (Managers know it, too. Why else would they grit their teeth and bring in "fun" consultants who promise to boost sagging employee morale?)

This culturally sanctioned slacking that results from job insecurity is a self-fulfilling prophecy. Over the past few years, technology has made it possible for work once done in U.S. offices to be performed just as easily anywhere in the world. National Public Radio's *Morning Edition* recently likened the current threat to white-collar jobs to steelworkers' complaints of a generation past. "Fewer and fewer jobs are safe," said Ethan Kapstein, a guest expert in international economic relations. "It means that all of us, people like myself as well, have to continually upscale, we have to continually invest in our skills to maintain our productivity levels."

"What [white-collar workers] need is a new model of unionism that focuses on assuring their employability, mobility, and earning power rather than protecting specific jobs or compensation packages," Will Marshall, president of the Progressive Policy Institute, writes in the January 2007 issue of

15

the *Democratic Strategist*. He echoes Kapstein, arguing that if U.S. white-collar workers want to keep their jobs, they'll have to focus on company productivity as much as on their own needs: "Modern labor associations...could operate, in short, like a back-to-the-future update on the old craft unions, which were defenders of quality workmanship as well as workers' interests."

To avert crisis, Kapstein and Marshall both call on the redeeming power of doing *good* work, of investing in skills and focusing on craftsmanship—which would require believing in the value of labor and the value of the laborer. Such a shift in mind-set could protect white-collar jobs, even transform domestic white-collar work. After all, the same technology that produced an outsourcing threat could just as easily make widespread telecommuting a reality. As Matt Bai writes in a November 2007 issue of the *New York Times,* "Why shouldn't more middle-class workers whose jobs can now be done remotely have the option to structure their own hours and still enjoy the security of a safety net? Why shouldn't . . . anyone who spends his day staring at a terminal in some sterile environment straight out of *Office Space* be able to work in shorts and spend more time around the kids?"

It's a lovely vision, shedding all those vestiges of cliché office work (the inflexible hours, the fluorescent-lit cubicles, the impossible work-home balance), but it can't happen if this generation of workers continues to find validation in checking out, backhandedly assuring themselves that they're better than their disappointing jobs and, in the process, proving to their employers that they're utterly replaceable and entirely outsourceable.

If white-collar workers seized this moment to check in, to believe in the value of their work and in themselves as workers, they might do more than save their jobs or even kick open the door for a reinvention of the workspace. They might remember what it feels like to care about what they do—or find out for the first time.

Analyze

1. How does *Office Space* function in Hanus's argument? What point does it help her to make?
2. Hanus explains that young professional workers are learning to "[r]eject loyalty and avoid betrayal." In your own words, explain the relationship between loyalty and betrayal. Why does it figure into jobs?
3. According to Hanus's article, what does it mean to be a "modern-day worker bee?"

4. Consider Hanus's following statement about disaffected white-collar workers: "This culturally sanctioned slacking that results from job insecurity is a self-fulfilling prophecy." In your own words, describe the situation. What is "culturally sanctioned slacking"? How does it come from job insecurity?

5. What solution does Hanus offer? How does that solution address the nature of the looming problem?

Explore

1. What kind of job do you want? Do you want to be a boss? A freelance professional? A worker bee? A skilled laborer? What are your reasons?

2. Do you imagine yourself as a loyal employee or a wary professional who's always ready to move on to a better opportunity?

3. How much of the white-collar problem described in this article is generational? In other words, do you think that your parents' generation had the same problems? Different work-related problems?

4. Hanus says, "It's a lovely vision, shedding all those vestiges of cliché office work (the inflexible hours, the fluorescent-lit cubicles, the impossible work-home balance), but it can't happen if this generation of workers continue[s] to find validation in checking out." What do you think she is suggesting? Why is her point valid or invalid?

5. This article was published in 2008—at the height of American job losses. What do you think has changed in the intervening years? Are conditions for white-collar workers better? Worse? Fundamentally different?

Patricia Ann McNair
I Go On Running

A fiction writing professor at Columbia College Chicago, Patricia Ann McNair is an essayist, short story writer, and travel writer. She has published fiction and creative nonfiction in numerous magazines and journals as well as the 2011 story collection *The Temple of Air*. In the following essay, McNair examines the relationship between creativity and work.

I run along the banks of the River Avon on a path shared with walkers, bicyclists, other runners. I'm an American in Bath, in England, where I've been invited to teach creative writing for four months at a local university. Can I say I live here? How long must one stay in one place to be able to call it home? Jane Austen lived here. In fact, my flat (a simple, one bedroom gut rehab in a Georgian-era shell of buttery stone with tall windows) is on a street around the corner from one of the places Miss Austen resided. We are neighbors from different centuries. I've heard it said that Jane Austen didn't like Bath, or at least a number of her fictional characters didn't: "Do you know I get so immoderately sick of Bath . . ." Isabella Thorpe says in *Northanger Abbey*.

> "Though I have built the best house I can build for you to stop at last and rest in, you go on running."
> —From "My Brother Running" by Wesley McNair

I, however, love everything about this place, starting with my morning run by the river. The path goes alongside walls built decades ago, some built centuries ago. It skirts a crescent of terraced homes curving around a wide, green lawn. It dips under low-slung bridges and passes gently bobbing houseboats. The machines of a paper factory chug noisily nearby while workers gather at a picnic table to smoke and drink coffee from paper cups. If I run this way, I reach a housing estate of lookalike buildings, dog walkers, and kids in school uniforms waiting under a shelter for their bus. If I go that way, in the other direction, I will run in the shadows of Pulteney Bridge, first built in the 1700s. I listen for the sound of wings, the heavy "whomp whomp" that I know means the swans are close by, swooping toward the river's surface. Nearly every morning as I run, I pass this pair of elegant and awesome birds, or they pass me.

I carry with me my keys, my identification, and my stories.

When I am home in Chicago, I run through the city streets that are lined with *Pho* cafés, restaurants that serve noodles morning, noon, and night. There is a large population of Asian immigrants here, and the bright sound of chatter surrounds me, whole conversations I do not understand called across the sidewalks, from the doorway of the train station and the bakery, spilling out from the Asian grocery store. I am heading for the lakefront where the running path goes for miles past high rises and restored prairie lands and beaches. I know this place; I've lived here for close to all of my life. When I first started kissing boys in cars, this was one of the parking lots where I did it, here at the foot of this beach where my run on the lakefront starts.

The stories I am writing take my attention as I run, I move my lips 5
around the dialogue I hear a character say, I try out opening sentences in
my head. Unlike Bath where I run full of the wonder that comes with a
brand new place, my Chicago run is like something on autopilot. I must
remind myself to look up from my story-making and out over the vast and
shimmering water toward Wisconsin, toward Michigan.

In Interlochen, Michigan, I run through woods and by wetlands, along
the curve of Green Lake (Wahbekenetta, it was once called, "Water Lingers
Again"). The dirt road I come to passes through a cottage community of
summer people mostly, folks who come to this place during warm months
to float and to fish, to swim and to make meals on grills to eat on decks. I'm
here to write and to teach, and it is the writing I mull over on my run, while
I look out toward the still, blue lake, while I feel the warmth of the sunlight
and cool of the tree shadow on my face, on my shoulders. I wind through
the woods and the marshes and watch for deer, for their horizontal movement amidst this vertical landscape. I can feel their presence even when
I can't see them, these deer. They are like an idea in the making: There.
Close. There.

Some say that writers need to be away from the place they want to write
about in order to make sense of that place. Sherwood Andersen wrote
Winesburg, Ohio while he lived in Chicago. James Joyce wrote *Dubliners*
while he resided in a number of European cities, none of them Dublin.
While living in Paris, Ernest Hemingway wrote stories of Northern
Michigan. In Bath I wrote about the Midwest; when I was in Interlochen,
I wrote about Cuba, where I'd stayed in January 2000, where I ran along
the sea. It wasn't until I was away from Interlochen that I could write about
that place, about the first morning of my classes there when two planes flew
into buildings in New York, when another crashed in DC, and another
went down in a field in the middle of our country. Some weeks after the
tragedy I flew home aboard a small plane; from the window I could see
below me Interlochen and the cabin I lived in, I could trace the path I ran.
We see best, perhaps, from some distance.

"The runner who's a writer is running through the land and cityscapes
of her fiction, like a ghost in a real setting," wrote Joyce Carol Oates in an
essay for *The New York Times*. In Prague I am not a ghost, judging from the
looks I get from the people I pass. Perhaps more like an apparition, a surprising thing that doesn't exactly make sense. Every day on my run near the
pension I share with my students, far away from the tourist section of the

city, a place with few strangers, I pass an old man who walks a fluffy white dog on a leash. The man stops and stares at me while I run by. I nod, smile. *Dobry den.* Good day, I say. But it isn't until I've lived in this place for three weeks and made this run every day that he finally tips his head to me, that he answers me. *Dobry den.* This happens on the same day I figure out my story, recognizing as I wait to get through a crowd of locals at a bus stop— moving in place—that I have tried too hard with the tale set in a small Midwestern town; I have told too much. I finish the last leg of my run— down a long hill and along a blacktopped road that leads to the door of my home-away-from home and sit down at my desk and try again.

In Johnson, Vermont, my run takes me under/over a covered bridge and for a short while on a quiet highway. I pass a small, clapboard house close to the road where I pass another old man. He has gray hair and a garden of tiger lilies that grow orange against the home's white siding. Sometimes the man sits on a metal chair, watching the world (and me) go by. We always say good morning. And then I am running on a dirt road past an old mill, a dilapidated barn, cows. There are birds and butterflies in the weeds. A loud and arrogant jay calls at me most days. I call back. I can only see so far on this run because I've left my glasses behind on my writing desk in the house I share with other writers and artists. It isn't until I wear my glasses on a walk with a friend along this same path that I see the reindeer high on a ridge. They look down at us as we go by, and I know they have watched me before; they have seen me moving my hands over the shape of a story I have almost finished, building the structure in the air, paragraph by paragraph, section by section. When I hear the final sentence in my head one day on this run, I whoop and punch my fists toward the sky.

10   I am lucky to have work I can carry with me, work that takes me to new places. I am lucky to have new roads to run. It is when I am in my room at my desk (wherever that might be) that I get the words on the page, but I need this other time, too, on the running path. In each new place I'm like a cat: circling and circling and circling until I can settle down. The rhythm of the steps on the road, the sound of my breath, the things I see on the way—these help me get to the story, that creative place I want to be. I run the streets I don't yet know and those that become familiar, sniffing the air, taking the long way.

I'll get there sooner or later, that place I need to be in the story. But until then, I mustn't stop, I can't give up. I will go on running.

Analyze

1. What is McNair's main idea about her work?
2. What does McNair suggest about the nature of work—what it is, what it can be?
3. Would you say that work is, for McNair, tied to the particular locations in her life or somehow placeless? Refer to specific passages to support your answer.
4. Explain how the references to Anderson, Joyce, and Oates function in McNair's essay. What idea do they support?
5. Consider the animals in McNair's essay (the cows, butterflies, birds, even the kindly old men). What idea do they help to show?

Explore

1. McNair focuses on the way she gets creative, which is crucial for her work. What other jobs depend entirely on creativity?
2. Even if you are not a writer (or don't know any personally), try to imagine the difficult parts of the job. What kinds of politics or entanglements might they encounter?
3. How do you think writers make a living? How many books do you think someone has to sell to make an average annual salary? Explain your arithmetic in your answer.
4. Do you think you could maintain an intensive work life if you were your own boss? If you didn't have an immediate supervisor or time clock, could you keep working? What intellectual or psychological habits would help or hurt your work?
5. Many economists and cultural theorists imagine that the next century will see far fewer people going to an office or factory. Instead, people will move around the world and carry their work with them. Do you think this is possible in your chosen field? Why or why not?

Jason Storms
In the Valley of the Shadow of Debt

The founding editor of *Echo Cognitio: A Journal of Research and Creative Writing*, Jason Storms is completing a BA in English and psychology. In the following essay, he dissects the cultural conversation about college debt. Part rhetorical analysis, part research project, and part argument, his essay reveals the complexity—and the dangerously flawed thinking—related to debt.

College graduation is one of the great achievements in life. The pageantry of the graduation ceremonies is truly a spectacle: for roughly one month, every day presents stadiums and arenas filled to capacity as the country's most prominent leaders, thinkers, creators and innovators tell thousands of freshly-minted graduates essentially the same thing: *Life is a long journey with obstacles along the way. But you are college graduates, and with your college education, you can do anything you want.*

Yes, having a bachelor's degree doubles earning potential (United States Census Bureau). It enables social mobility. It is becoming the new standard for obtaining employment. Yet, as a soon-to-be undergraduate, I'm tempted to call shenanigans on the whole thing. The line into the adult world of jobs and money is bottlenecked, and I'm scared as hell to graduate. Debt almost rivals death as my fundamental, existential fear. And I've accrued enough debt to make a down payment on a house, and will soon enter a bleak job market with this debt-child to feed and a wife in grad school to support.

On one hand, this fear of debt and the need to eat and pay bills and maintain sanity is rational, but I question how much of this fear is driven by recent political discourse that characterizes spending and debt as the Great Satan. Whether the government spends money on college funding, health care or social services, current political rhetoric names any spending whatsoever as an existential threat to the American lifestyle.

Some level of debt *is* necessary. For example, almost no one buys a house by merely opening their wallet and taking the appropriate amount of cash. Certain necessities *do require debt*. Debt is necessary for social mobility and basic qualities of life for a majority of our country's citizens. President Obama, an African American raised by a single mother, made his way through Columbia and Harvard Universities by taking on college debt, and could pay off his student loan debt a mere four years before his election as president. His story highlights the balances and payoffs of a college education—you pay more in the short term, but reap more in the long term.

None of this is to say that college funding doesn't have its flaws; the inner workings of various for-profit schools have aptly demonstrated this. One need only look at how much money the U.S. government doles out to for-profit institutions (e.g., University of Phoenix, ITT Tech., et al.) and those institutions' abysmal graduations rates compared with how much money public institutions receive—and keep for profit—and those institutions' graduation rates (Randazzo). Naturally, this information has found its way into college debt discourse. Republican politicians vying for the 2012 GOP presidential nomination offered numerous proposals for fixing higher education. Ron Paul proposed eliminating financial aid altogether, and requiring college students to pay out of pocket. But this would further stratify the social classes, with the result being the rich remaining rich and the poor remaining poor. Education is the key to social mobility. Blocking access to this key would be like eliminating food stamps and insisting that every man, woman, and child pay for their own food. This borders on a false comparison, but I'll offer it nonetheless: a college education is as important to financial and social health as food is to physical health.

Conversely, a slightly less destructive idea has worked its way into the debt discourse: erasing college debt altogether. The recently-created Consumers Financial Protection Bureau has pressed Congress to reverse a 1977 law prohibiting bankruptcy from forgiving student loans (Pianin). Currently, student loan debts are one of the few loans on which you *cannot default*—and with good reason. Meanwhile, the Forgive Student Loan Act would forgive a portion of student loan debt altogether, after students have paid ten percent of their discretionary income for ten years. This idea seems to work well enough on paper.

Yet, these ideas still seem unsatisfying to me. I have had the privilege to receive a higher education because a financial institution, with promises from the U.S. government, agreed to loan me—a financially risky twenty-something—thousands of dollars. Others in my situation before me received this gesture and paid their loans, which kept the institution in business and stable enough to fund my education. It's only fair that I do the same for those who come after me; doing otherwise would be selfish. And it seems better to address crushing student loan burdens rather than to

5

erase the debt altogether. Student loan bills must be paid so that those who attend college after this generation have the same access to education this generation has had.

The rub of this debt conversation comes when graduates can't get jobs or make their loan payments. It seems that the real specter is not debt but unemployment. My fear may not be debt, which has been a manageable constant in personal finance for decades. Rather, it's the intellectual arms race in which my cohorts and I find ourselves. As more people obtain college degrees, the competition for jobs increases, and I can't help but wonder if eventually the master's degree will become the new bachelor's degree, which seems on track to become the new high school diploma.

The conversation about college debt and funding really involves patterns of exclusivity, of finding ways we can preclude or include others in the ever-present quest to learn more and earn more. Right now, higher education, unlike primary and secondary education, costs money, and things like cost can act as a wall that financially or academically challenged individuals, and potentially their successive generations, have trouble breaking down. If we remove financial aid and college loans, we exclude a group—the financially needy—from having the option of attending college, and the subsequent opportunities a college education offers. If we make all funding based on academic merit, particularly academic merit in high school (as many college scholarships do), we keep a huge range of students who struggle through secondary education from having a second chance at social mobility.

10   One can't help but wonder if the hypothetical end of our country's technocratizing trajectory will result in graduates with too much knowledge but no flexibility or dynamism in their marketable job skills. My declared major is a good case in point here. With a bachelor's in English, I have numerous job options, such as writing, editing, teaching (market and geography depending, of course). These jobs may not pay me the same salary as, say, someone with a business or engineering degree, but a job still presents reliable income. Then comes grad school for English, and eventually, once a PhD is taken, there is really only one job available—teaching English in a college or university, and English PhDs only have a fifty-three percent chance of landing that coveted gig (Nared and Cerny, 2000). It seems that this could apply to almost any number of majors, particularly liberal arts majors that may not produce as much product as they do thought.

In the end, I view my college debt as a formidable adversary rather than the Grim Reaper. My wife has zero college debt. She actually had so much funding via scholarships and college trusts that she *made* money her senior year—and my debt is nothing that can't be wiped out quickly with modest living and aggressive repayment. It would have been a mistake *not* to attend college out of my fear of debt—a regret I've often seen in my mother, who turned down a basketball scholarship so she could live on my grandparents' farm for a few extra years and help with the chores. The only one of her siblings who went to college didn't graduate, and all of them churn up the rhetoric of debt each time they see me. But I am not afraid. Roughly a year from now, I will be everything a commencement keynote speaker will say I will be—a college graduate, capable of doing whatever I want in spite of life's obstacles. I just hope the commencement speech isn't too long and clichéd.

Works Cited

n.p. Educational Attainment. United States Census Bureau. Web. 22 August 2012.

Nared, Maresi & Cerny, Joseph. *From Rumors to Facts: Career Outcomes of English PhDs.* Modern Language Association, 2000. Web. 22 August 2012.

Pianin, Eric. "CFPB Pushes Bankruptcy Protection for Student Loans." *The Fiscal Times.* The Fiscal Times, 25 July 2012. Web. 22 August 2012.

Randazzo, Ryan. "For-Profit Colleges Bilking Public, Senator Says." *USA Today.* Gannett, 31 July 2012. Web. 22 August 2012.

Analyze

1. According to Storms, what is the core problem for graduating college students?
2. Of the possible solutions, which does Storms advocate?
3. Explain how personal testimony works for Storms. How does he use his own situation to provide insight on the complexity of the problem?
4. Explain how the sources operate in Storms's argument. What particular points do they support? How important are they in substantiating the claims?
5. Storms's essay might be seen as a two-layered argument. On one layer, he argues about college debt; on another, he argues about the way people argue. What is his concern about that second layer—or what he calls "the rhetoric of debt"?

Explore

1. To what degree are you concerned about college debt? On a scale of 1 to 10, are you mildly concerned (1) or terribly concerned (10)? Give reasons for your answer.
2. In the coming five years, how do you think college debt will figure into the economy at large?
3. Explain how student loans affected your college decisions: where you would attend, where you would live, what you would study, and so on.
4. Storms argues that college is the primary key to social mobility. Do you agree? And do you see the role of college education changing in the near future?
5. Storms explains that "the Forgive Student Loan Act would forgive a portion of student loan debt altogether, after students have paid ten percent of their discretionary income for ten years." What is your opinion of the Act? Why is it a good or bad idea?

Ross Perlin
Of Apprentices and Interns

Ross Perlin is a linguist and researcher for the Himalayan Languages Project in southwest China, where he studies the fading language Trung. He is the author of many articles on language and the 2011 book *Intern Nation: How to Earn Nothing and Learn Little in the Brave New Economy*. In the following magazine article, Perlin examines the historical and cultural value of internships.

After all the talk about amputating ears and public whippings, the Code of Hammurabi pauses to consider the plight of the intern. Well, not exactly—but that ancient litany of 282 laws, inscribed on diorite some 3700 years ago, did enjoin the master craftsmen of Babylon to pass on their trade and treat their apprentices fairly. Four millennia later, these are the basic rights that interns are still fighting for.

Interns, not apprentices, that is. Today, the contrast is stark, with the two groups seeming to inhabit completely different universes. The former are our favorite white-collar peons, often unpaid or paid a pittance, loaded with little indignities and unprotected in the workplace. Apprenticeships, on the other hand, represent a humane, professional model for training and beginning a career—the justified successor to the European tradition of craft apprenticeship, minus the cruelty, coercion, and familial arrangements, sensibly updated for the twentieth and now twenty-first centuries. If no longer ubiquitous, apprenticeships have nonetheless weathered the centuries. At this moment, there are nearly half a million active apprentices across the U.S. in fields as disparate as aerospace manufacturing, seafaring, cosmetology, and green energy.

Still, our archetypal apprentice is a cheerful, mildly rambunctious minion, probably straight out of medieval Europe (Goethe's "The Sorcerer's Apprentice," pre-Mickey Mouse), Colonial America (Ben Franklin), or Victorian England (a Dickens novel). Indeed, the institution has long since become a central model and metaphor for education more broadly. The Western apprenticeship tradition grew out of the medieval guilds, widely known in Latin as *universitates*. Some scholars assert that the first universities—early gatherings of scholars at Bologna, Paris, Oxford, and elsewhere—fancied themselves guilds of scholars, and that everything from set terms of student enrollment (inspired by indentures) to the concept of the dissertation (the "masterpiece" of a scholarly apprenticeship) drew on the model of guild apprenticeships.

In the English-speaking world, a typical term of "indenture" lasted seven years; the (mostly male) apprentices usually took up their indentures, with a nudge or a shove from their family, when they were around fourteen years old, the common-law "age of discretion." These indentures spelled out mutual obligations, more or less formally—the apprentice would work for such and such a period, at tasks relevant to the craft. (There were sometimes specific prohibitions against an apprentice performing grunt work considered the preserve of servants.) In return the master was obligated to teach the apprentice his trade, while also providing housing, meals, clothing, and so on. Numerous other kinds of stipulations also commonly bound both parties—that the apprentice should not marry during his term, for instance, or that the master should provide bedding or clothing of a certain quality.

In Britain, the Elizabethan-era Statute of Artificers enshrined this basic setup until 1814. In the U.S., it began to come apart during the American Revolution, ironically enough since almost all of the Founding Fathers had started out as apprentices. Apparently, the revolutionary spirit broadened the discourse of freedom in a way that threw indentures into a bad light, and runaway apprentices became an intractable problem. "Go West, young man," the Industrial Revolution, and the spread of mandatory schooling put further nails in the coffin of apprenticeship until the early twentieth century, when a coalition of enlightened employers, unions, and progressives managed to carve out the current, impressive niche.

So what about interns? In the late nineteenth century, the medical profession, eagerly standardizing, started pushing aspiring doctors to endure a year or two of purgatory between medical school and professional practice, "interning" them within the four walls of a hospital. Only after World War II did the model spread decisively to Washington, D.C., and corporate America. Yet the real internship boom is only three decades old—a sprawling, unstudied, unregulated mess gone global, allowing companies in every industry to save on costs and cut corners while millions of college students (and their families) scramble and sacrifice.

Every society has its gift economies—you probably don't pay a relative for babysitting, for instance—but young people working for free en masse is something new and frightening. What's amazing is how quickly we've become inured to it, how naturally we've accepted the idea of "investing in ourselves," bartering for connections and resume line-items. It's a useful reminder that the notion of work is hardly an eternal verity—more like a shifting, uneven landscape, fought over and redefined in every culture and in every age, in spite of hallowed old chiselings in stone.

Analyze

1. How does Perlin's reference to the Code of Hammurabi work? What idea or feeling does it help to establish for the article?
2. In your own words, describe a "gift economy." What part does the idea play in Perlin's thoughts about internships?
3. Why is it important, at least to this article, that apprenticeship may have begun with medieval universities?
4. How does the concept of "indenture" function in Perlin's article? How does it help to characterize or explain the value or peril of internships?
5. Is Perlin for or against modern internships? Or does he have some qualified stance? Refer to specific passages to substantiate your response.

Explore

1. Would you consider an unpaid internship in your chosen career field? Why or why not?
2. What is the most valuable aspect, from the perspective of a college student, of an unpaid internship?
3. Do you think the old-school method of training for a specific career is fundamentally better than getting a four-year university degree? Why or why not?
4. How young should someone start training for a career? Is there is a limit or should children begin as early as possible?
5. Consider the old-school method of adopting the family profession or craft. How do you think that would impact families? How would your family, for instance, be different if the children all supported or adopted the parents' profession?

Christian Williams
This, That, and the American Dream

Editor in chief for *Utne Reader,* Christian Williams writes on issues related to food, the environment, and politics. In his work, he strives to uphold *Utne's* mission in "capturing emerging culture." In the following blog post, Williams examines the validity of American cultural ideals.

Remember how it felt when you graduated college?

Perhaps you're like me, and you grew up learning that a college degree was the key to a successful future. You knew you didn't want to spend the rest of your life flipping burgers like you did every summer. So you did it: you graduated college, and you proudly walked across the auditorium stage with a big grin. As you shook the dean's hand, all that was left to do was ask, "What's next?"

Back then, a loaded question like that was easy to answer: entry level job in a chosen career, graduate school—the options were endless. It was a question that was exciting to answer because no matter what route you chose, the degree all but guaranteed you'd start higher on the ladder than you would have if you'd only finished high school like your older relatives. You could see and feel what had been promised if you applied yourself and got a degree: the American Dream was real, and you were ready to stake your claim.

It felt good to look back on the previous four years of balancing school and work, knowing now that it was all worth it. Soon, you'd be settling into your career, making a comfortable living, buying a house, and starting a family. Sure, there'd be bills to pay, but you'd rest easy at night knowing that you'd continue to work your way up to better paying jobs in your field, and that you'd comfortably pay back your student loans and meet your mortgage payments.

5   Eventually, the loans would become a distant memory, and you'd be saving your money for your kids' future. They would share their goals of having a career and starting a family, and you'd be happy to do what you could to help them realize their version of the American Dream. You'd even pay off your house one day and still have enough money left to set aside for your retirement, ensuring you wouldn't have to work the rest of your life.

In *that* life, "fair" was getting out what you put in, so you worked hard and were compensated appropriately. And you knew that if you ever found yourself being taken advantage of, your college degree was always in your pocket and able to open another door if need be. In *that* life, there were safeguards put in place to make sure that the greediest among us weren't able to keep you under their thumbs. In *that* life, we celebrated on graduation day because it represented a gateway to opportunity for everyone who earned the right to walk through it.

But in *this* life, the concept of "fair vs. unfair" has disintegrated into an accusation of laziness by the advantaged toward the disadvantaged. In *this* life, greed has infiltrated every nook and cranny of our society to the point where we don't know whom to trust anymore. And in *this* life, insurmountable student debt and the lack of real opportunities to reach our potential have drained graduation day of its optimism and replaced it with the burden of concern. Soon, the event might be more appropriately symbolized by handcuffs than a handshake.

Perhaps there is no alternate reality to *this* life; an existence where everyone truly has the opportunity to realize their full potential, be successful, and find happiness. Perhaps the American Dream has always been an unattainable illusion created by the powers that be.

But if it is an illusion, the false hope it's meant to sustain is quickly fading. While people will recognize the illusion for what it is, they'll remember something important: it sure sounded pretty nice. And maybe then, with nothing left to lose, we'll all stand together, ask "what's next?" and do what it takes to make *that* life a reality.

Analyze

1. Within the framework of this article, what is the American Dream? Point to specific passages that suggest a definition.
2. In your own words, explain the essential difference between that life and this life—the one that Williams remembers and the one he currently describes.
3. As a magazine editor, Williams is writing to a specific audience—to the people familiar with the *Utne Reader*. Given the nature of his argument, what can you infer about that audience? What kinds of political views do they have? What social class might they inhabit?
4. This article was published in 2012—as the United States was climbing out of the deepest recession in modern history and as a presidential election approached. How do you think those factors figure into Williams's tone?
5. Sometimes, writers fall prey to the golden age fallacy—a belief that the past was inherently better for everyone: more innocent, more ethical, more supportive, and so on. Do you think Williams is guilty of the golden age fallacy? Or does he manage to dodge it somehow? Explain specific passages to support your point.

Explore

1. Do you buy the American Dream? Do your friends and family?
2. What decisions have you made—or been invited to make—in support of the American Dream?
3. Williams says, "In *this* life, greed has infiltrated every nook and cranny of our society to the point where we don't know whom to trust anymore." To what extent is this accurate? In your experience, does this statement ring true?
4. Williams says, "Perhaps the American Dream has always been an unattainable illusion created by the powers that be." In this respect, what

are the powers that be? As specifically as you can, explain the forces, institutions, people, even ideas that comprise the powers.

5. What do you expect to do after you graduate from college? Will you pursue the American Dream or will you venture in some other, more or less defined, direction?

Mike Rose
Blue-Collar Brilliance

A research professor at UCLA's Graduate School of Education and Information Studies, Mike Rose is an expert on educational psychology, language, and teaching. He is the author of numerous magazine, newspaper, and journal articles as well as books dealing with issues related to education and work. In the following magazine article, Rose considers the relationship between intelligence and social class.

My mother, Rose Meraglio Rose (Rosie), shaped her adult identity as a waitress in coffee shops and family restaurants. When I was growing up in Los Angeles during the 1950s, my father and I would occasionally hang out at the restaurant until her shift ended, and then we'd ride the bus home with her. Sometimes she worked the register and the counter, and we sat there; when she waited booths and tables, we found a booth in the back where the waitresses took their breaks.

There wasn't much for a child to do at the restaurants, and so as the hours stretched out, I watched the cooks and waitresses and listened to what they said. At mealtimes, the pace of the kitchen staff and the din from customers picked up. Weaving in and out around the room, waitresses warned *behind you* in impassive but urgent voices. Standing at the service window facing the kitchen, they called out abbreviated orders. *Fry four on two,* my mother would say as she clipped a check onto the metal wheel. Her tables were *deuces, four-tops,* or *six-tops* according to their size; seating areas also were nicknamed. The *racetrack,* for instance, was the fast-turnover front section. Lingo conferred authority and signaled know-how.

Rosie took customers' orders, pencil poised over pad, while fielding questions about the food. She walked full tilt through the room with plates stretching up her left arm and two cups of coffee somehow cradled in her right hand. She stood at a table or booth and removed a plate for this person, another for that person, then another, remembering who had the hamburger, who had the fried shrimp, almost always getting it right. She would haggle with the cook about a returned order and rush by us, saying, *He gave me lip, but I got him.* She'd take a minute to flop down in the booth next to my father. *I'm all in,* she'd say, and whisper something about a customer. Gripping the outer edge of the table with one hand, she'd watch the room and note, in the flow of our conversation, who needed a refill, whose order was taking longer to prepare than it should, who was finishing up.

I couldn't have put it in words when I was growing up, but what I observed in my mother's restaurant defined the world of adults, a place where competence was synonymous with physical work. I've since studied the working habits of blue-collar workers and have come to understand how much my mother's kind of work demands of both body and brain. A waitress acquires knowledge and intuition about the ways and the rhythms of the restaurant business. Waiting on seven to nine tables, each with two to six customers, Rosie devised memory strategies so that she could remember who ordered what. And because she knew the average time it took to prepare different dishes, she could monitor an order that was taking too long at the service station.

Like anyone who is effective at physical work, my mother learned *to work smart,* as she put it, *to make every move count.* She'd sequence and group tasks: What could she do first, then second, then third as she circled through her station? What tasks could be clustered? She did everything on the fly, and when problems arose—technical or human—she solved them within the flow of work, while taking into account the emotional state of her co-workers. Was the manager in a good mood? Did the cook wake up on the wrong side of the bed? If so, how could she make an extra request or effectively return an order?

And then, of course, there were the customers who entered the restaurant with all sorts of needs, from physiological ones, including the emotions that accompany hunger, to a sometimes complicated desire for human contact. Her tip depended on how well she responded to these needs, and so she became adept at reading social cues and managing feelings, both the customers' and her own. No wonder, then, that Rosie was intrigued by psychology. The restaurant became the place where she studied human behavior, puzzling over the problems of her regular customers and refining her ability to deal with people in a difficult world. She took pride in *being among the public,* she'd say. *There isn't a day that goes by in the restaurant that you don't learn something.*

My mother quit school in the seventh grade to help raise her brothers and sisters. Some of those siblings made it through high school, and some dropped out to find work in railroad yards, factories, or restaurants. My father finished a grade or two in primary school in Italy and never darkened the schoolhouse door again. I didn't do well in school either. By high school I had accumulated a spotty academic record and many hours of hazy disaffection. I spent a few years on the vocational track, but in my senior year I was inspired by my English teacher and managed to squeak into a small college on probation.

My freshman year was academically bumpy, but gradually I began to see formal education as a means of fulfillment and as a road toward making a living. I studied the humanities and later the social and psychological sciences and taught for 10 years in a range of situations—elementary school, adult education courses, tutoring centers, a program for Vietnam veterans who wanted to go to college. Those students had socioeconomic and educational backgrounds similar to mine. Then I went back to graduate school to study education and cognitive psychology and eventually became a faculty member in a school of education.

Intelligence is closely associated with formal education—the type of schooling a person has, how much and how long—and most people seem to move comfortably from that notion to a belief that work requiring less schooling requires less intelligence. These assumptions run through our cultural history, from the post–Revolutionary War period, when mechanics were characterized by political rivals as illiterate and therefore incapable of participating in government, until today. More than once I've heard a manager label his workers as "a bunch of dummies." Generalizations about intelligence, work, and social class deeply affect our assumptions about ourselves and each other, guiding the ways we use our minds to learn, build knowledge, solve problems, and make our way through the world.

10   Although writers and scholars have often looked at the working class, they have generally focused on the values such workers exhibit rather than on the thought their work requires—a subtle but pervasive omission. Our cultural iconography promotes the muscled arm, sleeve rolled tight

against biceps, but no brightness behind the eye, no image that links hand and brain.

One of my mother's brothers, Joe Meraglio, left school in the ninth grade to work for the Pennsylvania Railroad. From there he joined the Navy, returned to the railroad, which was already in decline, and eventually joined his older brother at General Motors where, over a 33-year career, he moved from working on the assembly line to supervising the paint-and-body department. When I was a young man, Joe took me on a tour of the factory. The floor was loud—in some places deafening—and when I turned a corner or opened a door, the smell of chemicals knocked my head back. The work was repetitive and taxing, and the pace was inhumane.

Still, for Joe the shop floor provided what school did not; it was *like schooling,* he said, a place where *you're constantly learning.* Joe learned the most efficient way to use his body by acquiring a set of routines that were quick and preserved energy. Otherwise he would never have survived on the line.

As a foreman, Joe constantly faced new problems and became a consummate multitasker, evaluating a flurry of demands quickly, parceling out physical and mental resources, keeping a number of ongoing events in his mind, returning to whatever task had been interrupted, and maintaining a cool head under the pressure of grueling production schedules. In the midst of all this, Joe learned more and more about the auto industry, the technological and social dynamics of the shop floor, the machinery and production processes, and the basics of paint chemistry and of plating and baking. With further promotions, he not only solved problems but also began to find problems to solve: Joe initiated the redesign of the nozzle on a paint sprayer, thereby eliminating costly and unhealthy overspray. And he found a way to reduce energy costs on the baking ovens without affecting the quality of the paint. He lacked formal knowledge of how the machines under his supervision worked, but he had direct experience with them, hands-on knowledge, and was savvy about their quirks and operational capabilities. He could experiment with them.

In addition, Joe learned about budgets and management. Coming off the line as he did, he had a perspective of workers' needs and management's demands, and this led him to think of ways to improve efficiency on the line while relieving some of the stress on the assemblers. He had each worker in a unit learn his or her coworkers' jobs so they could rotate across stations to relieve some of the monotony. He believed that rotation would allow assemblers to get longer and more frequent breaks. It was an easy sell to the people on the line. The union, however, had to approve any modification in job duties, and the managers were wary of the change. Joe had to argue his case on a number of fronts, providing him a kind of rhetorical education.

15   Eight years ago I began a study of the thought processes involved in work like that of my mother and uncle. I catalogued the cognitive demands of a range of blue-collar and service jobs, from waitressing and hair styling to plumbing and welding. To gain a sense of how knowledge and skill develop, I observed experts as well as novices. From the details of this close examination, I tried to fashion what I called "cognitive biographies" of blue-collar workers. Biographical accounts of the lives of scientists, lawyers, entrepreneurs, and other professionals are rich with detail about the intellectual dimension of their work. But the life stories of working-class people are few and are typically accounts of hardship and courage or the achievements wrought by hard work.

Our culture—in Cartesian fashion—separates the body from the mind, so that, for example, we assume that the use of a tool does not involve abstraction. We reinforce this notion by defining intelligence solely on grades in school and numbers on IQ tests. And we employ social biases pertaining to a person's place on the occupational ladder. The distinctions among blue, pink, and white collars carry with them attributions of character, motivation, and intelligence. Although we rightly acknowledge and amply compensate the play of mind in white-collar and professional work, we diminish or erase it in considerations about other endeavors—physical and service work particularly. We also often ignore the experience of everyday work in administrative deliberations and policymaking.

But here's what we find when we get in close. The plumber seeking leverage in order to work in tight quarters and the hair stylist adroitly handling scissors and comb manage their bodies strategically. Though work-related actions become routine with experience, they were learned at some point through observation, trial and error, and, often, physical or verbal assistance from a coworker or trainer. I've frequently observed novices talking to themselves as they take on a task, or shaking their head or hand as if to erase an attempt before trying again. In fact, our traditional notions of routine performance could keep us from appreciating the many instances within routine where quick decisions and adjustments are made. I'm struck by the thinking-in-motion that some work requires, by all the mental activity that can be involved in simply getting from one place to another: the waitress rushing back through her station to the kitchen or the foreman walking the line.

The use of tools requires the studied refinement of stance, grip, balance, and fine-motor skills. But manipulating tools is intimately tied to knowledge of what a particular instrument can do in a particular situation and do better than other similar tools. A worker must also know the characteristics of the material one is engaging—how it reacts to various cutting or compressing devices, to degrees of heat, or to lines of force. Some of these things demand judgment, the weighing of options, the consideration of multiple variables, and, occasionally, the creative use of a tool in an unexpected way.

In manipulating material, the worker becomes attuned to aspects of the environment, a training or disciplining of perception that both enhances knowledge and informs perception. Carpenters have an eye for length, line, and angle; mechanics troubleshoot by listening; hair stylists are attuned to shape, texture, and motion. Sensory data merge with concept, as when an auto mechanic relies on sound, vibration, and even smell to understand what cannot be observed.

Planning and problem solving have been studied since the earliest   20
days of modern cognitive psychology and are considered core elements in Western definitions of intelligence. To work is to solve problems. The big difference between the psychologist's laboratory and the workplace is that in the former the problems are isolated and in the latter they are embedded in the real-time flow of work with all its messiness and social complexity.

Much of physical work is social and interactive. Movers determining how to get an electric range down a flight of stairs require coordination, negotiation, planning, and the establishing of incremental goals. Words, gestures, and sometimes a quick pencil sketch are involved, if only to get the rhythm right. How important it is, then, to consider the social and communicative dimension of physical work, for it provides the medium for so much of work's intelligence.

Given the ridicule heaped on blue-collar speech, it might seem odd to value its cognitive content. Yet, the flow of talk at work provides the channel for organizing and distributing tasks, for troubleshooting and problem solving, for learning new information and revising old. A significant amount of teaching, often informal and indirect, takes place at work. Joe Meraglio saw that much of his job as a supervisor involved instruction. In some service occupations, language and communication are central: observing and inter-preting behavior and expression, inferring mood and motive, taking on the perspective of others, responding appropriately to social cues, and knowing when you're understood. A good hair stylist, for instance, has the ability to convert vague requests (*I want something light and summery*) into an appro-priate cut through questions, pictures, and hand gestures.

Verbal and mathematical skills drive measures of intelligence in the Western Hemisphere, and many of the kinds of work I studied are thought to require relatively little proficiency in either. Compared to certain kinds of white-collar occupations, that's true. But written symbols flow through physical work.

Numbers are rife in most workplaces: on tools and gauges, as measure-ments, as indicators of pressure or concentration or temperature, as guides to sequence, on ingredient labels, on lists and spreadsheets, as markers of quantity and price. Certain jobs require workers to make, check, and verify calculations, and to collect and interpret data. Basic math can be involved, and some workers develop a good sense of numbers and patterns. Consider, as well, what might be called material mathematics: mathematical func-tions embodied in materials and actions, as when a carpenter builds a cabinet or a flight of stairs. A simple mathematical act can extend quickly beyond itself. Measuring, for example, can involve more than recording the dimensions of an object. As I watched a cabinetmaker measure a long strip of wood, he read a number off the tape out loud, looked back over his shoul-der to the kitchen wall, turned back to his task, took another measurement, and paused for a moment in thought. He was solving a problem involving the molding, and the measurement was important to his deliberation about structure and appearance.

In the blue-collar workplace, directions, plans, and reference books rely on illustrations, some representational and others, like blueprints, that require training to interpret. Esoteric symbols—visual jargon—depict switches and receptacles, pipe fittings, or types of welds. Workers them-selves often make sketches on the job. I frequently observed them grab a pencil to sketch something on a scrap of paper or on a piece of the material they were installing.

Though many kinds of physical work don't require a high literacy level, more reading occurs in the blue-collar workplace than is generally thought, from manuals and catalogues to work orders and invoices, to lists, labels, and forms. With routine tasks, for example, reading is integral to understanding production quotas, learning how to use an instrument, or applying a product. Written notes can initiate action, as in restaurant orders or reports of machine malfunction, or they can serve as memory aids.

True, many uses of writing are abbreviated, routine, and repetitive, and they infrequently require interpretation or analysis. But analytic moments can be part of routine activities, and seemingly basic reading and writing can be cognitively rich. Because workplace language is used in the flow of other activities, we can overlook the remarkable coordination of words, numbers, and drawings required to initiate and direct action.

If we believe everyday work to be mindless, then that will affect the work we create in the future. When we devalue the full range of everyday cognition, we offer limited educational opportunities and fail to make fresh and meaningful instructional connections among disparate kinds of skill and knowledge. If we think that whole categories of people—identified by class or occupation—are not that bright, then we reinforce social separations and cripple our ability to talk across cultural divides.

Affirmation of diverse intelligence is not a retreat to a softhearted definition of the mind. To acknowledge a broader range of intellectual capacity is to take seriously the concept of cognitive variability, to appreciate in all the Rosies and Joes the thought that drives their accomplishments and defines who they are. This is a model of the mind that is worthy of a democratic society.

Analyze

1. Explain the role of Rose's mother in this article. What does she help to show or represent?

2. Cognitive variability is central to Rose's argument. He says, "In manipulating material, the worker becomes attuned to aspects of the environment, a training or disciplining of perception that both enhances knowledge and informs perception." Explain this concept in your own words.

3. Rose explains that "Verbal and mathematical skills drive measures of intelligence in the Western Hemisphere, and many of the kinds of work I studied are thought to require relatively little proficiency in either." How does this point fit into his main idea about work?

4. In your own words, explain the position or attitude that Rose seems to be pushing against. What assumptions is he trying to correct?

5. What is the strongest part of Rose's article? What passage strikes you as the most powerful and effective in getting you to celebrate the complexities of blue-collar work?

Explore

1. Are you from a blue-collar or white-collar family? How do you think your upbringing influenced your understanding of work?
2. How did your upbringing influence your understanding of intelligence? Be as specific as possible in your explanation. What kinds of intellectual skills did you learn to value or ignore?
3. Rose argues that "we rightly acknowledge and amply compensate the play of mind in white-collar and professional work, [but] we diminish or erase it in considerations about other endeavors—physical and service work particularly." Do you agree or disagree? What experiences support your position?
4. Rose argues, "Our culture—in Cartesian fashion—separates the body from the mind, so that, for example, we assume that the use of a tool does not involve abstraction." Consider a tool that you're familiar with—something you use often. Explain how that tool involves abstraction.
5. Rose explains that his mother studied human behavior in her job. How much do you, as a worker or college student, have to study and attend to the complexities of human behavior? In short, how are you a psychologist? How might you be better at your job if you knew more psychology?

Forging Connections

1. How much does work depend on social media? Consider a specific job—one that you have or may have someday. In an essay, explain how specific social media sites and services support or undermine the success of the work. Borrow insights from the following writers in Chapter 4: Lucy P. Marcus ("What It Means Today To Be 'Connected'"), Cynthia Jones ("Lying, Cheating, and Virtual Relationships"), Michael Erard ("What I Didn't Write About When I Wrote About Quitting Facebook"), or Steven D. Krause ("Living Within Social Networks").

2. Analyze the language of work. If you have a job, examine the particular phrases, words, and language habits of your associates. What specific words or phrases have unique meaning among you and your associates? What codes do you use? How do you conceal meaning from customers or bosses? In an essay, describe that language as thoroughly as possible. Consider the workplace as its own culture—or what is sometimes called a *microculture.* Describe specific situations and exchanges to help characterize the nature of the communication. Borrow insights and strategies from writers in Chapter 3, "Language: What We Mean," specifically Blake Gopnik ("Revolution in a Can"), Richard Chin ("The Science of Sarcasm? Yeah, Right"), and Autumn Whitefield-Madrano ("Thoughts on a Word: Fine").

Looking Further

1. Research the average salary in your chosen career field—or one that you're interested in. Does the salary depend on geography or advanced degrees? Or does it depend entirely on experience? Make a case that workers in your field should, on average, be paid more than professional athletes, movie stars, or even rock stars. Explain the particular value your field adds to the civilization. Take on and correct misunderstanding or inaccurate portrayals of people in your field. If necessary, point to mischaracterizations in popular culture. Integrate images, charts, or graphs to thoroughly present the sophistication and value of your field.

2. Look further into college loan debt. What might it mean for you and your generation? How will it impact the culture of college and broader trends in American culture? Think big. Make connections between financial struggles in your generation and broader academic practices. How might the cost of college and the shrinking government contributions to higher education impact students? How will that, in turn, impact the shared values and beliefs beyond college life?

2 Consumerism: How We Spend

It's impossible to deny: If you attend college, work, drive, eat, use a computer, wear clothes, or talk on the phone, you're a consumer—not just a person who acquires things but an economic and cultural force. The average American citizen impacts the world simply by purchasing goods and services. Our needs and desires ripple outward. We influence labor trends, currency, production, and even political policy around the globe. In short, how we shop impacts how millions of others live.

Of course, we don't usually see ourselves in this light. We tend to see our purchasing decisions as personal—simple extensions of our own yearnings and needs. But while we select our next pair of pants, cell phone plan, caffeinated beverage, or house, we are being studied and tracked. Like at no other time in history, shoppers are being watched. Our next consumer move has been predicted, imagined, and charted out by those who want to shape our desires and then capitalize on them. In an unprecedented international spy game, we have been labeled according to our geography, age, race, gender, and fashion sense. In other words, as consumers, we are both agents and objects—targets of study and engines of commerce. We have immense power; yet, we are always nudged into decisions by trends and forces beyond us. And whether we admit it or not, American consumers are largely predictable and profoundly obedient to the marketing messages that surround us.

The readings in this chapter focus on the tensions of consumerism—on the forces behind and the effects of our consumption. Sara Davis, Dan Heath and Chip Heath, and Sharon Begley and Jean Chatzky all examine the power of products to lure us in and even dictate our tastes. Drew Harwell shows how appetites work in a particular social setting. David E. Procter and Charles Kenny show the holes in our otherwise powerful system of production and consumption. Fredrik deBoer and Sharon Angel reveal the historical complexity of our own desires. Finally, Damien Walter calls for a new culture entirely—one that supports creativity rather than consumption.

Sara Davis
Freshly Minted

A PhD candidate in literature, Sara Davis is the advertising and direct mail manager at University of Pennsylvania Press and a freelance puzzle editor for Kappa Publishing Group. She writes and blogs on the intersection of food and culture. Her columns appear in the online magazines *Table Matters* and *The Smart Set*. In the following *Smart Set* article, Davis examines a common ingredient in an everyday product.

O nce, and only once, I saw a stranger behaving curiously in the toothpaste aisle. He was standing with his arms crossed and brow furrowed; his eyes seemed to scan everything from the top shelf to bottom, then back to the top again. I waited some time for him to move before I realized that he was doing the same thing I had come to do: Read the labels and frown. Cool Mint, Strong Mint, Radiant Mint, Fresh Mint, Clean Mint, Vanilla Mint, Spearmint, Cinnamint, Now With Intense Mint Flavor: There were no options without mint.

I can't speak for the stranger, but my disappointment with this stunning variety was dermatological. In my early 20s I was diagnosed with a skin condition that was aggravated by among other things, mint oil. At the time, I was a serious mint user: I always had a pack of gum in my bag and thought Altoids were a required final course after every meal. I replaced the breath mints with xylitol-based fruit gums and the old-fashioned remedy of fresh fruit after a meal, but mintless toothpaste is a specialty item, difficult to find: for most toothpastes, mint is an essential feature, not an optional flavor.

But in the history of dental hygiene, the ubiquity of mint is a relatively recent phenomenon. Humankind has devised itself breath fresheners and dental abrasives throughout recorded time, but these varied greatly among cultures, depending mostly on what materials were available. Crushed shells, chalk or brick dust, and even powdered bone could serve to scrub teeth and clean the gums until the invention of toothpaste in the late 19th century. To sweeten the breath, medieval Europeans could crush herbs into their tooth scrub or vinegar mouthwash; mint was sometimes used for this purpose, but so were rosemary, parsley, and sage. Other cultures chewed aromatic seeds—fennel seeds, cardamom, star anise—to abrade and sweeten the mouth; some of these fragrant seeds still appear in the bowls of colorful mukhwas you see at Indian restaurants.

The twentieth century brought several changes to this homemade, all-natural dental care: improved science led to a better understanding of hygiene and new technology led to the industrialization of materials that had previously been made in the home, as well as brand new products. One of these products, Listerine, made good use of another twentieth-century device—advertising.

5   The Listerine company didn't invent halitosis—neither the word nor the condition—but they did invent an extremely effective marketing campaign for an extremely foul-tasting liquid. Originally a surgical antiseptic, Listerine destroys the primary cause of malodorous breath, bacteria that live in the mouth. But science aside, the acrid antiseptic won its way into the mouths of the American public by way of social insecurities. No one wants

bad breath, and if everyone else is gargling with Listerine, then those who don't will become social pariahs.

A campaign like that, which exaggerates a social ailment and normalizes the cure, can rewrite cultural history. Suddenly, daily mouth care was considered the new normal, a recognizable routine that other products could capitalize on. By 1932, Lifesavers advertisements could not only borrow a character from Listerine's campaign, reanimating the halitosis-suffering social and romantic outcast, but could also build on the normalized practice of mouthwash. It's not enough to rinse the mouth, these ads claimed; you should be ready to pop a breath-sweetening candy throughout the day.

There's not a single ingredient in a Lifesaver that combats halitosis or cleans the mouth, but each of the candies offered in that period features a flavor agent that has historically been used as a breath freshener: Pep-O-mint, Wint-O-green, Cl-O-ve, Lic-O-rice, Cinn-O-mon, and Vi-O-let. Violet and licorice seem like old-fashioned flavors to us now, but both have sweet and slightly astringent tastes that made them good crossover candies for a breath-saving sweet. Clove and cinnamon still appear in toothpastes today, particularly European and Middle Eastern brands, thanks to their strong and fiery flavors. But for an early twentieth century American manufacturer, mint oils would have been the cheapest and easiest breath-freshening flavor agent to obtain. Mint farms flourished in cool, damp regions near the Great Lakes and in the Pacific Northwest; some companies had already made a fortune distilling mint oils for export and medicinal use (peppermint was thought to ease digestive distress), and the addition of the manufacture of candies and toothpastes was a lucrative leap.

> "A campaign like that, which exaggerates a social ailment and normalizes the cure, can rewrite cultural history."

But it wasn't accessibility alone that made peppermint the most popular Lifesaver flavor for years and, over time, the preferred flavor for dental hygiene products. It's the sensation, more than the scent or the taste, that causes us to associate mint with clean mouths. Mint makes the mouth feel cold.

That "fresh" sensation is a thermal illusion: the actual temperature of your mouth doesn't change. Mouths contain particular cells that that activate in the presence of hot or cold: the condition of extreme temperature "turns on" the cell, which then sends a message to the brain that the mouth is rather hot or rather cold. But menthol also "turns on" these cells, which send their message to the brain as directed, and we experience a coolness in the mouth that isn't there. By itself, mint doesn't make the mouth a less suitable environment for germs; it's the abrasives in toothpastes or the alcohols in mouthwashes that do the dirty work. But it's easy to see how minty freshness became associated with cleanliness: the illusory change of temperature and the sharp, distinctive taste remind us more of cleaning agents than candy.

10   At the same time, the cool feeling of mint is more appealing and marketable than the taste of actual astringent solutions. Classic Listerine doesn't cool, it burns: that fiery sensation is not a thermal illusion but a mild irritation of the sensitive mouth tissues as the antiseptic solution goes about its germ-killing business. Effective, but it doesn't make a strong case for its own daily use. And so, in an intriguing reversal of the invented demand for antiseptic mouthwash, the market compelled Listerine to introduce a gentler, mint-flavored antiseptic for the first time in 1992. As the company president remarked to the *New York Times,* they'd done their research, and they knew that mint is what the market wanted.

In the toothpaste aisle, it certainly seemed that other dental care companies were acting on the same research, deviating from mintiness only for children, who perhaps haven't yet acquired the taste for the strong, astringent flavor. Adult toothpastes tend to come with a maximized mint punch. Because we associate that cool sensation with a clean sensation, toothpastes promise us more intense mint flavor to create the illusion of a more intensely clean mouth.

The promise is not so appealing if you associate mint oil with a puffy, swollen mouth and itchy face, however. My mint reaction subsided as I got older, as often happens with allergies, so I now enjoy mint tea and can withstand a mildly minted baking soda toothpaste. But without the daily exposure to concentrated mint oils, the tastes of "mint expressions" and "curiously strong mints" are repellent to me.

Analyze

1. In your own words, explain how "social insecurities" figured into the success of Listerine.
2. How did the American public buy into the idea of mint toothpaste?
3. How does Davis's personal experience with mint figure into her main idea?

4. What does Davis's article say about consumerism and culture?

5. Consider the article by Sharon Begley and Jean Chatzky in this chapter. How does Begley and Chatzky's point about neuroscience relate to Davis's explanation of ad campaigns and the illusion of "freshness"?

Explore

1. What oral hygiene products do you use? Why do you select one type or brand over others?

2. Davis explains how a particular ad campaign "exaggerates a social ailment and normalizes the cure." In your own words, explain how a cure becomes normalized.

3. How do ad campaigns, like those for Listerine or toothpaste, change history?

4. What other ad campaign (or type of campaign) has impacted the way Americans think of themselves, their bodies, or their families?

5. Why do you think illusions like the "fresh sensation" of mint toothpaste work so well? Why do consumers buy into them?

David E. Procter
The Rural Grocery Crisis

The author of two books on community building, David E. Procter is the director of the Center for Engagement and Community Development and the Institute for Civic Discourse and Democracy at Kansas State University, where he works to revive rural and local communities. The following article originally appeared in the *Daily Yonder*, whose motto is to "keep it rural." Here, Procter considers the demise of the rural grocery store and possible implications for our lives as consumers and citizens.

"**W**e *are one of your statistics, I'm afraid. We are losing our grocery store in Protection. The owner has an illness and she must sell or go out of business. It will be a sad situation for an already depressed town."*

This e-mail, from an economic development director in Southwest Kansas, is one of many we've received at Kansas State University. Similar e-mails, letters, and phone calls are coming into non-profits, local governments, universities, and economic development offices, and all are making the same point.

Rural America's grocery stores are facing a crisis. These businesses are closing at an alarming rate. Almost daily another small-town, independently-owned store shuts its doors and closes up shop.

In Iowa, for example, 43% of grocery stores in towns with populations less than 1,000 have closed, while in Kansas, nearly one in five rural grocery stores has gone out of business since 2006. These disappearing businesses are creating a crisis, as rural grocery stores represent a critical piece of the infrastructure that sustains rural America.

5   Rural grocery stores are part of the economic engine that sustains rural communities. They are a significant source of local taxes, powering the creation and maintenance of civic services and amenities. They provide essential, stable jobs—butchers, cashiers, managers, and stockers—at a time when we are desperate for employment opportunities.

Dollars spent at a local, independently-owned grocery store cycle through the local economy more than do dollars spent in national chain stores at the edge of town, and certainly more so than when those dollars are spent at an out-of-town big-box market.

Rural grocery stores are also a vital source for nutrition and health, providing a supply of fresh fruits, vegetables, dairy and protein. Where no grocery store exists, rural citizens are living in a "food desert." Citizens in these food-deprived areas struggle simply to find healthy and nutritious food for their families and themselves.

From initial investigations out of our office at the Center for Engagement and Community Development at Kansas State University, it has become clear that many parts of rural America are facing a crisis of access to healthy foods. Research indicates that millions of rural Americans live in food deserts.

A majority of the land area in several states of the Midwest and Mountain West could be described as food desert. "Severe" food desert counties—area where citizens have to drive more than 10 miles to a grocery store—are still apparent in the western portions of the Great Plains states. Approximately 40% of Kansas counties are "severe food desert" counties, and a significant portion of the population in half of Oklahoma's 77 counties live in severe food deserts. The following map displays the food deserts

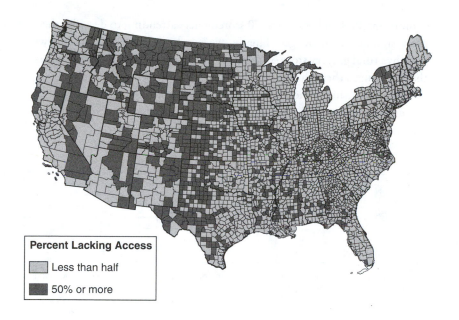

Percent Lacking Access

- Less than half
- 50% or more

throughout the U.S. and illustrates the severity of this problem in the central plains.

Grocery stores are also important vehicles for community development. They serve as gathering places, where folks see one another, talk about the latest issues affecting their towns, and dream together about what their communities could be. Just like our local schools, cafes, and post offices, rural grocery stores are important community assets, providing tangible evidence of local strength and stability.

So, the question is, why are these rural stores closing? Certainly, there are difficult economic and demographic trends that hurt rural grocery stores' chances to remain profitable. These include rural population decline, increased competition from larger chain stores, new shopping patterns, and changing food distribution models.

But we wanted to understand the crisis from the perspective of the rural grocery store owner and work to address those challenges. To understand the significant challenges rural grocery stores face, Kansas State mailed a survey to all rural grocery stores in Kansas communities with populations of 2,500 or less. Eighty-six of the 213 grocery stores responded.

Kansas State University and the Kansas Sampler Foundation—a Kansas non-profit dedicated to preserving rural Kansas—hosted a rural grocery summit in 2008 and asked the 70 storeowners attending to describe their most significant challenges. Finally, we conducted in-depth interviews with five rural grocery store owners and again asked them about the issues that challenged them the most.

From all of this, we identified the "Big Seven Challenges" facing rural grocery store owners. These challenges and the percentage of store owners identifying them as significant are illustrated in the graph below.

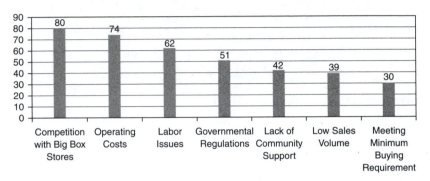

The most frequent, significant challenge identified by our rural grocers was competition with big box grocery stores.

15   In the past twenty years, we have seen a tremendous rise in the number of big-box, national-chain markets. In addition, big-box wholesalers have moved into the grocery business, and now many offer large food sections as part of their stores. Rural store owners view these stores as competition that threatens their very survival.

We also heard about the challenges of building maintenance, insurance, and shipping costs in the grocery business. The most significant operating expense is utilities, particularly energy. The costs of heating and cooling any store are significant.

By far, though, the operating cost of refrigeration is the greatest challenge. Many store owners struggle with outdated and inefficient coolers. A broken cooler could ruin a significant percentage of a grocery's inventory.

Many rural grocery stores struggle to find an adequate supply of reliable workers. Besides the challenge of finding "good help," in many small towns there is also the problem of finding any employees at all. In many rural communities, there is simply a lack of available folks to hire. This can be a real problem, because if the store owner and family are the only workers, they are likely to burn out or wear out.

Rural grocers must abide by a variety of regulations, such as those governing alcohol sales, food handling, WIC and SNAP participation, proper labeling, workers' comp, and federal and state wage laws.

Some grocers feel these government regulations are overly intrusive, but   20
for others the problem regulations pose is a matter of time and labor.

Lack of community support is one of the most frustrating challenges faced by rural grocers. Grocers say that they are asked to support a variety of community projects—the local ball team, church youth groups, the 4-H Club. They are frustrated when they notice adult sponsors and parents of these community groups traveling to distant big-box stores to do their grocery shopping.

This challenge of low sales volume is related to several others, and of course poses a basic problem. Nearly all rural grocery stores—certainly those in Kansas—are required to purchase a minimum dollar-amount of food each week from wholesale distributors. For small stores and especially those struggling with low sales volumes, this is a significant challenge.

If stores cannot meet the minimum, food distributors simply won't deliver food to their stores; they will literally drive right past and onto a store in the next town where the minimum can be met.

Analyze

1. Explain how Procter supports his statement: "Rural grocery stores are part of the economic engine that sustains rural communities."
2. According to this article, what is the biggest threat to rural grocery stores?
3. How does Procter make this about communities rather than stores?
4. How is the rural grocery store crisis about American culture? What does the disappearance of these stores say about change and resistance?
5. Compare Procter's article to Charles Kenny's "Haiti Doesn't Need Your Old T-Shirt" (in this chapter). What beliefs or assumptions do they share?

Explore

1. Explore "food deserts." What have other scholars and writers said about them?
2. In your area, what are the signs of community strength? What buildings, places, and events suggest cohesion and support?

3. In your area, what are the signs of community decay or weakness? Again, consider buildings, places, and events.
4. Why do you think sociologists and economists are interested in (and often concerned about) the decline of local stores?
5. How are consumers, rather than businesses, the main threat to local businesses?

Dan Heath and Chip Heath
How to Pick the Perfect Brand Name

Brothers Dan Heath and Chip Heath have coauthored several books, including, most recently, *Decisive: How to Make Better Choices in Life and Work* (2013). They are columnists for *Fast Company* magazine, which seeks to "inspire readers and users to think beyond traditional boundaries, lead conversations, and create the future of business." In the following article, the Heaths examine what contributes to, and results from, a successful brand name.

Even more than the crazy wigs and high-protein clothing, it's the name that makes Lady Gaga. If her name were Bethany Cranston (or, say, Stefani Germanotta), forget about it.

Everybody wants a Gaga name for their new product/website/startup. But if you've ever brainstormed about names, you know how deflating the process can be. The URLs for every four-letter word in the English language have long since been snatched up. Yet you crave something unique, something legally protectable. So here come the artful misspellings ("Gene-yus") and the syllable mashups ("TechnoRiffic"). Later, as you review your whiteboard full of gawky names, someone walks by with a BlackBerry and you seethe with envy. That's how it's done. (*Hey, has anyone trademarked Graype?*)

No one in the naming world has generated more envy than a boutique firm called Lexicon. You may not recognize the name. But Lexicon has created 15 billion-dollar brand names, including BlackBerry, Dasani, Febreze,

OnStar, Pentium, Scion, and Swiffer. Lexicon's steady success shows that great names do not come from lightning-bolt moments. (Nobody gets struck 15 times.) Rather, Lexicon's magic is its creative process.

Consider its recent work for Colgate, which was preparing to launch a disposable mini toothbrush. The center of the brush holds a dab of special toothpaste, which is designed to make rinsing unnecessary. So you can carry the toothbrush with you, use it in a cab or an airplane lavatory, and then toss it out.

Lexicon founder and CEO David Placek's first insight came early. When you first see the toothbrush, Placek says, what stands out is its small size. "You'd be tempted to start thinking about names that highlight the size, like Petite Brush or Porta-Brush," he says. As his team began to use the brush, what struck them was how unnatural it was, at first, not to spit out the toothpaste. But this new brush doesn't create a big mass of minty lather—the mouthfeel is lighter and more pleasant, more like a breath strip. So it dawned on them that the name of the brush should not signal smallness. It should signal lightness, softness, gentleness.

Armed with that insight, Placek asked his network of linguists—70 of them in 50 countries—to start brainstorming about metaphors, sounds, and word parts that connote lightness. Meanwhile, he asked another two colleagues within Lexicon to help. But he kept these two in the dark about the client and the product. Instead, he gave this team—let's call them the excursion team—a fictional mission. He told them that the cosmetics brand Olay wanted to introduce a line of oral-care products and it was their job to help it brainstorm about product ideas.

Placek chose Olay because he believed that beauty was an implicit selling point for the new brush. "Good oral care means white teeth, and white teeth are better looking," Placek says. So the excursion team began to come up with intriguing ideas. For instance, they proposed an Olay Sparkling Rinse, a mouthwash that would make your teeth gleam.

In the end, it was the insight about lightness, rather than beauty, that prevailed. The team of linguists produced a long list of possible words and phrases, and when Placek reviewed it, a word jumped out at him: *wisp*. It was the perfect association for the new brushing experience and it tested well; it's not something heavy and foamy, it's barely there. It's a wisp. Thus was born the Colgate Wisp.

Notice what's missing from the Lexicon process: the part when everyone sits around a conference table, staring at the toothbrush and brainstorming names together. ("Hey, how about ToofBrutch—the URL is available!") Instead, Lexicon's leaders often create three teams of two, with each group pursuing a different angle. Some of the teams, blind to the client and the product, chase analogies from related domains. For instance, in naming Levi's new Curve ID jeans, which offer different fits for different body types, the excursion team dug into references on surveying and engineering.

10   Necessarily, this often leads to wasted work—in the case of the Wisp, the excursion team found themselves at a dead end with the Olay project. But it's precisely this willingness to work in parallel, to endure some inefficiency, that often leads to a break in the case, as with the BlackBerry.

When Research in Motion engaged Lexicon, Placek and his team knew that they were fighting negative associations with PDAs: They buzz, they vibrate, they irritate us and stress us out. So he challenged the excursion team—again, unfamiliar with the actual client—to catalog things in the world that bring joy to people, that slow us down, that relax us. In other words, the antidotes to those negative PDA associations.

The list grew quickly. Camping, riding a bicycle, having a martini on Friday night. Taking a bubble bath, fly-fishing, cooking. Having a martini on Thursday night. Later, someone added "picking strawberries" to the list. Someone else plucked out the word *strawberry*. But one of Lexicon's linguists said, "No, strawberry sounds slow." (Think of the similar vowels in *drawl, dawdle, stall*.) Soon it was crossed out and replaced with the word blackberry underneath. *Hey, wait, the keys on the PDA look just like the seeds on a blackberry.* Epiphany!

Actually, no. "Most clients feel that they're going to know the perfect name as soon as they see it, but it doesn't happen that way," Placek says. Even "BlackBerry" was not easy to sell. The client had been leaning toward more descriptive names such as "EasyMail." (Interestingly, the same was true of past blockbuster names: Some at Intel had wanted to call the Pentium "ProChip," and some at P&G had wanted to call the Swiffer "EZMop." And no doubt someone wanted to call Budweiser "EZGut.")

As Lexicon's success demonstrates, a great name can make a big difference. When some smart marketer renamed the Chinese gooseberry a kiwi, the fruit became a huge hit. But we shouldn't overheroicize names. After all, we live in a world where some of the most powerful brands are called Microsoft, Walmart, and General Electric. Clearly, a mediocre name isn't destiny. For every Lady Gaga, there's a Katy Perry. So maybe there's hope for you after all, Bethany Cranston.

Analyze

1. What's so special about Lady Gaga—not the singer, but the name? Why is her name used in the introduction of the article?
2. Explain how the story of the *Wisp* functions in this article: why is the story told in detail? What does it help to show?
3. Explain how the point about kiwis, in the concluding paragraph, relates to the author's main point.
4. The title of the article promises to tell readers how to pick a perfect product name. In your own words, explain the brainstorming processes that the authors celebrate and one they seem to condemn.
5. The authors also make a subtle case against "lightning-bolt moments." Explain their case—and how they make it. Describe what examples or situations help to show their point.

Explore

1. Why is Katy Perry a worse name than Lady Gaga for a pop singer? And why is Bethany Cranston worse yet? How do the syllables, the vowels, and the word associations play into the effect of the names?
2. The authors suggest that BlackBerry, as a product name, is and should be envied. Why? How does *BlackBerry* function? Why do you think experts in the field of marketing would praise the name?
3. Name a product that you personally dislike but that also has a perfect name. Explain why the name, despite the product itself, is effective.
4. Companies spend millions of dollars every year on names and slogans. They carefully tweak words, fonts, and images to attract the target audience or primary consumer group. By and large, the process works. Americans respond very well to advertising. Explain how you have been part of this process. Tell of a specific product and how you were quietly attracted to its name, its slogan, or its packaging.

Charles Kenny
Haiti Doesn't Need Your Old T-Shirt

A development economist, Charles Kenny examines social and political trends related to growth and corruption. He is the author of numerous journal and magazine articles, books, and blog posts. The following article originally appeared in *Foreign Policy* magazine, which seeks to "combine original thinking with real-world illustrations of ideas in action." Here, Kenny questions the value of certain donated goods.

The Green Bay Packers this year beat the Pittsburgh Steelers to win Super Bowl XLV in Arlington, Texas. In parts of the developing world, however, an alternate reality exists: "Pittsburgh Steelers: Super Bowl XLV Champions" appears emblazoned on T-shirts from Nicaragua to Zambia. The shirt wearers, of course, are not an international cadre of Steelers die-hards, but recipients of the many thousands of excess shirts the National Football League produced to anticipate the post-game merchandising frenzy. Each year, the NFL donates the losing team's shirts to the charity World Vision, which then ships them off to developing countries to be handed out for free.

Everyone wins, right? The NFL offloads 100,000 shirts (and hats and sweatshirts) that can't be sold—and takes the donation as a tax break. World Vision gets clothes to distribute at no cost. And some Nicaraguans and Zambians get a free shirt. What's not to like?

Quite a lot, as it happens—so much so that there's even a Twitter hashtag, #SWEDOW, for "Stuff We Don't Want," to track such developed-world offloading, whether it's knit teddy bears for kids in refugee camps, handmade puppets for orphans, yoga mats for Haiti, or dresses made out of pillowcases for African children. The blog *Tales from the Hood*, run by an anonymous aid worker, even set up a SWEDOW prize, won by Knickers 4 Africa, a (thankfully now defunct) British NGO set up a couple of years ago to send panties south of the Sahara.

Here's the trouble with dumping stuff we don't want on people in need: What they need is rarely the stuff we don't want. And even when they do need that kind of stuff, there are much better ways for them to get it than for a Western NGO to gather donations at a suburban warehouse, ship everything off to Africa or South America, and then try to distribute it to remote areas. World Vision, for example, spends 58 cents per shirt on shipping, warehousing, and distributing them, according to data reported by the blog *Aid Watch*—well within the range of what a secondhand shirt costs in a developing country. Bringing in shirts from outside also hurts the local economy: Garth Frazer of the University of Toronto estimates that increased used-clothing imports accounted for about half of the decline in apparel industry employment in Africa between 1981 and 2000. Want to really help a Zambian? Give him a shirt made in Zambia.

The mother of all SWEDOW is the $2 billion-plus U.S. food aid program, a boondoggle that lingers on only because of the lobbying muscle of agricultural conglomerates. (Perhaps the most embarrassing moment was when the United States airdropped 2.4 million Pop-Tarts on Afghanistan in January 2002.) Harvard University's Nathan Nunn and Yale University's Nancy Qian have shown that the scale of U.S. food aid isn't strongly tied to how much recipient countries actually require it—but it does rise after a bumper crop in the American heartland, suggesting that food aid is far more about dumping American leftovers than about sending help where help's needed. And just like secondhand clothing, castoff food exports can hurt local economies. Between the 1980s and today, subsidized rice exports from the United States to Haiti wiped out thousands of local farmers and helped reduce the proportion of locally produced rice consumed in the country from 47 to 15 percent. Former President Bill Clinton concluded that the food aid program "may have been good for some of my farmers in Arkansas, but it has not worked. . . . I had to live every day with the consequences of the lost capacity to produce a rice crop in Haiti to feed those people because of what I did."

Bottom line: Donations of cash are nearly always more effective. Even if there are good reasons to give stuff rather than money, in most cases the stuff can be bought locally. Economist Amartya Sen, for example, has conclusively shown that people rarely die of starvation or malnutrition because of a lack of food in the neighborhood or the country. Rather, it is because they can't afford to buy the food that's available. Yet, as Connie Veillette of the Center for Global Development reports, shipping U.S. food abroad in response to humanitarian disasters is so cumbersome it takes four to six months to get there after the crisis begins. Buying food locally, the U.S. Government Accountability Office has found, would be 25 percent cheaper and considerably faster, too.

5

In some cases, if there really is a local shortage and the goods really are needed urgently, the short-term good done by clothing or food aid may well outweigh any long-term costs in terms of local development. But if people donate SWEDOW, they may be less likely to give much-needed cash. A study by Aradhna Krishna of the University of Michigan, for example, suggests that charitable giving may be lower among consumers who buy cause-related products because they feel they've already done their part. Philanthrocapitalism may be chic: The company Toms Shoes has met with considerable commercial success selling cheap footwear with the added hook that for each pair you buy, the company gives a pair to a kid in the developing world (it's sold more than a million pairs to date). But what if consumers are buying Toms instead of donating to charity, as some surely are? Much better to stop giving them the stuff we don't want—and start giving them the money they do.

Analyze

1. Kenny opens his article by alluding to football T-shirts. How does the image of Haiti's citizens wearing NFL shirts relate to his main point?
2. Why is the food aid program, explained in paragraph 5, "the mother of all SWEDOW"?
3. In your own words, explain Kenny's subtle argument about people who send their T-shirts and underwear to poor counties. What do those people not understand? How are their assumptions flawed? Where are they going wrong?
4. Even if you've never seen the word before, what can you infer about *philanthropicapitalism?* Given Kenny's concluding paragraph, how would you define the term?
5. Explain how Kenny's argument relates to Dan Heath and Chip Heath's article, "How to Pick the Perfect Brand Name" (in this chapter).

Explore

1. Do you give to charity? Why or why not?
2. If everyone in America read Kenny's article, what might change? How might Kenny's words impact people's thinking, shopping habits, or charity donations?
3. Kenny argues, "Here's the trouble with dumping stuff we don't want on people in need: What they need is rarely the stuff we don't want."

Explain why this might be true. Consider a specific item that might be shipped to a poor country. Further, explain how sending that item might do more harm than good.

4. Consider the following response to Kenny's article—posted to the *Foreign Policy* website by William O'Keefe, the Senior Director of Advocacy for Catholic Relief Services. Explain why you accept or do not accept O'Keefe's response:

> Though Mr. Kenny makes valid points in his critique of giving items such as clothing in the name of international charity, his brush gets a bit too broad when he uses it to condemn the entire food aid program of the United States. Certainly that program has its flaws and can be improved, but food from the U.S. keeps many people alive and healthy throughout the world. Today, millions in East Africa rely on food from the U.S. to get them through a horrendous drought. This is not the same as giving people t-shirts. Nor is it "dumping stuff we don't want on people in need." It is giving much needed nutrition to people who have no way else to get it.

Drew Harwell
Honey Buns Sweeten Life for Florida Prisoners

A business reporter for the *Tampa Bay Times*, Drew Harwell explores the politics of place. His articles often focus on real estate, housing, and property tax. In the following, Harwell considers the large role of a small commodity in the Florida prison system.

The honey buns enter lockup the same way anyone else does: bound, escorted through halls and sally ports, and secluded in small boxes solely opened from the outside. From there the honey buns languish for days, maybe longer, until they're gone.

They are a lowly, sturdy food designed for desperate cravings and vending machine convenience. They can endure weeks of neglect and even a mild mashing in a coat pocket or backpack. They are, it should come as no surprise, especially beloved by a similarly hardy but disrespected population: Florida's prison inmates.

Inmates in the Florida prison system buy 270,000 honey buns a month. Across the state, they sell more than tobacco, envelopes and cans of Coke. And they're just as popular among Tampa Bay's county jails. In Pasco's Land O'Lakes Detention Center, they're outsold only by freeze-dried coffee and ramen noodles.

Not only that, these honey buns—so puffy!—have taken on lives of their own among the criminal class: as currency for trades, as bribes for favors, as relievers for stress and substitutes for addiction. They've become birthday cakes, hooch wines, last meals—even ingredients in a massive tax fraud.

5   So what is it about these little golden glazed snacks? Is it that they're cheap, which is big, since the prisoners rely on cash from friends and family? That their sugary denseness could stop a speeding bullet? That they're easy, their *mise en place* just the unwrapping of plastic? What gives?

Maybe considering the honey bun can help us understand life behind bars.

Jailhouse cuisine is a closely calculated science.

A day's meals inside the mess hall must be hearty enough to meet the 2,750-calorie count, healthy enough to limit fat and sodium, easy enough for prison cooks to prepare and cheap enough to meet the state's average grocery bill—about $1.76 per inmate per day.

With all criteria met, meals behind bars achieve an impressive level of mediocrity. The portions are reasonable, the nutritional content adequate, the taste ordinary, the presentation dull, the blandness as inescapable as the facilities themselves. The meals are made to guarantee very little except survival.

10   Problem inmates don't have it any easier. Their punishment: "special management meals" of Nutraloaf, a tasteless lump of carrots, spinach and grits that resembles a sad fruitcake. Compared to that, honey buns are a revolution. Honey buns are fried dough in a bag. Honey buns meet next to none of the human body's needs and are impressively unhealthy.

The 6 ounces of a Mrs. Freshley's Grand Honey Bun, the favored pastry of Florida's prisons, serve up 680 calories, 51 grams of sugar and 30 grams of fat. The icing is sticky and frost white, like Elmer's Glue. The taste bears all the subtlety of a freshly licked sugar cube.

"As you can imagine," said Janice Anderson, a spokeswoman for Flowers Foods, which owns the Mrs. Freshley's brand, "this product is for those folks that feel like having something very decadent."

Decadent!

Inmates at the Maryland Correctional Institution for Women used honey buns as the base for a Christmas apple pie. Inmates at the Robeson County Jail in Lumberton, N.C., mixed in honey buns to sweeten a wine they fermented from orange juice. During his two-month stay in an Illinois jail cell, NFL defensive tackle Tank Johnson gulped down, after hearty meals of beef sticks and summer sausages, 40 honey buns for dessert.

Prisoners on death row have even turned to the sweets for their last   15
meals. Charles Roache, lethally injected in North Carolina in 2004, chose a sirloin steak, popcorn shrimp and a honey bun.

George Alec Robinson, an unemployed sanitation worker and father of three, paid his public defenders in honey buns after they saved him from Virginia's electric chair.

"He said, 'This is all in the world I can give you guys,'" attorney James C. Clark told the *Washington Post*. "They were good, too."

In September, the day after the New Orleans Saints beat the San Francisco 49ers in a Monday Night Football game, a fight broke out in the Alpha Pod of the Hernando County Jail. Inmate Ricardo Sellers, 21, had punched Brandon Markey, 23, in the face, sending Markey to a Brooksville hospital, according to Hernando deputies. Sellers was angry that Markey hadn't paid up after losing a bet over football.

His debt? Four honey buns.

For all their sweetness, honey buns have a history of involvement in   20
prison violence. In 2006, at the Kent County Jail in Michigan, inmate Benny Rochelle dragged his cell mate off the top bunk, killing the man, when he could not find his honey bun. And last year, at the Lake Correctional Institution west of Orlando, two men were sentenced to life in prison for stabbing with crude shivs the man they thought had stolen shaving cream, cigarettes and a honey bun from their footlockers.

Yes, murder over honey buns. Was it their decadence, or their status as jailhouse currency?

In Texas and Pennsylvania, inmates bartered honey buns for tablets of Seroquel, an addictive antipsychotic abused on the street as a sleeping pill.

In Sarasota, a millionaire businessman charged with child abuse earned the nickname "Commissary King" after fashioning honey buns into birthday cakes for inmates he felt he could sway to his defense.

In Naples, a bail bondsman was accused of giving an inmate hundreds of dollars' worth of honey buns over 13 years as rewards for referring him business.

25   And at the Graceville Work Camp, in the Panhandle, a Jacksonville trucker known for sharing his faith called it one of his great joys to sneak honey buns under inmates' pillows. In some cases, honey buns have proven too seductive for inmates' own good. At the Stock Island Detention Center, outside Key West, scheming inmates offered overnight arrestees in the jail's drunk tank an irresistible deal: their Social Security numbers for a honey bun. Using the numbers, they filled out tax forms with phony information—a scam that cost the IRS more than $1 million in fraudulent refunds.

As a retired Monroe County sheriff told the *Miami Herald,* "They were eating a lot of honey buns on the taxpayer."

After Ryan Frederick took the stand last year during his capital murder trial in Virginia, prosecutor James Willett made a strange request.

Stand up. Open your jacket. Turn sideways.

When he had been arrested for shooting a detective during a drug raid, Frederick had weighed 120 pounds, according to the *Virginian-Pilot.* After a year in lockup, he ballooned to 185.

30   Exhibit A: Frederick's gut.

"You're not exactly wasting away from regret and remorse now, are you?" Willett said.

Frederick's behavior at the Chesapeake City Jail was central to prosecutors' argument that he had bragged of the killing. His weight gain, they said, further proved his shamelessness.

But during his testimony, Frederick said the extra pounds stemmed from something else.

To deal with the stresses of jail, he said, he ate.

35   "I have a bad habit of doughnuts and honey buns," he told the jury.

Some inmates use honey buns to combat cravings deeper than a sweet tooth. At the Hernando County Jail, where honey buns are regulars atop the bestsellers list, the sweets have served as substitutes for other vices.

"Many people in jail are addicts or abusers of substances," said jail administrator Maj. Mike Page. "Alcohol is based in sugars generally, and the human body will receive some satisfaction of cravings from the honey bun as a substitute for the sugar."

Armon Power, an inmate at Alabama's Holman Correctional Facility who earned 30 cents an hour stamping license plates at the prison tag plant, explained it to a TV crew in simpler terms: "I crave honey buns. I buy honey buns," he said. "I can't buy no wine."

Convicted murderer Michael Caruso is a canteen operator at the Zephyrhills state prison. His is a prestigious job. Of all the tedious prison work, his pays the most ($75 a month) and affords him the sweetest office: front and center to the boxes of honey buns.

He sells about 60 sweets a day at this sprawling, razor-wired campus of mostly elderly prisoners in east Pasco. The men like to smother the honey buns with peanut butter Squeezers packets. Some inmates, he said, try to "manipulate" him into handing them over for free, though most think their $1.08 price tags, cheaper than foods like the $2.75 Big AZ Bubba Twins chili cheese dogs, are easier to stomach.

"It's the same as on the street," Caruso said. "When you get paid you drink Budweiser. After that you drink Black Label."

In prison, as in life, thrift wins. In 2009, when Florida upped its canteen prices, 60 families called and wrote letters to complain. Most of the anger, according to the Associated Press, centered on the price of honey buns, raised from 66 cents to 99 cents. (To, now, $1.08.)

But something funny happens, Caruso said. On Fridays, inmates will buy up honey buns for the weekend, when they gather in the dayroom to watch football. The prisoners share. Seems to happen all the time.

Maybe that's what it is with honey buns. They're sweet, when nothing else is.

Analyze

1. On its surface, this article is about honey buns. On a deeper level, it's about prison life. And on a deeper level still, what is this article about?

2. Harwell explains that the honey buns sold in the prison are "impressively unhealthy." How does this point fit into the main idea of the article? Why is it important that the honey buns are devoid of nutritional value?
3. How does the fight between two inmates, Markey and Sellers, support Harwell's main idea?
4. Explain how the issue of alcoholism relates to Harwell's main idea.
5. Consider Harwell's choice for a one-word paragraph: "Decadent!" What purpose does that single word (with an exclamation point!) serve?

Explore

1. In your own words, why are honey buns so sought after in prison?
2. Does this article make prison inmates seem more ordinary or less ordinary? Point to specific passages that support your thinking.
3. How might having a family member or loved one in prison impact readers' understanding of this article?
4. The United States jails more of its citizens than any country in the world. And most of the inmates come from abject poverty or working-class families. How do these facts figure into your thinking about honey buns? Is there some correlation between honey buns and poverty? Honey buns and socioeconomic class?
5. Consider Sara Davis's history of mint or Begley and Chatzky's point about neuroscience and spending habits. How do their articles (both in this chapter) shed light on the prisoners' attraction to honey buns?

Sharon Begley and Jean Chatzky
The New Science Behind Your
Spending Addiction

The senior health and science correspondent at Reuters, Sharon Begley writes on issues related to neuroscience and the brain's potential for change. She is the author of numerous magazine articles, blog posts, and books, including the 2012 book *The Emotional Life of Your Brain*. Jean Chatzky is the financial editor for NBC's *Today*. She writes and speaks on issues related to personal finance, debt, and wealth. Among her many publications is the 2012 book *Money Rules*. In the following article, Begley and Chatzky examine our consumer impulses, and how we can change them.

Like many colleges, Washington University in St. Louis offers children of its faculty free tuition. So Leonard Green, a professor of psychology there, did all he could to persuade his daughter to choose the school. He extolled its academic offerings, praised its social atmosphere, talked up its extracurricular activities—and promised that if Hannah chose Washington he would give her $20,000 each undergraduate year, plus $20,000 at graduation, for a nest egg totaling $100,000.

She went to New York University.

To many, this might seem like a simple case of shortsightedness, a decision based on today's wants (an exciting city, independence) versus tomorrow's needs (money, shelter). Indeed, the choice to spend rather than save reflects a very human—and, some would say, American—quirk: a preference for immediate gratification over future gains. In other words, we get far more joy from buying a new pair of shoes today, or a Caribbean vacation, or an iPhone 4S, than from imagining a comfortable life tomorrow. Throw in an instant-access culture—in which we can get answers on the Internet within seconds, have a coffeepot delivered to our door overnight, and watch movies on demand—and we're not exactly training the next generation to delay gratification.

"Pleasure now is worth more to us than pleasure later," says economist William Dickens of Northeastern University. "We much prefer current consumption to future consumption. It may even be wired into us."

5   As brain scientists plumb the neurology of an afternoon at the mall, they are discovering measurable differences between the brains of people who save and those who spend with abandon, particularly in areas of the brain that predict consequences, process the sense of reward, spur motivation, and control memory.

In fact, neuroscientists are mapping the brain's saving and spending circuits so precisely that they have been able to rev up the saving and disable the spending in some people (in the lab, alas; not at the cash register). The result: people's preferences switch from spending like a drunken sailor to saving like a child of the Depression. All told, the gray matter responsible for some of our most crucial decisions is finally revealing its secrets. Call it the "moneybrain." Psychologists and behavioral economists, meanwhile, are identifying the personality types and other traits that distinguish savers from spenders, showing that people who aren't good savers are neither stupid nor irrational—but often simply don't accurately foresee the consequences of not saving. Rewire the brain to find pleasure in future rewards, and you're on the path to a future you really want.

In one experiment, neuroeconomist Paul Glimcher of New York University wanted to see what it would take for people to willingly delay gratification. He gave a dozen volunteers a choice: $20 now or more money, from $20.25 to $110, later. On one end of the spectrum was the person who agreed to take $21 in a month—to essentially wait a month in order to gain just $1. In economics-speak, this kind of person has a "flat discount function," meaning he values tomorrow almost as much as today and is therefore able to delay gratification. At the other end was someone who was willing to wait a month only if he got $68, a premium of $48 from the original offer. This is someone economists call a "steep discounter," meaning the value he puts on the future (and having money then) is dramatically less than the value he places on today; when he wants something, he wants it now. The $21 person was, tellingly, an MD-PhD student. "If you're willing to go to grad school for eight years, you're really willing to delay gratification," says Glimcher.

More revealing was the reason for the differences. To measure brain activity while people considered whether to delay gratification, researchers slid their subjects into functional magnetic resonance imaging (fMRI) machines. The scientists found that activity in two regions—the ventral striatum, tucked deep in the brain, and the medial prefrontal cortex (PFC) right behind the forehead—closely tracked people's preferences. In someone who was offered a choice between $100 today or $100 next week, activity in these regions plunged when the next-week choice was considered, and fell even more as the payoff was postponed further and further into the future. These are spend-it-now, to-hell-with-tomorrow people who seek immediate gratification. In other people, however, activity in the ventral striatum and medial prefrontal cortex activity was the same whether they were thinking of having money today or down the road—indicating that they were just as happy either way.

For anyone who wants to save more but can't seem to do so, that raises the obvious question: how can I make my ventral striatum and medial prefrontal cortex as happy about rewards in the future as they are about rewards today?

It's something that scientists are actively studying. In one classic study from   10
the late 1960s, fondly known as the marshmallow experiment, scientists at Stanford University led by psychologist Walter Mischel (now at Columbia University) offered 4-year-olds a marshmallow, and left it invitingly in front of them. The hitch: if the kids waited to eat the marshmallow until the experimenter, who stepped out of the room, returned in a few minutes, they could have two marshmallows. More than a decade later, the children who waited and got the second marshmallow scored much higher on the SAT, supporting the idea that impulse control and other aspects of "emotional intelligence" are linked to academic performance. The reward delayers were also less likely to be obese, to have become addicted to illegal drugs, and to be divorced—outcomes that are more likely in people who go for immediate gratification.

The marshmallow children were tested every dozen years or so, says Mischel, and are now in their 40s. In a study reported in August in the *Proceedings of the National Academy of Sciences,* scientists led by psychobiologist B. J. Casey of Weill Cornell Medical College gathered 59 of the original kids and gave them an adult version of the delayed-gratification test. Using fMRI, they analyzed differences in brain activity between those who were good at delaying gratification and those who opted for instant rewards, marshmallows or otherwise. In high delayers, the brain's thoughtful, rational prefrontal cortex was more active, as was the right inferior frontal gyrus, which inhibits the "I want it now" impulse. Poor delayers had less activity in both regions, but higher activity in regions of the limbic system that respond to instant gratification. Identifying the regions of the brain that control such impulses is a first step in learning how to strengthen them and, ultimately, to enjoy saving.

Other studies, too, have shown the key role the prefrontal cortex plays in making us willing to defer gratification today in favor of saving for retirement. The dorsolateral PFC, in particular, sends "calm down" signals to the midbrain's "I want it now" circuits. As a result, in studies that use strong magnets to temporarily disable the dorsolateral PFC on human volunteers, "people get more impulsive," says NYU's Glimcher. That is, they strongly prefer immediate gratification. "But if you artificially activate it," he says, people become perfectly content to save for tomorrow.

The noninvasive "zapping" technology, called transcranial magnetic stimulation (TMS), is currently being studied at Columbia University and NYU, among other places. The technology works by inducing a weak electric current in targeted regions of the brain. In the lab, that allows scientists to pinpoint regions of people's brains responsible for specific functions. In other words, if zapping an area disables that area, then anything the person can no longer do is presumably controlled by that spot.

So far, none of the researchers using TMS to map the brain have wheeled the device to a shopping mall and aimed it at people who buy $300 sunglasses and $150 T-shirts despite having contributed $0 to their savings, but the notion isn't preposterous. TMS has been successfully used to treat chronic pain, major depression, tinnitus, and some symptoms of schizophrenia, in each case by revving up or shutting down activity in specific brain circuits that underlie the condition.

15   Since zapping your brain to rev up the dorsolateral PFC is not ready for prime time, scientists have begun searching for more practical ways to develop a moneybrain that has a talent for saving. One hint comes from the discovery that the size of the dorsolateral PFC differs from one person to another, notes neuroeconomist Paul Zak of Claremont Graduate University, as does the number and strength of its connections to the midbrain's circuits. Everything that's been discovered about the plasticity of the adult brain suggests that it should be possible to increase the number or strength of these connections so that the midbrain receives more calming signals.

Research has also shown that having a good short-term (or "working") memory is associated with being able to project yourself into the future and plan for it, which is a prerequisite of saving. That's partly because achieving a goal requires keeping it in mind. Brain scans back this up: the dorsolateral PFC is responsible for both. In one recent study, psychologist Warren Bickel of Virginia Tech put people through training exercises that improved their memory, and found they also developed "longer time horizons," meaning they valued the future more. "We're only at the beginning of figuring out how to change people's temporal horizons," says Bickel. "But the preliminary data are encouraging."

That seems to be what some of those original marshmallow-experiment children accomplished. Although the kids who remained in the same category—good at delaying gratification as toddlers as well as adults, or bad at both ages—have received the lion's share of the media attention, Mischel points out that many of the kids who gobbled up the marshmallow at the age of 4 learned to resist the lure of immediate gratification by the time they were young adults. "Being unable to delay gratification is not something we're stuck with for life," says Mischel. And a public that is infatuated with brain scans should know that just because a brain behaves in a particular way does not mean that it is hard-wired to do so.

To the contrary: even children can train their brains to recognize that forgoing pleasure now can bring a greater payoff later, says Claremont's Zak: doing homework tonight can bring good grades next month; saving a small allowance to buy one nice thing later rather than cheap junk every week. "You develop willpower and patience through practice," he says. "If you defer gratification, the payoff can be greater than with immediate gratification," says Zak, "but your brain has to learn that." He also finds that a squirt of the hormone oxytocin—known as the "love hormone" because of the role it plays in pair bonding and maternal behavior—makes people more patient: when people with a shot of the hormone are offered $10 now or $12 later, they are willing to wait 43 percent longer for that "later" to arrive (14 days rather than 10, for instance). "This tells us that people who are happier and have greater social support save more," says Zak. "Oxytocin reduces anxiety, so we can make decisions that are better for us." Not that we should be shooting ourselves up—but the research does suggest that any way we can reduce anxiety might also help us save for a rainy day.

This is good news for a generation of young people whose odds appear to be stacked against them. Research shows this group typically isn't willing to delay gratification, in part because they tend to be more impulsive and less patient, but also because they think they have plenty of time to save when they're older. "A college student who expects to graduate and obtain a high-paying job, or a young professional who expects to gain significant annual raises, will be apt not to save because they expect to be able to make up for lost time by saving more later," says economist Antony Davies of Duquesne University. "Another factor is inexperience. Young people are inexperienced at being old. A 22-year-old will perceive 20 years as an eternity. To ask this person to save for retirement is like asking the person to give his money to someone else: he cannot picture himself as a retiree."

Economists are waiting to see how the entitled, indulged children of helicopter parents will behave. On the one hand, many of them have been showered with every conceivable largesse, from private music lessons and pricey soccer camps to the SAT tutoring that got them into a top college. For many of those raised in two-career households, "no" was a word they seldom heard from their parents, so eager were Mom and Dad to compensate for their lack of quantity time by providing quality time—and experiences and stuff—instead. Even if they are inclined to save, they're facing real obstacles: many emerged from college with significantly more student-loan debt than those who came before them and are entering a job market getting weaker by the month.

20   Science has yet to identify whether the brains of the Twitter generation are any different from the rest of ours, but today's culture of one-click shopping and instant messaging doesn't merely satisfy our desire for instant gratification, it encourages it. "If you grow up in an environment marked by such short time horizons, of course you're going to satisfy your desires as quickly as you can," says Virginia Tech's Bickel. "Unless you're trained to control your impulses, why would you? Instant gratification is fun, and that's what today's technology is teaching us." What life teaches us, however, is another matter. Five years after she graduated, Hannah Green admits that, although she loved NYU, maybe she should have accepted that $100,000 from her father instead.

Analyze

1. This article is part report and part argument. What main point about neurology do Begley and Chatzky report? What point about instant gratification do they argue?
2. In your own words, what is the *moneybrain?* How does the concept relate to Begley and Chatzky's main idea?
3. Explain how the famous marshmallow experiments at Stanford correspond to the more recent findings of neuroeconomists.

4. Neuroplasticity, a relatively recent idea, involves the brain's ability to change—to develop new patterns and modes of thinking. How important is this concept to Begley and Chatzky's main idea? How does it fit into their subtle argument about training one's brain?

5. In the last two paragraphs, Begley and Chatzky admit that scientists have not yet determined generational differences in brain function. Why is that admission important? How does it function in their argument?

Explore

1. Are you one of those kids who wants the extra marshmallow or not? Would you like to change your reflex? Why or why not?

2. What's so bad about instant gratification? How might it negatively impact the typical college student?

3. Begley and Chatzy claim that "today's culture of one-click shopping and instant messaging doesn't merely satisfy our desire for instant gratification, it encourages it." Explain how that works. In your own experience, how does one-click shopping encourage instant gratification? Even if you've never shopped online, how do you think the typical online interface stimulates people's reflexes?

4. This article suggests that going to college—and then graduate school—might train the brain away from instant gratification. In other words, those with advanced degrees might be more inclined to save, to control impulsive buying habits. Why might this be true? Might there be some neurological cause/effect to getting a college degree?

5. A researcher from Virginia Tech says, "If you grow up in an environment marked by such short time horizons, of course you're going to satisfy your desires as quickly as you can." In your experience, how does this play out? Have you witnessed this or the opposite of this?

Sharon Angel
Sorting Out Santa

A songwriter, illustrator, and writer, Sharon Angel is currently pursuing a degree in liberal studies. In the following essay, written for a first-semester writing course, she explains the origin of Santa Claus and his particular role in American consumer culture. She also borrows some sophisticated concepts—such as *postmodernity, hyper-reality,* and *simulacrum*—to link Santa to broader cultural trends.

It's Black Friday. Forget peace on Earth and good will to men. It's time to find a parking space and avoid getting slush on your pant leg. Hopefully, you do not suffer from migraines because here comes Santa Claus, the bell-ringer. He is in his second hour of charitable arthritis of the wrist and fully habituated to the drip . . . drip . . . drip of icicle water torture. Confined to his windy hollow under the Wal-Mart eaves, he is meek and fierce and wise—or at least patient and maybe even compassionate.

Compassion is the essence of a Santa long forgotten by most Americans, a quality that has survived a journey of a thousand years. The voyage from human being to the symbol began with a Christian philanthropist named Nicholas, Bishop of Myra ("Saint Nicholas"; Haladewicz-Grzelak). Before his veneration to sainthood came acts of kindness. As with many historic figures, most details died[1] along with him or were recorded, and perhaps distorted, through legend and iconography. St. Nicholas' feast day, set on the anniversary of his death is still celebrated as a holiday by people abroad and in select areas of the U.S., on December 6th ("Saint Nicholas").

The origins of the Santa 21st century Americans recognize are based in numerous cultures, some predating Christianity[2] ("Santa Claus"; Haladewicz-Grzelak). What sets St. Nicholas' influence apart from other champions of compassion is that his character originated from a living, breathing person: the Bishop of Myra. But even when we refer to Saint Nicholas as "Saint Nick" (such as in the Christmas song "Up on the House Top") a saintly image is not conjured. Instead, what might pop into one's head is a giant red-clad elf, poised to deliver a new flat-screen.

Americans make a conscious choice to display Santa, but the modern image of Santa reflects Americans' willingness to accept increasingly cheapened versions of Santa to which we become accustomed. For example, my family has an annual tradition of visiting a drive-through Christmas light display near Detroit, MI. It is five miles long and set up on a road that is especially closed-off for the exhibit. The entry fee is a modest five dollars, and each display along the route is marked with an advertisement for the business that sponsors it. After dark, vehicles line up and slowly cruise through archways of twinkle lights and rolling hillsides featuring sparkling characters such as dinosaurs, elves, a sea serpent and a series of Santas. Certainly, children are entertained by the blinking lights. However, they are also trapped in a car, and the vast majority of vehicles do not pull aside at the end of the exhibit where visitors can stretch their legs, buy cocoa, or chat with an actor in a Santa suit. The experience for most visitors includes no walking, no fresh air, no stars, no outside interaction—just some family time in an automobile, gliding like a gondola through a digitally timed, theme machine.

The passengers in these vehicles may not feel as though they are being   5
intentionally taught to value a symbol or an icon or an artificial holiday, but they are learning to value something complex—and they are participating in the substitution of a natural environment by an artificial reality. Exit Bishop of Myra; enter the lighted, slightly kinked inflatable all-American Santa bobbing like a massage bed in a cheap motel. I think it is safe to say that the Bishop of Myra has been obliterated. This lawn decoration is our new reality. It has strategic advantages: mass production, distribution, media campaigns, hoards of willing consumers and hostages, consumers who *are* hostages. We live among the plastic Santas and there's nothing to indicate that they won't be back next December, or should I say November— or why not October? That's the beauty of this artificial consumer world: whichever items are selected most often from the menu will be offered again, while those items that are not chosen often enough to be profitable will be dropped from the menu—which makes choosing easier—and makes deviation more difficult.[3]

The model for our current Santa, by which all plastic Santas are cast, is most directly derived from an anonymous poem, which we now know as *'Twas the Night before Christmas* (later attributed to Clement C. Moore). This poem was published in the New York *Sentinel* magazine in 1823. Forty years later, an artist named Thomas Nast (who is also known for introducing the elephant and donkey political party images) drew inspiration from this poem and illustrated it in an 1863 issue of *Harpers' Weekly*. The images Nast drew were a marked departure from the white-garbed bishop, or stern St. Nicholas—and portrayed a very secular Santa ("Know Thy

History"). This Santa was jolly, plump, wore a fur-trimmed coat, and had a workshop where he could make toys. Nast continued to produce Santa illustrations of this genre until 1866 (El Santo).

Then, in 1890, in Brockton Massachusetts, something surreal happened. Santa began making appearances in James Edgar's department stores. Santa had now completed the transition from a real bishop, to an icon, and then to a real person *playing* an icon (surrounded by goods) in his own Santa-world setting. This transition is something cultural theorists, such as Jean Baudrillard, call simulacrum, or more commonly, hyper-reality. In his book entitled *Postmodernism for Beginners,* Jim Powell writes about Baudrillard's theory of how simulacra impact culture: "We are now in the Third Order of Simulacra—the era of postmodernity—the era of models. No longer is the simulacrum a counterfeit . . . or an infinite series, like automobiles rolling off the assembly line—but simulacrum becomes reality itself" (Powell 51).

As Jayme Stayer illustrates so well in his essay "Whales R Us," if we replace our own sense of reality in favor of interacting in an artificial "reality," simulacrum can be dangerous. Stayer speaks to the inability of the artificial Sea World to teach its visitors a true appreciation for creatures of the sea.

> Too occupied with obscuring the real moral, environmental, and scientific issues at stake, Sea World is constitutionally incapable of teaching respect for nature. Love of nature is spiritually informed and politically assertive. It is not the kind of passive, sentimental quackery Sea World prefers, and it cannot be taught with the crude tools in Sea World's lesson plans: glib moralizing, base pandering, and clichés masquerading as insights (Stayer 217).

Most people know when they are being solicited by this disengaged mentality. In the case of Disney World, we go willingly—to play. I was too young to remember believing in Santa Claus, and maybe I never did. However, I do remember playing along with the game on Christmas Eve and morning. The sock-filling, cookie eating, gifts under the magically lit Christmas tree experience made for some family moments that I treasure.[4] But my senses alert me, sometimes quietly and sometimes in abhorrence, when I encounter the hyper-real attempting to seduce me—or force me to participate.

But there's something, still, that seems real and vital about the Santa at Wal-Mart. Although statues of Nicholas the philanthropist have not found their way into the Christmas lawn and garden section, his qualities of benevolence and compassion are still vibrant. They are still working in the world of real human interaction. Compassion and good will may find purpose in the simulacrum, but they are somehow free to operate outside of it as well. Examples of unconditional generosity do exist within and beyond the scheme of consumerism. Last Christmas the Salvation Army bell ringers raised a record 147.6 million dollars through their Red Kettle charity campaign ("Poor Economy"). And then we have the Santa of letters and of listening. He receives the woes and wonders of our 21st century, the letters of the hopeful who wish to tap into his abundance, the requests of the desperate who speak concerns that have no solution except the healing power of being received by an empathetic reader.

Enthroned in a shopping mall, some Santas are there for the paycheck, and others are there to offer authentic Santa comfort—at least until they are exhausted due to the demands of our postmodern lifestyles. Inside these suits are "the real deal." They are the souls who dare to take on the children's hospitals, bringing the best they have to the terminally ill, and giving of themselves something priceless. If I were trapped on a hyper-real island, with several versions of Santa, this is the Santa I would choose.

10

Notes

1 The year of St. Nicholas' death varies from source to source. According to *Cultural Codes in the Iconography of St. Nicholas,* "The Bishop of Myra, St. Nicholas, died in Myra (Demre, Turkey) on the 6th of December (The year of his death is usually given within the span of 345–352 A.D.)" However, the online Wikipedia article "Saint Nicholas" entry gives the following dates; Born c. AD 270, died Dec. 6 343 (aged 73). Because of the ambiguity concerning the exact dates, I refer to St. Nicholas of Myra as having lived generally in the 4th century A.D.

2 The secularism of Santa is a natural result of his character's journey, from his pagan and pre-Christian folklore predecessors, through many significant cultural changes. The scope of this essay does not include details on (relatively recent) pertinent, historical events such as the Protestant Reformation (1517–1648) the Industrial "Revolution" (1750–1850) and the American Civil War (1861–1865). Further associations of interest would include the role of secularism as derived from the period of the Enlightenment.

3 These ideas refer to concepts introduced by J. Powell on pages 52 and 53 of *Postmodernism for Beginners:* "Thus our lives are controlled by a system of binary regulation—where the question/answer option of the test has been reduced to an either/or binary code. This system of binary choices acts as a 'deterrence model,' which suppresses radical change."

4   This essay addresses adults, focusing on the meaning and role of Santa Claus in Postmodern American "culture." This fact is not meant to downplay the impact of Santa Claus' role/folklore as it is passed down from parent to child. Janet Gill and Theodora Papatheodorou raise some interesting points regarding this parent-child interaction in their article "Perpetuating the Father Christmas Story: A Justifiable Lie?"

Works Cited

Dennis, Tami. "Poor economy? Yep, but red kettles set record for Salvation Army." *Los Angeles Times*. Tribune Company, 31 Jan. 2012. Web. 2 Feb. 2013.

Haladewicz-Grzelak, Malgorzata. "Cultural Codes in the Iconography of Saint Nicholas (Santa Claus)." *Sign Systems Studies* 39.1(2011): 105–45. *Ebscohost*. Web. 12 Nov. 2012.

"Know Thy History: Thomas Nast's Santa Claus." *Webcomicoverlook. com,* 14 Dec. 2010. Web. 10 Nov. 2012.

Powell, Jim. *Postmodernism for Beginners*. New York: Writers and Readers Publishing, Inc., 1998. Print.

"Saint Nicholas." *Wikipedia the Free Encyclopedia*. Web. 10 Nov. 2012.

"Santa Claus." *Wikipedia the Free Encyclopedia*. Web. 10 Nov. 2012.

Stayer, Jayme. "Whales R Us." *The Composition of Everyday Life: A Guide to Writing*, 4th ed. Ed. John Mauk and John Metz. Boston: Wadsworth Cengage Learning, 2013. 213–17. Print.

Analyze

1. Explain the function of Angel's opening paragraph. How does it relate to the rest of her essay?
2. What single sentence embodies Angel's main idea about Santa Claus?
3. Explain how the concept of "hyper-reality" relates to Angel's point about Santa Claus.
4. Explain the particular way the Stayer passage supports Angel's point about American consumerism.
5. How does Angel's point relate to one of the other works from this chapter? (For example, you might consider Begley and Chatzky or Charles Kenny's points about consumerism.)

Explore

1. Explain a time when you were "seduced by the hyper-real"—or, at least, beckoned by it.
2. Angel says that "Santa had now completed the transition from a real bishop, to an icon, and then to a real person *playing* an icon (surrounded by goods) in his own Santa-world setting." What other cultural figures have developed in this fashion—from real person, to icon, to person playing the icon?
3. Angel explains that compassion can, and does, exist outside of the hyper-real layer of everyday life. In your experience, what supports or opposes this idea?
4. Angel claims, "Most people know when they are being solicited by this disengaged mentality." Explain why you agree or disagree with her statement.
5. How is Santa Claus a representative figure of American consumer culture?

Fredrik deBoer
The Resentment Machine: The Immiseration of the Digital Creative Class

Fredrik deBoer is a doctoral student in rhetoric and composition at Purdue University and a self-professed "cranky lefty." The author of the political blog *L'Hôte,* he specializes in second language writing and inequality in higher education. His work has appeared in publications such as *Balloon Juice, Consider, The League of Ordinary Gentlemen, The New Inquiry,* and *Wunderkammer Magazine.* In the following *New Inquiry* article, deBoer dissects the notion of cultural consumption.

The popular adoption of the Internet has brought with it great changes. One of the peculiar aspects of this particular revolution is that it has been historicized in real time—reported accurately, greatly exaggerated, or outright invented, often by those who have embraced the technology most fully. As impressive as the various changes wrought by the exponential growth of Internet users were, they never seemed quite impressive enough for those who trumpeted them.

In a strange type of autoethnography, those most taken with the internet of the late 1990s and early 2000s spent a considerable amount of their time online talking about what it meant that they were online. In straight-forwardly self-aggrandizing narratives, the most dedicated and involved Internet users began crafting a pocket mythology of the new reality. Rather than regarding themselves as tech consumers, the most dedicated Internet users spoke instead of revolution. Vast, life-altering consequences were predicted for these rising technologies. In much the same way as those speaking about the importance of New York City are often actually speaking about the importance of themselves, so those who crafted the oral history of the Internet were often really talking about their own revolutionary potential. Not that this was without benefits; self-obsession became a vehicle for an intricate literature on emergent online technology.

Yet for all the endless consideration of the rise of the digitally connected human species, one of the most important aspects of Internet culture has gone largely unnoticed. The Internet has provided tremendous functionality, for facilitating commerce, communication, research, entertainment, and more. Yet for a comparatively small but influential group of its most dedicated users, its most important feature, the killer app, is its power as an all-purpose sorting mechanism, one that separates the worthy from the unworthy—and in doing so, gives some meager semblance of purpose to generations whose lives are largely defined by purposelessness. For the postcollegiate, culturally savvy tastemakers who exert such disproportionate influence over online experience, the Internet is above and beyond all else a resentment machine.

The modern American "meritocracy," the education/employment vehicle, prepares thousands of upwardly mobile young strivers for everything but the life they will actually encounter. The endlessly grinding wheel of American "success" indoctrinates young people with a competitive vision that most of them never escape. The numbing and frenetic socioacademic sorting mechanism compels most of the best and the brightest adolescents in our middle and upper class to compete for various laurels from puberty to adulthood. School elections, high school and college athletics, honors societies, finals clubs, dining clubs, the subtler (but no less real) social competitions—all make competition the natural habitus of American youth. Every aspect of young adult life is transformed into a status game, as academics, athletics, music and the arts, travel, hobbies, and philanthropy are all reduced to fodder for college applications.

This instrumentalizing of all of the best things in life teaches teenagers   5
the unmistakable lesson that nothing is to be enjoyed, nothing experienced purely, but rather that each and every part of human life is ultimately sub-servient to what is less human. Competition exists as a vehicle to provide the goods, material or immaterial, that make life enjoyable. The context of endless competition makes that means into an end itself. The eventual eats the immediate. No achievement, no effort, no relationship can exist as an end in itself. Each must be ground into chum to attract those who confer status and success—elite colleges and their representatives, employers.

As has been documented endlessly, this process starts earlier and earlier in life, with elite preschools now requiring that students pass tests and get references, before they can read or write. Many have lamented the rise of competition and gatekeeping in young children. Little attention has been paid to what comes after the competitions end.

It is, of course, possible to keep running on the wheel indefinitely. There are those professions (think: finance) that extend the status contests of childhood and adolescence into the gray years, and to one degree or another, most people play some version of this game for most of their lives. But for a large chunk of the striving class, this kind of naked careerism and straight-forward neediness won't do. Though they have been raised to compete and endlessly conditioned to measure themselves against their peers, they have done so in an environment that denies this reality while it creates it. Many were raised by self-consciously creative parents who wished for children who were similarly creative, in ethos if not in practice. These parents operated in a context that told them to nurture unique and beautiful butterflies while simultaneously reminding them, in that incessant subconscious way that is the secret strength of capitalism, that their job as parents is to raise their children to win. The conversion of the hippies into the yuppies has been documented endlessly by pop sociologists like David Brooks. What made this transformation palatable to many of those being transformed was the way in which materialist striving was wedded to the hippie's interest in cul-ture, art, and a vague "nonconformist" attitude.

It is no surprise that the urge to rear winners trumps the urge to raise artists. But the nagging drive to preach the value of culture does not go unnoticed. The urge to create, to live with an aesthetic sense, is admirable, and if inculcated genuinely—which is to say, in defiant opposition to the competitive urge rather than as an uneasy partner to it—this romantic artistic vision of life remains the best hope for humanity against the deadening drift of late capitalism. Only to create for the sake of creation, to build something truly your own for no purpose and in reference to the work of no other person—perhaps there's a chance for grace there.

But in context of the alternative, a cheery and false vision of the artistic life, self-conscious creativity becomes sublimated into the competitive project and becomes twisted. Those raised with such contradictory impulses are left unable to contemplate the stocks-and-suspenders lifestyle that is the purest manifestation of the competitive instinct, but they are equally unable to cast off the social-climbing aspirations that this lifestyle represents. Their parentage and their culture teach them to at once hunger for the material goods that are the spoils of a small set of professions, but at the same time they distrust the culture of those self-same professions. They are trapped between their rejection of the means and an unchosen but deep hunger for the ends.

Momentum can be a cruel thing. High school culminates in college acceptance. This temporary victory can often be hollow, but the fast pace of life quickly leaves no time to reckon with that emptiness. As dehumanizing and vulgar as the high-school glass-bead game is, it certainly provides adolescents with a kind of order. That the system is inherently biased and riotously unfair is ultimately besides the point. In the many explicit ways in which high-school students are ranked emerges a broad consensus: There is an order to life, that order indicates value, and there are winners and losers.

10   Competition is propulsive and thus results in inertia. College students enjoy a variety of tools to continue to manage the competitive urge. Some find in the exclusive activities, clubs, and societies of elite colleges an acceptable continuation of high-school competition. Others never abandon their zeal for academic excellence and the laurels of high grades and instructor approval. Some pursue medical school, law school, an MBA, or (for the truly damned) a PhD. But most dull the urge by persisting in a four-or-five-year fugue of alcohol, friendship, and rarefied living.

The end of college brings an end to that order, and for many, this is bewildering. Educated but broadly ignorant of suffering, scattershot in their passions, possessed of verbal dexterity but bereft of the experience that might give their words meaning, culturally sensitive 20-somethings wander into a world that is supposed to be made for them, and find it inhospitable. Without the rigid ordering that grades, class rank, leadership, and office provide, the incessant and unnamed urge to compete cannot be easily addressed. Their vague cultural liberalism—a dedication to tolerance and egalitarianism in generally vague and deracinated terms—makes the careers that promise similar sorting unpalatable. The economic resentment and petty greed that they have had bred into them by the sputtering machine of American capitalism makes lower-class life unthinkable.

Driven by the primacy of the competitive urge and convinced that they need far more material goods than they do to live a comfortable life, they seek well-paying jobs. Most of them will find some gainful employment without great difficulty. Perhaps this is changing: As the tires on the Trans Am that is America go bald, their horror at a poor job market reveals their entitlement more than anything. But the numbers indicate that most still find their way into jobs that become careers. Many will have periods of arty unemployed urbanism, but after awhile the gremlin begins whispering, "You are a loser," and suddenly, they're placing that call to Joel from Sociology 205 who's got that connection at that office. Often, these office jobs will enjoy the cover of orbiting in some vaguely creative endeavor like advertising. One way or the other, these jobs become careers in the loaded sense. In these careers, they find themselves in precisely the position that they long insisted they would never contemplate.

The competitive urge still pulses. It has to; the culture in which students have been raised has denied them any other framework with which to draw meaning. The world has assimilated the rejection of religion, tradition, and other determinants of virtue that attended the 1960s and wedded it to a vicious contempt for the political commitments that replaced them in that context. Culture preempts the kind of conscious understanding that attends to conviction, that all traditional designations of meaning are uncool.

If straightforward discussion of virtue and righteousness is socially unpalatable, straightforward political engagement appears worse still. Pushed by an advertising industry that embraces tropes of meaning just long enough to render them meaningless (Budweiser Clydesdales saluting fallen towers) and buffeted by arbiters of hipness that declare any unapologetic embrace of political ideology horribly cliché, a fussy specificity envelops every definition of the self. Conventional accounts of the kids these days tend to revert to tired tropes about disaffection and irony. The reality is sadder: They are not passionless, but many have invested their passion in a shared cultural knowledge that denies the value of any other endeavor worthy of personal investment.

15   Contemporary strivers lack the tools with which people in the past have differentiated themselves from their peers: They live in a post-virtue, post-religion, post-aristocracy age. They lack the skills or inspiration to create something of genuine worth. They have been conditioned to find all but the most conventional and compromised politics worthy of contempt. They are denied even the cold comfort of identification with career, as they cope with the deadening tedium and meaninglessness of work by calling attention to it over and over again, as if acknowledging it somehow elevates them above it.

Into this vacuum comes a relief that is profoundly rational in context—the self as consumer and critic. Given the emptiness of the material conditions of their lives, the formerly manic competitors must come to invest the cultural goods they consume with great meaning. Meaning must be made somewhere; no one will countenance standing for nothing. So the poor proxy of media and cultural consumption comes to define the individual. In many ways, cultural products such as movies, music, clothes, and media are the perfect vehicle for the endless division of people into strata of knowingness, savvy, and cultural value.

These cultural products have no quantifiable value, yet their relative value is fiercely debated as if some such quantifiable understanding could be reached. They are easily mined for ancillary content, the TV recaps and record reviews and endless fulminating in comments and forums that spread like weeds. (Does anyone who watches *Mad Men* not blog about it?) They are bound up with celebrity, both real and petty. They can inspire and so trick us into believing that our reactions are similarly worthy of inspiration. And they are complex and varied enough that there is always more to know and more rarefied territory to reach, the better to climb the ladder one rung higher than the person the next desk over.

There is a problem, though. The value-through-what-is-consumed is entirely illusory. There is no there there. This is what you can really learn about a person by understanding his or her cultural consumption, the movies, music, fashion, media, and assorted other socially inflected ephemera: nothing. Absolutely nothing. The Internet writ large is desperately invested in the idea that liking, say, *The Wire,* says something of depth and importance about the liker, and certainly that the preference for this show to *CSI* tells everything.

Likewise, the Internet exists to perpetuate the idea that there is some meaningful difference between fans of this band or that, of Android or Apple, or that there is a *Slate* lifestyle and a *This Recording* lifestyle and one for *Gawker* or *The Hairpin* or wherever. Not a word of it is true. There are no Apple people. Buying an iPad does nothing to delineate you from anyone else. Nothing separates a Budweiser man from a microbrew guy. That our society insists that there are differences here is only our longest con.

This endless posturing, pregnant with anxiety and roiling with class re-   20
sentment, ultimately pleases no one. Yet this emptiness doesn't compel people to turn away from the sorting mechanism. Instead, it draws them further and further in. Faced with the failure of their cultural affinities to define an authentic and fulfilling self, postcollegiate middle-class upwardly-oriented-if-not-upwardly-mobile Americans double down on the importance of these affinities and confront the continued failure with a formless resentment. The bitterness that surrounds these distinctions is a product of their inability to actually make us distinct.

The savviest of the media and culture websites tap into this resentment as directly as they dare. They write endlessly about what is overrated. They assign specific and damning personality traits to the fan bases of unworthy cultural objects. They invite comments that tediously parse microscopic distinctions in cultural consumption. They engage in criticism as a kind of preemptive strike against those who actually create. They glamorize petti-ness in aesthetic taste. The few artistic works they lionize are praised to the point of absurdity, as various acolytes try to outdo each other in hyperbole. They relentlessly push the central narrative that their readers crave, that consumption is achievement and that creators are to be distrusted and "put in their place." They deny the frequently sad but inescapable reality that consumption is not creation and that only the genuinely creative act can reveal the self.

This, then, is the role of the resentment machine: to amplify meaningless differences and assign to them vast importance for the quality of individuals. For those who are writing the most prominent parts of the Internet—the bloggers, the trendsetters, the über-Tweeters, the tastemakers, the linkers, the creators of memes and online norms—online life is taking the place of the creation of the self, and doing so poorly.

This all sounds quite critical, I'm sure, but ultimately, this is a critique I include myself in. For this to approach real criticism I would have to offer an alternative to those trapped in the idea of the consumer as self. I haven't got one. Our system has relentlessly denied the role of any human practice that cannot be monetized. The capitalist apparatus has worked tirelessly to commercialize everything, to reduce every aspect of human life to currency exchange. In such a context, there is little hope for the survival of the fully realized self.

Analyze

1. What exactly is the "resentment machine"? Explain it as precisely as possible—and integrate specific phrases or terms from deBoer.

2. DeBoer argues that "cultural products such as movies, music, clothes, and media are the perfect vehicle for the endless division of people into strata of knowingness, savvy, and cultural value." In your understanding of this article, what is a cultural product? What does it do? How does it function? How are movies, music, clothes, and media cultural products?

3. According to deBoer, how are Americans being conned by the media? In what particular way are we being deceived about ourselves?

4. In his second paragraph, deBoer says, "In a strange type of autoethnography, those most taken with the Internet of the late 1990s and early 2000s spent a considerable amount of their time online talking about what it meant that they were online." Consider this term: *autoethnography*. What does it mean? How does it fit into the main point of deBoer's article?

5. Explain how Begley and Chatzky's "The New Science Behind Your Spending Addiction" (in this chapter) relates to or supports deBoer's argument.

Explore

1. How are you part of, influenced by, or resistant to the resentment machine?

2. DeBoer argues that "the capitalist apparatus has worked tirelessly to commercialize everything, to reduce every aspect of human life to

currency exchange." Give some examples of this process. What behaviors, acts, or practices have been reduced to currency exchange? Can you think of any that have not?

3. DeBoer argues that mainstream television programs can "trick" viewers into identifying with the characters, the situations, and the values sold along with the program. What in your experience supports or challenges this idea?

4. Consider the essay by Richard Lawson and Jen Doll, "Lies Hollywood Told Us: Love and Romance Edition," in Chapter 6. How do their claims relate to deBoer's? In what way is deBoer going beyond the argument made by Lawson and Doll?

5. DeBoer concludes that "there is little hope for the fully realized self." First, what do you think he means by "the fully realized self?" Second, do you agree with his conclusion? Why or why not?

Damien Walter
Sparks Will Fly

The course director of the Certificate in Creative Writing at University of Leicester, Damien Walter specializes in the genre of weird fiction. Currently at work on his first novel, he has published stories in various literary publications and writes the "Weird Things" column for the newspaper the *Guardian*. The following article originally appeared in *Aeon* magazine, which describes itself as "open to diverse perspectives and committed to progressive social change." Here, Walter explains why consumerism and creativity are at odds—and how this fissure impacts our culture.

I arrived in Leicester in the late '90s as a student, a year after losing my mother to cancer. Having little support, I worked my way through university as a street sweeper, a factory worker, a waiter, a barman, a door-to-door salesman, a cleaner, recycling operative and grill chef. I wanted to be a writer but that seemed like an unattainable dream at the time. A few years later I began working for Leicester's library service as a literature development worker.

The first initiative I ran was a project to gather the reminiscences of senior citizens. There I was, in my mid-20s, in the meeting room of an older persons' lunch club. I had a circle of plastic stacking chairs, paper, pens and a dozen volunteers, most of them past their 80th birthday. At the time, I could manage (as I still can) a good line in cocky arrogance. I told everyone how things were going to be and what the project was going to achieve. We were to capture voices from under-represented stakeholders in the local community, thereby encouraging social cohesion. I hadn't yet learnt that the language of Arts Council England funding bids doesn't mean much to normal people. Patient smiles greeted my words.

After a long pause, a woman in her 90s started to speak. She had grown up in a children's home in Leicester, she told us. She had been abused by her father and then by another man at the home. She had worked in factories when she was old enough. Her husband died young, and so did her son. It took her half an hour to say this much. At the end, she said she'd never told anyone about her life before.

I was, in retrospect, unprepared for that project in every possible way. I spent the next fortnight doing a lot of listening and transcribing. The other stories were no easier to hear. Child abuse, abhorred in today's media, was so prevalent in the industrial communities of England before the Second World War that it had passed almost without comment.

5   We published a small pamphlet of writing from the project. It seemed puny and easily ignored, but it meant a great deal to the group. There was even a small reception to launch it. A few friends and relatives and a dignitary from the local council came along to enjoy the municipally funded wine and nibbles. The storytellers themselves had all made new friends, and had kept busy instead of sitting idle in care homes. They had had a chance to speak. And a few people had listened.

It would take me the best part of a decade to really understand why that was important.

In dozens of projects and hundreds of workshops, I tried to help people to develop everything from basic literacy to advanced creative writing skills. I worked with teenagers from local schools, who loved vampire novels and wrote their own hip-hop lyrics but said they didn't like English, until you told them that Mary Shelley was the first goth and 'rap' stood for

'Rhythmic American Poetry.' I worked with groups of factory workers and people caught in mind-numbing call-centre jobs who just wanted to find something, anything, to show that they were worth more than that. I sat in on daylong symposia of Urdu verse and learnt what it is to have Hindu and Muslim communities talk to each other through poetry. I ran projects with drug users and mental health service users, often the same people. A lot of these people were young men, my own age, from roughly the same background as me. I started to see how real the gaps in society are, and how easy they are to fall through.

This all happened in a midlands city of 330,000 people. Leicester now has the third-largest Hindu community in England and Wales, as well as substantial Muslim, Black African, Somali, Polish and Chinese populations. In the late 1800s it was an industrial powerhouse, the hosiery capital of Europe. By the start of the 20th century, it was home to some of the poorest wards in Britain. Throughout the industrial revolution, it had sucked in thousands of rural labourers to man its factories. When the factories closed, that population, lacking any history of education or development, was abandoned, left to subsist on state benefits and lower-than-minimum-wage jobs on huge sink estates. Decades later, many are still there.

I honestly have no idea, beyond individual stories, if the creativity work I did had any real effect. I still get e-mails from one or two of the school kids I worked with: they've gone on to write their own sci-fi books. But there's a guilt trap in almost any job where the aim is to help other people. Human need is infinite, and you quickly learn the limits of what can be achieved, or else you break from the pressure of attempting the impossible.

Even so, what I did see again and again was the real difference that a   10
sliver of creative life can make, even to people in the worst circumstances. I saw it most often through the discipline of writing, and I think that the written word makes a good route for many people. But any act that helps to empower a person creatively can ignite the imaginative spark without which life of any kind struggles—and in many senses fails—even to begin.

Between the years of 1914 and 1930 the psychiatrist and founder of analytical psychology Carl Gustav Jung undertook what he later termed a "voluntary confrontation with his unconscious." Employing certain techniques of active imagination that became part of his theory of human development, Jung incited visions, dreams and other manifestations of his imagination, which he recorded in writing and pictures. For some years, he kept the results of this process secret, though he described them to close friends and family as the most important work of his life. Late in his career, he set about collecting and transcribing these dreams and visions.

The product was the "Liber Novus" or "New Book," now known simply as *The Red Book*. Despite requests for access from some of the leading thinkers and intellectuals of the 20th century, very few people outside of Jung's close family were allowed to see it before its eventual publication in 2009. It has since been recognised as one of the great creative acts of the century, a magnificent and visionary illuminated manuscript equal to the works of William Blake.

It is from his work on *The Red Book* that all of Jung's theories on archetypes, individuation and the collective unconscious stem. Of course, Jung is far from alone in esteeming human creativity. The creative capacity is central to the developmental psychology of Jean Piaget and the constructivist theory of learning, and creativity is increasingly at the heart of our models of economic growth and development. But Jung provides the most satisfying explanation I know for why the people I worked with got so much out of discovering their own creativity, and why happiness and the freedom to create are so closely linked.

Jung dedicated his life to understanding human growth, and the importance of creativity to that process. It seems fitting that the intense process that led to *The Red Book* should also have been integral to Jung's own personal development. Already well into his adult life, he had yet to make the conceptual breakthroughs that would become the core of his model of human psychology. In quite a literal sense, the process of creating *The Red Book* was also the process of creating Carl Jung. This simple idea, that creativity is central to our ongoing growth as human beings, opens up a very distinctive understanding of what it means to make something.

15   Anyone who has performed any significant creative feat, whether writing a novel or founding a business, will acknowledge the element of inner transformation inherent in the act. The person who attends a writing class in her 20s isn't the same person who completes a great novel in her 50s, and it isn't only day-to-day life that shapes her in the meantime: the creative process itself will have been at work. The growth that comes from progress through the stages of any artistic discipline provides a backbone for our

intellectual and emotional development as human beings. And it is as a framework for growth that our creative endeavours should be judged. Commercial success more often than not follows growth, but it can become a fatal distraction from it, as we see in the trajectories of celebrities who ape creativity to achieve fame but remain stunted as human beings.

This point raises difficult questions about our society. Much about the way we have chosen to organise our lives, often with the goal of maximising material comfort, is bad for creativity. These problems are most pronounced for the bulk of the population who work inside the structures that support the creativity of others: the factories, offices, shops and other parts of the system of consumer capitalism.

If you are a production line worker at a Foxconn factory in China, a retail operative at Walmart or a call-centre assistant at the Next offices in Leicestershire, the chances of finding any measure of creativity in your work are slim. They are sure to be less than those of the graphic designer using the Apple iPad, the billionaire inheritors of the Walmart fortune, or me sitting here typing this essay on my laptop. As much as our social hierarchies are about limiting and controlling access to wealth, they are also about limiting and controlling access to creativity. Increasingly, the real benefit that money buys is the time, freedom and power to act creatively.

And yet, perhaps internal factors are the greatest barrier to creative fulfilment for most people. We are driven creatures. While our lust for status, money, power and sex can be harnessed towards creative ends, it is more likely to block any spark we might have had. Our consumer culture is happy to cater to these drives. We lose decades of our lives chasing money to buy luxury goods and climbing through artificial hierarchies in the workplace. We struggle with the health problems caused by high-calorie, high-fat diets. We become caught in webs of addiction, trying to distract our minds from the emptiness left by our lost creativity. The novelist Don DeLillo wrote that "longing on a large scale is what makes history." Our longings shape our lives and they shape the world around us. But it is our longing to create that is our deepest drive, and the one that makes us the most human. We ignore it at our own cost.

· ⁘ ·

Albert Einstein once said that "every child is born a genius." Educationalists ask: "What if every child could be made an Einstein?" The key to unlocking our full human potential lies in our creative drive. As a writer and critic of science fiction, I am fascinated by the prospect of a world where our full human potential has been realised, and I believe that a "creator culture" is the necessary next step on the path to achieving that vision. We are already well on the way; it might arrive much sooner than many of us expect. Moreover, some of our most pressing societal concerns—from economic decline to environmental collapse—exist because we are resisting the natural evolution of a more creative society.

20   What might a creator culture look like?

Firstly, it is not a utopia. It is much like the developed world today, with governments, businesses, financial systems, political parties, cities, nations and many other elements of modern, post-industrial life. But it is a society where human creativity has been made the first priority.

The arts and sciences are at the heart of a creator culture, but so are many other kinds of human creativity. Entrepreneurialism, community work, industry; there are many paths. The economic system will have been rebalanced to distribute wealth more fairly to all, permitting the 10–15 hour working week that John Maynard Keynes predicted nearly a century ago. While some people will still be richer than others, wealth will no longer be hoarded by a tiny minority. Poverty as we know it will no longer exist. A more equal society will allow everyone the time and freedom to follow their creative passions, without the paralysing question of whether they produce wealth.

The rise of automation in the workplace will have continued, and the physical work that remains will be distributed more fairly across society. Otherwise, employment in a creator culture will consist almost entirely of knowledge work. The rise of the knowledge worker was among the most remarkable developments of the 20th century, ushering in an era in the developed world that would already seem semi-utopian to the people of the 19th century. For software engineers, graphic designers, data analysts, writers, doctors, lawyers and a huge range of other kinds of worker, the key asset is knowledge rather than any capacity for physical labour. That will be the norm in a creator culture.

Most workers will be freelancers, and to earn a living wage, they will have to work an average of two days a week. Nevertheless, many people will work tirelessly on projects and jobs that relate to their creative interests. Networks will subsume hierarchical organisational structures. As has already happened with open-source software development, many business models will be challenged by networks of knowledge workers providing better products and services at better prices.

Technology is foundational to a creator culture. The focus of the net-   25
worked, knowledge-based workforce will be the invention and application of new technologies. The automation of most routine work tasks will provide the base of production that allows such a culture to flourish in the first place. But instead of allowing the wealth created by automation to accumulate in the hands of a few, it must be distributed to the many. We need the right technologies, implemented for the benefit of society; progress can't be driven by purely commercial imperatives. And to turn the disruptive effects of technology into positive social change we need to think far beyond the currently limited scope of our education system.

Education is the lubricant that allows a creator culture to function. Basic education will often continue into one's late 20s and early 30s. Most people will return to education many times between spells of employment. There will no longer be an artificial divide between the sciences, humanities and arts: all contribute holistically to a full education. The utilitarian demand for education that only leads to specific jobs will be as frowned upon in a creator culture as behavioural conditioning and corporal punishment are in our own society. The singular aim of education will be human development. Every person should be freed to achieve their full creative potential.

For many people, a creator culture will appear far from utopian. It will demand exceptional levels of independence and self-reliance from its citizens. Creativity, moreover, is always uncertain, always accompanied by the risk of failure. A creator culture will require universal lifelong education, the explicit redistribution of wealth and the deconstruction of many existing hierarchies and authority structures. These will be difficult ideas for political conservatives to accept. But it will also demand that the structures of government, education and social care that exist to support the bottom of society are continually reformed, and that they ultimately make themselves redundant, as the poverty they serve is eliminated. That, in practice, may be equally difficult for the political left to embrace.

Such a society would also change the shape of certain environmental issues. The climb out of poverty inevitably places demands on the natural resources of our planet. Yet consumerism is built on ever-increasing demand for goods, which fuels economic growth. A creator culture would lead to a plateau in demand and a levelling of growth. The energy we invest in buying consumer goods would instead go towards our creative activities. And though it is very unlikely that our demand for resources will do anything but increase over time, a creator culture might also help us to reach beyond the limits of our own planet.

That's because, though it isn't a utopia itself, a creator culture might eventually let us bring about the utopian visions of science fiction. Imagine our planet populated by billions of humans, educated to the standard of the greatest scientists and given the freedom to cultivate their full measure of creativity. At our disposal is any technology we can conceive and create. Within our reach is a universe of unlimited resources. In the whole of that universe, humans are the only beings we know with the power of creation. And there are only a few billion of us—a large number on a small planet perhaps, a vanishingly small one in an infinite cosmos. We're going to need the wondrous creativity of every single human being to knock this universe in to shape. I wonder, what will we create?

30   We are *Homo faber*, "Humankind the Creator." God did not create us in his image, we created god in our image. We might only be an insignificant species orbiting an insignificant star in an infinite and impassive universe. But we have, perhaps uniquely, the power of creation. Why, then, are we trapped on this ball of rock, repeating the same patterns of self-destructive behaviour, instead of fulfilling our creative potential?

We are caught in a consumer culture that works against our innate creativity. The economic crisis of 2008 might have heralded the collapse of that culture. The consumerist economic model—itself a set of ad hoc compromises following the death of the industrial model—has reached the end of its useful existence. It evolved for a world where technology placed creativity in the hands of the few and television communicated their message to the masses, in what the entrepreneur Seth Godin has called the TV-industrial complex. Today, the Internet has decentralised communications, and computers the size of an iPhone place vast creative resources in the hands of broad swathes of the population. The ongoing financial crisis is a symptom of an economy that has fallen behind its own technological capacities.

The instinctive response of our leaders is to reconstruct our consumer culture. The generation holding the reins of society is trained to think of us as passive consumers. It might take a generational shift before a world leader addresses a speech, not to the world's consumers, but to its creators.

Yet a creator culture is emerging from the ground up, driven by creators themselves. The crowd-funding platform Kickstarter is only three years old and last year it significantly outfunded the U.S. National Endowment for the Arts. It has allowed artists and entrepreneurs of all kinds to sidestep traditional forms of investment. Crowd-funded creativity is not driven by the commercial imperative of business or the political priorities of government, but by the creative passions of the crowd. "Maker" culture resurrects the spirit of craftsmanship and combines it with technologies, such as 3D printing, that promise to do for manufacturing what the Internet did for communication. The principles of "open source" are now being applied far beyond the software development community, invigorating academic and scientific research, politics and government, the media and education. Notice how many of the new voices that are emerging through social media—the cultural curator Maria Popova, an "interestingness hunter-gatherer" who started the Brain Pickings blog; the New York-based Big Think project to sift the "best thinking on the planet"; many TED talks—make creativity their central concern. All articulate our new understanding of creativity.

But the green shoots of a creator culture are only just bursting through the rubble of consumerism. Most of us are still plugged in to a mass media that equates creativity with branding and marketing and ignores its potential for human development. Businesses are still afraid of the ideas of their own employees, missing the fact that this creativity is their only hope of adapting to changing times. And our political landscape, dominated by a Left-Right dialogue that only engages with creativity as a source of economic growth, seems incapable of making the changes needed to bring about a creator culture.

In years of working with people struggling to reclaim their creativity, 35 I learnt one very important lesson. Creation is the start, not the end, of the process of growth. We do not escape our tedious jobs, our oppressive social hierarchies, our addictive and self-destructive behaviour, and then become creative. We begin to create; then the process of growth it sets in train helps to free us from the traps that life sets.

We need to learn this lesson as a culture. We have to place the human capacity to create at the very centre of our social and political life. Instead of treating it as a peripheral benefit of economic growth, we need to understand that our wealth only grows at the speed that we can develop our creative capacities. And we must realise that we can no longer afford to empower the creativity of the few at the cost of the many. Our systems of government, business and education must make it their mission to support the creative fulfilment of every human being.

Analyze

1. What single sentence in Walter's article best captures his main idea?
2. Explain how Walter's experience with the seniors in the Leicester home relates to his main idea.
3. Early in his article, Walter references the twentieth-century psychologist Carl Jung. Explain how Jungian thought matters here. How does Jung support Walter's main idea?
4. Walter argues, "As much as our social hierarchies are about limiting and controlling access to wealth, they are also about limiting and controlling access to creativity." Explain this point. What does he mean by "social hierarchies" and how do they limit access to creativity?
5. Articulate the specific differences between a consumer culture and a creative culture.

Explore

1. Are you free to create? Why or why not? What forces, processes, or people figure into your freedom (or lack thereof)?
2. Walter argues, "Increasingly, the real benefit that money buys is the time, freedom and power to act creatively." What have you experienced, witnessed, or read that supports this idea?
3. Walter also says that "Most of us are still plugged in to a mass media that equates creativity with branding and marketing and ignores its potential for human development." Consider your own life. How might you or your friends be plugged in to the system described here? How might your favorite attractions or pastimes be part of that system?
4. What are the obstacles to Walter's proposal? Who or what would stand in the way of moving toward a creative culture?
5. How does Walter's article impact your thinking about college—your chosen academic major, your potential career, even the classes you might take in the future?

Forging Connections

1. Marketers try to fuse consumer products to identity. Everything from pickup trucks to mascara is pitched to reinforce a type of man, woman, or child—the gruff outdoorsy type, the well-groomed metropolitan type, or even the edgy hipster who resists labels and types. Consider a particular product in your life, one that is important to you practically, and explain how it has become part of your identity, part of your understanding of yourself. Resist the urge to say that you are beyond the influence of marketing and consumption trends. Be honest. Try to probe the subtle ways that the product has nestled up close to your identity—and vice versa. Borrow insights from Fredrik deBoer ("The Resentment Machine"), Mike Rose ("Blue-Collar Brilliance," Chapter 1), or even James Gleick ("What Defines a Meme?," Chapter 4).

2. How is consumerism related to work? How do our jobs invite us to adopt a lifestyle and, therefore, buy particular products? How does working in a specific field prompt people to adopt some consumer reflexes? Consider your own job or career choice—or those among your family members. Develop an essay that forges a connection between work and consumption. Also, you might borrow insights from writers in the Work chapter. For instance, Elizabeth Dwoskin ("Why Americans Won't Do Dirty Jobs," Chapter 1) might shed light on this subtle connection.

Looking Further

1. Being a consumer means belonging to a group—not consciously buying products but behaving in a pattern: buying the same types of shirts as others in your demographic, eating at the same restaurants as others in your age range, and so on. Examine your own consumer patterns—where you eat, what you eat, what you drink, or what you wear. Write an ethnographic essay that examines your own consumption patterns. Describe yourself as part of a particular demographic: single college students under 25, married students with no children, 50+ college students returning for a second career, and so on. Borrow insights from the writers in this chapter to help explain how your peer group gets identified as consumers. Integrate images and specific advertisements to illustrate the types of products and services that are pitched to you.

2. Begley and Chatzky make reference to the work of the neuroeconomist Paul Glimcher. What is neuroeconomics? Research the field and find out its focus. Try to understand the trends, the claims, and even the debates within the field. In an analytical essay, explain what the work of neuroeconomics means for American culture. Use the information you discover to help generate insights about the state of consumerism in modern American life.

3 Language: What We Mean

As a child, the writer Helen Keller lived without language. Blind and deaf, she had no understanding of herself or the world around her until she came to understand the meaning and function of signs. Years after Keller learned language, she explained her awakening: "When I learned the meaning of 'I' and 'me' and found that I was something, I began to think. Then consciousness first existed for me." Keller knew that language is not simply a tool for communication, nor is it simply a mode of expression. It is, rather, the way we know ourselves and others. It is the most basic ingredient of consciousness and the way a culture knows itself.

In America, we have always wrestled with the power and role of language. U.S. citizens are allowed, under the First Amendment, to say plenty without fear of legal punishment. It's not a crime to condemn the government. But we can get into all kinds of trouble if we say the wrong things to the wrong people: if we lie about others, if we spread rumors that injure someone's reputation or career, if we foment hatred against others, if we say something that gets someone else hurt. In other words, we have laws about language. Speech is free but not entirely free. If we slander or promote riots, we have crossed a line of legality. As we grow up and participate in mainstream culture, we hopefully learn the power of language—that it makes or breaks lives, that it starts countries and ends them, that it makes careers and kills them, and that it forges friendships and destroys them. We learn, in short, how to speak—and speak within—our culture.

The writers in this chapter begin with an understanding that language makes consciousness and culture work. Blake Gopnik and Juliette Kayyem show the political force of language—its role in shifting power from one group to another. Richard Chin and Fleda Brown explore the bond between thought and language. Julie Traves, Robert Lane Greene, and Autumn Whitefield-Madrano reveal the complex sociological function of the English language.

Julie Traves
The Church of Please and Thank You

Julie Traves is the deputy arts editor for *The Globe and Mail*, where she works "to enhance the *Globe*'s cultural presence in digital media." The following article originally appeared in *This Magazine*, which considers itself "the leading alternative Canadian magazine of politics, pop culture, and the arts." Here, Traves examines the role of English in shaping global culture.

Michelle Szabo smiles encouragingly as a young businessman talks about his hobbies in broken English. She is a Canadian teacher at Aeon's language school in Kawagoe, Japan. He is a prospective student she's charged to recruit as part of her job. The two meet in a drab five-storey office building outside the train station. The room is so small it fits only a table and two chairs. But making the sell to would-be learners has little to do with décor. What counts is Szabo's final handshake.

More than contact with an attractive young woman, her personal touch symbolizes a grasp on a better life. In the competitive marketplace of Japan, English test scores make or break job applications. Getting ahead means getting into classes with teachers like Szabo. "I would ask so many people, 'do you expect to use English in your life?' And most people would say 'No, no, no, I just need this test score,'" says Szabo. "I think it's sort of a given for all families—it's like food, shelter, English." Some sarariiman (salarymen) were so excited they trembled when they took her hand.

In addition to the 380 million people worldwide who use English as their first language, it's estimated there are 350 million to 500 million speakers of English as a foreign language (EFL)—and the number is growing. For people from affluent and developing nations alike, it is clear that the secret passwords to safety, wealth and freedom can be whispered only in English. Even 66 percent of French citizens, linguistic protectionists *par excellence,* agreed they needed to speak English in a 2001 Eurobarometer poll. While thinkers such as John Ralston Saul proclaim the death of globalization, locals from countries around the world are clamouring for English training.

Enter thousands of Westerners who spread the English gospel overseas each year. Like the Christian missionaries who came before them, many are young, have a blind faith in the beliefs they've grown up with and are eager to make their mark on the world. Unlike the 19- to 26-year-olds who proselytize for the Latter-day Saints, however, these new missionaries are also out for adventure, good times—and hard cash. Part of a $7.8-billion industry, instructors can earn $400 a month plus room and board in China and up to $4,000 a month in Japan. That's a lot more than a McJob back home.

But students expect more than lessons in syntax and style. EFL teachers 5 are also hired to share Western customs and values. "'Let's have lunch sometime' doesn't mean stop by my office tomorrow and we'll go out and have lunch. It means something more general, like 'It's been nice talking to you and maybe at some point I'd like to continue the conversation,'" says Diane Pecorari, a senior lecturer at the University of Stockholm. "When you're teaching formulae like 'Please,' 'Thank you,' 'Can I split the cheque?' you also have to teach the context in which they come up. That means teaching culture."

But what is the effect of that culture on students' dialects, customs—their very identity? Ian Martin, an English professor at York University's Glendon College in Toronto, points to a troubling precedent for the current explosion of EFL. "One of the big moments in the spread of English took place in India in 1835. [British politician] Thomas Babington Macaulay proposed that English be used to create a class of Indian middlemen who would be sympathetic to British interests, without the necessity of large numbers of British citizens coming out and running the show." Instead of invading India at great economic and human cost, English allowed the British to transform the country from within. With English on the tip of their tongues, Indians could much more easily swear allegiance to England.

> "Where once English facilitated the staffing of colonial offices, now it helps fill the cubicles of multinational corporations."

Today's linguistic imperialism has a similar goal. Where once English facilitated the staffing of colonial offices, now it helps fill the cubicles of multinational corporations. Teaching locals Western speech and when it's appropriate to use it no longer transforms them into perfect Englishmen, it makes them into perfect business-men and women. The politics of English haven't changed—the language simply serves a new corporate master.

To be sure, even those who are fascinated by the countries where they teach sometimes can't help transforming "the natives" as part of their work abroad. Canadian Michael Schellenberg, who taught in Japan more than a decade ago, loved learning about Japanese customs but also sheepishly admits he urged students to express themselves—quite against the Japanese grain. "One of the sayings in Japan is that the nail that sticks up will get pounded down. They wanted people to conform," he says. "I remember classes where I'd be like, 'Just be yourself!' As someone in my early 20s, I had a pretty good sense of how I thought the world should be. I felt pretty confident being forthright about that."

Teaching materials subtly suggest the superiority of Western values. Produced primarily in the U.S. and UK, textbooks propagate the advantages of materialism, individualism and sexual liberation. For example, Ian Martin recalls an Indian friend's reaction to one textbook that showed Jack and Jane meeting in lesson one and dancing alone together by lesson three. "Where are the parents?" his friend wondered.

Some newer textbooks are more culturally sensitive. But in many of the 10 books currently in circulation, says Martin, "there's nothing about environmentalism, nothing about spirituality, nothing about, say, respecting nonnative [English] speakers. And there's very little realism in any of the language learning material that I've seen. It's this mythic world of dream fulfillment through consumerism and Westernization." The Aeon language franchise in Japan uses Cameron Diaz and Celine Dion as its poster girls.

Of course, not all teachers aggressively peddle a mythic world—some have their soapbox thrust upon them. In her book *The Hemingway Book Club of Kosovo,* California writer Paula Huntley chronicles her experience teaching English to the survivors of the area's brutal ethnic clashes. Huntley doesn't believe her language and culture are better than any other. She wants to learn from the Kosovars as much as they want to learn from her. It's her students who are convinced that the American way is the way forward, that English is the true language of progress.

Before leaving for Kosovo, Huntley crams for four weeks to complete an English as a second language instructors' certificate. But this is not what impresses the owner of the Cambridge School in Kosovo, a man named Ahmet whose house and library of 5,000 books were destroyed by the Serbs. Barely looking at her CV, he tells her she's hired. "'You are an American,'" he says. "'So you can teach our students more than English. You can teach them how to live together, with others, in peace. You can teach them how to work, how to build a democracy, how to keep trying no matter what the odds.'"

Then there is the conflicted experience of Kathy Lee. She teaches at Guangdong Industry Technical College in China. In a suburb called Nanhai, the school is putting up satellite facilities eight times larger than the main campus. Teaching labs have banks of computers and a plasma screen TV. But like so much of the country, there is such impatience to forge ahead that Lee conducts her three classes a week amid construction because the school is expanding so fast.

Her pupils are equally anxious to take part in the country's massive business boom. Though most of them have been studying English since primary school, their fluency is strained. They tell her: "The world is growing and many people speak English. If I want to do business with them, I must speak English well too!" What students want is a foreign teacher to help them get up to speed. That's why the college has hired the 23-year-old Canadian at 4,000 RMB a month, two to three times the average salary for Chinese teachers.

15   The payoff is more than just monetary for Lee. Born in China but raised in Canada, she accepted the job so she could live in Hong Kong, within a short train ride from her sick grandmother. But now, her feelings have deepened. "When the schools were asking me why I wanted to teach in China, I BS'd and said it's because I wanted to learn about my 'other' culture," she says. "But the more I said it, the more I believed it. Now, I feel that I need to be here and learn what it means to be a Chinese person."

Yet the way of life Lee is trying to understand is challenged by her methodology in the classroom. By the end of term, her students will be well practised in communication modes that are entirely un-Chinese. Lee worries about this—and the general English fever sweeping the country that even includes television programs that aim to teach English.

"I know that if everyone spoke English in the world there would still be cultural differences, but the differences between cultures will become less and less," she says. "Why is China pushing English so hard? [My students] get the sense that their own language is not good enough. To prosper, they need English. What was wrong with the way it was before? Why do you have to be Western to be competitive in business?"

If it is tough for teachers to come to terms with these questions, it is even more complex for students. While some are in what Martin calls a "process of self-assimilation," others are much more ambivalent about the course they are on. These students may be struggling with the political implications of learning English in places where the language is associated with American or British hegemony. Or they may simply recognize that as English proliferates, the survival of their own customs and dialects is under threat.

Take 27-year-old Sanghun Cho of South Korea. He is a graduate student in Toronto and has a Canadian girlfriend. But when he thinks of English he also thinks of the U.S. "It's a kind of dilemma for Koreans," he says. "I don't like America in Korea because they want to control the Korean government, but to survive in this kind of competitive environment I have to speak English and I have to know what English culture is."

20   Another South Korean student puts it even more bluntly. Part of a multinational research project Martin has been conducting over the past five years to examine why students study English as a foreign language, the student was asked to draw a picture of his future with English, and describe the picture. He sketched Uncle Sam extending a fishing line from the U.S. across the Pacific Ocean, a hook dangling above the student's open mouth.

His description: "English is the bait that Americans are using to catch Koreans in their net."

Marta Andersson is a part of the last generation of Poles forced to learn Russian in school. When she was able to study English after the fall of communism, she was thrilled. On the one hand, it paid off: she got a good job in Poland, is now studying abroad and speaks English at home with her husband. On another level, though, Andersson is aware that using English is eroding part of what her people fought for. "I have just started to lose the sense of my native language and just wait when it will become moribund," she says, "Yet I cannot imagine my future without the presence of English."

Swede Hélène Elg is also concerned about the fate of her language as English words invade it the way they do in "Chinglish" and "Franglais." "I think it's important to separate the languages in order to 'protect' our own," she says. "I realize that languages evolve, allowing new words to come into use, but we should be aware of that development and be cautious about it. The reason I feel this is because languages are so much more than just words. Words have cultural connotations. As with languages, cultures evolve, but that development should not be about adopting another culture."

Can students fight back? It's arguable that withdrawing from English would exact too high a cost for those who want to be a part of a global economy. Instead, what's changing is how people from around the world use English. Rather than simply conforming to an English steeped in Western values, many students are co-opting the language for themselves.

On an Internet discussion board for EFL teachers, one teacher writes: "I feel the need of reminding our students and young colleagues that the purpose of learning English is not for us to 'speak and act' like an English person . . . but to 'speak English' as an educated Indonesian." Similarly, one Cuban who participated in Martin's project drew a picture of a rocket being launched into the sky with the description: "English is the rocket which will allow Cuba to tell its own stories to the world."

A new "global" English is emerging that is a bridge language between cultures, not simply a language that supplants other cultures. As Salman Rushdie is quoted as saying in the best-selling history *The Story of English,* "English, no longer an English language, now grows from many roots; and those whom it once colonized are carving out large territories within the language for themselves. The Empire is striking back."

Along with students, many teachers are joining the fight to create a more egalitarian English. They do not want to be cultural colonialists. As David Hill, a teacher in Istanbul, writes in *The Guardian Weekly:* "English is global for highly dubious reasons: colonial, military and economic hegemony, first of the British, now of the U.S. . . . If we are not to be imperialists then we must help our students to express themselves, not our agenda."

To do that, new programs are emerging, like the Certificate in the Discipline of Teaching English as an International Language, which Martin coordinates at Glendon College. It pays close attention to issues of cultural sensitivity and autonomy when training teachers. As Martin says, "We're trying to come to grips with the effect of globalization on language teaching. Do we want a globalization that is going to be assimilationist to Western models of communication only? Or, do we want to help people gain a voice in English?"

Michelle Szabo is one teacher who has tried to give her students a voice. After her stint in Japan, she took a job at Chonbuk National University in South Korea from 2003 to 2004. On one November morning, she recalls encouraging discussion about the power of English. Her hope was to give pause to students who'd never considered the impact of studying English on their lives—as well as a place for those who had thought about it—a rare place to vent.

And there was plenty of venting as students heatedly debated face-to-face from desks arranged in a conversation-friendly horseshoe configuration. "One side was feeling very pressured and resentful," says Szabo, "and one side was saying, 'No, [English is] opening doors for us.'" Szabo tried to "equalize" the class by sitting among the students. She also said little. She wanted a forum that conveyed the message, "I'm not here to change you, to acculturize you, to force my beliefs on you," she says.

30   But even Szabo's new self-consciousness about what it is she is selling to her students along with English grammar has limits. English has irrevocably changed and acculturated the world already. Even if locals don't want to participate in the global capitalist machine, they need English to truly challenge it. As one of Szabo's students couldn't help but point out during the debate, "Isn't it ironic we're discussing the effect of English—in English?"

Analyze

1. Traves's article is, in part, a profile of Michelle Szabo. Like all profiles, Traves's uses its primary subject to make a broader point. Explain that broader point.
2. What do you think Traves means by "the English gospel" in paragraph 4?
3. What do you think Traves means by "linguistic imperialism" in paragraph 7?
4. Traves explains the increasing global influence of English. But she also describes some complicating factors. Identify specific statements that show some exceptions or qualifiers in the growing influence of English.
5. How is this article about American culture? Even though Traves focuses on a Canadian teacher, what does the article suggest about the nature of U.S. culture, the way it changes, spreads, impacts others, or those within its boundaries?

Explore

1. Traves argues that "English has irrevocably changed and acculturated the world already." How so? Explain how the English language has "acculturated the world."
2. According to David Hill, "English is global for highly dubious reasons: colonial, military and economic hegemony." Why do you think English has become the dominant global language? What forces, institutions, or trends are responsible?
3. How many languages do you know? What personal factors, social forces, or cultural conditions are responsible for your answer? Why do you know one, two, three, or more languages?
4. What would a "more egalitarian English" look like?
5. How might social media impact the role of English around the world?

Richard Chin
The Science of Sarcasm? Yeah, Right

A clinical professor at the University of California, San Francisco, Richard Chin works in drug development. Named one of the ninety-nine youngest public company CEOs by *Businessweek* in 2006, he is the author of numerous blog posts, magazine articles, and textbooks on issues related to clinical trial medicine and global health care. In the following *Smithsonian* article, Chin considers the scientific underpinnings of sarcasm.

"**S**arcasm detector? That's a *really* useful invention," says another character, the Comic Book Guy, causing the machine to explode.

Actually, scientists are finding that the ability to detect sarcasm really is useful. For the past 20 years, researchers from linguists to psychologists to neurologists have been studying our ability to perceive snarky remarks and gaining new insights into how the mind works. Studies have shown that exposure to sarcasm enhances creative problem solving, for instance. Children understand and use sarcasm by the time they get to kindergarten. An inability to understand sarcasm may be an early warning sign of brain disease.

Sarcasm detection is an essential skill if one is going to function in a modern society dripping with irony. "Our culture in particular is permeated with sarcasm," says Katherine Rankin, a neuropsychologist at the University of California at San Francisco. "People who don't understand sarcasm are immediately noticed. They're not getting it. They're not socially adept."

Sarcasm so saturates 21st-century America that according to one study of a database of telephone conversations, 23 percent of the time that the phrase "yeah, right" was used, it was uttered sarcastically. Entire phrases have almost lost their literal meanings because they are so frequently said with a sneer. "Big deal," for example. When's the last time someone said that to you and meant it sincerely? "My heart bleeds for you" almost always equals "Tell it to someone who cares," and "Aren't you special" means you aren't.

5   "It's practically the primary language" in modern society, says John Haiman, a linguist at Macalester College in St. Paul, Minnesota, and the author of *Talk Is Cheap: Sarcasm, Alienation, and the Evolution of Language*.

Sarcasm seems to exercise the brain more than sincere statements do. Scientists who have monitored the electrical activity of the brains of test subjects exposed to sarcastic statements have found that brains have to work harder to understand sarcasm.

That extra work may make our brains sharper, according to another study. College students in Israel listened to complaints to a cell phone company's customer service line. The students were better able to solve problems creatively when the complaints were sarcastic as opposed to just plain angry. Sarcasm "appears to stimulate complex thinking and to attenuate the otherwise negative effects of anger," according to the study authors.

The mental gymnastics needed to perceive sarcasm includes developing a "theory of mind" to see beyond the literal meaning of the words and understand that the speaker may be thinking of something entirely different. A theory of mind allows you to realize that when your brother says "nice job" when you spill the milk, he means just the opposite, the jerk.

Sarcastic statements are sort of a true lie. You're saying something you don't literally mean, and the communication works as intended only if your listener gets that you're insincere. Sarcasm has a two-faced quality: it's both funny and mean. This dual nature has led to contradictory theories on why we use it.

Some language experts suggest sarcasm is used as a sort of gentler insult,   10 a way to tone down criticism with indirectness and humor. "How do you keep this room so neat?" a parent might say to a child, instead of "This room is a sty."

But other researchers have found that the mocking, smug, superior nature of sarcasm is perceived as more hurtful than a plain-spoken criticism. The Greek root for sarcasm, *sarkazein,* means to tear flesh like dogs. According to Haiman, dog-eat-dog sarcastic commentary is just part of our quest to be cool. "You're distancing yourself, you're making yourself superior," Haiman says. "If you're sincere all the time, you seem I."

Sarcasm is also a handy tool. Most of us go through life expecting things to turn out well, says Penny Pexman, a University of Calgary psychologist who has been studying sarcasm for more than 20 years. Otherwise, no one would plan an outdoor wedding. When things go sour, Pexman says, a sarcastic comment is a way to simultaneously express our expectation as well as our disappointment. When a downpour spoils a picnic and you quip, "We picked a fine day for this," you're saying both that you had hoped it would be sunny and you're upset about the rain.

We're more likely to use sarcasm with our friends than our enemies, Pexman says. "There does seem to be truth to the old adage that you tend to tease the ones you love," she says.

But among strangers, sarcasm use soars if the conversation is via an anonymous computer chat room as opposed to face to face, according to a study by Jeffrey Hancock, a communications professor at Cornell University. This may be because it's safer to risk some biting humor with someone you're never going to meet. He also noted that conversations typed on a computer take more time than a face to face discussion. People may use that extra time to construct more complicated ironic statements.

15   Kids pick up the ability to detect sarcasm at a young age. Pexman and her colleagues in Calgary showed children short puppet shows in which one of the puppets made either a literal or a sarcastic statement. The children were asked to put a toy duck in a box if they thought the puppet was being nice. If they thought the puppet was being mean, they were supposed to put a toy shark in a box. Children as young as 5 were able to detect sarcastic statements quickly.

Pexman said she has encountered children as young as 4 who say, "smooth move, mom" at a parent's mistake. And she says parents who report being sarcastic themselves have kids who are better at understanding sarcasm.

There appear to be regional variations in sarcasm. A study that compared college students from upstate New York with students from near Memphis, Tennessee, found that the Northerners were more likely to suggest sarcastic jibes when asked to fill in the dialogue in a hypothetical conversation.

Northerners also were more likely to think sarcasm was funny: 56 percent of Northerners found sarcasm humorous while only 35 percent of Southerners did. The New Yorkers and male students from either location were more likely to describe themselves as sarcastic.

There isn't just one way to be sarcastic or a single sarcastic tone of voice. In his book, Haiman lists more than two dozen ways that a speaker or a writer can indicate sarcasm with pitch, tone, volume, pauses, duration and punctuation. For example: "Excuse me" is sincere. "Excuuuuuse me" is sarcastic, meaning, "I'm not sorry."

20   According to Haiman, a sarcastic version of "thank you" comes out as a nasal "thank yewww" because speaking the words in a derisive snort wrinkles up your nose into an expression of disgust. That creates a primitive signal of insincerity, Haiman says. The message: These words taste bad in my mouth and I don't mean them.

In an experiment by Patricia Rockwell, a sarcasm expert at the University of Louisiana at Lafayette, observers watched the facial expressions of people making sarcastic statements. Expressions around the mouth, as opposed to the eyes or eyebrows, were most often cited as a clue to a sarcastic statement.

The eyes may also be a giveaway. Researchers from California Polytechnic University found that test subjects who were asked to make sarcastic statements were less likely to look the listener in the eye. The researchers suggest that lack of eye contact is a signal to the listener: "This statement is a lie."

Another experiment that analyzed sarcasm in American TV sitcoms asserted that there's a "blank face" version of sarcasm delivery.

Despite all these clues, detecting sarcasm can be difficult. There are a lot of things that can cause our sarcasm detectors to break down, scientists are finding. Conditions including autism, closed head injuries, brain lesions and schizophrenia can interfere with the ability to perceive sarcasm.

Researchers at the University of California at San Francisco, for example, recently found that people with frontotemporal dementia have difficulty detecting sarcasm. Neuropsychologist Katherine Rankin has suggested that a loss of the ability to pick up on sarcasm could be used as an early warning sign to help diagnose the disease. "If someone who has the sensitivity loses it, that's a bad sign," Rankin says. "If you suddenly think Stephen Colbert is truly right wing, that's when I would worry." 25

Many parts of the brain are involved in processing sarcasm, according to recent brain imaging studies. Rankin has found that the temporal lobes and the parahippocampus are involved in picking up the sarcastic tone of voice. While the left hemisphere of the brain seems to be responsible for interpreting literal statements, the right hemisphere and both frontal lobes seem to be involved in figuring out when the literal statement is intended to mean exactly the opposite, according to a study by researchers at the University of Haifa.

Or you could just get a sarcasm detection device. It turns out scientists can program a computer to recognize sarcasm. Last year, Hebrew University computer scientists in Jerusalem developed their "Semi-supervised Algorithm for Sarcasm Identification." The program was able to catch 77 percent of the sarcastic statements in Amazon purchaser comments like "Great for insomniacs" in a book review. The scientists say that a computer that could recognize sarcasm could do a better job of summarizing user opinions in product reviews.

The University of Southern California's Signal Analysis and Interpretation Laboratory announced in 2006 that their "automatic sarcasm recognizer," a set of computer algorithms, was able to recognize sarcastic versions of "yeah, right" in recorded telephone conversations more than 80 percent of the time. The researchers suggest that a computerized phone operator that understands sarcasm can be programmed to "get" the joke with "synthetic laughter."

Now that really would be a useful invention. Yeah, right.

Analyze

1. Chin explains that sarcasm is "a true lie." Explain this apparent contradiction in your own words.
2. What is Chin's main point about sarcasm? Either point to a specific sentence or write out the idea in your own words.
3. Explain how the study about children and their ability to detect sarcasm fits into Chin's main point.
4. Katherine Rankin, a researcher from the University of California, says, "If you suddenly think Stephen Colbert is truly right wing, that's when I would worry." Explain how Rankin's words relate to Chin's main point.
5. Chin suggests that sarcasm is not a style or choice but a neurological ability. What passages most support that idea?

Explore

1. On a scale of one to ten, how sarcastic are you? To what or whom do you attribute your sarcasm level? A parent, teacher, sibling, favorite television show, or even something broader such as your generation?
2. Chin suggests that modern American society is "dripping with sarcasm." Try to support Chin's point by alluding to material from popular culture, politics, and entertainment. Explain how specific ads, shows, characters, or famous statements are "dripping with sarcasm."
3. Chin cites a study that notes a big difference between Northerners' and Southerners' use and understanding of sarcasm. What do you think about this difference? What might other people think?
4. How might sarcasm be necessary or crucial in a tense situation? When is it needed? Describe a specific situation.
5. Explain the last time you used or heard sarcasm that didn't work. Did it create tension or misunderstanding or worse? Why did it fail?

Blake Gopnik
Revolution in a Can

An art and design writer for *The Daily Beast,* Blake Gopnik studies the culture of aesthetics, or the philosophical basis for art and beauty. In his work, Gopnik analyzes particular artworks and artistic movements, working toward a more refined cultural understanding of art. In the following *Foreign Policy* article, Gopnik examines graffiti as a particular kind of language art.

The worst moment in the history of graffiti came during what was also its heyday, in the early 1980s in New York. That was when mainstream culture adopted graffiti as something called "art." A counterculture medium that had, at least for a bare moment, been about communication and empowerment became saddled with the oldest high-culture clichés. Graffiti came to be about "personal style," "aesthetic innovation," and "artistic self-expression"; about looking good and catching the eye; about stylistic influence and the creation of a self-conscious visual tradition. That left it perfectly positioned to be co-opted by consumerist culture. You could say that the grand murals of graffiti art, known to their makers as "pieces"— short for "masterpieces," another hoary cliché—were a kind of stand-in for missing advertising billboards, made by artists from neighborhoods that had been left out of Calvin Klein's underwear ad buy. It was only by chance that those murals had no commodity to sell—until they realized they could sell themselves, as that high-end good called art.

Then, by way of contrast, think about graffiti as it appears to us around the world today, in places where painting on a wall is about speaking truth to power. The Arab Spring was marked by spray-painted taunts to dictators, and Haiti's chaos led to impassioned scrawls. A crackdown against anti-regime graffiti in the town of Daraa was even the inspiration this year for Syria's tank-defying protest movement. In many of these cases, the artfulness of the graffiti takes a distant second place to what someone is actually trying to say. "Free doom—Get out Hamad," reads one spray-painted text from Bahrain. During the rebellion in Libya, "Freedom=Aljazeera" written on a wall makes the value of a free press perfectly clear; on another wall, the simple tracing of an AK-47 is enough to invoke an entire ethos of rebellion. In Guatemala City, stenciled portraits of the "disappeared" of Guatemala's long civil war, with the Spanish words for "Where are they?" written below, stand as eloquent witness to one of the country's most crucial concerns. (The portrait style is loosely derived from the British street artist Banksy.)

In all these cases, graffiti is being used as a true means of communication rather than as purely aesthetic exchange. These 21st-century scrawls leap-frog back to a prehistory of graffiti, when wall writing was mostly about voicing forbidden thoughts in public. And they take us back to the first years of graffiti in New York, when some members of the underclass declared their incontrovertible presence by "tagging" every square inch of the city as they transgressed the normal boundaries set by class and race. As German scholar Diedrich Diederichsen has written, "graffiti was a form of cultural and artistic production that was illegible from the dominant cultural perspective." When some of those same taggers realized that they could also make "pieces" that would count as something called "art," they began quickly buying into the values of the mainstream they'd once confronted.

By now, grand graffiti gestures are as tired as could be, at least in the context of the Western art world. But across the rest of the planet, the static language of the American "piece" has moved on to a second life as the visual lingua franca of genuine political speech. The most elaborate images from Egypt, Libya, and Haiti today look very much like the 1980s paint jobs on New York subway cars and warehouse facades, and yet their point is not to function as art but to work as carriers of content and opinion. In Managua, the swooping letters developed for New York graffiti spell out the initials of the Sandinista party. In the Palestinian West Bank, a big-eyed figure you'd expect to see decorating a wall in Los Angeles wears a keffiyeh and proclaims a longing for a "free Palestine," as the text beside him says, in English.

5   It's not clear whether the use of English in so much of this wall-painting represents a desire to speak to Western eyes or whether English has simply become the standard idiom for political protest, even of the local variety. (It could be that the two are almost the same.) But it does seem clear that the stylistic clichés of graffiti in the West—the huge loopy letters, the exaggerated shadows dropped behind a word—have become an inter-national language that can be read almost transparently, for the content those clichés transmit. Look at New York–style graffiti letters spelling "Free Libya" on a wall in Benghazi or proclaiming "revolution" in Tahrir

Square: Rather than aiming at a new aesthetic effect, they take advantage of an old one that's so well-known it barely registers.

That thing called "art" in the West is essentially an insider's game, thrilling to play but without much purchase on the larger reality outside. We have to look at societies that are truly in crisis to be reminded that images—even images we have sometimes counted as art—can be used for much more than game-playing. In a strange reversal, the closer graffiti comes to being an empty visual commodity in the West, the better it serves the needs of the rest of the world's peoples, who eagerly adopt it to speak about their most pressing concerns. It is as though Coca-Cola, as it spread across the globe, turned out to be a great nutritional drink.

Analyze

1. What do you think Gopnik means by calling graffiti "a self-conscious visual tradition?" Why is graffiti "self-conscious"?
2. What is Gopnik's point about cliché and art? How does it relate to his characterization of graffiti?
3. What sentence in Gopnik's article best captures his main idea?
4. In his conclusion, Gopnik says that art "in the West is essentially an insider's game." Explain how this point relates to his claims about graffiti.
5. Explain Gopnik's final statement. How is graffiti like Coca-Cola—at least in the United States and Europe?

Explore

1. Given Gopnik's statements about graffiti, how do you think he'd define art?
2. Do you think graffiti is art? Why or why not?
3. Gopnik says that graffiti was originally "about voicing forbidden thoughts in public." In your estimation, what is the value of voicing forbidden thoughts in public? Why might historians, sociologists, and writers like Gopnik see value in that act?
4. What other art forms are like graffiti? Or might graffiti be unique in some way?
5. Examine some definitions of cliché, and then consider these questions: What art form has become completely cliché? Why does it thrive? What's the value of or attraction to cliché art?

Autumn Whitefield-Madrano
Thoughts on a Word: Fine

A contributing editor to *The New Inquiry*, Autumn Whitefield-Madrano explores the intersection between culture and beauty. The author of numerous articles on topics related to personal appearance, she writes the blog *The Beheld*, which seeks "to foster a larger conversation about beauty and what it means." The following blog post is part of Whitefield-Madrano's *Thoughts on a Word* series, in which she interrogates language that sustains the culture of feminine beauty.

Fine is dignity, elegance, class. Fine is edges that manage to be clean yet soft. Fine is a low, respectful whistle emitted under one's breath. Fine is manners, fine is taste—but if she's so fine, why is there no telling where the money went? Fine is the root of *refined*. Fine is delicacy, fine is restraint, fine is *thin*. Fine is balanced on the palate, hints of tannin and leather, aged in oak barrels. Fine is *please* and *you're welcome*—and, depending on who's speaking, *wham bam thank you ma'am* too.

Fine—unblemished, pure, of superior quality—stems from the Latin *finis*, meaning *end*, for once you've reached the end you can't get any better, can you? Used since the mid-15th century to express admiration or approval, it quickly became applied to women's appearances. From Jeremy Collier's *Essays Upon Several Moral Subjects*, published in 1700: "Why should a fine Woman, be so Prodigal of her Beauty; make Strip and Waste of her Complexion, and Squander away her Face for nothing?" First Lady Elizabeth Monroe was repeatedly described as *fine* by newspapers of the time; a 1798 report of a woman's travels in France describes *une femme* as "A fine-looking woman, evidently above the vulgar class." Indeed, class, refinement, and elegance were tethered to the quality of being fine: A woman in the underclass might be plenty pretty or beautiful or even handsome, but *fine*? Hardly. Manners and affect of fineness mattered just as much as looks, and occasionally writers would delineate being fine from being pretty: "The elder was a fine-looking woman . . . Yet no one would call her a beauty" (*McBrides*, 1898).

It would be a mistake, however, to think that *fine* is always used with wholehearted approval. Even fairly early on, *fine* could be used as a double-edged sword. For all the elegance implied with *fine,* the word can also reek of *She thinks she's all that.* When applied homogeneously among members of the same class, *fine* tends to be a straightforward compliment; in the hands of someone with lower socioeconomic status than the person labeled *fine,* it can turn sour. That fine little number needs to be put in her place—and the one sneering *fine* knows just the fellow for the job. "She's so fine that she thinks no one that comes up-stairs in dirty shoes worth speaking to" (1860). "Why, she's so fine she can't eat eggs outen chickens that costs less than maybe a hundred dollars the dozen" (1918). "[S]he's so fine herself. That sort of a woman always finds her happiness in making some unworthy sort of a devil happy" (1911). And filed under U for "uppity women," we find this entry from a 2001 *Ebony*: "There was a time where . . . all you needed to do was turn on the charm, whisper a few sweet nothings and that fine woman was yours."

Its appearance in *Ebony* is hardly incidental. If *fine* tends to be a compliment when uttered by someone who considers himself to be of equal class to the fine lady, it can also be inverted by someone wishing to create class differences within members of the same group. Historically speaking, plenty of black men have been eager to diminish black women—motherhood may be held in reverence, but one glance at the catalogue of misogynist rap and hip-hop lyrics shows that black women aren't necessarily held in high esteem by their male counterparts. It was actually a rap song that first alerted me to the subverted use of *fine*—"She's So Fine She Can Ride My Face," by C-Boyd, aka "Mr. Ride My Face." (Argue all you want for a song about cunnilingus to be a positive turn for women; the lyrics include gems like "I'm gonna take her home if she's wasted"—presumably *not* for a glass of Alka-Seltzer—so I'm sticking with my initial distaste to the phrase "ride my face.") Then there's hip-hop artist Akon's take on fine women. "See that girl think that she's so fine/I must believe her 'cuz I'm losing my mind/Look like the type that love to wine and dine/But I plan to get it without spending a dime": Akon may have plenty of problems, but treating this bitch like she's fine ain't one.

Yet the turnaround use of *fine* is hardly the word's dominant usage in the black community: "She's so fine, I'd drink her bathwater," exclaimed a Halle Berry fan in a 1999 Ebony. "'Damn, all that fine body going to waste,'" quoth a black lesbian of what men sigh upon finding out she's gay, in a 2005 report in Atlanta magazine of black women living on the down low. Going back to the word's original meaning—that of class, elegance, and visibly "good breeding," a *fine* woman is something to behold—that is, she is something to be seen. It's an (unintended?) nod to the controversial idea of conspicuous consumption within black communities—that black and Latino populations spend more on visible goods (clothing, cars, jewelry) than white populations of comparable income. It's been disputed by plenty who cite racial stereotyping ("rims!") as the root of this theory; the 2008 study that examined race and spending concluded there was something to the notion, and that stereotyping *does* play a role—that conspicuous consumption in black communities comes from the need to prove one's middle-class status when you're assumed to not be middle-class by dint of race. Whatever the truth of race and spending, the prevalence of *fine* in regards to black women is notable: One of Google's "related searches" options for the search term "fine women" is "fine black women," while black women remain absent from suggested searches for *beautiful, pretty, cute,* and *lovely* women. And image-wise, none of the top 10 searches for those others sorts of ladies yielded a single woman of visibly African descent—while three appeared in the top 10 for "fine women," including the lead result.

Hip-hop aside, the sheer number of songs about fine women is initially perplexing. Bruce Springsteen, Jimi Hendrix, Clarence Garlow, The Easybeats, Flash Cadillac, Big Boy Myles, Roscoe Dash—all of these artists have recorded a song entitled "She's So Fine," and none of them are the same. Compare that with the single entry of *him* being so fine ("He's So Fine" by The Chiffons), and something seems askew—something, that is, besides the oodles of tributes penned to women in general, automatically tipping the balance in favor of fine ladies. For a word that has the potential to be applied evenly to the sexes—after all, men too can be elegant, classy, reeking of quality—the overwhelming number of times *fine* is tacked onto women makes not only the class aspect of the word clear, but the *possession* aspect as well. (It's worth noting that in the black community, the word appears to be more equitably applied, if things like the Fine Black Men Tumblr and Flickr pool are any indication.) Fineness in women is a good, a commodity; much like the fineness in material goods, in women the quality is something to be detected, pursued, and won over. It takes knowledge and discernment to distinguish something—or someone—that's fine from its more common sisters. And if you have the skills to make that distinction, why wouldn't you want to possess so fine a good? The songsters tell us this over and over. Lucky for them, *fine* rhymes with *mine*.

Analyze

1. Explain Whitefield-Madrano's opening paragraph. What point does it make?
2. How do the historic references (in the second and third paragraphs) work in the blog post? What point do they help to support?
3. Explain, in your own words, Whitefield-Madrano's connection between *fine* and "conspicuous consumption" in the black community.
4. What does Whitefield-Madrano mean by "the possession aspect" in her concluding paragraph?
5. How is this blog about culture—and the way ideas, words, or things become normal?

Explore

1. Why do you think *fine*—as a descriptor for women—is more frequently associated with black women?
2. How are terms for physical attraction connected to class?
3. How are terms for physical attraction connected to race?
4. Whitefield-Madrano argues that words can shift from compliments to subtle digs or insults according to the situation. Consider another word, something other than fine, and explain how it shifts from compliment to insult.
5. Consider the word from your previous response and research it in the *Oxford English Dictionary*. Briefly report its etymology—its origin and primary use through history.

Juliette Kayyem
Never Say "Never Again"

A lecturer in public policy for Harvard University's John F. Kennedy School of Government, Juliette Kayyem is an expert on counterterrorism and emergency management. Named one of CNN/*Fortune* magazine's People to Watch, she is the national security and foreign policy columnist for the *Boston Globe* and the author of numerous articles and books. In the following *Foreign Policy* article, Kayyem considers the cultural impact of a particular phrase.

There will be no politicians at the 11th anniversary of the 9/11 attacks on the World Trade Center. They are no longer invited. Organizers of the memorial have now decided that they want to make the solemn events more intimate. The decision also reflects the continuing struggle between New York City, New York state, and New Jersey over the memorial, the museum, control of the site, and, as a consequence, the memory of 9/11. Last year, on this same day, the political grandstanding got so outlandish that it led to a showdown between Gov. Andrew Cuomo and Mayor Michael Bloomberg over the choice of readings.

But, whatever the motivation, the United States may be ready for a change on how to remember 9/11 too. It is time to make it personal again, to make it less an event or even a call to action. The burden of tragedy is private, but the 9/11 families lost possession of a day that was ultimately theirs. So many of them—embracing new lives, spouses, children, professions, but forever cognizant that it might have been so much different—have, at long last, carried on. America needs to do the same.

This last decade has been summed up by a series of mottos that captured its zeitgeist. The War on Terror. Mission Accomplished. With Us or Against Us. The Surge. Heck of a Job. One Percent Doctrine. Red (Orange, Yellow, Green, Purple, Hazy) Alert. The System Worked. Security Theater. Bin Laden Is Dead.

But surely none has so animated the way we think about, and organize around, America's security than the two words uttered by President George W. Bush as early as Sept. 14, 2001, and repeated to defend policies as far ranging as the war in Iraq to the establishment of the NYPD's massive counterterrorism unit: Never Again.

"Never again." It is as simplistic as it is absurd. It is as vague as it is   5
damaging. No two words have provided so little meaning or context; no
catchphrase has so warped policy discussions that it has permanently confused the public's understanding of homeland security. It convinced us that
invulnerability was a possibility.

The notion that policies should focus almost exclusively on preventing the
next attack has also masked an ideological battle within homeland-security
policy circles between "never again" and its antithesis, commonly referred
to as "shit happens" but in polite company known as "resiliency." The
debate isn't often discussed this way, and not simply because of the bad
language. Time has not only eased the pain of that day, but there have
also been no significant attacks. "Never again" has so infiltrated public
discourse that to even acknowledge a trend away from prevention is considered risky, un-American. Americans don't do "Keep Calm and Carry On."
But if they really want security, the kind of security that is sustainable and
realistic, then they are going to have to.

I have spent most of my career in counterterrorism and homeland
security in both state and federal government. And though it may look
thoughtless, even numbingly dumb at times, there is actually a theory
behind it. Homeland security has rested on four key activities: prevention,
protection, response, and recovery. And while the U.S. Department of
Homeland Security (DHS)—created in 2003 out of some 40 agencies—is
part of the national security apparatus, it is as much about the "homeland"
as it is about "security."

There is little acknowledgment of the almost impossible balance that
homeland security seeks to maintain every day. A country like the United
States—a federal structure with 50 governors all kings unto themselves,
hundreds of cities with transit systems that only function when on time,
commercial activity across borders that makes Amazon.com so successful
and gas so plentiful, respect (sometimes nodding) for civil rights and civil
liberties, the flow of people and goods taken as a God-given right, and, oh
yes, public money in an economic downturn that must be distributed to
not only security efforts but schools, health care, transportation, and every
other issue that people care about—was never going to succeed at "never
again." But somehow that's what Americans bought into. The terrorist
attacks on 9/11 and the fear that animated so many decisions then made us
forget this obvious fact: As a nation, we are built unsafe.

But "never again" would hear none of it, though it soon became clear
that doing "everything possible" to prevent another attack was a lot, probably

too much, and very, very expensive. The die had been set; the way we talked about homeland security no longer was some attempt to balance security needs with everything else or to prepare the public for the inevitable harm and the need to be resilient. Instead, over the past 10 years, the United States has spent nearly $640 billion on homeland security throughout almost every federal agency. To give a sense of how far-reaching the apparatus is, consider a study by the National Priorities Project, which found that of the "$71.6 billion requested for homeland security in FY2010, only $37 billion is funded through DHS." The rest flowed mostly through the departments of Defense, Health and Human Services, and Justice.

10   But "never again" was not just fiscally outrageous; it was, somewhat ironically, myopic in its scope. "Never again" what, exactly? In 2005, Hurricane Katrina came barreling through New Orleans and the Gulf states and reminded us that a country too focused on one threat was surely going to miss the more common, and blameless, ones.

Perhaps the worst legacy of this exclusive focus on prevention was that it bred a nearly unstoppable institutional inertia. It made changes, modifications, reassessments, even total abandonment almost impossible to discuss, let alone enforce. What should have been an easy example—the vilified color-coded system that had been publicly rejected by former Secretaries of Homeland Security Michael Chertoff and Tom Ridge—took DHS over a year to amend. The alert system had so infiltrated every aspect of public safety, down to the smallest of local police departments, which had planned and trained around it, that it wasn't so simple to say, "It's over."

Ratcheting up is easy, ratcheting down not so much. For political leadership, the fear that the antiquated policy or unsuccessful program that is defunded or rejected ends up being the one policy or program that would have stopped the terrorists—a fear that has sometimes been manipulated by local and state first responders during budget decisions—has paralyzed the kind of analysis that is routine in other public policy arenas. Chertoff faced a backlash when he famously, and rightly, acknowledged in defense of the department's priorities that not every piece of critical infrastructure could be protected. As he remarked on the obvious, that the bridge near his suburban home was not as significant as the Golden Gate Bridge, he faced a barrage of criticism from, mostly, senators who lived near suburban bridges.

I saw the phenomenon up close when I entered state government as Gov. Deval Patrick's homeland security advisor in 2007. At that time,

19 members of the National Guard, deployed in late 2001, were still sitting outside our only nuclear facility in Pilgrim, Massachusetts. The Pavlovian response triggered by 9/11, then re-enforced by Governor Mitt Romney during his tenure, persisted nearly six years later, even though the guardsmen had no real function in securing the perimeter or the interior of the structure. Removing those National Guard members was not operationally questionable—if anything, their armed presence in a residential neighborhood was more troublesome—but it was politically difficult. We had to convince the public that we weren't abandoning "never again," leaving them vulnerable to an attack, but instead balancing costs and benefits and acknowledging that other mechanisms—like better lighting—were more effective.

I experienced that same sense of unease, that cautiousness, when I later served on President Barack Obama's transition team for DHS. As we heard about the multiple programs, assessments, and policies that the exiting regime had established, and were clamoring to protect, it became clear that "change" was going to be slow and methodical. Every piece of the homeland security pie had a constituency that believed that this one program (you name it, because there are plenty) was the reason why America had not been attacked again and that removing it would endanger the whole nation. It is not easy to prove them wrong.

I wouldn't yet call the policies that seek to give more nuance to the homeland security effort a movement. But the limitations and delusions inherent in "never again" are surely taking a beating. This has been necessary because of how destructive that term has become to the very apparatus established to enforce it. "Never again" set a multibillion-dollar effort on a wayward course, a fool's errand. Throughout government, there are countervailing, and complementary, approaches to preventive security that suggest that the entire apparatus is beginning to acknowledge what couldn't be admitted 11 years ago: Bad things will happen, they most definitely will, and then, guess what, they will happen again.

One such shift has been in the acceptance of an "all-hazards" approach to emergency management planning, with an emphasis on areas that pose the greatest risk. When DHS started to distribute funds to state and local governments, it was animated by the notion that terrorism anywhere, anytime had to be prevented. Everything had to be new and shiny, every gizmo purchased to stop another 9/11. While that may have led to nice new cars for a willing police department, often the approach had no coherent philosophy behind it. The Office of Management and Budget hated the program for that reason: what exactly were state and localities buying with this money? I had once been on the receiving end of this funding when in state government and could never quite understand the policies behind the department's directives; one year, it asked all states to spend 25 percent of their homeland security funding on preventing IED explosions, as if Boston were Baghdad.

By 2008, though, and more aggressively since then, funding to states and local governments shifted from new gizmos and counterterrorism planning to approaches that would be relevant for any threat and any known response. By this year, the department had so modified what it was willing to fund that it explicitly focused its guidance on "mitigating and responding to the evolving threats," without a mention of preventing terrorism. The department had once, at its peak, considered nearly 100 cities—ranging from New York City to Bakersfield, California—as high-threat areas that would be granted additional funding. This year, the number is a much more realistic 31 high-density areas.

In addition, the department no longer pretends it is something it is not. "Never again" was, of its many flaws, inherently paternalistic. It created a mythology that politicians and terrorism experts have been allowed to ride for over a decade: The government could actually achieve perfect protection. It gave the American people an easy out, absolving them of responsibility. The famous utterance by Secretary Janet Napolitano, my former boss, that the "system worked" in explaining how a *passenger* stopped the underwear bomber in December 2009 may have been criticized, but it was utterly honest. Why would we be offended by it unless we had handed government all our own responsibilities as citizens, as well as our expectations for perfect safety? There are 1.5 million people in the air, every day. Honestly, grow up. This concept, dare I say it, that it takes a village is described in the department's most recent planning as the "homeland security enterprise," defined as the broad scope of contributions to security from all federal agencies, levels of government, businesses, nongovernmental organizations, individuals, families, and communities. It is an admission by the agency formed to enforce "never again" that it is now delegating.

"Never again" had not allowed for that, and the Department of Homeland Security—a department known more for its public flaws than its unacknowledged successes—will surely thrive in the next decade if it can model itself more on the Education Department than the Defense

Department. When parents think about their children's education, they do not immediately think of a federal agency. They focus on their own children, their local schools, the options available to them, and the options they can afford. The Education Department sends money to state and local entities, sets standards, and enforces areas that are exclusively in the federal domain. But no one thinks the department owns education. The same could be true for homeland security. Phrases like "first 72 on you" (a motto emergency managers use to urge the public to plan for the possibility that services will not be restored after a disaster for at least three days, and so to have food, water, and resources available at home) or the more controversial "see something, say something" (which is self-descriptive and came into play when a car bomb started to smoke in Times Square in May 2010) are essential efforts to engage the public. It's a little bit of tough love.

But the most significant shift has been in the institutionalization of resiliency as a core mission of homeland security and the department. Obama spoke of it in his speech for the 10th anniversary of 9/11, giving voice to a philosophy that had barely been mentioned. Resiliency isn't only about the capability to bounce back but how to actually do that. It isn't just a state of mind, though that surely helps, but also a set of policies and procedures that would help a community come back from the brink. The National Security Council has a resiliency directorate, and the DHS has explicitly reoriented its mission to make resiliency a fifth core function (beyond prevention, protection, response, and recovery). This may sound like bureaucratic lingo, but the reality is that much of what the federal government does is to help communities get back on their feet after a disaster. This includes providing quick access to funding, planning procedures to ensure adequate and inclusive local efforts, and ensuring that essential services are functioning so that communities can begin to rebuild. And after each disaster, levees are built stronger, sheltering facilities are made more livable, and access to emergency funds are made more efficient—because there will always be a next time.

I saw the same sentiment play out when I served on the leadership of the National Incident Command, the ad hoc entity established to deal with the BP oil spill in the Gulf of Mexico. It looked ugly, I know, but over two years later, at the fear of sounding like a BP ad campaign, the Gulf thrives. That's because the operational response was perfectly cognizant of one simple fact that seemed to catch both the media and the public off-guard: Oil would hit shore. Everyone working the spill knew that within weeks of the rig going down and the blowout preventer failing, there were going to be oiled pelicans. So, even as they tried almighty to keep the oil offshore, planners spent as much time preparing for when it inevitably did. If a port had to close due to oil, then the most important question was "How the heck do we reopen it?" If oil closed a fishing area, the planning focused on establishing standards so that the government would reopen it as quickly and safely as possible. Oil was going to hit shore—stuff happens—and the goal was to make sure as little of it came onto land as possible, but once it did to make sure its impact was felt for as little time as possible.

All these efforts are moving us from resistance and revenge to resilience. And it is sort of amazing to see. I experienced this firsthand at the one-year anniversary of the Joplin, Missouri, tornado. How does a community that lost so many and suffered so much actually bounce back, which it surely had within a year? There, the Federal Emergency Management Agency had established a long-term recovery framework for the kind of planning that a very grassroots effort, and a devastated community, needed in areas such as housing, education, and mental services. The federal government didn't fill in the details; it merely had the resources and even objectivity to help launch a very local effort to find the answers. If resiliency is a state of mind, the government can do much to help those actually impacted to embrace it.

The ideological debates within homeland security should be understood by the American public because acknowledgment is the first step toward acceptance. Prevention and resiliency are obviously complementary, but only one has been given voice. While the Bush administration embraced prevention as a unifying mantra, those still abusing it range in ideological and financial motivations. There is still a lot of money in the game, and it is simply much easier to galvanize support on Capitol Hill, win government contracts, and lure consulting fees with two quick words. How do you find a constituency in what is essentially a mood, a spirit of resiliency?

In many respects, what is happening is that many of the disciplines that make up the homeland security enterprise have tired of the focus and funding going to law enforcement and police departments. Emergency managers, public health officials, and fire departments can make a pretty strong case that in a world of hurricanes, H1N1, and massive forest fires, and with a terrorist threat that has changed and waned so significantly, we ought to adapt as well. Sure, this doesn't explain the NYPD's attitude—to this day, its motto hasn't changed. While they may have history to support them, it is jarring that every time they are criticized—such as for extending an odd and quite likely ineffective "demographics" program to conduct surveillance of Muslim communities in New Jersey—they retreat, literally word by word, to "never again" as a defense, rather than an explanation. But, they are more an aberration than the norm, purposefully conflating "never forget" with "never again."

Just as the threat has changed, so has the homeland. There are 49 new   25 governors since 9/11. (The only exception: Rick Perry from Texas.) My last role in government was to support the homeland security transition planning of 23 new governors who came in 2010, many of them without any government experience. They met at the Old Executive Office Building and with the president at Blair House. They were in a crisis, but it wasn't one made by al Qaeda. State budgets had created a new enemy. None had a "homeland security" platform to speak of. And, to be honest, that did not seem entirely objectionable.

All these internal shifts and funding debates over priorities and planning are barely understood by the public. The ideological tensions will exist side by side, and perhaps it will take more years of relative calm interrupted by dramatic jolts (a virus, a spill, a hurricane, a loner with a bomb) for the public to realize that there has never been such a thing as peace in the homeland. But having traveled throughout most of the "homeland," I have some hope that resiliency is taking shape in more than theory. Maybe it is in the long lines for the H1N1 vaccine, lines that were not filled with angry parents but accepting citizens who understood that, given our interconnected world, germs will spread. Or the planning meetings in Joplin, with bean dip and potato chips, where citizens openly discuss what they want their community to look like. Or the design of major new bridges that are no longer built to withstand an earthquake, but to literally sway with the movement. Or in how we choose to remember today, if we choose to remember today, with less anger and quiet acceptance.

And one day it will be acceptable, politically and publicly, to argue that while homeland security is about ensuring that fewer bad things happen, the real test is that when they inevitably do, they aren't as bad as they would have been absent the effort. Only our public and political response to another major terrorist attack will test whether there is room for both ideologies to thrive in a nation that was, any way you look at it, built to be vulnerable.

Analyze

1. In your words, explain Kayyem's problem with "never again."
2. In paragraph 8, Kayyem says, "The terrorist attacks on 9/11 and the fear that animated so many decisions then made us forget this obvious fact: As a nation, we are built unsafe." How is this statement related to Kayyem's argument about the phrase "never again"?
3. In paragraph 11, what does Kayyem mean by "unstoppable institutional inertia" and how is the concept related to "never again"?
4. Throughout her article, Kayyem argues that "never again" (the phrase itself) wouldn't allow certain actions. How does her treatment of the phrase influence your thinking? How does it impact your understanding of her main idea?
5. Explain how "never again" has become tangled in state, national, and local budgets. Point to a particular passage from Kayyem's article that best shows the entanglement.

Explore

1. Kayyem says, "Bad things will happen, they most definitely will, and then, guess what, they will happen again." Why do you think politicians get voted out or publicly condemned when they say something similar? Why don't Americans accept this idea? Or why don't they want political leaders to admit it?
2. What percentage of a national budget do you think ought to go for defending against terrorist attacks? What programs would you be willing to discard to maintain such defenses?
3. What evidence in your community supports the idea that the United States was "built to be vulnerable"?
4. Kayyem focuses on the power of "never again" to control governmental policies over a decade. What other phrases or statements have had power over our institutions?
5. Now think in less political terms. Consider the phrases and statements that have populated your education, your religious training, your family life. What statements have had the most power in your decision-making?

Robert Lane Greene
OMG, ETC

A New York-based journalist and multilinguist, Robert Lane Greene writes about language and culture. A business correspondent and blogger for *The Economist* magazine, he is the author of numerous articles and the 2011 book *You Are What You Speak: Grammar Grouches, Language Laws, and the Politics of Identity*. In the following magazine article, Greene examines the cultural significance of acronyms.

Perhaps the perfect modern movie is the cult classic *Office Space*. The anti-hero, Peter, begins his working day with a dressing-down from a droning boss about forgetting to put the cover-sheets on his TPS reports. We never find out what a TPS report is. Nor do we have to; the name alone tells us all we need to know about the life seeping out of Peter's days, three capital letters at a time.

Acronyms have become so prevalent that they suffer what anything does when coined without end: devaluation. "Oh, my God" still packs quite a punch in the right circumstances. "OMG," by contrast, is barely effective as a plaything any more. ("OMG he's cute." "OMG is it ten already?") LOL began life as "laughing out loud," a way for Internet chatterers to explain a long pause in typing. Now, LOL means "you just said something so amusing my lip curled for a moment there." And how many BFFs will truly be best friends forever? Teens, with their habit of bleaching once-mighty words (from "awesome" to "fantastic"), can quickly render a coinage banal.

The kids are not ruining the language, though. Grown-ups play the same inflationary game. Walk into any business and a cloud of three-lettered titles surrounds you. The one who used to be just the boss, or the managing director, now styles himself the CEO, for chief executive officer. This alone would be one thing, but it turned into a viral infection: CIO, CTO, CFO, COO, CLO, and so on, for what used to be the heads of technology, finance and operations, and the company lawyer. The so-called C-suite is an allegedly prestigious club, but whither prestige as its ranks swell? Throw in the VPs and SVPs who swarm all over American offices—not just vice-presidents, but senior ones—and everyone is a manager.

A study of LinkedIn, the networking site, found the number of C- and VP-level members growing three to four times faster than the membership overall. Who, then, is managed anymore?

All this seems natural in a technological age, when almost anything we do depends on computers. The first modern computers had acronymic names (ENIAC and UNIVAC), and they set the tone for the subsequent half-century; in fact ever since IBM gave us the cheap PC, homes have been flooded with CPUs (central processing units) that grow in power at an alarming rate, progressing from reading CD-ROMs to downloading MP3s (formerly known as songs) to controlling your HDTV. No one knows what the future of technology holds, but we can be confident it will arrive in a swirl of capital letters.

5 Acronyms have become so ubiquitous that we look for them even where they don't exist. They are a major source of the folk etymologies that ping around the Internet, etymologies for words that aren't actually acronyms. "Fuck" isn't short for "for unlawful carnal knowledge," "posh" has nothing to do with "port out, starboard home," and a "tip," while it might be to insure promptness, certainly doesn't derive its name from that phrase. All these words are much older than the profusion of acronyms in English. When, in fact, did we start talking in acronyms, and why?

The armed forces have much to do with it. And the American army seems to have contributed more than its share. But acronyms don't have a particularly long pedigree. You won't find them in the papers of GEN George Washington or LTG Ulysses Grant. (Grant was occasionally referred to as USG, but this was long before the "United States Government" he fought for was universally known by those same letters in bureaucratese, as it is today.) David Wilton, a linguist, says that a 19th-century "smattering" turned into a flood with the First World War, when one of the most famous among them, AWOL ("absent without leave"), is definitively attested for the first time.

The smattering became a smorgasbord with the coming of FDR—the first president (1933–45) to be known so frequently by his initials alone. Roosevelt brought the New Deal economic programme, and many a pointy-headed planner, to Washington, DC. In the midst of the Great Depression, these idealists thought they could remake society with a host of new government programmes. The long names begged for a shorthand: when the Tennessee Valley Authority and the Works Progress Administration were being rushed out of the door, it was natural to dub them the TVA and the WPA.

There may have been another temptation as well. The use of letters as symbols began with the physical sciences: Jons Jacob Berzelius had invented the one- and two-letter system for the chemical elements in 1813, and physicists had unlocked the secrets of the universe with insights from F=MA to E=MC². By analogy, perhaps, something that had an acronym felt scientific and controllable, tempting to government planners in the chaotic world of the mid-20th century. Enter the FBI to police the country, the CIA to spy on others, and the SEC to wrestle with financial markets.

If acronyms meant trying to define something so it could be controlled, this was especially tempting in medicine. Diseases, physical and mental, used to get curt, Germanic names: mumps, measles, madness. (When my paediatrician told me my son had croup, I felt transported to a mud-and-thatch hut in medieval Europe.) But as science progressed, the ailments began to get more Latin- and Greek-derived names: typhoid, cholera, mania, melancholy. Then the late-20th-century version of this trend came along: stringing together a long series of polysyllables to describe an illness—acquired immunodeficiency syndrome, chronic obstructive pulmonary disease and so on. It's only natural that these would become AIDS and COPD. If croup were discovered today, its lovable monosyllable would have no chance: it would be called acute laryngeal irritation disorder or ALID.

At the same time, clever marketing people seized the chance to get into the medical, or quasi-medical acronym game. Having a hard time getting men to talk to their doctor about certain boudoir-related issues? A clever two-step solves the problem: dub it "erectile dysfunction," and then since nobody wants to say that either, "ED." Before you know it, celebrities are advertising your medication.

The principle of inflation applies here too, though. When I first saw an advertisement promising treatment for "restless leg syndrome, or RLS," I thought "now they're just making it up," trying to sell drugs. It turns out that RLS is a real thing, also known as Wittmaack-Ekbom's syndrome (as usual, after two of its discoverers). The names of a German and a Swedish scientist seem to me to give a lot more solidity to the syndrome than that triad of capital letters.

Psychology is another realm where many are not convinced that acronymic new "syndromes" and "disorders" are real. No one is insane any more, or even eccentric, or highly strung; they have BPD or OCD (borderline personality disorder or obsessive-compulsive disorder). And it's tempting to think that we might be over-medicalising kids when we talk about their

ODD (oppositional-defiant disorder) and ADHD (attention-deficit hyper-activity disorder). In the old days, conservatives grumble, we had a different label for these kids—"badly behaved"—and we treated their condition with a good hard swat. The grumpy reaction against acronymic inflation may be making us ignore real advances in psychology, throwing the scientific baby out with the alphabet-filled bathwater.

The conservative anti-acronym crusader may grind to a halt when considering the business world, which is a long-standing source of acronymy. In 1901 the National Biscuit Company sought a trademark for a new short form of its name—Nabisco. The "co" trend took off, especially with oil companies (Texaco, Conoco, Sunoco), using a different kind of acronym, one that pulls together first syllables, not just letters. But the rise of the initialism and acronym proper were not far off; the stock-ticker and other space-compressed media did not cause, but helped accelerate, the trend towards shorter names. The century-long process that gave birth to IBM, GE and AT&T has culminated with many companies preferring not to be known by their original names. IBM may still do international business but it no longer makes most of its money selling machines. GE does so much more than electronics that it rarely refers to itself as General Electric. AT&T would prefer you forget the "telegraph" in its name, though American iPhone users might prefer a telegraph to the much-derided voice service bundled with their handset by AT&T. The desire to shed an old association goes doubly for the second word in Kentucky Fried Chicken, now served up by a company called KFC. God bless Radio Shack for resisting the trend. But how long before they become RS.com?

There's a whiff of the American about many acronyms. This may be the reason that a Chinese ministry, which went unnamed in press reports, quietly told media outlets to stop using roman-letter acronyms; F1 (Formula One motor racing) and the NBA (America's National Basketball Association) were no longer to be so called in the columns of Chinese newspapers. But even the mighty Chinese government can only do so much; CCTV, the state-controlled Chinese Central Television, still has a large Roman "CCTV" in its logo, perhaps because its web address consists of those letters, not the Chinese characters, which cannot be used in web addresses.

15   There is nothing inherently American, or even Anglo-phone, about acronyms. Chinese itself has them, despite its remarkable character-based writing system. Many words consist of more than one character, and

Chinese acronyms will use one character from each word (often, but not always, the first one). But of course acronyms are more suited to alphabets. The fish became a Christian symbol largely because the Greek word for it, *ichthos,* is an acronym for *iesous christos theou ouios soter,* "Jesus Christ, Son of God, Saviour." The Jews enjoyed making acronyms too, and even the name of the Bible is the *tanakh,* an acronym for *torah nevi'im ketuvim,* "Torah, prophets, writings," the three main sections of the Hebrew Bible.

The proliferation of acronyms through texting seems particularly Anglophone. The standard term for a text in America is itself a set of capitals (SMS, short message service). Now other languages are following suit. In German, the initialism SMS has become an acronym proper, pronounced "zims." It has also been made into a verb, *smsen,* so that it's perfectly natural to say *Ich habe ihr gesmst,* "I texted her."

The French too are playing with text-speak. Though many will happily import LOL from English tout court, they may also write MDR, *mort de rire,* "dead from laughing." And just as English texters can play with the rebus principle to write things like CUL8R ("see you later"), so the French have @+ (*à plus,* short for "see you later") and OQP, *occupé,* "busy."

This trend points to good news as we drown in ever more acronyms. They are a mere microcosm of language, sharing most of the properties of language generally. So just as the bureaucrats coin jargon, waffle and acronyms, the grunts and drones will continue to fight back against the plodding predictability of acronymic churn. And kids will continue to speed up the process by replacing anything that catches on too broadly— to the next generation, "LOL" could be about as groovy as "groovy" is today.

Slang initialisms and nonce-acronyms survive in the crowded market-place of language because they fill a useful function. A SNAFU (situation normal: all fucked up) filled a void; it's not just any screw-up, it's the screw-up caused by some title-inflated CTO or SVP trying to impose TQM (total quality management) on his remaining subordinates. Soldiers, who have to face the reality of life and death on the battlefield along with the fact that they work for a giant bureaucracy, are a prolific source of subversive acronyms. The American military mindset that gave us CENTCOM (Central Command), NORAD (North American Aerospace Defence Command) and NETWARCOM (Naval Network Warfare Command) has also come up with SNAFU and FUBAR (fucked up beyond all recognition). In the famous profile in *Rolling Stone* that led to Stanley McChrystal's resignation as America's commander in Afghanistan, some troops were quoted as mocking the non-Americans serving with them in the International Stabilisation Force for Afghanistan: ISAF, they said, really stood for "I suck at fighting." Soldiers will subvert acronyms as long as superiors think they can drive off the fog of war with the seductive quasi-certainty of the caps-lock key.

20   Ultimately, there's nothing wrong with acronyms. They may be a quint-essentially modern annoyance, fooling us into thinking we have a greater grip on life's complexities than we really do. But that goes hand in hand with the wonders of the modern world: I'll take COPD and modern drugs over tuberculosis in 1910 any day. Acronyms are tools, no better or worse than the people who enliven or burden our lives with them.

Analyze

1. Greene spends much of his article giving acronym examples from around the world, across different traditions, and across age groups. How do those examples help to prove, enrich, or thicken his main idea?

2. Identify several phrases that suggest Greene's attitude about acronyms. Explain how each speaks (or whispers) of his overall feeling about acronymic behavior.

3. Identify a passage in which Greene defends or at least acknowledges some value of acronyms. Explain how the passage comes to the side of acronyms or their use in a specific situation.

4. Green says, "There's a whiff of the American about many acronyms," but later says, "there is nothing inherently American, or even Anglo-phone, about acronyms." Explain why these two statements are not contradictory—and how they help to make a broader point in Greene's article.

5. Greene explains that acronyms provide soldiers with a "seductive quasi-certainty." How does this characterization relate to Greene's overall point?

Explore

1. How do you think acronyms are influencing language use in general?

2. In his conclusion, Greene says that acronyms "[fool] us into thinking we have a greater grip on life's complexities than we really do." Explain

how this works. How do acronyms make people think they understand something when they might not?

3. In his conclusion, Greene also explains that "acronyms are tools." If that's true, what do they help people to accomplish? Beyond making words shorter, what do acronyms accomplish?

4. Greene suggests that most people, whether they realize it or not, use acronyms. Are you an avid or reluctant acronym user? Do you willingly embrace the acronyms of the day or resist them? Why? What's behind your choice?

5. Consider how Greene's article relates to Richard Chin's article, "The Science of Sarcasm? Yeah, Right." How do you think acronym use is similar or contrary to sarcasm?

Fleda Brown
Art and Buddhism: Looking for What's True

The previous poet laureate of Delaware and a Buddhist practitioner, Fleda Brown explores the connections between poetry and spirituality. A regular contributor to the radio show *Michigan Writers on the Air,* she is the author of six poetry collections, a collection of memoir-essays, and the *On Poetry* column for the *Record-Eagle* newspaper. In the following essay, Brown compares the languages of art and Buddhism.

Is beauty truth, and truth beauty, as the nineteenth-century English poet John Keats says at the end of his famous "Ode on a Grecian Urn"? Poetry—all art, in fact—is passionately engaged with the question of truth: what it is, where it can be seen, what it has to do with beauty, and what beauty means. This subject is nothing new for Buddhists, either. They've been doing a great deal of deep thinking about this for over 2,500 years, asking questions like, "What is truth? What is real? Are there objects 'out there' that embody ultimate truth? Are there objects (art, music, dance, poetry, fiction, etc.) that can be deliberately created in some way to 'stand for' truth?"

The goal of Buddhist meditation is to see what is true. Not to "understand" what's true, which assumes that truth can be reached by logic—that it's rational. Its goal is to "see," in the sense that truth can only be perceived, not explained. The goal of all art, also, seems to be to show us what we have no words to explain, a truth that's embodied in the work itself, inseparable from our relation to the work. As the poet W. B. Yeats said, "How can we know the dancer from the dance?" (line 64).

It may be that meditation in the Buddhist sense and the doing of art (as well as our role as the audience of art) are the same thing. Take visual art, for example. Ever since photography became widely available, paintings and art installations have turned away from representation and toward attempting to mirror the way the mind filters and interprets the "exterior" world, or attempting to make a map of what the artist's mind is doing. Take for example Jackson Pollack's *Full Fathom Five,* 1947. What happens on canvas is interdependent with what happens in our minds as we look at it and what happens in Pollack's mind as he makes the image. What would that image be without us? We're doing the work of making its meaning together. That doesn't mean that it can mean anything we want it to mean. There's actual paint on an actual canvas in a particular pattern. We can't ignore that and drift off with our own daydream of what it might "be."

The origin of the painting, then, is in the sensual experience of paint itself. We invent Pollack. Our minds invent everything, actually, through the compounding Buddhists call *mind-aggregates.* Here is how we invent our world: we see (or experience with one of our senses) a form, we have a feeling about it (love, hate, indifference), we start developing concepts about it, we recall other things in our past that seem to be like this object, and we put it into a category. Finally, we run riot with our minds, fitting the image into all sorts of ideas, theories, memories, and random thoughts about it. The Buddhists note that this is the way our minds get confused—by building up this material, and then *believing in* all these inventions that begin surrounding the simple truth of what "is." (Our minds, of course, follow that path every moment. It's our *belief* that what we're seeing is true that distorts the truth.)

5   Okay, if we are the artist, we paint. If we want to come close to a truth, we don't dwell among the concepts; we don't paint in order to prove any idea or to promote an ideal. We make what seems right to us, what seems true to us. If we are the audience for art, we are its co-makers. We don't come at it with our preconceived ideas. We look at what's actually there, on the canvas. We don't overlay our own meaning. We look. We look as if we

were meditators. We simply watch our own preconceptions come and go. We allow the art to be made in the relationship between our mind and the mind of the painter.

The artist/poet is working as hard as possible to come close to the truth of things. And as the work comes closer, the gaps between what can be said and what is the case begin to be more obvious. It is as if we lowered a high-powered microscope on an atom. We begin to see that there's more space there than there is matter! The poem "Dan's Bugs" by Jim Harrison seems pretty simple. In it, the speaker laments bugs he's killed. But as we invest ourselves more and more in the poem, we see that it begins to open out into a space that eludes language:

> On the way to town to buy wine and a chicken
> I stopped from 70 mph to pick up
> a wounded dragonfly fluttering on the yellow line.
> I've read that some insects live only for minutes,
> as we do in our implacable geologic time. (lines 12–16)

Did the speaker really stop from 70 mph to pick up a wounded dragonfly? We'll never know. But the act is a generosity and an awareness of our own fragility. We're like that dragonfly when you think of us living inside the vast space of time. But my brief paraphrase isn't the poem itself. The poem lifts us into a sense of wonder. We go to town to buy wine and chicken, while we are also living within this vastness. There's such sympathy for us as well as for all creatures, but it's not said. It's located in what we see in the poem.

When art tries to see into what can't exactly be seen or said, it is a meditation. It is pointing toward the unknowable. Art and religion both struggle toward what can't be said. They use symbols and they stretch their words as far into wordlessness as possible. There's a suffering in that longing. We can hear it in Harrison's poem.

The four Noble Truths the Buddha taught are (1) suffering is real and not to be denied, (2) there is an identifiable cause of suffering, (3) there is an actual end to suffering possible, and (4) there is a way to get there. (He then explains further, of course.) Art is made of suffering—oh, maybe not earthshaking suffering, although it can be. If we look closely at our own artistic attempts, we feel the frustration, the sense of not-quite-getting-it-right, never quite saying or painting what we mean. According to Buddhist teachings, this is exactly our route toward freedom. We stay at it and gradually begin to see in a new way that no longer binds us to our preconceptions. We see into the actual truth and the vibrant beauty of things.

Works Cited

Harrison, Jim. "Dan's Bugs." *Songs of Unreason*. Port Townsend: Copper Canyon, 2011. 51–52. Print.

Pollock, Jackson. *Full Fathom Five*. 1947. Oil on canvas. The Museum of Modern Art, New York.

Yeats, W. B. "Among School Children." *The Collected Poems of W. B. Yeats*. Ed. Richard J. Finneran. Rev. 2nd. ed. New York: Simon, 1996. 215–17. Print.

Analyze

1. Brown begins with a difficult question: "Is beauty truth and truth beauty?" Having read her essay, how do you answer the question? How are truth and beauty related?

2. In her second paragraph, Brown explains that art, like meditation, seeks to "see" rather than "understand" what is true. Explain the difference, at least in the scope of Brown's point, between seeing and understanding.

3. What are *mind aggregates* and how do they relate to Brown's point about meaning and art?

4. Explain how Jim Harrison's poem, "Dan's Bugs," figures into Brown's essay. What does the poem help to illustrate?

5. In Brown's understanding, how are the four Noble Truths of Buddhism related to art?

Explore

1. How is art like meditation?

2. Brown says that "Art and religion both struggle toward what can't be said. They use symbols and they stretch their words as far into wordlessness as possible." Apply her point to your own religion or one that you've experienced. Explain how a specific religious verse, text, or statement reaches "into wordlessness."

3. Using Brown's discussion of the Jackson Pollock painting, explain how people create or co-invent meaning in art.

4. Discuss your favorite art form; for example, painting, music, or dance. Explain how a particular piece "stretches . . . as far as possible into wordlessness."

5. Do you think most people would accept the idea that art is like meditation? Why or why not?

Forging Connections

1. How has social media impacted language use? Write an analytical essay that explains the function of specific terms and phrases on the site. If you can, avoid the common complaint that social media is diminishing linguistic complexity. Instead, explain the micro-culture of that social media. Borrow insights from Robert Lane Greene's "OMG, ETC" and Autumn Whitefield-Madrano's "Thoughts on a Word: Fine" in this chapter, and Robert Fulford, "How Twitter Saved the Octothorpe"; Roger Scruton, "Hiding Behind the Screen"; and James Gleick, "What Defines a Meme?" in Chapter 4, "Social Media: How We Communicate."

2. How has war become part of everyday language? What terms, phrases, and metaphors have worked into the language that you hear and use daily? Write an analytical essay that both describes military language in everyday use and explains the subtle effects of that language. Consider how the military language shapes the way you and others think. Focus on specifics. How does a term such as "surrender" or phrases such as "target audience" and "on the home front" reinforce beliefs or values? How does this language quietly impact our culture? For extra guidance, consider the way Robert Lane Greene ("OMG, ETC") narrows in on specific terminology. Even though his article focuses on social media, you might borrow his strategy of detailing specific linguistic elements. Also, consider the terms and phrases that writers in Chapter 9, "War: How We Fight" use or suggest.

Looking Further

1. Like Juliette Kayyem, focus on a specific phrase that has power over your life—in schools, public settings, or family life. Consider how that

phrase maintains control, how it persuades people to believe in a course of action, how it reinforces policies, and even how it shapes values and assumptions. In an illustrated essay, show the phrase in context. Show where it gets printed, how it gets disseminated. As thoroughly as possible, explain the function of the phrase in your life.

2. When does language move from everyday use to art? What distinguishes basic communication from artistic expression or conscious performance? Consider the essays by Richard Chin, Blake Gopnik, and Fleda Brown in this chapter. How do they help to make some distinctions? What phrases, terms, and insights do they offer? Write an argumentative essay that clearly establishes the mark of artistic language. Integrate your own experiences and insights to support your position.

 4 Social Media: How We Communicate

When it launched in 2003, MySpace introduced the era of online social networking. By 2006, it was the most accessed website in the world. Millions of people on every continent signed up to post intimate details about their lives. And then along came Facebook, whose popularity dwarfed MySpace. On its way to one billion users, Facebook currently serves three times the number of people in the United States. In short, social media are normal. They now operate at the center of culture, in the daily routine of millions. People of different countries, age groups, religions, and entirely different worldviews convene in the same social media. Business owners, artists, politicians, and even religious leaders now see Facebook and Twitter as necessary. However, it hasn't been a quiet process. From the moment they first came along, social media have been debated. They have been blamed and celebrated, condemned and defended. For instance, some media scholars credited Twitter for the civic uprising in Egypt—and even more broadly for the Arab Spring, which saw democratic protests in Saudi Arabia, Egypt, Libya, Iran, and Syria. Others have blamed Twitter for the end of the English language. Still others have said that Twitter and Facebook have doomed civilization to a future of teenage silliness and shallow self-involvement.

The readings in this chapter take on a range of issues related to social media. In her essay, "What It Means Today To Be 'Connected,'" Lucy P. Marcus celebrates networking technology. She argues that relationships forged across huge distances can be deeper and more profound than those confined by traditional boundaries. As the chapter proceeds, the articles introduce doubts. In "Lying, Cheating, and Virtual Relationships," Cynthia Jones examines the way multiplayer online games enable, even cultivate, dishonesty. Michael Erard explores the real effects of social media addiction in "What I Didn't Write About When I Wrote About Quitting Facebook." When he tries to quit Facebook, he finds himself pulled back, face-to-face with his own yearning. Both Jones and Erard see a definite tension between real (nondigital) life and the allure of an online identity. Toward the end of the chapter, writers pose even tougher questions: Roger Scruton claims in "Hiding Behind the Screen" that online identity—a life of avatars— lacks "risk, embarrassment, suffering, and love." And in "What Defines a Meme?" James Gleick explains how the rise of social media is cultivating a new kind of human—a new step in the very nature of the species.

Lucy P. Marcus
What It Means Today To Be "Connected"

Lucy P. Marcus was named one of the most influential voices on Twitter in 2011 and 2012. An expert on global economic trends and business ethics, Marcus is the founder and CEO of Marcus Ventures, whose mission is "to build strong funding businesses." She writes frequently for *Business-Week*, *CSRWire*, *Harvard Business Review*, the *Huffington Post*, and *Reuters*. In the following *Harvard Business Review* blog post, Marcus explores the value of online relationships and the meaning of "real" connections.

Only connect! That was the whole of her sermon. Only connect the prose and the passion, and both will be exalted, and human love will be seen at its height. Live in fragments no longer. Only connect, and the beast and the monk, robbed of the isolation that is life to either, will die.

—E.M. Forster, Howards End (1910)

I was recently selected as one of Britain's "best connected" women by *Director*, a business magazine. This prompted me to reflect on what it actually means to be "connected." I began to explore the meaning of connectedness, both in person, and in an ever more virtual world, and to consider whether the two forms are so different. I considered it both in my role as a board director, but also in a wider framework of building relationships and gathering, synthesizing and sharing knowledge.

Connecting with people and innovative ideas is more important than ever. To my mind, in a world where new and interesting ideas can come from anywhere, true value is found by breaking through the silos of sector-only or country-only knowledge and relationships. In such a world, it is not about the number of people you know or the mountain of business cards you collect, but rather about the depth and authenticity of the relationships you build and sustain, the depth and maturity of the connection you have with one another, and about valuing and nurturing the free flow of ideas.

The integration of social media tools, like Twitter, LinkedIn, Google Plus, and Facebook, and the use of technologies like video Skype means that when used to best effect, the online and offline exchange of ideas can be seamless and without the restrictions of distance and time. We need only keep an open mind and be on both "transmit" and "receive" to be able to find new, dynamic ways to work together and make the most of the synergies thus created. One of the most exciting developments that technological advances have facilitated is the breaking down of the hierarchy of ideas, allowing great ideas to bubble to the surface from virtually anywhere. This means that it matters little whether an idea originates from a young woman entrepreneur in Japan or an elder statesman in Africa.

> "For me, the insight is more important than the size of the input."

I have found myself asking a question via Twitter, sending the query out into the ether, only to have some of the most creative and interesting solutions coming back in very short order. I am struck by the fact that some of the best, most considered answers can come from unlikely sources, and I'm encouraged that oftentimes the most compelling answers do not come from "experts" but rather from someone I had not heard of before. More and more I look at the answer or the new idea before I look to see who sent it. This marks an extraordinary and complete shift in power to the idea, and away from the source. Ideas are increasingly judged on their merit, no longer requiring "validation" on the basis of their source before they are taken seriously. This opportunity for innovation to flourish and for talent to shine will only reach its full potential if connectedness is based on authenticity, depth and continuity.

5   Why? To me authenticity is the key to building relationships both online and offline. It is easy to see, either in person or over social media, when someone is putting on an act, or is genuinely interested in a particular issue. Connectedness is not an end in itself. It is not about the number of connections you have on LinkedIn, the number of followers on Twitter or the number of friends on Facebook, but about the relationship that you have with them. The real measure of connectedness is both how much you give and how much you get, and how much anyone cares or trusts what you say. It is that relationship that PeerIndex and Klout try, in part, to measure. As the kind of connectedness that social media and technologies like Skype facilitate crosses and blurs the boundaries between social and professional networks, the depth of the relationships that result is often profound. For me, the insight is more important than the size of the input: a light-hearted quip is often more helpful and insightful than a long post or link to a book, or more often now, an e-book. It is about sharing ideas,

developing them together, and putting them jointly to good use—this depth increases with the degree of connectedness you have, and in turn sustains it over time.

The most interesting part of social media is how it enables more meaningful connections with friends, colleagues, and advisers. Connectedness in this sense is also about the seamless way in which our communication continues, irrespective of whether we are meeting over a cup of tea or meeting over Skype, sending each other direct messages on Twitter or writing on each other's Facebook walls, or sharing links and holding conversations in LinkedIn or Google Plus.

When done well, with authenticity, depth and continuity, being connected, both online and offline, facilitates constant learning, synthesizing, evolving, and sharing that is, for me, the most exciting and rewarding part of being "connected."

Analyze

1. For Marcus, authenticity is a key dimension of a connected life. What do you think she means by *authenticity*?

2. Marcus also says that depth and continuity are key qualities of a connected life. What do you think she means by *depth* and *continuity*?

3. Marcus uses quotation marks around the word *connected*. What might those quotation marks mean? Why are there no quotation marks around other words, such as *connectedness* or *communication*?

4. An epigraph is a statement or quotation that comes at the beginning of an article and connects to the article's main idea. Writers use them to establish a way of thinking—a perspective or overall vision for their work. Explain the relationship between Marcus's epigraph, which comes from the novel *Howards End,* and her main idea.

5. Explain the overall purpose of this article. Is Marcus defending, celebrating, or familiarizing social media? Is she doing something else? Point out particular passages that support your answer.

Explore

1. Marcus says that "true value is found by breaking through the silos of sector-only or country-only knowledge and relationships." What are "the silos of sector-only or country-only knowledge?" Explain how you might exist in such silos.

2. Give an example of an authentic and an inauthentic online relationship.

3. Explain a relationship that hovers between authentic and inauthentic—that is not clearly one or the other. Explain, then, how this gray area might pose problems in professional or personal life.

4. Marcus mentions PeerIndex and Klout—companies that measure and manage online influence. Check out both of these companies online. What are the plusses and minuses of such companies? Why might they be crucial in a connected age? What questions do they raise?

5. In "Hiding Behind the Screen" (later in this chapter), Roger Scruton explains that social media such as Facebook diminish the real complexity of friendship. He argues that "by placing a screen between yourself and the friend, while retaining ultimate control over what appears on that screen, you also hide from the real encounter—denying the other the power and the freedom to challenge you in your deeper nature and to call on you here and now to take responsibility for yourself and for him." Do you think Scruton's point about Facebook challenges anything in Marcus's article? Does Scruton make you think differently about Marcus's characterization of social media?

Steven D. Krause
Living Within Social Networks

An English professor at Eastern Michigan University, Steven D. Krause studies the intersection between writing and technology. An avid blogger, he has written articles for such publications as the *Chronicle of Higher Education, College Composition and Communication Online, Computers and Composition,* and *Kairos.* In the following essay, Krause considers the social impact of social media.

In 2011, Toyota ran an amusing commercial that played off of the worst fears we have about social media sites like Facebook. The commercial opens with a college-aged woman sitting at a tidy desk in front of her laptop and speaking directly to the camera about an article (or "part of an article") she read online about how older people were becoming more antisocial. She explains that this was the reason why she was "really aggressive with my parents about joining Facebook," and while she speaks, the scene turns to her parents: smiling, attractive and active 50-somethings driving their Toyota Venza Sports Utility Vehicle down a dirt road into the wilderness. The couple parks and takes the mountain bikes off the roof of the sporty car. The scene goes back to the young woman who proclaims aloud her parents are up to "19 friends now," though she immediately mouths silently into the camera "*so sad*" since that is such a pathetically small number of Facebook friends. We jump back to her parents who are now on their bikes in the real world, joining real friends for a real bike ride through real nature. The scene switches back to our Facebook enthusiast a final time. "I have 687 friends," she says in a deadpan tone. "*This* is living."[1]

Of course, the intention of the commercial is the exact opposite: that is, sitting in front of your laptop looking at pictures of puppies on Facebook all day is decidedly *not* living. Rather, "living" means getting out in nature and being active with others in a real—not virtual—space. And it helps to do all this in a stylish new Toyota, too.

The ad works well because it plays humorously off of some of the greatest fears of Facebook and other social media, that they leave us alone and inactive, involved in what is at best superficial "friendships" in a pretend space. Stephen Marche presumes we know the answer to the question "Is Facebook Making Us Lonely?" in his May 2012 *The Atlantic* article of the same name:

> We are living in an isolation that would have been unimaginable to our ancestors, and yet we have never been more accessible. Over the past three decades, technology has delivered to us a world in which we need not be out of contact for a fraction of a moment. . . . Yet within this world of instant and absolute communication, unbounded by the limits of time or space, we suffer from unprecedented alienation. We have never been more detached from one another, or lonelier. (61–2)

It's a dramatic claim, but is it a claim that is broadly supported by evidence and experiences? There's a fairly good chance that you the reader has a Facebook account—after all, almost a billion people have one, and most college students and fellow professors that I encounter use Facebook and social media to some extent. Do *you* feel detached and lonely because of it?

5   Facebook is but one of the many Internet services that have been called social media, software tools and websites that make it easy for anyone with access to write content for the Internet, something that wasn't nearly as simple just a few years ago. Facebook allows its users to write original updates about anything, to share web links—serious stories about the anti-social behavior of senior citizens or humorous pictures of puppies—and to "like" the postings and sharings of the people users know on Facebook, their "friends." Readers who have a Facebook account already know what I'm talking about.

But in considering social media as a whole, it's important to not think of only Facebook but rather to think about the rise of the many ways we quickly add and share content online and its likely importance in the way that we will interact into the foreseeable future. As Steven Johnson points out in his 2009 *Time* magazine article about one of Facebook's rivals, "How Twitter Will Change the Way We Live," "Social networks are notoriously vulnerable to the fickle tastes of teens and 20-somethings. . . ." Johnson asks, "Remember Friendster?" And I would add, "Remember MySpace?" or, maybe in the not so distant future, perhaps even, "Remember Facebook?"

But tools *like* Facebook are not going away. The shift to social media—tools and online spaces which allow anyone to easily create, share, and comment on the content created by others—shifts the paradigm as to how we understand and relate to the things we read and watch online, and indeed, how we "read" and "watch" each other.

Is this new wave of Internet interaction, social media, ironically making us more apart, lonely, or unproductive? There's been a fair amount of research on these questions and the results are often surprising and con-tradictory. For example, in their *First Monday* essay "Facebook and Aca-demic Performance: Reconciling a Media Sensation with Data," Josh Pasek, eian more, and Ester Hargittai follow and replicate the claims of an earlier study by Aryn Karpinski called "A Description of Facebook Use and Academic Performance Among Undergraduate and Graduate Stu-dents." In that study, Karpinski found that Facebook use had a negative impact on students' grades, and even though Karpinski's was a small study, it became a bit of a "media sensation" in 2009. Pasek, moore, and Hargittai repeated Karpinski's study with a larger and more diverse group of students, and they found just the opposite. Not only was there no evidence of a negative relationship between Facebook and grades, Pasek and his colleagues found that Facebook use was more common among students with higher grades.

Even the answer to the question asked by Marche's *Atlantic* article, "Is Facebook Making Us Lonely?" is less than clear. According to John Cacioppo, who is the director of the Center for Cognitive and Social Neuroscience at the University of Chicago and is called by Marche "the world's leading expert on loneliness," it depends. Facebook is merely a tool, he says, and like any other tool, its effectiveness will depend on its user. "If you use Facebook to increase face-to-face contact," he says, "it increases social capital." So if social media let you organize a game of football among your friends, that's healthy. If you turn to social media instead of playing football, however, that's unhealthy. To extend this example a bit: the college student who uses Facebook as a way of connecting with her professor about assignments, follows useful research sources via Twitter, and collaborates with classmates on a Blogger site seems to me to be making the most of the power of social media. On the other hand, the obsessive Facebook-er who uses it and similar tools to *escape* connections between him and his classmates and professors is being victimized by social media.

So, to turn back to my opening example for a moment: paradoxically, I'd   10
suggest that *both* the older couple with their snazzy SUV and the college-aged woman with her laptop are indeed "living," depending on what we don't know about what their lives beyond the commercial entail. Assuming that college-aged Facebook fan does indeed leave her apartment to interact with at least *some* of her 687 "Friends"—people who probably range from actual and "real life" friends to mere acquaintances to the famous who make their fans Facebook friends—then yes, this *is* living. And if those retired parents are obsessed with their mountain biking and otherwise cut off from the day-to-day world and the interactions of those around them—including things like Facebook—well, maybe they aren't living to their potential after all.

Note

1   See "2011 Toyota Venza Commercial—Social Network," http://www.youtube .com/watch?v=TUGmcb3mhLM

Works Cited

Johnson, Steven. "How Twitter Will Change the Way We Live." *Time Magazine.* 5 June 2009. Web. 20 Sept. 2012.

Marche, Stephen. "Is Facebook Making Us Lonely?" *The Atlantic.* May 2012, 60–69. Print.

Pasek, Josh, eian more, and Hargittai, Eszter. "Facebook and Academic Performance: Reconciling a Media Sensation with Data." *First Monday* 14. 4 May 2009. Web. 20 Sept. 2012.

Analyze

1. Explain how the Toyota ad works in Krause's argument: how does it support, develop, or shape his ideas?
2. Krause says, "The shift to social media . . . shifts the paradigm as to how we understand and relate to the things we read and watch online, and indeed, how we 'read' and 'watch' each other." Explain why Krause uses quotation marks around *read* and *watch*. What is he suggesting?
3. Krause offers a range of insights and answers to the question: Is Facebook making us lonely? What is his answer? (Note: It's more complicated than "it depends.")
4. For Krause, what is living? What does it mean?
5. How does Krause's position align with or oppose claims made by Roger Scruton ("Hiding Behind the Screen")?

Explore

1. Is Facebook making us lonely? Does social media make you lonely?
2. How do you use social media? As a way to connect with professors, family, and friends or as a way to hide away from the relationships that may benefit you?
3. Is Facebook merely a tool—like a hammer or a saw? Or is it more like a car? Or is it something altogether different than a tool?
4. How do you think the shift to online social media has shifted the way you (or others) think?
5. Are Facebook and Twitter forms of consumption? Why or why not?

Cynthia Jones
Lying, Cheating, and Virtual Relationships

A professor of philosophy at the University of Texas, Pan American, Cynthia Jones is the director of the Pan American Collaboration for Ethics in the Professions (PACE), which seeks to "promote interdisciplinary research and engagement on issues in diverse fields of professional ethics." The author of several scholarly and popular articles, she co-edited the book *A Future for Everyone: Innovative Social Responsibility and Community Partnerships* (2004) with David Maurrasse. In this article from *Global Virtue Ethics Review*, Jones explores the ethical questions surrounding virtual dating.

Gem and Zupy were married earlier this year in a beautiful ceremony atop a snow-covered mountain with a breathtaking view. They met last year and dated for seven months before officially taking the plunge. Theirs is a fairly common story, except the couple has never been in the same city together or even in the same state. And Gem and Zupy are both married to other people irl (in real life). Their wedding ceremony, and their entire relationship, is virtual, having taken place in the virtual world of *Second Life*. How does virtual dating compare to traditional face-to-face dating? Since they are both legally married to other people, does Gem and Zupy's virtual relationship and marriage count as cheating or even as polygamy?

Continually improving technology has made virtual dating more attractive than in the past. The advent of social virtual worlds like *Second Life,* and the popularity of other kinds of virtual worlds such as MMORPGs (massively multiplayer online role-playing games) like the immensely popular *World of Warcraft,* have made purely virtual relationships and dating more appealing than in the past when the available options were online chat rooms and dating websites. And not all virtual dating remains purely virtual as some online relationships later turn into "real-world" relationships. Virtual dating offers a host of perks that dating in real life cannot, such as: sexual encounters without fear of disease or pregnancy, anonymity, and, for some, a chance to "cheat" on a partner without ever leaving home. This paper will explore the ethical and prudential aspects of virtual dating, focusing on moral issues like lying and on prudential issues like satisfying urges for different partners within a committed relationship without ever touching another person.

Dating, Cybersex, and Virtual Worlds

Virtual dating, online relationships, and online sexual encounters (which I will group under the category *cybersex*) can take place in a number of ways and in a number of virtual venues, but perhaps the easiest places for such encounters to take place in are virtual worlds. Virtual dating, online relationships and cybersex are in no way restricted to virtual worlds, however virtual worlds like the popular *Second Life* and *World of Warcraft* offer subscribers far more visual stimulation, as well as more potential partners, than most other online venues. Having spent over four years playing *World of Warcraft* and a few months wandering around some very interesting places in *Second Life*, I can say that both worlds are far more "social" than one might suspect. While online dating experiences and cybersex encounters surely can vary greatly, a look at these two most popular virtual worlds can offer some insight into purely virtual relationships.

For those who have never encountered a virtual or online world, the idea of dating in one may be strange indeed. But virtual worlds have amassed a huge number of subscribers and their popularity only continues to grow. Linden Lab's *Second Life* (SL, for short) and Blizzard's *World of Warcraft* (commonly known as WoW) each claim to have more than 12 million subscribers worldwide, and WoW has servers in many different countries.

5   The difference, in general, between social virtual worlds like SL and MMORPGs like WoW is the general purpose of the worlds: social vs. gaming. Most people initially log on to WoW to play the game, although the social aspect is often significant for subscribers as well. *Second Life*, on the other hand, is not a game, even though one can find some games to play within the world, and it did not begin its life as a computer game like WoW did, before the online aspect became popular. From personal experience, I can say that if I create a new character in WoW, one whose name is unknown to any of my online friends, I can be online for hours without anyone talking to me. If I don't want to be bothered and ignore anyone who talks to me in chat, probably no one would care. Logging in to SL, on the other hand, as a new avatar (the name given the virtual characters of the subscribers) you will find your virtual self greeted by many other avatars before you even figure out how to walk forward. Other avatars may follow you around and talk to

you, even if you try to ignore them. As such, SL is purely intended to be a social enterprise, so to speak, and those who log on should expect the social aspect. Everyone in SL is in the same world, although the world is huge, and individuals can buy virtual space and modify and add to the world itself. WoW, on the other hand, has a large number of servers in many different countries, each is identical and each supports approximately 20K–50K users.

There is a cost difference between SL and WoW as well. One cannot log on to WoW without paying the monthly subscription fees (roughly $15 a month, although a free short-term trial is possible) and without purchasing the software. SL, on the other hand, can be accessed without purchasing anything, although some subscribers pay real money to have enhanced graphics, in-game money, and more "bling" for their avatars. This makes SL more accessible to the general public since it is free to join and log on.

Both virtual worlds have their own currency. The currencies of WoW and SL can be purchased online—the Linden of SL and virtual gold from WoW. The main difference here is that Blizzard's rules forbid the buying and selling of WoW gold outside of the game, an offense which is punishable, if discovered, by having one's account banned. In contrast, SL encourages its subscribers to buy and sell Lindens outside of and inside of SL and Linden Labs sells virtual land in SL for real money to individuals, companies, schools, and even countries to be developed and populated.

But what about dating? Independently-run websites exist for both SL and WoW subscribers interested in "hooking up"[1] although the SL sites seem more popular, which is perhaps not surprising given that SL is social rather than game-based. The upshot is that SL is far more popular for dating. SL avatars and the world itself can be significantly modified by users in a manner that WoW does not permit. Although character movement in virtual worlds is of course scripted, SL subscribers can write scripts or buy them for their avatars to allow them to have sex—an aspect utilized by many SL subscribers. Avatars can thus move and gyrate and appear to have sex in ways that WoW toons or characters cannot. There are even whole areas for sexual encounters in SL and specific "mature" zones dedicated to fetishisms and other kinds of sex-related activities like bondage and discipline, S & M, and dominance and submission. But dating and sex in SL has its critics, even amongst people who admittedly engage in virtual dating and cybersex. One such critic argues that a significant attraction of cyber-sex, the imagination and creativity of the participants, is compromised in a virtual world like SL, especially since one can use pre-written "canned" lines while engaged in the act. (Welles, 2007)

Real Virtual Couples

Reports in the media of couples who met online, had online relation-ships, were married online, or found their partners "cheating" online are easy enough to find.[2] There are even books in print about virtual dating and infidelity. A few stories about virtual couples have received large amounts of publicity, like the story of Dave Barmy and Laura Skye (David and Amy Pollard irl). (Cable, 2008) In real life, the couple is an unemployed and rather overweight British pair who met in SL, married in SL and irl, and not long after divorced in both worlds after Amy caught David's SL avatar in compromising positions with other women. Both Amy and David have moved on, Amy to a beau from WoW and David to a hostess at the club he operates in SL. Comparing Amy and David's irl personas to their handsome, fit, successful, and trendy online personas has afforded the media a chance to poke fun at and generalize virtual relationships, making them seem absurdly fake and made-up.

10   But despite the media's interest appearing to lie solely in exploiting the "freak factor" involved in virtual dating and relationships, a large number of people choose to not only flirt and date virtually but to become sexually and emotionally involved in a purely virtual manner. And the number grows daily. Some people move from virtual dating to a "normal" relation-ship with a former virtual partner, but many others prefer to keep it virtual. So what's the attraction, you may ask?

The Perks and the Problems of Virtual Dating

There are obvious advantages to virtual dating. First, one can engage in a heavy dose of fantasy if dating virtually. Even those who choose to cyber (engage in cybersex) via webcams where they can actually see their partners can still remain considerably removed from the reality of messy real-world relationships and feel free to role-play. (One cannot help but wonder if virtual daters would choose to go back into the Matrix after being freed if they were promised great bodies, well-endowed organs, and wealth and success . . .)

A second attractive perk of online dating is the cost. Anyone with a computer and Internet access can engage in a virtual relationship for little to no cost. Going out with your best girl in SL is considerably cheaper than the irl counterpart. But the lower costs of virtual dating aren't just financial. You can extend less of yourself in a virtual relationship and so the emotional costs can be quite lower. I remember an interview with a very attractive young woman on the popular HBO show *Real Sex,* detailing her numerous online relationships and sexual encounters. She argued that a cost/benefit analysis of virtual dating and cybersex vs. their irl counterparts had led her to date exclusively online. Virtual dating is free from most emotional and financial costs, fear of physical abuse, and the chance of contracting STDs and unwanted pregnancy. It also offered her the chance to engage with multiple partners without the baggage of jealousy, messy entanglements, and the ties that an irl relationship carried.

The anonymity aspect of virtual dating and cybersex can clearly be counted as a third appealing perk. Anonymity can free a person to do things they would never dream of doing irl. For those who wish to explore lifestyles that are not socially accepted or are even illegal, virtual dating, online relationships, and cybersex offer them the freedom to explore their desires anonymously. One can only hope that some of these illicit desires can be satisfied virtually, especially if they involve harm to unwilling others. (Of course anonymity can unquestionably have a serious moral component as well, but we'll come to that in the next section.)

A final obvious perk of virtual dating and cybersex over real-life relationships and sex the old-fashioned way is the freedom to disengage. It is considerably easier to walk away from a relationship in which you never have to look your partner in the eye and say "It's over." And there is less fear of being stalked by crazy ex's if they don't have your personal information. What about problems or potential costs of virtual dating, online relationships, and cybersex, in comparison to the "real deal?" Most of the benefits we have just discussed have another side. The costs of virtual dating may be considerably lower than irl dating, but the satisfaction gained from such relationships may be considerably lower as well. It is fun to role-play, but having a partner who knows you for who you really are carries an immeasurable benefit. One downside of anonymity is that if you never see or speak to the person on the other end of the ravishingly handsome avatar with whom you're flirting or cybering, you have no idea of the gender, age, attractiveness, or mental health of said individual. Although the costs may be lower, the potential payoffs are lower as well. The old adage "nothing ventured, nothing gained" comes to mind.

15   One prudential question we can ask of virtual marriages in particular, apart from the other aspects of these relationships, is whether a virtual marriage legally counts as polygamy if one or both partners happen to be married irl to someone else. Virtual marriages do not, of course, currently count as "real" in terms of polygamy, however, virtual adultery or infidelity has begun to be cited as a reason for divorce. The divorce laws in the U.S. vary, but I wouldn't be surprised if virtual infidelity was soon counted among the plausible grounds for divorce in some places.

Many relationships end due to infidelity. Virtual relationships seem to some to offer a way to technically remain monogamous, if monogamy and sex are defined in physical terms, while having guilt-free virtual relations with a variety of partners. Have we finally found a way to have the best of both worlds? Can you cheat on your partner without ever touching someone else? This raises related but distinct questions regarding the moral aspects of virtual dating and cyber [dating].

Two Ethical Aspects of Virtual Dating: Lying and Cheating

I believe the two most compelling ethical questions arising from virtual dating and virtual relationships are as follows. First, is it permissible to lie to one's virtual partners, given that role-playing and taking on virtual identities which are quite distinct from one's irl persona are generally assumed to be the norm in an online environment? Second, do virtual relationships and cybersex count as cheating, assuming the existence of real-world partners who are unaware of the virtual hanky-panky?

Let's discuss lying first. What can one expect in virtual dating, online relationships, and cybersex in terms of truth-telling? It seems that any reasonable person in a virtual world should expect to doubt the absolute honesty of potential virtual partners. However, anyone who has been in a successful and meaningful relationship would probably say that honesty and communication are integral components of a healthy relationship. Where does this leave virtual dating and online relationships? This is surely a problem if one expects to find a satisfying relationship, in terms of honesty and communication, in a virtual world. And the anonymity that we counted as a perk in the previous section is not without moral implications. Anonymity affords virtual partners certain protections and perks, but it also makes it exceedingly easy to lie. Nonetheless, honest encounters are possible in virtual worlds, if one is careful. Assuming that it is morally problematic to lie to a partner irl, is it wrong to lie to a virtual partner?

What do ethicists say about lying in general? Some ethicists argue that lying is always wrong, regardless of the circumstances or the consequences. (Rachels, 2009) Kantian ethics, for example, argues that lying to a person treats that person as merely a means to an end, or uses them—and that is wrong. (Rachels, 2009) Undoubtedly, lying is usury. But what if lying is expected? Is lying morally problematic in virtual dating, virtual relationships, and cybersex if it is generally acknowledged that people are lying about themselves? Let's look at a different ethical theory.

Utilitarian ethics, which focuses on maximizing benefit and avoiding   20
harm, would argue that lying is typically morally problematic because it has the potential to harm others in a significant way. (Rachels, 2009) Lying, however, is not always wrong on utilitarian grounds. Lying may be justified if the circumstances and consequences warrant not telling the truth. Benefiting others and avoiding harm are central to morality on utilitarian grounds. If virtual partners expect that the individuals with whom they are virtually interacting are likely not being completely truthful, then they are less apt to be harmed. Further, if virtual partners tell tall tales to heighten the sexual experience and the role-playing involved for both partners, and this is expected, then lying in such a scenario wouldn't seem to be problematic on this account.

Notice that the issue of lying, as we've discussed it, differs from the issue of cheating in an important way. The worry in lying is directed towards not harming the person on the other end of the computer connection, whereas the issue of cheating involves possible harm caused to a person outside of the virtual relationship, namely the irl partners of those engaging in virtual dating, virtual relationships, and cybersex. Of course cheating involves a component of lying as well, but the issues involved in lying to one's irl partner can be delineated from lying to virtual partners.

We now turn to the issue of cheating. So what really counts as cheating? It may plausibly count as cheating if one engages in multiple online relationships without informing one's multiple virtual partners, however the cheating I would like to address is cheating on irl partners with virtual partners. Do I have to physically touch another person in order to count as cheating on my husband, for example? (I can't help but be reminded of the amusing debate during the Clinton presidency when pundits debated whether intercourse was required for sex.)

From what I can tell, more women than men think that engaging in online relationships is morally problematic, when one has a partner irl who is unaware of the virtual relationships. Perhaps an important component here is honesty as well; that is, if one's partner irl is aware of and has no problems with their partner engaging in virtual relationships, it would be harder to argue that cheating occurred. But what about those who engage in online dating, virtual relationships, or cybersex without informing their irl partners?

It is reasonable to assume that virtual dating and cybersex can be damaging to a real-world relationship, especially if lying to one's irl partner plays a role. It is easy enough to find media accounts of husbands and wives who argue that their spouses neglected them for a virtual partner or partners. Even if virtual sex isn't grounds for divorce per se, neglect is.

25   Cheating is typically much more complex than just sex. And sex may not have to be involved for one to cheat on a partner. If this is the case, then virtual relationships can clearly count as cheating on irl partners. Again, lying or betrayal plays a role. The sense of betrayal involved in cheating is complicated. An irl partner can find their position and their time usurped by a virtual partner, and this usurping can be just as real if the relationship is virtual. Further, the intimacy involved in many virtual relationships can be just as intense as irl. Intimacy with a partner outside of a committed relationship surely seems to be cheating, especially if we take cheating to encompass emotional infidelity. It may reasonably be argued that emotional infidelity is more harmful to a relationship than physical infidelity. For example, just like finding out in the real world that your partner has engaged in "meaningless" sex with a prostitute, finding out that your partner has engaged in "meaningless" cybersex with a virtual partner whose real name is unknown seems to me at least to be less worrisome than finding out that your partner has decided he or she is in love with and desires to commit to and marry someone else, even if it is "only virtual."

Real or Not?

So what can we conclude from our foray into the world of virtual dating, online relationships, and cybersex? Perhaps that these are as real as you allow them to be and that the emotions involved in virtual relationships can be seriously detrimental to irl partners, if you have them. Lying is clearly a worry, as is emotional attachment and emotional infidelity, if one is juggling a virtual partner and an irl partner.

Virtual dating offers a host of perks that irl relationships may not, and virtual dating may be a springboard to an irl relationship, if that's your cup of tea, but use with caution.

Notes

1   www.avmatch.com and www.datecraft.com, respectively.
2   For examples, see http://www.time.com/time/world/article/0,8599,1859231,00 .html and http://online.wsj.com/article/SB118670164592393622.html.

References

Cable, A. (2008). *Divorced from Reality: All Three Accounts of the Second Life Love Triangle that Saw a Woman Separate from Her Husband for Having a Cyber-Affair.* July 30; http://www.dailymail.co.uk/femail/ article-1085915/Divorced-reality-All-accounts-Second-Life-love-triangle- saw-woman-separate-husband-having-cyber-affair.html

Rachels, J. and Rachels, S. (2009). *The Elements of Moral Philosophy* (6 ed.). New York: McGraw-Hill.

Welles, D. (2007). *The Ins and Outs of a Second Sex Life.* July 30; http:// www.theregister.co.uk/2007/01/09/good_sex_in_second_life/

Analyze

1. According to Jones's analysis, what are the primary ethical questions about virtual dating?
2. Much of this article analyzes the ethical tensions related to virtual dating. But Jones also makes some direct claims about those tensions. Identify passages that demonstrate Jones's stance on virtual dating.
3. Jones explains that virtual communities such as *World of Warcraft* and *Second Life* "are far more 'social' than one might suspect." Why is this statement crucial to her examination of virtual relationships?

4. Jones explains several dimensions to *World of Warcraft* and *Second Life,* such as the infrastructure, the currency, and even the real estate. Why are these dimensions important to her analysis of virtual dating?

5. Compare Jones's writing style to that of Lucy B. Marcus in "What It Means Today To Be 'Connected.'" Beyond the different ideas each has about the Internet and connectedness, how are the two articles different? How does Jones approach the issues in a way that's different from Marcus?

Explore

1. How is cybersex different from sex?

2. If you have cybersex with someone other than your significant other, is it cheating? Why or why not?

3. How is falling in love in virtual reality similar to or different from falling in love with someone you meet at a bar or in a college classroom?

4. Jones says that "Cheating is typically much more complex than just sex. And sex may not have to be involved for one to cheat on a partner." What, then, constitutes cheating on a significant other? How is it more than sex? How are issues such as betrayal and intimacy involved?

5. How does Jones's analysis of virtual dating relate to Roger Scruton's claims in "Hiding Behind the Screen" about online friendship? What tensions or questions seem to be operating in both articles?

Michael Erard
What I Didn't Write About When I Wrote About Quitting Facebook

As a linguist, Michael Erard studies the slips, stumbles, and elegant perfor-mances of daily language. He has written for a range of newspapers and magazines, including *Psychology Today*, the *Atlantic*, the *New York Times*, *Reason*, *Science*, *Slate*, and *Wired*. For this article, he set out to examine and even dramatize the way people quit social media such as Facebook. The article first appeared on *The Morning News*, which describes itself as "an online magazine of essays, art, humor, and culture published weekdays since 1999." According to its website, the editors of *The Morning News* "believe in good writing, tight editing, wit, curiosity, making mistakes, and solving them with tequila."

The first thing I didn't write about quitting Facebook was a status update to my friends saying, I'm quitting Facebook.

I also did not write a proposal for the nonfiction book I imagined, which was about quitting Facebook. In the book, I would indulge the conceit that my Facebook friends are, actually, my good friends, and that the social net-work comprises a sort of community when taken as a whole. Then, as one does with one's friends, I would call each person up or visit them and tell them I was leaving Facebook, which would create an opportunity to talk about Facebook and this whole social media thing, but mainly it would be to get to know something about who they actually were and why we were linked in the first place and what it all might have meant.

Eighteen weeks of five interviews a day would get me through my friend list, I calculated. Friends from high school and college and grad school. Friends of friends. Editors. Siblings and a couple of cousins, my in-laws. Random admirers and hangers-on. The resulting book would reflect our conversations about how much Facebook had enhanced our friendships and our lives in general, or maybe it hadn't, and we'd talk about that, too. And we'd exchange info, and say goodbye, and then linger, and wave, and wave, until we couldn't see each other any more—one of those departures where you look away out of exhaustion with the moment, then when you look up find they've gone, vanished, as if they hadn't been there at all.

At the end of the book, I would actually unplug from Facebook, and I would write about that, too, and the heartwarming account of the ties that bind us would inspire you to hold your Facebook friends close, so close, because the time we pass in this mortal coil is so fleeting; we are truly encountering only the passing of the person, not the person in themselves.

5   But I didn't write this, nor did I write a status update about leaving. When I quit, there were no goodbyes. No interviews. Just, I'm outta here.

Another thing I did not write about quitting Facebook was that one of the great social pleasures in my life has been to leave gatherings or parties unannounced. You know, when the party is socked in solid from the front door to the kitchen, and the conversation is drying up like old squeezed limes, it's easiest to keep heading out the back. How cool the night. How open and unquestioning the darkness. "French leave," we English speakers say. ("English leave," the French say.) Often I went to parties to be able to vanish from them. But the disappearing act rarely happens any more; I could never get away with it. Such pleasures one has to give up because they're so unsuited to middle-aged life. You get trained, after a while, to going to every person in the room. Hey, great to see you again. See you later. Send me a note about that thing. Yes, let's do that. Goodbye, bye. The book idea was, in a way, testing out the durability of that social grace. But I didn't write about either topic.

I did, however, start an essay that could have been about why I quit Facebook, except that I got distracted by the emergence of a genre you could call the Social Media Exile essay, and I wondered whether I could meet the conventions of that genre if I ever tried to write about why I quit Facebook, though the truth is, I didn't really want to write another version of the Social Media Exile Essay, dramatizing the initial promise of this or that social media or network, the enthusiastic glow of online togetherness, then the disillusionment, the final straw, the wistful looking back. I did write that it seems like so many people have had their crack at "The Day I Quit Blogging" or "Why I Tweet No More," which aren't real essay titles but could have been, also like "How Google Broke My Heart" or "Farewell MySpace" or "*Je Ne Regrette Rien,* Friendster." So this essay never got written.

I was also writing e-mails to former Facebook friends who had noticed that I was gone from their friend list and who were taking my disappearance personally, all because of what I hadn't written about quitting Facebook—which I didn't start writing, because I had to placate my

Photo Gallery 1

"Photographs allow me to hold on to what I notice as I pass through time and place."
—Benjamin Busch

The readings throughout this book give voice to culture. With their written language, the authors respond to, defend against, and even cultivate change. But formal writing is only one way to read a culture. We can witness a civilization's development by listening to its music, watching its films, or studying the images it leaves behind. If culture is a living thing, then photographs are memories—individual recollections of past moments. In those moments, we can read values, hopes, fears, and any number of cultural reflexes.

The photographs in this gallery, taken by Benjamin Busch, show artifacts and scenes from everyday life. Examine them closely. Consider how each image speaks—what it argues, what it suggests, and what it whispers about contemporary American culture. For example, a photograph of plastic bags caught in trees says something about the way we keep, transport, and discard goods. An image of a plastic doll says something about our fixation with the human form. Consider, too, how the photographs resonate with articles throughout the chapters. Some relationships are obvious: How does the image of Santa's house connect to Sharon Angel's essay, "Sorting Out Santa" (Chapter 2)? Some relationships are more subtle: How might the image of Revlon products connect to articles about brand names or spending addictions? You might even see the photographs as assertions that support or respond to the articles. For example, imagine how the image of two concrete deer reinforces Stephanie Mills's "Some Words for the Wild" (Chapter 7).

Finally, remember that photographs are not objective accounts. They come from a particular person holding a camera at an angle, at a specific point in time, and for a reason. If photographs are a kind of memory, they are selective memory. Sometimes, photographs are observational accidents: they capture something more pronounced than the photographer's artistic hopes or plans. And sometimes, they are carefully constructed statements. This gallery contains a range of both. In other words, you might sense the photographer's decisions—in which case, you can read him as part of the culture as well.

Soil

Revlon

Deer and Forest

Mermaid

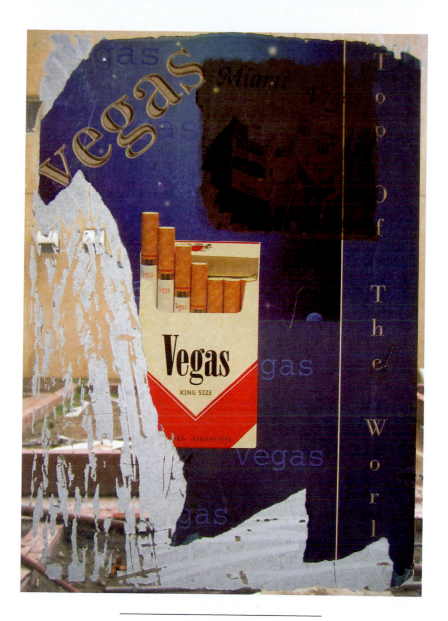

Vegas, baby

Santa's House

friends. Really, it wasn't because of you, it was because of the whole enterprise, I wrote, which had begun to throw salt on my misanthropy. I went no farther than that—I feared offending them if I wrote about how difficult it became to have peaceable face-to-face relationships with people who projected unlikeability online.

I did tweet the observation that Facebook isn't going to pay you a pension or 401k for all the time you spent there, and quite a lot of people liked this. So that was one veiled thing I wrote about why I quit Facebook.

I didn't write about the shock of finding out that the two dear sons of one 10 of my Facebook "friends" had been tragically killed in an auto accident, not recently but two years ago. Somehow I had missed this fact, until an anniversary post by one of the grieving parents—the status update elliptical, scourged by grief—pointed me toward the incident. I do not know what I would have done or written if I had known before. I did not write anything to them now because I felt so ashamed of my ignorance amidst a wealth of things to click on and know about. A wealth of things that may not matter so much. It's always been a world in which you can lose your children or your parents in an instant, but somehow I have made it this far without knowing that in my gut.

Instead of writing about any of this, once I was not on Facebook anymore, I found myself sending e-mails with some witty insights or photos of my baby, but it just wasn't the same; a request for housing help for a friend via e-mail got no responses. However, I was now *talking* a lot about quitting Facebook, and this for a time became the most interesting thing about me. Fueled by how interesting I now was, I wrote a draft of an essay about writing about why I quit Facebook, which was clever but did not contain any of the things I have already said I didn't write about. Plus, as the editor pointed out, I didn't actually explain why I had quit. I hadn't written about feeling like Facebook was a job. Like I was running on a digital hamster wheel. But a wheel that someone else has rigged up. And a wheel that's actually a turbine that's generating electricity for somebody else. That's how I felt, which is what I should have written.

I thought about how I didn't want to write about why I quit, only about how great it feels to be free, because how often do you get to leave a job? Something along the lines of, you stand up at your desk, you un-pin the photo of your dog or loved one from the cubicle wall, and you walk right out the door, don't take the elevator because it's slower than the stairs, and you bid the thrumming hive adios. Leaving Facebook felt like that. The sun singing on your face like springtime. The birds all whistling your theme song.

In the standard Social Media Exile essay, one doesn't mention or announce when one returns to blogging or Twitter. For each platform or network one leaves, there's another one to return to. Sometimes they're the same. So I'm going to close this piece by breaking that convention and mentioning how easy it turns out to be to reactivate Facebook. When you sign back in, all your stuff is there, as if you'd never left. It's like coming back to your country after a month in a foreign land, and it makes one feel that the whole reason for leaving is to make the place seem strange again. Being away from Facebook was certainly that. But I had to come back. That's where all the people are. I've got a book coming out, and I need to let my friends know. Anyway, you know where to find me and what to talk about when you do. I'll have some cookies baked.

Analyze

1. In one sentence, try to articulate Erard's point about Facebook and the process of quitting.
2. Throughout the article, Erard repeats the phrase "what I didn't write about." What effect does this repetition have on you? What point might that repetition make?
3. Much of this article is *confessional*. Erard is telling us a good deal about his personal struggle. Explain the function of his confessions: How do they relate to or help support the main idea?
4. In paragraph 6, Erard describes the way he would leave parties unannounced. How does this information support his main idea? How does it relate to the point about Facebook and the struggle to leave it?
5. This article might be considered *parody*. In other words, Erard might be spoofing or mocking the way people sound (what they say, what they don't say) when they try to quit Facebook. Identify passages that make you think the article might, in part, be a parody.

Explore

1. Do you know anyone addicted to Facebook? Are you addicted? What is it like? Does Erard capture the feeling? Which passages or comparisons from the article seem accurate to you? Which don't?
2. What do you think is worse for people: Facebook or Twitter? What particular qualities or reflexes does each bring out?

3. Apparently, enough people have tried to quit Facebook that Erard discovered an entire genre (or category) of writing that he calls the Social Media Exile essay. What do you think this says about Facebook itself, people's daily lives in 21st-century America, or people's inabilities?

4. It's easy to defend Facebook against naysayers. After all, it connects people who might otherwise lose track of one another. It allows shy people to have a voice. It makes people feel better about their days. But what else does Facebook do for people? What other, less acknowledged, value does it have?

5. Erard's article drew a range of comments—both sympathetic to and condemning of chronic Facebookers. Consider the following three comments. What do they say about Facebook and its role in public life?

   - "I just didn't like what I was hearing about snooping by employers or even prospective employers. And FB's policy of making unannounced changes compromising user privacy really bites. I simply don't trust FB."—banshee
   - "Got all Facebook'ed up and quit within the month because of no self discipline—it was taking over my life. Went back several months later and stayed longer this time, but still quit the scene—again, too much time spent with too little actual benefit."—Guest
   - "Quitting Facebook is so 2009."—Jungberg

Robert Fulford
How Twitter Saved the Octothorpe

A columnist for the *National Post* and *Toronto Life*, Robert Fulford is a Toronto-based journalist, editor, and broadcaster. His work focuses on art, entertainment, and culture, often through a Canadian lens. He is the author of numerous articles, reviews, and books, including the 1999 book *The Triumph of Narrative: Storytelling in the Age of Mass Culture*. In the following article, Fulford considers the value of the octothorpe.

When punctuation geeks assembled earlier this month at Punctuacon, our annual convention, we spent the usual two or three hours whining about the pathetic size of our gathering, compared to Comic-Con International in San Diego, Dragon*Con in Atlanta or any of those tiresome Star Trek conventions that draw multitudes to worship at the shrine of William Shatner.

We have no heroes like Shatner, just ourselves and our proud tradition of judging and promoting the images and ideograms of language—and our totally imaginary convention.

That should be enough, but a love for punctuation, signage and graphic symbols remains a lonely passion. It's hard not to be bitter.

Why can't the rest of the world understand that a well-designed semicolon or an expertly made STOP sign is every bit as enthralling as a mint *Batman* first edition, an early sketch of the Jedi, or a photograph signed by Margot Kidder herself? Why can't they care about the tragically missing apostrophe on the logo of a certain coffee-shop chain?

5   Still, Punctuacon was happier this year than usual, mostly because we could forget about what had become at previous conventions the most melancholy issue on the agenda: Who will save the octothorpe?

The Big O is a sign with deep historical and cultural roots, part of our heritage. It didn't deserve the neglect it suffered in recent times. It's lived under many names: the hash, the crunch, the hex (that's in Singapore), the flash, the grid. In some circles it's called tic-tac-toe, in others pig-pen. From a distance it looks like the sharp sign on a musical score. Whether you call it a pound sign or a number sign or anything else, it retains its identity. It's so majestically simple that it always looks good, even if drawn by someone utterly without graphic talent. Good old #. It can't go wrong.

Even so, it was in decline for years. After generations of vigorous life everywhere in the retailing world where numbers were written, it lost out to computerized invoices and receipts that simply ignored its value. In literature, after centuries showing printers where to put spaces, it was abolished by computers that do the same job with the touch of a keyboard.

It lost its proud place alongside the & and the @, on a shelf higher than both the © and the ®. After a while # appeared mostly in a cameo role on touch-tone phones, a serious comedown.

But lately the pendulum has swung again. On Twitter, the home of microbloggers, the octothorpe has a new career, reborn as the "hashtag."

Tweeters use hashtags to catalogue their tweets. Someone writing about Miles Davis, for instance, will tag his name #Miles. Anyone coming after will be able to find all the tweets dealing with Miles. (You don't have to wade through phrases like "miles to go before I sleep" or "I'd go a million miles for one of your smiles.")

Tech for Luddites, a valuable online resource ("Providing tips, tricks, and   10
techniques for navigating the digital world"), says hashtags allow tweeters to build interest-based communities. It's heartening that this function has been created spontaneously, unplanned by the Twitter hierarchy—just as, long ago, copyist monks in monasteries invented their own working language.

This year *GQ* magazine, a major arbiter of the cool, has anointed # "symbol of the year." *GQ* explains: "Hashtags have changed the way we think, communicate, process information. # is everywhere." What we have here is one of the great comeback stories in the history of competitive punctuation. Today, & © and ® have been left in the dust (of course @ retains its status in e-mail).

And what about the name, octothorpe? It's been replaced, obviously, but there's no reason to be upset. Change is the law of usage. That term now becomes, at least for the immediate future, a historical artifact. Its own history will be the subject of discussion for generations to come, whenever punctuation geeks gather.

It was born somewhere in the Bell system in the 1970s, when touchtone became established. The first half of the name was easy, though rich in cultural reference. Since the # has eight points the name fell within the order of eight, where an eight-sided figure is an octagon, a sea creature with eight suckered arms is an octopus, eight notes are an octave and octopush (an underwater game played by two teams of scuba divers pushing a lead puck on the bottom of a swimming pool) originally had eight players a side.

And where did "thorpe" come from? The *American Heritage Dictionary* says it honours James Edward Oglethorpe, the 18th-century British general who helped found the colony of Georgia in 1732. A more popular story has an engineer at Bell Labs deciding to honour Jim Thorpe, an Indian athlete who won the pentathlon and decathlon for the U.S. at the 1912 Olympics; he had his gold medals taken from him when his background as a professional athlete was disclosed, a decision that was reversed three decades after his death.

A third explanation was endorsed in 1996 by the *New Scientist,* an ex-   15
cellent journal in Britain. On ancient maps you can sometimes find the #

used to indicate the presence of a village; it looks like a primitive plan of eight fields of identical size, with a village square in the middle. It's possible that octothorpe derives from the Old Norse word for village, which survives today in some British town names, such as Scunthorpe in North Lincolnshire.

The fourth story, backed by evidence as strong as the sources for the other three, emerged in 2006, a year after an earlier column I wrote on the octothorpe. It blames a weird form of anonymous malice perpetrated by Bell Labs engineers (people named Schaak, Uthlaut, Asplund and Eby) who devised a sound that speakers of various languages would find difficult to pronounce. Probably this etymological mystery will go unsolved and we'll never know the truth.

Through all these troubled times, we octothorpe supporters remained loyal, like hockey fans who wear Maple Leafs sweaters despite all the years of pain. Even though Punctuacon is a fictional organization (though metaphorically vibrant), you can understand why the members of our little band were pleased to raise a glass to the hash mark in its new life on Twitter.

Analyze

1. Explain the effect of Fulford's first four paragraphs. What idea do they establish? How does that idea serve the rest of the article?
2. Consider Fulford's characterization of the hashtag on Twitter: "It's heartening that this function has been created spontaneously, unplanned by the Twitter hierarchy—just as, long ago, copyist monks in monasteries invented their own working language." Why do you think he's heartened by the spontaneous role? Why is it good that the Twitter hierarchy didn't plan on the function of #?
3. Fulford gives several versions of the octothorpe's history. What is the purpose of the different versions? What idea do they serve or support?
4. Fulford values the tradition of language but he also seems to value change. Identify a passage that shows Fulford's values—a place where he accepts change yet celebrates the history of language.
5. Explain what assumptions or beliefs Fulford's article shares with Steven D. Krause's, "Living Within Social Networks."

Explore

1. Do you tweet? Why or why not?
2. Are you a "tech Luddite?" Why or why not?
3. Fulford says, "Change is the law of usage." What other linguistic change has occurred in your lifetime or at least recently enough that your parents recall a different usage? Explain the change—and why you think it happened.
4. What is the role of punctuation in a culture? What does it do besides regulate language? What quieter, more subtle, functions does it have?
5. What's your personal role in the maintenance of English punctuation? Are you obedient, transgressive, unconcerned, dismissive, ignorant, or passive? Explain your role in detail.

Roger Scruton
Hiding Behind the Screen

A philosopher, essayist, critic, novelist, and poet, Roger Scruton serves as a scholar at the American Enterprise Institute, a visiting professor at both Oxford University and at the University of St. Andrews in Scotland. The author of numerous books, including *The Face of God: The Gifford Lectures* and *How to Think Seriously About the Planet: The Case for an Environmental Conservatism* (both 2012), he is currently exploring the influence of neuroscience on culture. In the following essay, which was adapted from a lecture, Scruton considers the limitations of human development in online contexts.

Human relations, and the self-image of the human being, have been profoundly affected by the Internet and by the ease with which images of other people can be summoned to the computer screen to become the objects of emotional attention. How should we conceptualize this change, and what is its effect on the psychic condition of those most given to constructing their world of interests and relationships through the screen? Is this change as damaging as many would have us believe, undermining our capacity for real relationships and placing a mere fantasy of relatedness in their stead? Or is it relatively harmless, as unproblematic as speaking to a friend on the telephone?

First, we should make some distinctions. We all now use the computer to send messages to our friends and to others with whom we have dealings. This sort of communication is not different in any fundamental respect from the old practice of letter writing, except for its speed. Of course, we should not regard speed as a trivial feature. The rapidity of modern communications does not merely accelerate the process whereby relationships are formed and severed; it inevitably changes how those relationships are conducted and understood. Absence is less painful with the Internet and the telephone, but it also loses some of its poignancy; moreover, e-mails are seldom composed as carefully as letters, since the very slowness with which a letter makes its way to its destination prompts us to put more of our feelings into the words. Still, e-mail is reality, not virtual reality, and the changes it has brought about are changes in real communication between real people.

Nor does the existence of social networks like Facebook, which are also for the most part real communication between real people, involve any attempt simply to substitute a virtual reality for the actual one. On the contrary, they are parasitic on the real relationships they foster, and which they alter in large part by encouraging people to put themselves on display, and in turn to become voyeurs of the displays of others. Some might claim that the existence of these networking sites provides a social and psychological benefit, helping those who shy away from presenting themselves directly to the world to gain a public place and identity. These sites also enable people to keep in touch with a wide circle of friends and colleagues, thereby increasing the range of their affections, and filling the world with goodwill and happy feelings.

Yet already something new is entering the world of human relations with these innocent-seeming sites. There is a novel ease with which people can make contact with each other through the screen. No more need to get up from your desk and make the journey to your friend's house. No more need for weekly meetings, or the circle of friends in the downtown restaurant or bar. All those effortful ways of making contact can be dispensed with: a touch of the keyboard and you are there, where you wanted to be, on the site that defines your friends. But can this be real friendship, when it is pursued and developed in such facile and costless ways?

Friendship and Control

Real friendship shows itself in action and affection. The real friend is the one who comes to the rescue in your hour of need; who is there with comfort in adversity and who shares with you his own success. This is hard to do on the screen—the screen, after all, is primarily a locus of information, and is only a place of action insofar as communication is a form of action. Only words, and not hands or the things they carry, can reach from it to comfort the sufferer, to ward off an enemy's blows, or to provide any of the tangible assets of friendship in a time of need. It is arguable that the more people satisfy their need for companionship through relationships carried out on the screen, the less will they develop friendships of that other kind, the kind that offers help and comfort in the real trials of human life. Friendships that are carried out primarily on the screen cannot easily be lifted off it, and when they are so lifted, there is no guarantee that they will take any strain. Indeed, it is precisely their cost-free, screen-friendly character that attracts many people to them—so much so, students of mine tell me, that they fear addiction, and often have to forbid themselves to go to their Facebook account for days on end, in order to get on with their real lives and their real relationships.

What we are witnessing is a change in the *attention* that mediates and gives rise to friendship. In the once normal conditions of human contact, people became friends by being in each other's presence, understanding all the many subtle signals, verbal and bodily, whereby another testifies to his character, emotions, and intentions, and building affection and trust in tandem. Attention was fixed on the other—on his face, words, and gestures. And his nature as an embodied person was the focus of the friendly feelings that he inspired. People building friendship in this way are strongly aware that they appear to the other as the other appears to them. The other's face is a mirror in which they see their own. Precisely because attention is fixed on the other there is an opportunity for self-knowledge and self-discovery, for that expanding freedom in the presence of the other which is one of the joys of human life. The object of friendly feelings looks back at you, and freely responds to your free activity, amplifying both your awareness and his own. As traditionally conceived, friendship was ruled by the maxim "know thyself."

When attention is fixed on the other as mediated by the screen, however, there is a marked shift in emphasis. For a start, I have my finger on the button; at any moment I can turn the image off, or click to arrive at some new encounter. The other is free in his *own* space, but he is not really free in *my* space, over which I am the ultimate arbiter. I am not risking myself in the friendship to nearly the same extent as I risk myself when I meet the other face to face. Of course, the other may so grip my attention with his messages, images, and requests that I stay glued to the screen. Nevertheless, it is ultimately a *screen* that I am glued to, and not the face that I see in it. All interaction with the other is at a distance, and whether I am affected by it becomes to some extent a matter of my own choosing.

In this screenful form of conducting relationships, I enjoy a power over the other person of which he himself is not really aware—since he is not aware of how much I wish to retain him in the space before me. And the power I have over him he has too over me, just as I am denied the same freedom in his space that he is denied in mine. He, too, therefore, will not risk himself; he appears on the screen only on condition of retaining that ultimate control himself. This is something I know about him that he knows that I know—and vice versa. There grows between us a reduced-risk encounter, in which each is aware that the other is fundamentally *withheld,* sovereign within his impregnable cyber-castle.

But that is not the only way in which cyber-relationships are affected by the medium of their formation. For instance, while "messaging" is still very much alive on Facebook, much of it is depersonalized in nature: the use of private messages has for many been supplanted by posting messages on a friend's public "Wall," meaning that the entire network is now participant in the communiqué. And while the Wall post still maintains the semblance of interpersonal contact, probably the most common form of communication on Facebook is the "status update," a message that is broadcast from one person to everyone (or, put another way, to no one in particular).

10   All of these communications, along with everything on the screen, appear in competition with whatever else might be called up by the mouse. You "click on" your friend, as you might click on a news item or a music video. He is one of the many products on display. Friendship with him, and relationships generally, belong in the category of amusements and distractions, a commodity that may be chosen, or not, depending on the rival goods. This contributes to a radical demotion of the personal relationship. Your friendships are no longer special to you and definitive of your moral

life: they are amusements, things that have no real life of their own but borrow their life from your interest in them—what the Marxists would call "fetishes."

There is a strong argument to be made that the Facebook experience, which has attracted millions of people from all around the world, is an antidote to shyness, a way in which people otherwise cripplingly intimidated by the venture outwards into society are able to overcome their disability and enjoy the web of affectionate relationships on which so much of our happiness depends. But there is an equally strong argument that the Facebook experience, to the extent that it is supplanting the physical realm of human relationships, hypostatizes shyness, retains its principal features, while substituting an ersatz kind of affection for the real affection that shyness fears. For by placing a screen between yourself and the friend, while retaining ultimate control over what appears on that screen, you also hide from the real encounter—denying the other the power and the freedom to challenge you in your deeper nature and to call on you here and now to take responsibility for yourself and for him.

I was taught growing up that shyness (unlike modesty) is not a virtue but a defect, and that it comes from placing too high a value on yourself— a value that forbids you to risk yourself in the encounter with others. By removing the *real* risks from interpersonal encounters, the Facebook experience might encourage a kind of narcissism, a self-regarding posture in the midst of what should have been other-regarding friendship. In effect, there may be nothing more than the display of self, the others listed on the website counting for nothing in themselves.

Freedom Requires Context

In its normal occurrence, the Facebook encounter is still an encounter— however attenuated—between real people. But increasingly, the screen is taking over—ceasing to be a medium of communication between real people who exist elsewhere, and becoming the place where people finally achieve reality, the only place where they relate in any coherent way to others. This next stage is evident in the "avatar" phenomenon, in which people create virtual characters in virtual worlds as proxies for themselves, so enabling their controllers to live in complete self-complacency behind the screen, exposed to no danger and yet enjoying a kind of substitute affection through the adventures of their cyber-ego.

The game *Second Life* offers a virtual world and invites you to enter it in the form of an avatar constructed from its collection of templates. It has its own currency, in which purchases can be made in its own stores. It rents spaces to avatars as their homes and businesses. By late 2009, the company that created *Second Life* announced that its user base had collectively logged more than a billion hours in the system and had conducted business transactions worth more than a billion dollars.

15   *Second Life* also provides opportunities for "social" action, with social positions achieved by merit—or, at any rate, virtual merit. In this way people can enjoy, through their avatars, cost-free versions of the social emotions, and can become heroes of "compassion," without lifting a finger in the real world. In one notorious incident in 2007, a man attempted to sue an avatar for theft of his *Second Life* intellectual property. The property itself was an "adult entertainment" product—one among many such *Second Life* products now available that enable your cyber-ego to realize your wildest fantasies at no risk to yourself. There have been many reports of couples who have never met in person conducting adulterous affairs entirely in cyberspace; they usually show no guilt towards their spouses, and in fact proudly display their emotions as though they had achieved some kind of moral breakthrough by ensuring that it was only their avatars, and not they themselves, that ended up in bed together.

Most people probably would see this as an unhealthy state of affairs. It is one thing to place a screen between yourself and the world; it is another thing to inhabit the world on that screen as the primary sphere of your relationships. In vesting one's emotional life in the adventures of an avatar, one retreats completely from real relationships. Instead of being a means to augment relationships that exist outside of it, the Internet could become the sole arena of social life—but an unreal life involving unreal people. The thought of this reawakens all of those once-fashionable claims of alienation and the fetishism of commodities of which Marx and his followers accused capitalist society. The nerd controlling the avatar has essentially "placed his being outside of himself," as they would have put it.

The origin of those critiques lies in an idea of Hegel's, an idea of enduring importance that is constantly resurging in new guises, especially in the writings of psychologists concerned with mapping the contours of ordinary happiness. The idea is this: we human beings fulfill ourselves through our own free actions, and through the consciousness that these actions bring of our individual worth. But we are not free in a state of nature, nor do we, outside the world of human relations, have the kind of consciousness of self that allows us to value and intend our own fulfillment. Freedom is not reducible to the unhindered choices that even an animal might enjoy; nor is self-consciousness simply a matter of the pleasurable immersion in immediate experiences, like the rat pressing endlessly on the pleasure switch. Freedom involves an active engagement with the world, in which opposition is encountered and overcome, risks are taken and satisfactions weighed: it is, in short, an exercise of practical reason, in pursuit of goals whose value must justify the efforts needed to obtain them. Likewise, self-consciousness, in its fully realized form, involves not merely an openness to present experience, but a sense of my own existence *as an individual,* with plans and projects that might be fulfilled or frustrated, and with a clear conception of what *I* am doing, for what purpose, and with what hope of happiness.

All those ideas are contained in the term first introduced by the philosopher Johann Gottlieb Fichte to denote the inner goal of a free personal life: *Selbstbestimmung,* self-determination or self-certainty. Hegel's crucial claim is that the life of freedom and self-certainty can only be obtained through others. I become fully myself only in contexts which compel me to recognize that I am another in others' eyes. I do not acquire my freedom and individuality and then, as it were, try them out in the world of human relations. It is only by entering that world, with its risks, conflicts, and responsibilities, that I come to know myself as free, to enjoy my own perspective and individuality, and to become a fulfilled person among persons.

In the *Phenomenology of Spirit* and the *Philosophy of Right,* Hegel tells many pleasing and provocative parables about the way in which the subject achieves freedom and fulfillment through his *Entäusserung*—his objectification—in the world of others. The status of these parables— whether they are arguments or allegories, conceptual analyses or psychological generalizations—has always been a matter of dispute. But few psychologists now would dispute the fundamental claim that underpins them, which is that the freedom and fulfillment of the self come about only through the recognition of the other. Without others, my freedom is an empty cipher. And recognition of the other involves taking full responsibility for my own existence as the individual who I am.

In his efforts to "set Hegel on his feet," the young Marx drew an important contrast between the true freedom that comes to us through relationships with other subjects and the hidden enslavement that comes when our ventures outwards are not towards subjects but towards objects. In other words, he suggested, we must distinguish the *realization* of the self, in free relations with others, from the *alienation* of the self in the system of things. That is the core of his critique of private property, and it is a critique that is as much bound up with allegory and storytelling as the original Hegelian arguments. In later writings the critique is transformed into the theory of "fetishism," according to which people lose their freedom through making fetishes of commodities. A fetish is something that is animated by a *transferred* life. The consumer in a capitalist society, according to Marx, transfers his life into the commodities that bewitch him, and so loses that life— becoming a slave to commodities precisely through seeing the market in goods rather than the free interactions of people; as the place where his desires are brokered and fulfilled.

These critiques of property and the market, it should be noted, do not merit endorsement. They are flamboyant offshoots of a Hegelian philosophy which, properly understood, endorses free transactions in a market as much as it endorses free relations between people generally—indeed, it sees the one as an application of the other. Rather, the crucial idea from which we may still learn is that of the *Entäusserung,* the realization of the self through responsible relations with others. This is the core contribution of German Romantic philosophy to the understanding of the modern condition, and it is an idea that has direct application to the problems that we see emerging in our new world of social life conducted on the Internet. In the sense in which freedom is a value, freedom is also an artifact that comes into being through the mutual interaction of people. This mutual interaction is what raises us from the animal condition to the personal condition, enabling us to take responsibility for our lives and actions, to evaluate our goals and character, and both to understand the nature of personal fulfillment and to set about desiring and intending it.

This process of raising ourselves above the animal condition is crucial, as the Hegelians emphasized, to the growth of the human subject as a self-knowing agent, capable of entertaining and acting from reasons, and with a developed first-person perspective and a sense of his reality as one subject among others. It is a process that depends upon real conflicts and real resolutions, in a shared public space where each of us is fully accountable for what he is and does. Anything that interferes with that process, by undermining the growth of interpersonal relations, by confiscating responsibility, or by preventing or discouraging an individual from making long-term rational choices and adopting a concrete vision of his own fulfillment, is an evil. It may be an unavoidable evil; but it is an evil all the same, and one that we should strive to abolish if we can.

Television and the Trend Toward Self-Alienation

Transferring our social lives onto the Internet is only one of the ways in which we damage or retreat from this process of self-realization. Long before that temptation arose (and preparing the way for it) was the lure of television, which corresponds exactly to the Hegelian and Marxist critique of the fetish—an inanimate thing in which we invest our life, and so lose it. Of course we retain ultimate control over the television: we can turn it off. But people don't, on the whole; they remain fixed to the screen in many of those moments when they might otherwise be building relationships through conversation, activities, conflicts, and projects. The television has, for a vast number of our fellow human beings, destroyed family meals, home cooking, hobbies, homework, study, and family games. It has rendered many people largely inarticulate, and deprived them of the simple ways of making direct conversational contact with their fellows. This is not a question of TV's "dumbing down" of thought and imagination, or its manipulation of people's desires and interests through brazen imagery. Those features are familiar enough, and the constant target of despairing criticism. Nor am I referring only to its addictive quality—though research by the psychologists Mihaly Csikszentmihalyi and Robert Kubey offers convincing evidence that TV is addictive in the same way as gambling and drugs.

The concern is rather the nature of television as a replacement for human relationships. By watching people interacting on TV sitcoms, the junkie is able to dispense with interactions of his own. Those energies and interests that would otherwise be focused on others—in storytelling, arguing, singing together, or playing games; in walking, talking, eating, and acting—are consumed on the screen, in vicarious lives that involve no engagement of the viewer's own moral equipment. And that equipment therefore atrophies.

We see this everywhere in modern life, but nowhere more vividly than in the students who arrive in our colleges. These divide roughly into two   25 kinds: those from TV-sodden homes, and those who have grown up talking. Those of the first kind tend to be reticent, inarticulate, given to aggression when under stress, unable to tell a story or express a view, and seriously hampered when it comes to taking responsibility for a task, an activity, or a relationship. Those of the second kind are the ones who step forward with ideas, who go out to their fellows, who radiate the kind of freedom and adventurousness that makes learning a pleasure and risk a challenge. Since these students have had atypical upbringings, they are prone to be subjects of mockery. But they have a head start over their TV-addled contemporaries. The latter can still be freed from their vice; university athletics, theater, music, and so on can help to marginalize TV in campus life. But in many other public or semi-public spaces, television has now become a near necessity: it flickers in the background, reassuring those who have bestowed their life on it that their life goes on.

These criticisms of television parallel criticisms of the "fetishizing" nature of mass culture made by Max Horkheimer, Theodor Adorno, and other members of the neo-Marxist Frankfurt school. Interestingly enough, the Frankfurt school ideas have been recently put to use in criticizing another way in which we can now achieve instant and cost-free stimulation: the iPod. In his 2008 book *Sound Moves,* Michael Bull draws on the "cultural theory" of Horkheimer and Adorno to argue that, thanks to the iPod, urban space has in many ways ceased to be public space and has become fragmented and privatized, each person retreating into his own inviolable sphere and losing his dependency upon and interest in his fellows. This process not only alienates people from each other, it enables people to retain control over their sensations, and so shut out the world of chance, risk, and change.

Although there is good reason to be sympathetic with Bull's argument, as well as those original criticisms of the consumer economy made by Adorno and Horkheimer, their criticisms had the wrong target: namely, the system of capitalist production and the emerging culture industry which forms part of it. The object of Adorno and company's scorn was the substitution of risk-free and addictive pleasures for the pleasures of understanding, freedom, and relationship. They may have been right in thinking that the culture industry has a propensity to favor the first kind of pleasure, for this kind of pleasure is easily packaged and marketed. But take away the healthy ways of growing up through relationships and the addictive pleasures will automatically take over, even where there is no culture industry to exploit them—as we witnessed in communist Europe. And, just like the theater, the media of mass culture can also be used positively (by those with critical judgment) to enhance and deepen our real sympathies. The correct response to the ills of television is not to attack those who manufacture televisions or who stock them with rubbish: it is to concentrate on the kind of education that makes it possible to take a critical approach to television, so as to demand real insight and real emotion, rather than kitsch, Disney, or porn. And the same is true for the iPod.

To work towards this critical approach means getting clear about the virtues of *direct* rather than vicarious relations. Why, as Villiers de l'Isle-Adam said, do we go to the trouble of living rather than asking our servants to do it for us? Why do we criticize those who eat burgers on the couch, while life plays out its pointless drama on the screen? Get clear about these questions, and we can begin to educate children in the art of turning off the television. The avatar can therefore be seen as merely the latest point in a process of alienation whereby people learn to "put their lives outside of themselves," to make their lives into playthings over which they retain complete, though in some way deeply specious, control. (They control physically what controls them psychologically.) And this is why it is so tempting to look back to those old Hegelian and Marxist theories. For they were premised on the view that we become free only by "moving out-wards," embodying our freedom in shared activities and mutually respon-sible relations. And the Hegelians distinguished a true from a false way of "moving outwards": one in which we gain our freedom by giving it real and objective form, as opposed to one in which we lose it by investing it in objects that alienate us from our inner life. Those theories show how the thing that we (or at any rate the followers of Hegel) most value in human life—self-realization in a condition of freedom—is separated by a thin dividing line from the thing which destroys us—self-alienation in a condition of bondage.

Impressive though they are, however, the Hegelian-Marxist theories are shot through with metaphor and speculation; they are not anchored in em-pirical research or explanatory hypotheses; they rely for their plausibility entirely on *a priori* thoughts about the nature of freedom, and about the metaphysical distinction between subject and object. If they are to be of use to us we will have to translate them into a more down-to-earth and practi-cal language—one that will tell us how our children should be educated, if we are to bring them out from behind the screen.

The Necessary Risks of Life Off the Screen

30   We must come to an understanding, then, of what is at stake in the current worries concerning the Internet, avatars, and life on the screen. The first issue at stake is risk. We are rational beings, endowed with practical as well as theoretical reasoning. And our practical reasoning develops through our confrontation with risk and uncertainty. To a large extent, life on the screen is risk-free: when we click to enter some new domain, we risk nothing immediate in the way of physical danger, and our accountability to others and risk of emotional embarrassment is attenuated. This is vividly apparent in the case of pornography—and the addictive nature of pornography is familiar to all who have to work in counseling those whom it has brought to a state of distraught dependency. The porn addict gains some of the benefits of sexual excitement, without any of the normal costs; but the costs are part of what sex means, and by avoiding them, one is destroying in oneself the capacity for sexual attachment.

This freedom from risk is one of the most significant features of *Second Life,* and it is also present (to an extent) on social networking sites like Facebook. One can enter and leave relationships conducted solely via the screen without any embarrassment, remaining anonymous or operating under a pseudonym, hiding behind an avatar or a false photograph of oneself. A person can decide to "kill" his screen identity at any time, and he will suffer nothing as a consequence. Why, then, trouble to enter the world of real encounters, when this easy substitute is available? And when the substitute becomes a habit, the virtues needed for the real encounter do not develop.

It should not go unmentioned that the habit of reducing risk is one that is widespread in our society, and indeed encouraged by government. An unhealthy obsession with health and an unsafe craze for safety have confiscated many of the risks that previous generations have not merely taken for granted but incorporated into the process of moral education. From the padding of children's playgrounds and the mandating of helmets for skateboarders to the criminalization of wine at the family table, the health-and-safety fanatics have surrounded us at every point with a web of prohibitions, while encouraging the belief that risks are not the concern of the individual but a matter of public policy. Children are not, on the whole, encouraged to risk themselves in physical ways; and it is not surprising if they are reluctant, in consequence, to risk themselves in emotional ways either.

But it is unlikely that this is either the source of risk-avoidance in human relationships, or a real indication of the right and the wrong way to proceed. No doubt children need physical risk and adventure if they are to develop as responsible people, with their full quota of courage, prudence, and practical wisdom. But risks of the soul are unlike risks of the body; you don't learn to manage them by being exposed to them. As we know, children exposed to sexual predation do not learn to deal with it but, on the contrary, tend to acquire the habit of *not* dealing with it: of altogether closing off a genuine emotional engagement with their sexuality, reducing it to a raw, angry bargaining, learning to treat themselves as objects and losing the capacity to risk themselves in love. Much modern sex education, which teaches that the only risks of sex are medical, exposes children to the same kind of harm, encouraging them to enter the world of sexual relations without the capacity to give or receive erotic love, and so learning to see sex as lying outside the realm of lasting relationships—a source of pleasure rather than love.

In human relations, risk avoidance means the avoidance of *accountability*, the refusal to stand *judged* in another's eyes, the refusal to come *face to face* with another person, to give oneself in whatever measure to him or her, and so to run the risk of rejection. Accountability is not something we should avoid; it is something we need to learn. Without it we can never acquire either the capacity to love or the virtue of justice. Other people will remain for us merely complex devices, to be negotiated in the way that animals are negotiated, for our own advantage and without opening the possibility of mutual judgment. Justice is the ability to see the other as having a claim on you, as being a free subject just as you are, and as demanding your accountability. To acquire this virtue you must learn the habit of face-to-face encounters, in which you solicit the other's consent and cooperation rather than imposing your will. The retreat behind the screen is a way of retaining control over the encounter, while minimizing the need to acknowledge the other's point of view. It involves setting your will outside yourself, as a feature of virtual reality, while not risking it as it must be risked, if others are truly to be encountered. To encounter another person in his freedom is to acknowledge his sovereignty and his right: it is to recognize that the developing situation is no longer within your exclusive control, but that you are caught up by it, made real and accountable in the other's eyes by the same considerations that make him real and accountable in yours.

35   In sexual encounters it is surely obvious that this process of "going out" to the other must occur if there is to be a genuine gift of love, and if the sexual act is to be something more than the friction of body parts. Learning to "go out" in this way is a complex moral process, which cannot be simplified without setting sex outside the process of psychological attachment. And it seems clear—though it is by no means easy to give final proof of it—that attachment is increasingly at risk, and that the cause of this is precisely that sexual pleasure comes without justice or commitment. It is surely plausible to suggest that when we rely on the screen as the forum of personal development, we learn habits of relationship without the discipline of accountability, so that sex, when one arrives at it (as even the screen addict may eventually), will be regarded in the same narcissistic way as the vicarious excitements through which it has been rehearsed. It will occur in that indefinable "elsewhere" from which the soul takes flight, even in the moment of pleasure.

Perhaps we can survive in a world of virtual relations; but it is not a world into which children can easily enter, except as intruders. Avatars may reproduce on the screen: but they will not fill the world with real human children. And the cyber-parents of these avatar-children, deprived of all that makes people grow as moral beings—of risk, embarrassment, suffering, and love—will shrink to mere points of view, on a world in which they do not really occur.

Analyze

1. Scruton begins his article by making "some distinctions" (in paragraphs 2–4). Explain those distinctions and why they are critical to his argument about human relationships.

2. As best you can, summarize Scruton's claim in each section: Friendship and Control, Freedom Requires Context, Television and the Trend Toward Self-Alienation, and The Necessary Risks of Life Off the Screen. Try to capture the full dimension of his points.

3. In paragraph 10, Scruton explains the idea of a "fetish." Explain how this idea fits into his overall argument about social media.

4. In paragraph 11, Scruton describes an argument for the value of Facebook. Halfway through the paragraph, he then responds to that argument with an "equally strong argument." This move, often called a *turnabout paragraph*, allows Scruton to counter opposing positions. Find another turnabout paragraph and explain the opposing position that Scruton counters.

5. Scruton borrows some concepts from 19th- and 20th-century philosophers (such as Hegel, Marx, and Adorno). Focus on one of those philosophers and explain his role in Scruton's argument.

Explore

1. In his first sentence, Scruton explains that humans are used as "objects of emotional attention" on the Internet. Consider this phrase. What does it make you think or feel? What argument can you sense lurking inside of the phrase?

2. Scruton explains that Facebook removes "*real* risk" from friendship. How is this true or false? What have you witnessed or read that supports or contradicts this point?

3. Scruton claims that "e-mail is reality, not virtual reality." What does he mean? Why does he state it in this way?

4. In his conclusion, Scruton claims that "risk, embarrassment, suffering, and love" make people grow into "moral beings." Examine each of these phenomena: risk, embarrassment, suffering, and love. How do they prompt us to become moral beings?

5. Look up *phenomenology* online and then describe why it might be an important idea in discussions about virtual life.

James Gleick
What Defines a Meme?

Award-winning author and Pulitzer Prize finalist James Gleick has published numerous books, including *The Information: A History, a Theory, a Flood* (2011), from which the following essay was adapted. A former editor and reporter for *The New York Times,* he founded an Internet service in 1993 that launched the first full-featured graphical user interface to connect online. This article originally appeared in *Smithsonian* magazine, which was "created for modern, well-rounded individuals with diverse interests." Here, Gleick considers the ways in which culture reproduces itself, both biologically and virtually.

"**W**hat lies at the heart of every living thing is not a fire, not warm breath, not a 'spark of life.' It is information, words, instructions," Richard Dawkins declared in 1986. Already one of the world's foremost evolutionary biologists, he had caught the spirit of a new age. The cells of an organism are nodes in a richly interwoven communications network, transmitting and receiving, coding and decoding. Evolution itself embodies an ongoing exchange of information between organism and environment. "If you want to understand life," Dawkins wrote, "don't think about vibrant, throbbing gels and oozes, think about information technology."

We have become surrounded by information technology; our furniture includes iPods and plasma displays, and our skills include texting and Googling. But our capacity to understand the role of information has been sorely taxed. "TMI," we say. Stand back, however, and the past does come back into focus.

The rise of information theory aided and abetted a new view of life. The genetic code—no longer a mere metaphor—was being deciphered. Scientists spoke grandly of the *biosphere:* an entity composed of all the earth's life-forms, teeming with information, replicating and evolving. And biologists, having absorbed the methods and vocabulary of communications science, went further to make their own contributions to the understanding of information itself.

Jacques Monod, the Parisian biologist who shared a Nobel Prize in 1965 for working out the role of messenger RNA in the transfer of genetic information, proposed an analogy: just as the biosphere stands above the world of nonliving matter, so an "abstract kingdom" rises above the biosphere. The denizens of this kingdom? Ideas.

5   "Ideas have retained some of the properties of organisms," he wrote. "Like them, they tend to perpetuate their structure and to breed; they too can fuse, recombine, segregate their content; indeed they too can evolve, and in this evolution selection must surely play an important role."

Ideas have "spreading power," he noted—"infectivity, as it were"—and some more than others. An example of an infectious idea might be a religious ideology that gains sway over a large group of people. The American neurophysiologist Roger Sperry had put forward a similar notion several years earlier, arguing that ideas are "just as real" as the neurons they inhabit. Ideas have power, he said:

> Ideas cause ideas and help evolve new ideas. They interact with each
> other and with other mental forces in the same brain, in neighboring

brains, and thanks to global communication, in far distant, foreign brains. And they also interact with the external surroundings to produce in toto a burstwise advance in evolution that is far beyond anything to hit the evolutionary scene yet.

Monod added, "I shall not hazard a theory of the selection of ideas." There was no need. Others were willing.

Dawkins made his own jump from the evolution of genes to the evolution of ideas. For him the starring role belongs to the replicator, and it scarcely matters whether replicators were made of nucleic acid. His rule is "All life evolves by the differential survival of replicating entities." Wherever there is life, there must be replicators. Perhaps on other worlds replicators could arise in a silicon-based chemistry—or in no chemistry at all.

What would it mean for a replicator to exist without chemistry? "I think that a new kind of replicator has recently emerged on this very planet," Dawkins proclaimed near the end of his first book, *The Selfish Gene*, in 1976. "It is staring us in the face. It is still in its infancy, still drifting clumsily about in its primeval soup, but already it is achieving evolutionary change at a rate that leaves the old gene panting far behind." That "soup" is human culture; the vector of transmission is language, and the spawning ground is the brain.

For this bodiless replicator itself, Dawkins proposed a name. He called   10
it the meme, and it became his most memorable invention, far more influential than his selfish genes or his later proselytizing against religiosity. "Memes propagate themselves in the meme pool by leaping from brain to brain via a process which, in the broad sense, can be called imitation," he wrote. They compete with one another for limited resources: brain time or bandwidth. They compete most of all for *attention*. For example:

> *Ideas.* Whether an idea arises uniquely or reappears many times, it may thrive in the meme pool or it may dwindle and vanish. The belief in God is an example Dawkins offers—an ancient idea, replicating itself not just in words but in music and art. The belief that Earth orbits the Sun is no less a meme, competing with others for survival. (Truth may be a helpful quality for a meme, but it is only one among many.)
>
> *Tunes.* This tune has spread for centuries across several continents.
>
> *Catchphrases.* One text snippet, "What hath God wrought?" appeared early and spread rapidly in more than one medium. Another,

"Read my lips," charted a peculiar path through late 20th-century America. "Survival of the fittest" is a meme that, like other memes, mutates wildly ("survival of the fattest"; "survival of the sickest"; "survival of the fakest"; "survival of the twittest").

Images. In Isaac Newton's lifetime, no more than a few thousand people had any idea what he looked like, even though he was one of England's most famous men. Yet now millions of people have quite a clear idea—based on replicas of copies of rather poorly painted portraits. Even more pervasive and indelible are the smile of Mona Lisa, *The Scream* of Edvard Munch and the silhouettes of various fictional extraterrestrials. These are memes, living a life of their own, independent of any physical reality. "This may not be what George Washington looked like then," a tour guide was overheard saying of the Gilbert Stuart portrait at the Metropolitan Museum of Art, "but this is what he looks like now." Exactly.

Memes emerge in brains and travel outward, establishing beachheads on paper and celluloid and silicon and anywhere else information can go. They are not to be thought of as elementary particles but as organisms. The number three is not a meme; nor is the color blue, nor any simple thought, any more than a single nucleotide can be a gene. Memes are complex units, distinct and memorable—units with staying power.

Also, an object is not a meme. The hula hoop is not a meme; it is made of plastic, not of bits. When this species of toy spread worldwide in a mad epidemic in 1958, it was the product, the physical manifestation, of a meme, or memes: the craving for hula hoops; the swaying, swinging, twirling skill set of hula-hooping. The hula hoop itself is a meme vehicle. So, for that matter, is each human hula hooper—a strikingly effective meme vehicle, in the sense neatly explained by the philosopher Daniel Dennett: "A wagon with spoked wheels carries not only grain or freight from place to place; it carries the brilliant idea of a wagon with spoked wheels from mind to mind." Hula hoopers did that for the hula hoop's memes—and in 1958 they found a new transmission vector, broadcast television, sending its messages immeasurably faster and farther than any wagon. The moving image of the hula hooper seduced new minds by hundreds, and then by thousands, and then by millions. The meme is not the dancer but the dance.

For most of our biological history memes existed fleetingly; their main mode of transmission was the one called "word of mouth." Lately, however, they have managed to adhere in solid substance: clay tablets, cave walls, paper sheets. They achieve longevity through our pens and printing presses, magnetic tapes and optical disks. They spread via broadcast towers and digital networks. Memes may be stories, recipes, skills, legends or fashions. We copy them, one person at a time. Alternatively, in Dawkins' meme-centered perspective, they copy themselves.

"I believe that, given the right conditions, replicators automatically band together to create systems, or machines, that carry them around and work to favor their continued replication," he wrote. This was not to suggest that memes are conscious actors; only that they are entities with interests that can be furthered by natural selection. Their interests are not our interests. "A meme," Dennett says, "is an information-packet with attitude." When we speak of *fighting for a principle* or *dying for an idea,* we may be more literal than we know.

Tinker, tailor, soldier, sailor. . . . Rhyme and rhythm help people remember bits of text. Or: rhyme and rhythm help bits of text get remembered. Rhyme and rhythm are qualities that aid a meme's survival, just as strength and speed aid an animal's. Patterned language has an evolutionary advantage. Rhyme, rhythm and reason—for reason, too, is a form of pattern. *I was promised on a time to have reason for my rhyme; from that time unto this season, I received nor rhyme nor reason.* 15

Like genes, memes have effects on the wide world beyond themselves. In some cases (the meme for making fire; for wearing clothes; for the resurrection of Jesus) the effects can be powerful indeed. As they broadcast their influence on the world, memes thus influence the conditions affecting their own chances of survival. The meme or memes comprising Morse code had strong positive feedback effects. Some memes have evident benefits for their human hosts ("Look before you leap," knowledge of CPR, belief in hand washing before cooking), but memetic success and genetic success are not the same. Memes can replicate with impressive virulence while leaving swaths of collateral damage—patent medicines and psychic surgery, astrology and Satanism, racist myths, superstitions and (a special case) computer viruses. In a way, these are the most interesting—the memes that thrive to their hosts' detriment, such as the idea that suicide bombers will find their reward in heaven.

Memes could travel wordlessly even before language was born. Plain mimicry is enough to replicate knowledge—how to chip an arrowhead or start a fire. Among animals, chimpanzees and gorillas are known to acquire behaviors by imitation. Some species of songbirds learn their songs, or at least song variants, after hearing them from neighboring birds (or, more recently, from ornithologists with audio players). Birds develop song repertoires and song dialects—in short, they exhibit a birdsong culture that predates human culture by eons. These special cases notwithstanding, for most of human history memes and language have gone hand in glove. (Clichés are memes.) Language serves as culture's first catalyst. It supersedes mere imitation, spreading knowledge by abstraction and encoding.

Perhaps the analogy with disease was inevitable. Before anyone understood anything of epidemiology, its language was applied to species of information. An emotion can be infectious, a tune catchy, a habit contagious. "From look to look, contagious through the crowd / The panic runs," wrote the poet James Thomson in 1730. Lust, likewise, according to Milton: "Eve, whose eye darted contagious fire." But only in the new millennium, in the time of global electronic transmission, has the identification become second nature. Ours is the age of virality: viral education, viral marketing, viral e-mail and video and networking. Researchers studying the Internet itself as a medium—crowdsourcing, collective attention, social networking and resource allocation—employ not only the language but also the mathematical principles of epidemiology.

One of the first to use the terms "viral text" and "viral sentences" seems to have been a reader of Dawkins named Stephen Walton of New York City, corresponding in 1981 with the cognitive scientist Douglas Hofstadter. Thinking logically—perhaps in the mode of a computer—Walton proposed simple self-replicating sentences along the lines of "Say me!" "Copy me!" and "If you copy me, I'll grant you three wishes!" Hofstadter, then a columnist for Scientific American, found the term "viral text" itself to be even catchier.

> Well, now, Walton's own viral text, as you can see here before your eyes, has managed to commandeer the facilities of a very powerful host—an entire magazine and printing press and distribution service. It has leapt aboard and is now—even as you read this viral sentence— propagating itself madly throughout the ideosphere!

Hofstadter gaily declared himself infected by the *meme* meme.   20

One source of resistance—or at least unease—was the shoving of us humans toward the wings. It was bad enough to say that a person is merely a gene's way of making more genes. Now humans are to be considered as vehicles for the propagation of memes, too. No one likes to be called a puppet. Dennett summed up the problem this way: "I don't know about you, but I am not initially attracted by the idea of my brain as a sort of dung heap in which the larvae of other people's ideas renew themselves, before sending out copies of themselves in an informational diaspora.... Who's in charge, according to this vision—we or our memes?"

He answered his own question by reminding us that, like it or not, we are seldom "in charge" of our own minds. He might have quoted Freud; instead he quoted Mozart (or so he thought): "In the night when I cannot sleep, thoughts crowd into my mind. . . . Whence and how do they come? I do not know and I have nothing to do with it."

Later Dennett was informed that this well-known quotation was not Mozart's after all. It had taken on a life of its own; it was a fairly successful meme.

For anyone taken with the idea of memes, the landscape was changing faster than Dawkins had imagined possible in 1976, when he wrote, "The computers in which memes live are human brains." By 1989, the time of the second edition of *The Selfish Gene,* having become an adept programmer himself, he had to amend that: "It was obviously predictable that manu-factured electronic computers, too, would eventually play host to self-replicating patterns of information." Information was passing from one computer to another "when their owners pass floppy discs around," and he could see another phenomenon on the near horizon: computers connected in networks. "Many of them," he wrote, "are literally wired up together in electronic mail exchange. . . . It is a perfect milieu for self-replicating pro-grams to flourish." Indeed, the Internet was in its birth throes. Not only did it provide memes with a nutrient-rich culture medium, it also gave wings to the *idea* of memes. *Meme* itself quickly became an Internet buzzword. Awareness of memes fostered their spread.

A notorious example of a meme that could not have emerged in pre-   25
Internet culture was the phrase "jumped the shark." Loopy self-reference characterized every phase of its existence. To jump the shark means to pass a peak of quality or popularity and begin an irreversible decline. The phrase

was thought to have been used first in 1985 by a college student named Sean J. Connolly, in reference to an episode of the television series "Happy Days" in which the character Fonzie (Henry Winkler), on water skis, jumps over a shark. The origin of the phrase requires a certain amount of explanation without which it could not have been initially understood. Perhaps for that reason, there is no recorded usage until 1997, when Connolly's roommate, Jon Hein, registered the domain name jumptheshark.com and created a web site devoted to its promotion. The web site soon featured a list of frequently asked questions:

> *Q. Did "jump the shark" originate from this web site, or did you create the site to capitalize on the phrase?*

> *A. This site went up December 24, 1997, and gave birth to the phrase "jump the shark." As the site continues to grow in popularity, the term has become more commonplace. The site is the chicken, the egg and now a Catch-22.*

It spread to more traditional media in the next year; Maureen Dowd devoted a column to explaining it in *The New York Times* in 2001; in 2002 the same newspaper's "On Language" columnist, William Safire, called it "the popular culture's phrase of the year"; soon after that, people were using the phrase in speech and in print without self-consciousness—no quotation marks or explanation—and eventually, inevitably, various cultural observers asked, "Has 'jump the shark' jumped the shark?" Like any good meme, it spawned mutations. The "jumping the shark" entry in Wikipedia advised in 2009, "See also: jumping the couch; nuking the fridge."

Is this science? In his 1983 column, Hofstadter proposed the obvious memetic label for such a discipline: *memetics*. The study of memes has attracted researchers from fields as far apart as computer science and microbiology. In bioinformatics, chain letters are an object of study. They are memes; they have evolutionary histories. The very purpose of a chain letter is replication; whatever else a chain letter may say, it embodies one message: *Copy me.* One student of chain-letter evolution, Daniel W. VanArsdale, listed many variants, in chain letters and even earlier texts: "Make seven copies of it exactly as it is written" (1902); "Copy this in full and send to nine friends" (1923); "And if any man shall take away from the words of the book of this prophecy, God shall take away his part out of the book of life" (Revelation 22:19). Chain letters flourished with the help of a new 19th-century technology: "carbonic paper," sandwiched between sheets of writing paper in stacks. Then carbon paper made a symbiotic partnership with another technology, the typewriter. Viral outbreaks of chain letters occurred all through the early 20th century. Two subsequent technologies, when their use became widespread, provided orders-of-magnitude boosts in chain-letter fecundity: photocopying (c. 1950) and e-mail (c. 1995).

Inspired by a chance conversation on a hike in the Hong Kong mountains, information scientists Charles H. Bennett from IBM in New York and Ming Li and Bin Ma from Ontario, Canada, began an analysis of a set of chain letters collected during the photocopier era. They had 33, all variants of a single letter, with mutations in the form of misspellings, omissions and transposed words and phrases. "These letters have passed from host to host, mutating and evolving," they reported in 2003.

> Like a gene, their average length is about 2,000 characters. Like a potent virus, the letter threatens to kill you and induces you to pass it on to your "friends and associates"—some variation of this letter has probably reached millions of people. Like an inheritable trait, it promises benefits for you and the people you pass it on to. Like genomes, chain letters undergo natural selection and sometimes parts even get transferred between coexisting "species."

Reaching beyond these appealing metaphors, the three researchers set out to use the letters as a "test bed" for algorithms used in evolutionary biology. The algorithms were designed to take the genomes of various modern creatures and work backward, by inference and deduction, to reconstruct their phylogeny—their evolutionary trees. If these mathematical methods worked with genes, the scientists suggested, they should work with chain letters, too. In both cases the researchers were able to verify mutation rates and relatedness measures.

Still, most of the elements of culture change and blur too easily to qual- 30 ify as stable replicators. They are rarely as neatly fixed as a sequence of DNA. Dawkins himself emphasized that he had never imagined founding anything like a new science of memetics. A peer-reviewed *Journal of Memetics* came to life in 1997—published online, naturally—and then faded away after eight years partly spent in self-conscious debate over status, mission and terminology. Even compared with genes, memes are hard to mathematize or even to define rigorously. So the gene-meme analogy causes uneasiness and the genetics-memetics analogy even more.

Genes at least have a grounding in physical substance. Memes are abstract, intangible and unmeasurable. Genes replicate with near-perfect fidelity, and evolution depends on that: some variation is essential, but mutations need to be rare. Memes are seldom copied exactly; their boundaries are always fuzzy, and they mutate with a wild flexibility that would be fatal in biology. The term "meme" could be applied to a suspicious cornucopia of entities, from small to large. For Dennett, the first four notes of Beethoven's Fifth Symphony (quoted above) were "clearly" a meme, along with Homer's *Odyssey* (or at least the idea of the *Odyssey*), the wheel, anti-Semitism and writing. "Memes have not yet found their Watson and Crick," said Dawkins; "they even lack their Mendel."

Yet here they are. As the arc of information flow bends toward ever greater connectivity, memes evolve faster and spread farther. Their presence is felt if not seen in herd behavior, bank runs, informational cascades and financial bubbles. Diets rise and fall in popularity, their very names becoming catchphrases—the South Beach Diet and the Atkins Diet, the Scarsdale Diet, the Cookie Diet and the Drinking Man's Diet all replicating according to a dynamic about which the science of nutrition has nothing to say. Medical practice, too, experiences "surgical fads" and "iatro-epidemics"— epidemics caused by fashions in treatment—like the iatro-epidemic of children's tonsillectomies that swept the United States and parts of Europe in the mid-20th century. Some false memes spread with disingenuous assistance, like the apparently unkillable notion that Barack Obama was not born in Hawaii. And in cyberspace every new social network becomes a new incubator of memes. Making the rounds of Facebook in the summer and fall of 2010 was a classic in new garb:

> *Sometimes I Just Want to Copy Someone Else's Status, Word for Word, and See If They Notice.*

Then it mutated again, and in January 2011 Twitter saw an outbreak of:

> *One day I want to copy someone's Tweet word for word and see if they notice.*

By then one of the most popular of all Twitter hashtags (the "hashtag" being a genetic—or, rather, memetic—marker) was simply the word "#Viral."

In the competition for space in our brains and in the culture, the 35 effective combatants are the messages. The new, oblique, looping views of genes and memes have enriched us. They give us paradoxes to write on Möbius strips. "The human world is made of stories, not people," writes the novelist David Mitchell. "The people the stories use to tell themselves are not to be blamed." Margaret Atwood writes: "As with all knowledge, once you knew it, you couldn't imagine how it was that you hadn't known it before. Like stage magic, knowledge before you knew it took place before your very eyes, but you were looking elsewhere." Nearing death, John Updike reflected on

> *A life poured into words—apparent waste intended to preserve the thing consumed.*

Fred Dretske, a philosopher of mind and knowledge, wrote in 1981: "In the beginning there was information. The word came later." He added this explanation: "The transition was achieved by the development of organisms with the capacity for selectively exploiting this information in order to survive and perpetuate their kind." Now we might add, thanks to Dawkins, that the transition was achieved by the information itself, surviving and perpetuating its kind and selectively exploiting organisms.

Most of the biosphere cannot see the infosphere; it is invisible, a parallel universe humming with ghostly inhabitants. But they are not ghosts to us—not anymore. We humans, alone among the earth's organic creatures, live in both worlds at once. It is as though, having long coexisted with the unseen, we have begun to develop the needed extrasensory perception. We are aware of the many species of information. We name their types sardonically, as though to reassure ourselves that we understand: urban myths and zombie lies. We keep them alive in air-conditioned server farms. But we cannot own them. When a jingle lingers in our ears, or a fad turns fashion upside down, or a hoax dominates the global chatter for months and vanishes as swiftly as it came, who is master and who is slave?

Analyze

1. In your own words, define a meme and explain how it works.
2. Gleick gives a range of examples to illustrate the nature and function of memes. Which example in this article is most helpful to you? Which helps you to best understand?
3. This article begins with a statement about information technology and then progresses along a chain of connected ideas (often called a *line of reasoning*). Trace the line of reasoning. Explain how Gleick goes from the nature of information technology to the concept of an infosphere.
4. According to Gleick, why is the Internet such a vital step in the evolution of the meme?
5. Gleick says that "Language serves as culture's first catalyst. It supersedes mere imitation, spreading knowledge by abstraction and encoding." As best you can, explain this point in your own language. (Imagine that you're explaining this point to someone who hasn't read the article.)

Explore

1. How have you, or people you know, participated in the spreading a meme?
2. Gleick suggests that humans do not choose language but that language chooses us—that it works through us to pollinate others. Clearly, this idea runs contrary to most people's thinking. What have you experienced that either supports or opposes Gleick's suggestion?
3. Gleick explains, "Ideas have 'spreading power.' An example of an infectious idea might be a religious ideology that gains sway over a large group of people." Give another example of an infectious idea, one that takes hold of many people and maintains control of thought and behavior.
4. What social or political forces get in the way of memes? Can you think of any specific situations in which a policy, law, group, or organization hindered the replication (or spreading) of a meme?
5. In his conclusion, Gleick boldly claims, "Most of the biosphere cannot see the infosphere; it is invisible, a parallel universe humming with ghostly inhabitants. But they are not ghosts to us—not anymore." After reading this article, do you think people are developing the "extrasensory perception" that he describes? Explain why you accept or do not accept Gleick's claim.

Forging Connections

1. How do social media influence users' relationship to nature? Do social media make people more distant from the patterns and complexities of the natural world? Does life in virtual reality somehow undermine or enrich human understanding of their place in the ecosystem? Consider articles in Chapter 7, "Nature: How We Share the Planet," specifically those by Rob Dunn ("Fly on Wall Sees Things It Wishes It Hadn't"), David P. Barash ("Two Cheers for Nature"), or Michael Shellenberger and Ted Nordhaus ("Evolve"). How do their claims make you think about life on social media sites? Develop your thinking in a written essay. Integrate photos or graphics from social media sites to illustrate your claims.

2. How do social media influence people's identities? For instance, how might Facebook impact the way individual users identify themselves according to gender, ethnicity, or sexual orientation? Or how might MMORPGs like WoW stretch, reinforce, or shatter players' identities? Consider Sameer Pandya ("The Picture for Men: Superhero or Slacker") or other writers in Chapter 5 and the points they make about the role of media in maintaining identity. Develop your thinking in a written essay and integrate specific references to social media. Consider specific scenes, gaming rules, or even direct player exchanges.

Looking Further

1. Explore a particular feature on a social media site. For instance, you might focus on the way Facebook organizes friends or how it sends notifications to an e-mail account. In an essay, explain how that feature enhances or deepens the virtual experience. Explain the subtle effects, the quiet ways in which people are influenced or impacted. Try to avoid selling the feature or just flatly condemning it. Instead, try to *understand how it operates* in the broader culture of social media, how it works to reinforce the virtual world. Borrow insights from the writers in this chapter to help explain the subtle effects.

2. James Gleick concludes "What Defines a Meme?" with a profound note on human nature: "Most of the biosphere cannot see the infosphere; it is invisible, a parallel universe humming with ghostly inhabitants. But they are not ghosts to us—not anymore. We humans, alone among the earth's organic creatures, live in both worlds at once. It is as

though, having long coexisted with the unseen, we have begun to develop the needed extrasensory perception." To what extent do you think social media is changing human nature? How is the *infosphere* changing how humans operate, even what humans are? Make your case in an argumentative project that employs both written passages and images. Integrate photos or graphics from social media sites to illustrate your claims.

5 Identity: Who We Are

In America, identity is and always has been a tough issue. On one hand, we are anxious to identify with a group. We openly call ourselves Democrats, Republicans, conservatives, liberals, Spartans, Falcons, Phoenixes, Texans, flatlanders, gangsters, cheeseheads, hipsters, or Jeep owners. We are glad not simply to join a group, but also to adopt that group's history, present, and future. We get flags, bumper stickers, particular shoes, t-shirts, hats, and even body paint to make sure that everyone else knows how to label us. When our favorite team loses to the dreaded archrival, we take it personally. And when the candidate from another political party gets into office, some of us even argue that the world is ending. But Americans also buy into the idea that we are each individuals with no shared identity. Consider some clichés that circulate in everyday language:

Everyone is different. Everyone is an individual. I'm my own person. Such statements eclipse the ongoing practice of managing our group identities and affiliations. In short, Americans are serious but also unsure about identity. Is it personal or shared? The answer seems to be both.

Identity also has a dark side. Once we figure out "who we are," we also tend to figure out who isn't us—who doesn't belong, who shouldn't have power, who should stay away or be silenced. Our struggle is nothing new. For hundreds of years, slavery was an official institution. In the 1800s, Irish and Dutch immigrants were condemned as inherently dirty, unintelligent, and naturally immoral. Similar statements were made, at different times, about Chinese, Jews, Africans, Arabs, and homosexual and transgendered people. And if you've attended high school or watched how Congress works, you know that such identity politics still thrive.

The readings in this chapter explore the tensions of identity—the conflict and cleavage created by change. Sameer Pandya and Cristina Black deal with shifts in gender. Doug LaForest examines popular culture and race. S. Alan Ray and Eboo Patel discuss identity conflicts on college campuses, and Leila Ahmed examines the intersection of gender and religious identity.

Sameer Pandya
The Picture for Men: Superhero or Slacker

A lecturer in the Department of Asian-American Studies at the University of California, Santa Barbara, Sameer Pandya writes the Research of Culture blog for *Pacific Standard* magazine, where the following post first appeared. A writer of fiction and nonfiction, he has published works on cultural topics such as education, sports, religion, race, and entertainment. Here, Pandya examines the restrictive nature of American masculine identity.

At the end of the fourth season of the critically loved and chronically underwatched *Friday Night Lights*, the former football star Tim Riggins martyrs himself for the sake of his brother and newborn nephew.

For much of the season, he and his brother Billy have been stripping down stolen cars and making the type of fast cash they cannot make legitimately. Tim wants the quick cash to fund his desire to buy a bit of sun-drenched Texas countryside, and Billy needs it for his new duties as a father.

As the season finale starts, the brothers are talking to a lawyer and working through their options after they have both been arrested and released. Through the duration of the television hour, it becomes clear that Tim is going to take the fall so that his brother can be a present father to his new son. Their own father had run out on the brothers early in their lives. In a couple of truly emotionally stirring scenes, Tim tells his brother of his decision and then heads into the sheriff's office to turn himself in.

In the show, the character of Tim Riggins is a poster child for what Hanna Rosin has provocatively referred to, in a recent *Atlantic* cover story, as "The End of Men." Rosin argues that in our postindustrial society, women are succeeding in a way in which men cannot keep up. Women are attending and graduating from college and professional schools at a higher rate, and women are entering and ascending in the work force in greater numbers and more successfully.

And in the recession we are living through, men have been hit the hardest. "The worst-hit industries were overwhelmingly male and deeply identified with macho: construction, manufacturing, high finance."

Riggins had plenty going for him: handsome, athletically gifted, a full scholarship at a state university to play football. But in line with the self-destructive behavior the character has displayed—quick to throw punches, quiet on verbal communication—he throws much of this away. A year after the end of high school, he has abandoned college and returned home to open a mechanics shop with his brother, where business is quite slow. 5

In contrast, his love interest has long abandoned the small Texas town where the show takes place and moved on to her new life at Vanderbilt.

If the makers of *Friday Night Lights* and Rosin are to be believed, there is a simple message being transmitted: Men are screwed. Or to put it another way, for a large subsection of American men, their options in life have become severely limited.

The possible reasons for this are layered and complicated. But recent research points to one possible culprit: traditional forms of masculinity.

In two different studies presented Aug. 16 at the American Psychological Association meetings in San Diego, researchers examined the lives of boys.

10   Sharon Lamb, a distinguished professor of mental health at the University of Massachusetts–Boston along with her co-authors Lyn Mikel Brown and Mark Tappan of Colby College, found that media images, particularly of superheroes, severely limit the models of boys' behavior. Today's movie superheroes offer a basic template for superhero behavior: nonstop violence when in costume, and the exploitation of women, the flaunting of money, and wielding guns when not.

In the past, Lamb argues, comic book heroes "were heroes the boys could look up to and learn from because outside of their costumes, they were real people with real problems and many vulnerabilities."

> "Today's movie superheroes offer a basic template for superhero behavior: nonstop violence when in costume, and the exploitation of women, the flaunting of money, and wielding guns when not."

Now, boys between the ages of 4 and 18 have only two choices.

"In today's media, superheroes and slackers are the only two options boys have. Boys are told if you can't be a superhero, you can always be a slacker. Slackers are funny, but slackers are not what boys should strive to be; slackers don't like school and they shirk responsibility. We wonder if the message boys get about saving face through glorified slacking could be affecting their performance in school."

Lamb suggests teaching boys to distance themselves from these images by helping them recognize the problems with them.

15   Lamb's fellow researcher on the panel, Carlos Santos of Arizona State University, offers another set of questions and solutions to this larger question of masculinity. Santos examined 426 middle school boys and posed a series of sharp research questions. Are middle school boys able to resist being emotionally stoic, autonomous, and physically tough—the traditional, stereotypical markers of masculinity—as they moved from the sixth to the eighth grade? What difference does ethnicity make? Do relationships with families and peers foster resistance? Does resistance affect psychological health?

His conclusions provide a certain amount of hope, given the right type of influences. Santos found that boys who remained close to their mothers, siblings, and peers did not act as tough or shut down emotionally. However, close relationships with fathers encouraged greater autonomy and detachment from friendships.

One assumes that these fathers had learned how to be men from their own fathers, thus maintaining a certain cycle of traditional masculinity.

How can the cycle be broken? "If the goal is to encourage boys to experience healthy family relationships as well as healthy relationships, clinicians and interventionists working with families may benefit from having fathers share with their sons on the importance of experiencing multiple and fulfilling relationships in their lives," Santos said.

Santos also found that boys from diverse ethnic and racial backgrounds were able to resist masculine stereotypes, thus breaking another type of stereotype about the hyper-masculinity of certain ethnic minorities.

Time is of the essence in resistance. Santos suggests that the ability to   20
resist internalizing macho images declines as the boys grow older.

And what happens to these boys when they grow older is that they encounter Hanna Rosin announcing their end even before they have had an opportunity to begin.

Certainly, changing media images and encouraging broad-ranging relationships are both important in subverting traditional, and often socially harmful, markers of masculinity. But there is another factor that might also contribute to broadening the choices beyond gun-slinging superhero and slacker: the availability and variety of work.

Of course, making work available now and in the future is no simple task. Among the bad job and unemployment numbers that seem to come out every week, it is clear that there is a bumpy road ahead not only for men, but also for the economy as a whole.

As much as I am worried about my two young boys being bombarded by superhero-slacker images, I am even more worried about the jobs that might not be available to them when they hit adulthood.

And here the studies by Lamb and Santos come back into play. Rethinking   25
certain masculine traits for boys—stoic, autonomous, tough—may be the key for the men they will become to survive in a postindustrial economy. Rosin writes, "The attributes that are most valuable today—social intelligence, open communication, the ability to sit still and focus—are, at a minimum, not predominantly male."

We may not be able to control the availability of jobs, but we can control how boys prepare for them.

Analyze

1. In your own words, explain the problem with the superhero and slacker male images in the media.

2. How does the scene from *Friday Night Lights* figure into this article? What point does it help to establish?

3. What is the postindustrial economy? How might it relate to gender and to jobs?

4. What do you think Pandya means by "traditional masculinity"? What are the negative or positive qualities that this article attributes to traditional masculinity?

5. Explain how the Lamb and Santos study figures into Pandya's article. What points does the study help to make?

Explore

1. Which image, superhero or slacker, has had more impact on you or the men you know?

2. What other identifiers, beyond superhero or slacker, can you imagine? Make a list of terms that characterize the type of men, fictional or real, in your life.

3. What popular culture texts (films, songs, or television shows) support the slacker image that Pandya explains?

4. What popular culture text (film, song, or television show) might push against or complicate the slacker image? Explain how the text works— what it does to make the slacker image unattractive or somehow different than what the audience might expect.

Cristina Black
Bathing Suit Shopping with Annette Kellerman, the Australian Mermaid

The entertainment editor for *Foam* magazine, Cristina Black writes on various pop culture topics ranging from surfing to fashion. Her work has appeared in such publications as *Dazed & Confused, Nylon, Time Out New York*, and the *Village Voice*. The following blog post originally appeared in *The Hairpin*, a website that targets a primarily female readership. In it, Black explores the changing nature of women's swimsuit fashion, and what it might mean for female identity.

t's the same thing every spring: You peruse the magazines, grit your teeth, and go bathing suit shopping. But when you get into the dressing room, it's a big old mess. Your limbs are pale, lumpy, mottled, and large-looking. You shouldn't have eaten so much pasta/drunk so much wine. You should have started around mid-February cutting out carbs/going to the gym. So you head home empty handed, in a haze of disgust and frustration.

Before you get fitted for a burqa, though, think of this: A hundred years ago, you wouldn't have been in this position, shopping for a bathing suit, because there was no such thing. You would be rummaging through your summer storage trunk for your stockings, bloomers, and sailor dress, which would be made of wool, because that's actually what women wore to the beach until one lady came along and changed all that. Annette Kellerman, known in her time as "the Australian Mermaid," was a competitive swimmer, diver, model, actress, stuntwoman, fitness guru, and, yes, professional mermaid in vaudeville and movies, who originally sewed stockings onto a man's racing suit for less drag in the water. Then, one day, circa 1908, she forewent those old leg coverings and appeared on a Boston beach in a skin-tight onesie with the legs cut off mid-thigh. She was arrested. Later, in court, she explained she was not a provocateur but a pragmatist. She simply wanted to swim freely, and was that so wrong? "I may as well be swimming in chains," she complained. Before long, she had created her own line of women's swimwear, when there really was no such thing, and long before celebrities regularly leveraged their fame to sell clothes. The "Annette Kellerman" was the first modern swimsuit for women. And, in many ways, its namesake was one of the first modern women.

By the time of her famous beach arrest, Kellerman, still in her early 20s, was already a world-class swimmer. She had beaten dozens of men in long distance races; swum the Thames, the Seine, and the Danube; and had attempted to cross the English Channel three times—then the only woman who had dared to try—making it three-quarters of the way before succumbing to frigid temperatures and seasickness. "The men wore no clothes, but I was compelled to put on a bathing suit," she recalled of her first Channel swim. "Small as it was, it chafed me. When I finished, the flesh under my arms was raw and hurt fearfully."

When long distance swimming failed to pull her and her father-manager out of poverty, Kellerman turned to high-diving in Chicago and quickly became the highest paid act on the vaudeville circuit. Meanwhile, she invented the sport of synchronized swimming with a water ballet performance in a glass tank at the New York Hippodrome. After a 1908 study of 3,000 female figures, a Harvard University faculty member named Kellerman "the Perfect Woman" because of the similarity of her physical attributes to the Venus de Milo. She was uncomfortable with the label. "I don't want to be just a pretty fish," she complained.

5   It's worthwhile to note that Kellerman was not particularly thin by today's standards. At 5' 4", she measured 33 inches in the chest, 26 at the waist. Her hip measurement was never recorded, but from photos, it looks like it never dipped too far south of 40. Most of the bathing-beauty pinups she spawned had similar figures, round-butted and full-thighed, but for a long time, Kellerman was considered the prettiest fish of them all. When she tired of flopping into the water like a trick seal, she parlayed her rising star into a silent film career, becoming the first major actress to do a nude scene (in *A Daughter of the Gods* in 1916). Later in life, Kellerman became a celebrity fitness guru when there was no such thing, and opened a health food store in Long Beach when everybody still drank whole cow's milk and ate steak for dinner. She was a vegetarian many decades before it stopped seeming strange. And right up to her death at age 88, she bragged that she could still bend over and touch her toes, a picture of perfect health until the end.

Well into the '70s, Annette Kellerman swam every day. "There is nothing more democratic than swimming," she wrote. "Bathing is a society event but swimming out beyond the surf line is just plain social. Everyone is happy and young and funny. No one argues. No one scolds. There is no time and no place where one may so companionably play the fool and not be called one." When she puts it that way, it seems a little silly to think that bathing suit shopping is excruciating for women because we are frightened at the thought of baring so much skin. We forget how fragile is the freedom to go swimming and sunning in clothes that let us feel the water and wind and sun on our skin. Ladies, relish the skimpiness of today's suits! If it makes you more comfortable, go ahead and wear a maillot cut low on the legs, high in the neck. Just be glad you have a choice.

Analyze

1. For whom is this article written? What gender, age group, or race? Everyone? Anyone in particular? What specific passages support your answer?
2. What is Black's main idea? Is this article about gender? Fashion changes? Body size? Sports? In your own words, explain Black's main idea.

3. Black explains that Kellerman was a "picture of perfect health until the end." Why is this point important to the article? How does it help to support Black's main idea?

4. Kellerman once described swimming as democratic. In your understanding, what does that mean? How is swimming democratic?

5. Compare Black's point about women to the point Sameer Pandya makes in "The Picture for Men: Superhero or Slacker" about young men. How are these articles similar? How do they point to similar cultural tensions?

Explore

1. Black's article shows how cultures change. What attitudes or beliefs changed or faded so that Kellerman's one-piece bathing suit went from scandalous to normal to modest?

2. What is the biggest change in fashion you've seen in your lifetime? What attitudes or beliefs were behind that change? What ideas about men, women, sex, and freedom might have spurred that change?

3. Compare Kellerman to a contemporary female celebrity. Are there any women in today's media who have served a similar function?

4. People like Annette Kellerman have helped to create choices for us today. She established a broader range of possible behaviors and options. Name another person in history who did this. Explain the choices that he or she made available to others.

Doug LaForest
Undocumented Immigrants

Douglas LaForest is pursuing a degree in computer information technology. In the following essay, developed for a second-semester writing course, he examines the role of language in shaping cultural notions of *other*. With a range of sources, personal testimony, and appeals, he argues against the use of a common phrase.

Language is power. This is especially true of language which maligns a person. A friend of my family is aware of this. She hands out pamphlets asking that people consider the language they use when discussing Down's syndrome. She has championed local projects that advocate for people living with Down's syndrome, which includes her daughter. Her volunteer work reminds people that her daughter is a person first. She's not a "Down's child." It does not define her. This is not merely a matter of semantics; it's validating an individual's humanity. My friend understands that this issue is a cornerstone to building upon issues of justice and quality of life for her daughter as well as other individuals who live with Down's syndrome.

I think of my friend's work when I hear of the current debates over immigration. Immigration laws are outdated and unjust. But before any changes can be made to the system, we have to begin to use language which acknowledges the humanity of the individuals who are affected by the immigration system. We cannot begin to have just conversations and make legal changes within the immigration system without taking action regarding the language we use. One of the primary reasons we have not been able to justly reform our immigration system is based on our inability to use language which validates the humanity of individuals who are also undocumented immigrants.

Not too long ago, I heard another friend mention a local incident which involved an "illegal alien." Apparently, the man was to be deported to Mexico after his home was swarmed by armed policeman. My friend's description of the man, the "illegal alien," shocked me. This is a friend whom I think of as tolerant and thoughtful of others. When I suggested he use the phrase "undocumented immigrant" rather than "illegal alien," he agreed. He confessed that his poor choice was simply a result of the jargon he was accustomed to hearing and therefore using.

The conversation between my friend and me is precisely the reason why Jose Antonio Vargas, a Pulitzer Prize–winning journalist, decided to "come out." He wanted to draw attention to the need for just immigration reform, and to insist that we begin using language in conversations and media that validates an individual's humanity. Vargas was tired of hearing all of the pejorative language used to describe individuals in immigrant communities: "illegal aliens," "illegal immigrants" or simply "illegals." Working in journalism, he had heard these derogatory descriptions used in writing and in political campaigns. But at some point, he was done with it all and was willing to take personal risk. What was the personal risk? He himself struggles in a complicated life which includes the experience of being an undocumented immigrant.

In this summer's June 6th issue of *The New York Times*, Vargas shared   5
his life story, and ever since, he has risked being deported. Filipino born,
Vargas was put on a plane at the age of twelve to join his grandparents in
California. His grandparents, like many families, wanted for their grandson
a good education and a better life as a United States citizen. Though Vargas
didn't know it for many years, he was an undocumented immigrant. Unable
to find a legal route to obtain citizenship for their grandson, his grandparents hoped that he would one day marry a citizen and thereby obtain a
green card. But, as it turns out, Vargas is gay and did not want to live with
the lie of a fraudulent marriage.

Vargas bravely revealed his life story. He was compelled to do it when
time after time he was suffering and realizing that there was an "undeni-
able" consensus that the media framing around illegal immigration was
"stuck in simplistic, us-versus-them, black-or-white, conflict-driven narrative." As he had hoped, by sharing his life story, a debate once again emerged
surrounding immigration, but this time there was an urgency to humanize
the issue. Furthermore, the media has responded to Vargas's insistence that
the phrase undocumented immigrant be used (Ly). Currently, television
networks and newspapers are engaged in a debate as to how to describe the
individuals struggling within the immigration system. Vargas has argued
fervently that the media needs to lead the way in using the phrase undocumented immigrant, and nothing else.

Again, this is not simply a matter of semantics. What comes to mind
when reading text that defines the person in the article as an illegal immigrant or simply illegal? The word "criminal" comes to mind, right? Some
newspapers are responding to Vargas's request. They're beginning to dis-
continue such negative descriptions. For example, *The Cornell Daily Sun*
wrote an editorial underlying the humanity of this community. "No
human being is illegal." And though the "first person to coin the phrase
may have done so out of convenience, naivety or xenophobia," *The Cornell
Daily Sun* agreed that the term conveyed criminality. The editorial concludes by saying that "it is the action of entering the United States without
permission that is illegal, not the immigrant him or herself ("What Does It
Mean?").

Claudia Melendez Salinas, an education reporter at the *Monterey
County Herald* convinced her newspaper to change its wording to "undocumented immigrant." How? "I told them 'illegal' was offensive and

compared it to other offensive labels like 'spic.' That's how people use it, if you think about it" (qtd. in Ly).

So what might be one of the reasons for derogatory language? Perhaps there's an anti-immigrant sentiment that is especially fearful of the changing demographics of our nation; there's a growing Hispanic population. Vargas notes in his June *Time Magazine* article that the Hispanic population is growing. The Pew Hispanic Center reports that 56% of the nation's growth from 2000–2010 was Hispanic (Rubio 52). Some of that percentage, as Vargas reports, is the percentage of undocumented immigrants: 59% of the undocumented immigrants being from Mexico. He writes, "Whites represent a shrinking share of the total U.S. population." And he goes on to argue that "The immigration debate is impossible to separate from America's unprecedented and culture-shifting demographic make-over."

10   Could it be that our nation's resistance to using respectful language is wrapped in a "white" vs. "Hispanic" sentiment? My sense is that as a nation, this is true and based on fear of diverse peoples. Vargas writes about "white conservatives" who would quickly complain to him of "other" people joining their schools and churches and the discomfort of overhearing Spanish in Wal-Mart (Vargas 42).

Consider the following experience: The Leelanau Children's Center, where my three-year-old son attends, had a parenting night. It was early in the fall and new families were coming together to share an evening of introductions and to create community. I think of the Children's Center as being progressive—progressive in the sense that community building is emphasized and everyone is welcome, regardless of race, economic status and any other potential category of differences. Many of the parents were first generation immigrants from Mexico. To start off the evening, the directors of the Children's Center requested parents sit in a circle with one another and introduce ourselves. It seemed friendly enough. Like any introductory circle, there were plenty of shy folks and some nervous laughter. Circle participants would often respond with welcoming words or gestures in response to a parent's introduction. As the introductions progressed, there was a growing sense of comfort. Then, one Hispanic man began to introduce himself and speak of his children. Only he spoke in Spanish. The minute he finished sharing, there was silence. You could have heard a pin drop. I realized that no one knew how to respond. Or was it that there was a general discomfort in the room with his choice of language? Had he just crossed the line of an unspoken rule? I left thinking about that exchange and a general "tolerance" of immigration that might have been tested. Did I witness and perhaps participate in a very subtle anti-immigration sentiment?

Language is power. As a nation we have only begun to reconsider language that respects an individual's humanity when speaking about the lives of people in immigrant communities. Using the phrase "undocumented immigrants" instead of derogatory phrases such as "illegal immigrant," "illegal alien," and "illegal" is fundamental to validating a person's life. It's not just a matter of semantics. Perhaps one of the reasons that derogatory language continues is that, as a nation, we are struggling to accept the shifting demographics of the population: In the U.S. Hispanics will soon outnumber folks from European descent.

Vargas urges us to challenge ourselves to get beyond the fear. He insists that we look at the issue of immigration, the language we use in describing immigrant communities and the changing demographics of this nation in a holistic light. Vargas concludes his personal coming out story in *Time Magazine* with a question: "when will you realize that we are one of you?"(43).

Works Cited

Ly, Phuong. "Vargas' Essay Renews Attention to Media's Use of 'Illegal' and 'Undocumented.'" *Poynter.org*. The Poynter Institute, 6 July 2011. Web. 6 Apr. 2013.

Rubio, Angelica. "Undocumented, Not Illegal: Beyond the Rhetoric of Immigration Coverage." *NACLA Report on the Americas* 44.6 (2011): 50–52. *Academic Search Elite*. Web. 15 May 2013.

Vargas, Jose Antonio. "Just Not Legally." *Time* 179.25 (2012): 34–44. Print.

———. "My Life as an Undocumented Immigrant." *The New York Times*. n. p. New York Times, 22 June 2011. Web. 25 May 2013.

"What Does it Mean to be 'Illegal?'" Editorial. *The Cornell Daily Sun* [Ithaca]. n. p. Cornell Daily Sun, 16 Oct. 2012. Web. 8 Apr. 2013.

Analyze

1. Explain why LaForest begins and ends his essay with the point that "language is power." Why is this statement so critical to his main idea?

2. LaForest devotes much of his essay to analyzing the cause of certain phrases. In your words, explain LaForest's conclusion. What is behind the persistence of phrases such as *illegal alien*?
3. Near the end of his essay, LaForest connects derogatory language to fear. Explain how that connection supports his main idea.
4. LaForest argues that this discussion is "not merely a matter of semantics." Why does he make this point? What assumption or belief is countering?
5. LaForest uses a range of support strategies throughout his essay. He relies on personal testimony and on the testimony of journalists. Which passage do you think is most powerful? What situation seems most supportive or revealing?

Explore

1. Why might *undocumented immigrant* be more humane than *illegal alien*?
2. Of the two phrases, *undocumented immigrant* and *illegal alien*, do you think one is more accurate? Or if both are accurate, why would one be used more than the other?
3. Throughout American history, language has been central to issues of race, gender, and sexual orientation. Why? Why are the labels and terms we assign to others so important? Why do they generate concern and even outrage?
4. Are you part of a community that has been labeled by others? What is the label? What power does it have in your life?

S. Alan Ray
Despite the Controversy, We're Glad We Asked

President of Elmhurst College, S. Alan Ray is a professor of religion and society. In describing Elmhurst, he explains, "We think about how the things we learn can be related to the world beyond college. . . . We don't have the problem of reconciling reflection and action. Here, reflection and action have always gone hand in hand." In the following *Chronicle of Higher Education* article, Ray describes the effects of a college application question that asks about students' sexual orientation.

When we decided this year to make one of our routine annual revisions in the application for undergraduate admission at Elmhurst College, we weren't expecting to make national headlines as a result. But we did. What landed Elmhurst in the media spotlight last month was a new application question. Like some others, the question was optional. It asked: "Would you consider yourself a member of the LGBT (lesbian, gay, bisexual, transgender) community?"

Like many other institutions, our private liberal-arts college in Chicago's western suburbs, long affiliated with the United Church of Christ, has included optional questions on our admission applications for many years. They ask about matters like ethnic identity, religious affiliation, and languages spoken at home. But this new question generated levels of interest and controversy that those other questions never did.

Our revised application became news when the national organization Campus Pride sent out a press release congratulating us for "setting the bar" by becoming the first college in the United States to ask prospective undergraduates about sexual orientation and gender identity on its application. The Campus Pride release was quickly followed by articles in newspapers, segments on national radio shows, and stories on major news-media Web sites. We hadn't sought this wave of publicity, but we were proud to have so much attention focused on our efforts to build a campus that is diverse, open, and affirming to all students.

Of course, the coverage also occasioned some commentary that challenged our wisdom and motivation. That the new application question produced some controversy will not surprise anyone familiar with online comment strings and call-in radio, which too often are more about heat than light. The application question had placed us in the middle of a national discussion about diversity and sexual identity—one that continues to stir passions and challenge established beliefs.

Perhaps the most common question I heard from our supportive but 5 surprised friends was simply this: Why did we do it? One way of explaining is simply to quote our application, which notes that Elmhurst is "committed to diversity and connecting underrepresented students with valuable resources on campus." For years we have asked students about their personal interests, high-school activities, and faith traditions, among other things, so we can connect them with campus support and gauge their eligibility for certain opportunities, including scholarships.

This year we decided to include self-identified LGBT students in the process. We wanted them to know that they, like all our students, would find abundant resources at Elmhurst to enable them to succeed. We wanted them to know that they would not feel isolated on our campus because of their sexual orientation or gender identity. On the contrary: We clearly, openly, emphatically want them here.

Beyond that, there are substantive reasons to reach out directly to LGBT students, who still experience hostility and discrimination on some campuses. Studies show that they are at significantly higher risk for harassment compared with their heterosexual peers, and many have reported experiencing a difficult or hostile campus climate or actual harassment. A recent survey found that 13 percent of gay students said they feared for their physical safety; the number rises to 43 percent for transgender students.

Media coverage of our decision was overwhelmingly positive, but the public's reaction ran the gamut from grateful praise to harsh criticism, clearly reflecting the sharp divisions over this issue. Most of the negative response was based on a misunderstanding of what the application question says and how responses to the question will be used. One sticking point for some critics was the availability of scholarship money for students who identified themselves as lesbian, gay, bisexual, or transgender. Over the years, Elmhurst has awarded what we call Enrichment Scholarships to talented students whose presence would add to the diversity and richness of campus life. Now gay and transgender students are eligible for these scholarships, too. That does not, as some uninformed commentators suggested, deprive another deserving student of a scholarship. We offer scholarships of varying kinds to all qualifying admitted students; they are not capped at a certain number. Thus one student's gain is not another student's loss.

It is becoming ever more clear to educators that students learn best when they engage with a wide spectrum of individuals, both like and unlike themselves—that is, if they are part of a campus community that resembles our diverse society and multicultural world. That's why Elmhurst and many other colleges and universities make an extra effort to recruit students of color, international students, first-generation students, and many others. Encouraging talented, self-identified gay and transgender students to come to Elmhurst enhances the education of every one of our students.

10   It is also the right thing to do. The United Church of Christ, with which Elmhurst is affiliated, is a Protestant denomination with a long and proud history of shattering our society's color and gender barriers. The tradition

that made the church the first mainstream American denomination to ordain an African-American minister, the first to ordain a female minister, and the first to ordain an openly gay minister is one that resonates with our own core values. The church describes itself as "extravagantly welcoming." Elmhurst is, too.

It is possible, as some people have suggested, that students will misrepresent themselves as gay or lesbian on applications solely to qualify for a scholarship. I think it also is unlikely. There have always been opportunities for fraud in the application process, but I have seen no evidence that this happens much at Elmhurst or elsewhere.

It is also possible that some students will object to the question as intrusive or inappropriate. But we hope that many more students will recognize it as part of our sincere effort to meet them, and understand them, as they really are. After all, one of the great aims of higher education is to help students to attain—as Elmhurst's sixth president, the theologian H. Richard Niebuhr, put it—an "effective individuality." That can happen only if students and educators alike are willing to take on the deepest matters of identity with unflinching honesty and open minds.

One of the unanticipated benefits of this episode is the opportunity it has afforded Elmhurst to clearly communicate two of its core values—its unyielding commitment to diversity and profound respect for individuals—to people who previously were unfamiliar with us. I think that those around the country who read or heard about Elmhurst for the first time as a result of our application question encountered a principled institution in the process of uncovering new ways to do right by its students. We are hoping the discussion that resulted from our action encourages other colleges and universities to follow our lead.

Analyze

1. Consider Ray's opening strategy. How does it impact your entry into the article—and the issue it raises?

2. How does Ray address positions or claims that might oppose the Elmhurst College application questions? Focus on a specific passage and explain how Ray deals with opposition.

3. Much of Ray's article focuses on the reason Elmhurst asked the question. In one or two sentences, summarize the reason.

4. Ray explains that online commentary and radio talk shows often generate "more about heat than light." How does this point help his case?

5. Read "Is Your Campus Diverse?" by Eboo Patel (later in this chapter). What underlying belief or value do Ray and Patel share? Explain how that shared belief functions in each article.

Explore

1. Do you think your campus is welcoming to LGBT students? Why or why not?

2. Do you think an application question about sexual orientation is intrusive, inappropriate, or inviting? What's your reasoning? What beliefs are behind your answer?

3. According to Ray, the United Church of Christ has played a critical role in "shattering our society's color and gender barriers." How does this point impact your thinking about religion, gender equality, or race?

4. Why do you think policy issues related to sexual orientation generate so much controversy? What fears, beliefs, or assumptions are driving that controversy?

Eboo Patel
Is Your Campus Diverse?
It's a Question of Faith

Named one of America's Best Leaders of 2009 by *U.S. News & World Report*, Eboo Patel focuses on advancing the interfaith movement across colleges worldwide. He has published three books on issues related to religious identity and frequently contributes to CNN, The Huffington Post, National Public Radio, *USA Today*, and the *Washington Post*. In the following *Chronicle of Higher Education* article, Patel considers the importance of religious diversity on college campuses.

It came as no surprise to me to read the recent *New York Times* article indicating that Muslim students feel particularly welcome on Roman Catholic campuses—precisely because of their faith. "Here people are more religious, even if they're not Muslim, and I'm comfortable with that," a Muslim student said of her experience at the University of Dayton.

That was my father's experience at the University of Notre Dame 35 years ago. He was a Muslim immigrant from India in the land of gray snow and white Catholics. While the priests didn't always understand his faith, they always respected it, and he felt that the broader environment nurtured it. When he missed home, he'd go to the Grotto of Our Lady of Lourdes, where the flickering candles reminded him of the line in the Koran that God is light upon light.

When I went to the University of Illinois at Urbana-Champaign, in the mid-1990s, we were focused on other forms of identity. The Rodney King beating and its aftermath had sparked a rise in campus activism around race. You couldn't walk 10 feet in any direction without seeing a copy of Cornel West's *Race Matters* or running into a heated discussion about the role of black women in the feminist movement. Freshman orientation, resident-adviser training, speeches by the football coach at pep rallies— race was a theme in all of these.

Part of the rationale for 1990s-era campus multiculturalism was to remedy the racial bias in the broader society: to lift up underrepresented narratives, to remind people that many communities have contributed to the American project, to ensure that our perceptions of race were not driven by the crime reports on the evening news. Gender, sexuality, class, and ethnicity all got some airtime, but mostly we talked about race. And one form of identity was almost totally excluded: faith.

Now that the evening news is full of stories of faith-based violence, and 5 our public discourse has a constant undercurrent of religious prejudice (Barack Obama is a Muslim! Mitt Romney isn't a Christian!) colleges can no longer ignore faith identity. For many of the same reasons that they actively engaged race, so should they now actively and positively engage faith identity.

That Catholic colleges are welcoming places for people from other religions is very good news on one front. It means that Samuel Huntington's "clash of civilizations" thesis—the idea that people of different faith backgrounds are inherently in conflict with one another—is not inevitable, at least not everywhere. On American Catholic campuses, it appears, the clear and proud expression of one faith identity isn't a barrier that separates people of different faiths, it's a bridge that invites them in.

And it's not just Catholic colleges. A few years ago, I was invited to speak at Berea College, a nondenominational Christian college, and my podium was set up right in front of a large cross. The minister asked if I would feel more comfortable if it was covered. Not at all, I told him. Berea's understanding of that cross was the key reason the college had such a diverse student body, and precisely why they had invited a Muslim speaker to address the community. I was proud to speak in front of that cross. In fact, its presence allowed me to open my talk with a Muslim prayer.

But interfaith work is not just for religious campuses, and creating a "safe space" for different faiths cannot be the ultimate goal. In the most religiously diverse nation in human history and the most religiously devout nation in the West at a time of global religious conflict, how people from different faith backgrounds get along and what they do together is a crucial question. And so it must be a central question for our public universities as well.

Robert Putnam, who teaches American politics at Harvard, emphasizes that faith communities are the single largest repository of social capital in America, but that they operate mainly within their own restrictive networks. Certainly faith groups can continue to work in isolation. The tension among religions in America can grow, faith can become a weapon, and we can move directly into the open conflict we see in other religiously diverse societies. Or we can encourage more social capital among faith communities (and between them and philosophically secular ones), and help them cooperate to serve the common good. Colleges are miniature civil societies that can nurture that vision of interfaith respect and cooperation, and train a critical mass of leaders to help achieve it.

10   What if campuses took religious diversity as seriously as they took race? What if recruiting a religiously diverse student body, creating a welcoming environment for people of different faith and philosophical identities, and offering classes in interfaith studies and co-curricular opportunities in interfaith leadership became the norm? What if university presidents expected their graduates to acquire interfaith literacy, build interfaith relationships, and have opportunities to run interfaith programs during their four years on campus? What impact might a critical mass of interfaith leaders have on America over the course of the next generation?

I'm pretty convinced that one reason Barack Obama is president is because of the 1990s-era multiculturalism movement on campuses. A generation of college students caught a vision of what a multicultural nation should look like—and those were the people who staffed the moonshot Obama campaign. Imagine the impact a 21st-century campus interfaith movement could have on the nation over the course of the next 30 years. Perhaps we won't be Googling "Sikh" when we hear of a hate-fueled murder in Milwaukee; perhaps we'll be electing a Sikh president.

Analyze

1. What single sentence best captures Patel's main idea?
2. Explain how Patel uses current events to develop his point about college campuses.
3. Patel invites readers to encourage "more social capital among faith communities." What does he mean by this? What is social capital and how can it function among communities?
4. According to Patel, what is the relationship between the culture of college campuses and the politics of the nation? How do college campuses figure into cultural change?
5. Patel uses the phrase "underrepresented narrative." If narrative is a story, what is an underrepresented narrative? And how is the concept important to this article?

Explore

1. Is your campus diverse? In what specific ways? In what ways is it not diverse?
2. Patel compares religious diversity and racial diversity. How are these concepts similar? What do race and religious affiliation have in common? How are they different?
3. Look up Samuel Huntington's "clash of civilizations" thesis online. What have you seen, read, or experienced that supports or challenges Huntington's thesis?
4. Should diversity among groups always be encouraged? Why is diversity helpful?
5. When is diversity unhelpful, dangerous, or ruinous?

Leila Ahmed
Reinventing the Veil

A professor at Harvard Divinity School, Leila Ahmed studies Islam's role in constructing female identity. She is the author of numerous articles and books, including the 2011 book *A Quiet Revolution: The Veil's Resurgence, from the Middle East to America*. In the following *Financial Times* article, Ahmed examines the cultural impact of a particular Islamic tradition.

I grew up in Cairo, Egypt. Through the decades of my childhood and youth—the 1940s, 1950s and 1960s—the veil was a rarity not only at home but in many Arab and Muslim-majority cities. In fact, when Albert Hourani, the Oxford historian, surveyed the Arab world in the mid-1950s, he predicted that the veil would soon be a thing of the past.

Hourani's prophecy, made in an article called *The Vanishing Veil: A Challenge to the Old Order*, would prove spectacularly wrong, but his piece is nevertheless a gem because it so perfectly captures the ethos of that era. Already the veil was becoming less and less common in my own country, and, as Hourani explains, it was fast disappearing in other "advanced Arab countries," such as Syria, Iraq and Jordan as well. An unveiling movement had begun to sweep across the Arab world, gaining momentum with the spread of education.

In those days, we shared all of Hourani's views and assumptions, including the connections he made between unveiling, "advancement" and education (and between veiling and "backwardness"). We believed the veil was merely a cultural habit, of no relevance to Islam or to religious piety. Even deeply devout women did not wear a hijab. Being unveiled simply seemed the modern "advanced" way of being Muslim.

Consequently the veil's steady "return" from the mid-1980s, and its growing adoption, disturbed us. It was very troubling for people like me who had been working for years as feminists on women and Islam. Why would educated women, particularly those living in free Western societies where they could dress as they wished, be willing (apparently) to take on this symbol of patriarchy and women's oppression?

5   The appearance of the hijab in my own neighbourhood of Cambridge, Massachusetts, in the late 1990s was the trigger that launched my own

studies into the phenomenon. I well remember the very evening that generated that spark. While I was walking past the common with a friend, a well-known feminist who was visiting from the Arab world, we saw a large crowd with all the women in hijab. At the time, this was still an unusual sight and, frankly, it left us both with distinct misgivings.

While troubling on feminist grounds, the veil's return also disturbed me in other ways. Having settled in the U.S., I had watched from afar through the 1980s and 1990s as cities back home that I had known as places where scarcely anyone wore hijab were steadily transformed into streets where the vast majority of women now wore it.

This visually dramatic revolution in women's dress changed, to my eyes, the very look and atmosphere of those cities. It had come about as a result of the spread of Islamism in the 1970s, a very political form of Islam that was worlds away from the deeply inward, apolitical form that had been common in Egypt in my day. Fuelled by the Muslim Brotherhood, the spread of Islamism always brought its signature emblem: the hijab.

Those same decades were marked in Egypt by rising levels of violence and intellectual repression. In 1992, Farag Foda, a well-known journalist and critic of Islamism, was gunned down. Nasr Hamid Abu Zayd, a professor at Cairo University, was brought to trial on grounds of apostasy and had to flee the country. Soon after, Naguib Mahfouz, the Egyptian novelist and Nobel Laureate, was stabbed by an Islamist who considered his books blasphemous. Such events seemed a shocking measure of the country's descent into intolerance.

The sight of the hijab on the streets of America brought all this to mind. Was its growing presence a sign that Islamic militancy was on the rise here too? Where were these young women (it was young women in particular who wore it) getting their ideas? And why were they accepting whatever it was they were being told, in this country where it was entirely normal to challenge patriarchal ideas? Could the Muslim Brotherhood have somehow succeeded in gaining a foothold here?

My instinctive readings of the Cambridge scene proved correct in some 10 ways. The Brotherhood, as well as other Islamist groups, had indeed established a base in America. While most immigrants were not Islamists, those who were quickly set about founding mosques and other organisations. Many immigrants who grew up as I did, without veils, sent their children to Islamic Sunday schools where they imbibed the Islamist outlook—including the hijab.

The veiled are always the most visible, but today Islamist-influenced people make up no more than 30 to 40 per cent of American Muslims. This is also roughly the percentage of women who veil as opposed to those who do not. This means of course that the majority of Muslim American women do not wear the veil, whether because they are secular or because they see it as an emblem of Islamism rather than Islam.

My research may have confirmed some initial fears, but it also challenged my assumptions. As I studied the process by which women had been persuaded to veil in Egypt in the first place, I came to see how essential women themselves had been in its promotion and the cause of Islamism. Among the most important was Zainab al-Ghazali, the "unsung mother" of the Muslim Brotherhood and a forceful activist who had helped keep the organisation going after the death of its founder.

For these women, adopting hijab could be advantageous. Joining Islamist groups and changing dress sometimes empowered them in relation to their parents; it also expanded job and marriage possibilities. Also, since the veil advertised women's commitment to conservative sexual mores, wearing it paradoxically increased their ability to move freely in public space—allowing them to take jobs in offices shared with men.

My assumptions about the veil's patriarchal meanings began to unravel in the first interviews I conducted. One woman explained that she wore it as a way of raising consciousness about the sexist messages of our society. (This reminded me of the bra-burning days in America when some women refused to shave their legs in a similar protest.) Another wore the hijab for the same reason that one of her Jewish friends wore a yarmulke: this was religiously required dress that made visible the presence of a minority who were entitled, like all citizens, to justice and equality. For many others, wearing hijab was a way of affirming pride and rejecting negative stereotypes (like the Afros that flourished in the 1960s among African-Americans).

15   Both Islamist and American ideals—including American ideals of gender justice—seamlessly interweave in the lives of many of this younger generation. This has been a truly remarkable decade as regards Muslim women's activism. Perhaps the post-9/11 atmosphere in the West, which led to intense criticism of Islam and its views of women, spurred Muslim Americans into corrective action. Women are reinterpreting key religious texts, including the Koran, and they have now taken on positions of leadership

in Muslim American institutions: Ingrid Mattson, for example, was twice elected president of the Islamic Society of North America. Such female leadership is unprecedented in the home countries: even al-Ghazali, vital as she was to the Brotherhood, never formally presided over an organisation which included men.

Many of these women—although not all—wear hijab. Clearly here in the West, where women are free to wear what they want, the veil can have multiple meanings. These are typically a far cry from the old notions which I grew up with, and profoundly different from the veil's ancient patriarchal meanings, which are still in full force in some countries. Here in the West—embedded in the context of democracy, pluralism and a commitment to gender justice—women's hijabs can have meanings that they could not possibly have in countries which do not even subscribe to the idea of equality.

But things are changing here as well. Interestingly, the issue of hijab and whether it is religiously required or not is now coming under scrutiny among women who grew up wearing it. Some are re-reading old texts and concluding that the veil is irrelevant to Islamic piety. They cast it off even as they remain committed Muslims.

It is too soon to tell whether this development, emerging most particularly among intellectual women who once wore hijab, will gather force and become a new unveiling movement for the 21st century: one that repeats, on other continents and in completely new ways, the unveiling movement of the early 20th century. Still, in a time when a number of countries have tried banning the hijab and when typically such rules have backfired, it is worth noting that here in America, where there are no such bans, a new movement may be quietly getting under way, a movement led this time by committed Muslim women who once wore hijab and who, often after much thought and study, have taken the decision to set it aside.

Occasionally now, although less so than in the past, I find myself nostalgic for the Islam of my childhood and youth, an Islam without veils and far removed from politics. An Islam which people seemed to follow not in the prescribed, regimented ways of today but rather according to their own inner sense, and their own particular temperaments, inclinations and the shifting vicissitudes of their lives.

I think my occasional yearning for that now bygone world has abated 20 (not that it is entirely gone) for a number of reasons. As I followed, a little like a detective, the extraordinary twists and turns of history that brought about this entirely unpredicted and unlikely "return" of the veil, I found the story itself so absorbing that I seemed to forget my nostalgia. I also lost the vague sense of annoyance, almost of affront, that I'd had over the years at how history had, seemingly so casually, set aside the entirely reasonable hopes and possibilities of that brighter and now vanished era.

In the process I came to see clearly what I had long known abstractly: that living religions are by definition dynamic. Witness the fact that today we have women priests and rabbis—something unheard of just decades ago. As I followed the shifting history of the veil—a history which had reversed directions twice in one century—I realised that I had lived through one of the great sea changes now overtaking Islam. My own assumptions and the very ground they stood on had been fundamentally challenged. It now seems absurd that we once labelled people who veiled "backward" and those who did not "advanced" and that we thought that it was perfectly fine and reasonable to do so. Seeing one's own life from a new perspective can be unsettling, of course—but it is also quite bracing, and even rather exciting.

Analyze

1. What does Ahmed mean by "reinventing" the veil?
2. In several passages, Ahmed draws attention to her own thinking—and how it changed during her research. Consider, for instance, paragraphs 12 through 14. How do these passages function in the article? How do they show something crucial? How do they support her main idea?
3. Explain Ahmed's point about context and the meaning of hijab. Which single sentence best characterizes her point?
4. Ahmed calls religions "dynamic." What does she mean? And how does that meaning figure into her main idea?
5. People often imagine that society advances through history—that civilizations move forward in some collective way toward a more enlightened or more free state. Explain how Ahmed's conclusion complicates or challenges the idea of such progress.

Explore

1. Why do you think hijab generates so many questions or concerns? Why does the veil carry so much cultural weight?

2. Can something as old as hijab be reinvented? What cultural forces keep something from being reinvented?

3. How do religious traditions figure into cultural change or cultural stasis? Consider a religious practice or ritual other than Islamic dress to develop your point.

4. *Cultural context* is key to Ahmed's analysis of hijab. Broadly speaking, what is the relationship between meaning and context—between the meaning of a specific act and the culture surrounding it?

5. Have you ever been able to view your own life from a new perspective? If so, what happened? What prompted the new vision? If not, what forces or habits or social patterns have kept you from a new perspective?

Forging Connections

1. How does identity get used to sell products and services? Explain how a particular advertisement or advertising campaign targets a specific demographic: young heterosexual men, middle-aged white women, young Hispanic women, gender-neutral teens, older rural or suburban white men, and so on. Explain how specific elements in the ad appeal to the target audience. To help explain the relationship between marketing and identity, borrow insights from Robert Moor, "Mother Nature's Sons" (Chapter 7) and Fredrik deBoer, "The Resentment Machine" (Chapter 2).

2. What happens to identity on social media? How does it get complicated or simplified? In what ways does identity flatten out or change? In an essay, argue that social media either enriches or diminishes personal identity. Make a case that relies on your own experience and your research of specific social media. Integrate quotations, descriptions, even terms of agreement between users and social media providers. Borrow insights from any of the writers in Chapter 4, "Social Media: How We Communicate."

Looking Further

1. How are personal identity and culture related? How do the two concepts influence one another? Does one cause the other? Does one fold into the other? Does one challenge or animate the other? In an analytical essay, explain the relationship. Although you are dealing with

concepts, try to ground your ideas with specific examples and situations. Use your own life experience to dramatize ideas. Allude to popular culture or history to illustrate your thinking. Integrate images and photographs to flesh out especially abstract points.

2. Eboo Patel and S. Alan Ray deal with identity issues on college campuses. Explore the demographics of your own campus. Research changes in one specific category: race, gender, religion, or sexual orientation. In an essay, explain how the student body has changed, in that one respect, over the past decade, and over several decades. Explain what institutional or social forces may have influenced that change, and finally, explore the relationship between your college campus and the surrounding culture. Is your campus a microcosm—a representation of the broader American culture? Or is it distinct in some way?

Entertainment: What We Watch, How We Listen

6

If we want to understand the intellectual trends of a culture, we would do well to explore its schools, colleges, and universities. But if we want to understand a culture's emotional reflexes, we should study its entertainment. What a culture reads, watches, and listens to says something about its collective desires, hopes, and fears. After all, when we're listening to music or watching our favorite programs, we are not simply escaping daily life; we are escaping *into* something—into an invented reality that resonates with how we feel or how we want to feel for a while.

Entertainment is a form of escape, but it is also a reflection of shared fears and hopes. Consider, for instance, how many thousands of films and novels focus on the horrors of technology gone wrong—humanity's own creation taking over. From *Frankenstein* to the *Matrix* films, plenty of works dramatize the fear of our own creations. Or consider the many happy endings in Hollywood movies, those that show peace between races, reconciliation of enemies, the utter destruction of evil, or the discovery of true love. Such works dramatize what millions of people quietly yearn for in their own lives. In other words, entertainment gives shape to and reflects a range of deep emotions. It embodies what people hate, love, need, crave, and fear.

It is no wonder, then, that scholars, writers, and everyday citizens want the most popular forms of entertainment to reflect their lives. They want to see themselves—or people like themselves—on the screen and inside of the drama. They want to escape into someone else's life, but they also want that life to resemble their own. This is the tension of contemporary entertainment, and the writers in this chapter deal with it directly. Whether it's a need for community, a hope for realism, or a longing to see men and women who resemble those in our lives, the articles and blogs in this chapter examine specific works from popular culture and explain how they reveal or resemble parts of our own identities.

Laura Bennett
Fallon and Letterman and the Invisible Late Show Audience

A staff writer at *The New Republic*, Laura Bennett explores issues related to TV and film entertainment. She is the author of numerous magazine articles, book reviews, and blog posts. In the following magazine article, Bennett examines the ways late-night TV audiences build a sense of community.

Last night both Jimmy Fallon and David Letterman sent their studio audiences home for the storm and did their shows for an empty theater. The result was an eerie kind of performance art: all those rows of empty chairs, the coughs and cleared throats from crew members, the strange clarity of each single peal of laughter from someone backstage. Both shows opened with their respective hosts standing outside in the whipping rain like weathermen, explaining that the show would go on. "There's no audience tonight," Fallon said into the camera. "So you are the audience. So imagine laughter. Imagine fun. Imagine excitement."

The bands had clearly been instructed to play extra loudly to cover up the silence as the hosts jogged on stage. "Please, please, keep it down," Fallon joked as the studio echoed with straggling claps from cameramen and producers. Letterman had a crew member hold up hand-written cards with alternate names for Hurricane Sandy that included "Trumpical Storm" and "Oprah Windy," a gag that called attention to just how far this comedy landscape has drifted from the analog world. (Fallon read from a list of viewer submissions to the hashtag #halloweendisaster.) "You're performing as if there was an audience," said announcer Steve Higgins to Fallon as he paused between jokes. "I'm assuming that people at home will be watching either on their laptops or with their generators out, and they'll want to leave room for laughs," he said.

Both *Late Night* and *The Late Show* highlighted just how much the studio audience has become ingrained in the format—the way Fallon occasionally hands cue cards for failed jokes to people in the crowd, or dispenses high-fives as he leaves the theater, and how Letterman is a master of playing up the casual one-on-one chat with an audience member for laughs. It was hard not to miss that classic moment when Letterman stands and smiles and soaks up the applause before his monologue. Or the way he pauses and rides out a joke, riffing over the laughter, letting it sink in. And watching Letterman and Fallon was to become newly attuned to the art of the segue: the sudden, uneasy emptiness of between-joke pauses, accompanied by an impulse to doubt whether the thing you heard was as funny as it seemed since it felt so newly strange that no other voices were laughing.

Todd VanDerWerff of The AV Club wrote last year that the "illusion of community," especially for TV comedy, is becoming less and less important. He attributed this to the fact that audiences have increasingly been raised on "setup-punchline humor" that makes it hard for us to be surprised by anything, and the way the Internet "provides an instant community for viewers." "We don't need ghost voices to laugh with us," he wrote, "when we have our friends online spitting out LOLs." In the era of TV blogs and Twitter we have substituted reliance on the arbitrary tastes of the studio audience for a curated, engaged, and informed community of our own making.

Granted, both shows last night were hilarious. Fallon was absurdist and   5
fidgety; Letterman was calm and resolute—the joke was his pretending that nothing was different at all. Both used shots of the empty seats to great comic effect. And generally speaking both shows made for excellent

television, offering up a totally new angle on the late-night experience that hinged on the thrill of being privy to behind-the-scenes dynamics: the particular jokes the crew laughed at, the amped-up rapport between Letterman and wingman Shaffer and the crew, and between Fallon and announcer Steve Higgins and the Roots and everyone else on set. But instead of convincing me that the live studio audience is a bygone trick, a vestigial limb of the late-night format, it reminded me why the on-set community is still key to the experience of these shows.

Watching *The Late Show,* I thought of a great old clip from 1986 when Letterman led his whole audience in an enthusiastic rendition of "O, Canada," an off-key chorus of random voices filling the small studio. It was a display of rowdy, impromptu, human-to-human community, and it was so much fun to watch. Today the illusion of community is everywhere, but the late night show is the one place where it does not unfurl in a sidebar of piecemeal commentary but in the midst of the action, in a way that allows the host to participate and respond. So last night's Letterman and Fallon were ultimately a reminder that the talk show still relies on in-person community—even in the age of hashtags, there is something weirdly comforting about that filled-up room.

"In the era of TV blogs and Twitter we have substituted reliance on the arbitrary tastes of the studio audience for a curated, engaged, and informed community of our own making."

Analyze

1. Bennett suggests that live studio audiences have an inherent value—something, perhaps, beyond entertainment. What is that value? And what passage or sentence from the article best characterizes that value?

2. Explain how *community* figures into Bennett's main idea. What does she mean by *community?* How is it connected to live studio audiences?

3. Explain how Todd VanDerWerff's point in paragraph 4 fits into Bennett's overall point. How does VanDerWerff's description of prevailing trends in entertainment support or reinforce something critical in Bennett's article?

4. Analyze Bennett's final statement. What does "weirdly comforting" suggest? How does it relate to the rest of the article?

5. The chapter introduction claims that entertainment "embodies what people hate, love, need, crave, and fear." How does Bennett's article speak to this claim?

Explore

1. Bennett explains that "illusion of community is everywhere." What does she mean by "illusion" and how does that contrast with something more real or genuine?

2. Point to other situations in the media—or in daily life—that support or conjure the illusion of community.

3. What is your favorite hosted television program? Explain its particular qualities or values—what it does for viewers, what kind of entertainment it provides.

4. How does community "unfurl in a sidebar of piecemeal commentary?" What do you think Bennett is describing?

5. The chapters of this book argue that culture is filled with, and even defined by, the tension between tradition and change. What cultural tensions does Bennett describe in her article? What do you think is the most important or critical tension related to late-night television shows?

Richard Lawson and Jen Doll
Lies Hollywood Told Us:
Love and Romance Edition

Writers for *The Atlantic Wire*, Richard Lawson and Jen Doll explore the quirky underside of popular culture and entertainment news. In the following article, they dissect several romantic myths that Hollywood films perpetuate.

Love is hard. Romantic movies make it harder. We've lived through life-times of rom-coms and romances and the occasional dramas that make relationships seem ever so simple or sometimes complicated but still beauti-ful. . . . If you only wait it out and sleep in your makeup and make sure to attend weddings with your gay best friend, and love dogs and do the right thing and are fully aware of when he or she is or is not just that into you. And we are tired. Tired of the lies. Tired of the misleading details. Tired of being fooled into thinking that real life works this way, and therefore our expectations are completely and totally reasonable and why hasn't anyone flown a plane overhead explaining how devoted they are to us? Sure, *The Five-Year Engagement* may have been a flop, but that doesn't mean it didn't imperil thousands of Americans with unrealistic romantic expectations, and, further, continue a long tradition of movies cementing bad habits and relationship turmoil. Let's put a stop to it, here and now. Here are the ways in which Hollywood lies. It probably cheats, too.

You will never have to choose between two amazing men (or women) who love you equally and utterly but in completely opposite ways. One will not be a brunette, and one will not be a blonde, because you either like blondes or you like brunettes. One will also not be a hunter while the other is a bread-maker, and one will not be courageous and strong and your best friend while the other loves you unconditionally, even, maybe, after he's been driven mad by corrupt governmental forces. Neither of them will want to kill you, unless you're complaining about taking out the garbage again, and in that case, it's only figuratively. Nor will you have to choose between your adoring, perfect boyfriend or girlfriend and his/her annoying, perfect best friend. More likely, you will tolerate the annoying best friend who's always making the dumb jokes or talking about shopping because your beloved adores that person, foul piece of humanity he or she may be, and, more importantly, when you make fun of the BFF your beloved tends to get really annoyed and denies you sex.

You will not find someone ten years after you met them but did not give them your number because you were being weird or whimsical and, at the time, coyly believed in fate. You will not be able to track them down using old receipts and half-disappeared memories, they will not appear magically at a skating rink when it has just begun to snow. And even if they do, even if you and your wacky friend do somehow manage to track this person down, it will have been ten years and you only met them the once so it will be awkward and you will very quickly realize that the connection you felt all those years ago was just a quick, passing thing, a ribbon of lightning gone as quick as it came. You're both older now and you have different values and you live all the way across the country and this whole adventure will suddenly feel sad and strange instead of exciting and romantic. You will realize that if you were interested a decade ago you should have just given them your stupid phone number and he or she would have called and you would have gone on some dates and maybe it would have worked out and maybe it wouldn't have, but at least it would be then, and you would know, rather than wasting all this money on airplanes to New York ten long years later.

Your hook-up buddy will never be more than your hook-up buddy. Same with your sperm donor.

There will never be a last-minute chase scene as you board the plane   5 to Dubai/New York City/Los Angeles/Singapore/Iowa City, Iowa, in which your lover, former lover, or best friend not yet your lover has finally realized his or her grave mistake, and that he or she needs you desperately after all. This person will not stop you before you board and will certainly not board the plane himself, eyes wild, rushing through the seats to find you and ask for your hand in marriage. For one thing, in this day and age of air travel, that is impossible. Further: He will not be carrying flowers, or gifts, or even a bottle of water. There will be no grand gesture. More likely, if your lover does decide he wants to try again after you fly to Singapore, he will e-mail you and schedule a time in which you can Skype. It will probably be some months from the time you depart, around the same time that you start dating someone else, because former lovers have that sort of radar. Maybe he will convince you to come back, and maybe he won't. But he will not arrive at your doorstep, if you even have a doorstep, without telling you he's coming, and then get down on one knee and proffer a ring/a sign that says "To Me You Are Perfect"/a bottle of champagne/something important that only the two of you know about. If, on the very rare occasion, he actually does arrive, you will probably have to take out a restraining order, or, alternatively, pick him up at the airport.

You will never fall in love with a hooker with a heart of gold, or, if you are a hooker, your john will not fall in love with you and also happen to be a very wealthy businessman and a very nice person, too, who takes you on shopping sprees and cleans you up and makes you presentable and teaches you what fork to use at the dinner table and introduces you to high society. When you consider going back to your old ways, he will not climb a fire escape and rescue you and get down on one knee and promise to make you an honest woman. You will not watch Lucille Ball stomp on grapes together and congratulate yourselves on your good fortune in finding each other, and there will not be a kindly hotel manager who looks like Hector Elizondo to take anyone under his wing at the Regent Beverly Wilshire.

Your male friend will not suddenly realize he loves you. He will not have any romantic epiphany in which he remembers great, unwittingly sexy times you had together and realize suddenly that they make up a perfect patchwork quilt of love. If you have had this friend for years and years and he has not shown an interest then he is either a gay person or really just not into you. Either way, he will not show up at your house in the rain and tell you a story about something you two did when you were kids, he will not make an awkward, embarrassing speech at a party, in front of everyone. Your other friends will not nod and smile knowingly, because they thought you two would get together all along. (And if they did, wouldn't they be not very good friends for having never said anything to you?) There will not be a nice old jazz song that plays. There will be no end credits.

Your marriage will not be interrupted by the person who's actually right for you, at the altar, when the minister asks if anyone would like to speak out against said marriage. If anyone does disapprove of the marriage (and surely, someone, somewhere, will), they will never say anything until and unless your marriage ends, years later, possibly, and then that person will say something to the tune of, "I never liked him/her anyway." This person is more likely to be a relative than the person who has hidden away their love for you, like a locket underground, for many, many years because they only wanted you to be happy, even though you clearly weren't. Additionally, you will not be a wedding planner who falls in love with a client, or a client who falls in love with a wedding planner, or, for that matter, an escort who falls in love with a client, or a client who falls in love with an escort, and you will certainly not marry someone you meet when you are a bridesmaid at a wedding, or a guest at a funeral.

That slacker guy who got you pregnant? Chances are, he's not going to reform and suddenly become wonderful. But you never know!

10   **You will not fall in love with someone you fight with all the time**, be they neighbor or coworker or obnoxious magazine writer. If you fight with them all the time it means you do not like each other and do not get along and should not, will not, date. Why would you want to date the asshole across the hall anyway? Why would that smug jerk at the rival advertising

company suddenly seem appealing? This will not happen. You are enemies, not future lovers. Stay away from this person because they make you mad and you do stupid things to get back at them, stupid wacky zany things that no one will find cute, they will just think you're annoying and you will probably get fired or evicted and it will all be because of this complete ass who you will never fall in love with.

There will not be a makeover montage. There just won't be.

You will not meet on a boat, or on a plane, or in a school or florist's shop or mall, or via a professional male matchmaker, and be of two different social and economic classes yet know from the minute your eyes meet that you are kindred spirits destined to be together despite the odds, despite impending tragedy. You will not save one another over and over again, from water, from fire, from certain death, from bad humans, from falling back into your own sad life. You will not, in the end, attempt to climb atop a board together—once, only once—and fail, and then stop trying. You will not freeze to death in the cold, cold sea waters after the *Titanic* has sunk.

There will not be a comedy of manners or tiny, insurmountable offenses, in which he says one thing and you take it the wrong way and then you say something else, and then other people stick their noses in and sway you in one way or the other, but then he saves your sister from ill repute, and you finally realize what a good man he is, and how he love-love-loves you.

There will not be a "happy ever after." There might be a happy sometimes. For best chances of such, stop believing what you see in romantic movies.

Analyze

1. Explain the function of Lawson and Doll's opening statement. How does their first claim relate to or support their main point?
2. Unlike many articles, especially more formal works written in an academic setting, this article uses the second-person pronoun *you* to address readers directly. How does that affect your understanding of the point? How does it influence the way you read it?
3. Lawson and Doll take on and refute a range of typical romance movie formulas—and *suggest* specific movies along the way. How does this strategy work for the overall success of the article? Why is it better or worse not to continue listing specific characters or plots throughout the article?

4. Lawson and Doll explain, to some degree, their purpose in writing the article. In your own words, what is their purpose? What are they trying to do with this article? What do they want for their audience?

5. What other article, book, or even television show has the same purpose as Lawson and Doll? Explain, as specifically as possible, how another author or person is aiming for the same effect.

Explore

1. Does a small part of you still cling to the romantic formulas that Lawson and Doll mention? Or do you know someone who still clings to these romantic ideals? If so, why? What's the attraction? Why can't some people (or most people) let these ideals go?

2. Lawson and Doll argue that Hollywood makes romantic relationships even harder than they naturally are. How does your experience support or challenge that claim?

3. What other unhealthy ideals do Hollywood movies project? (If you can, give specific movie titles or scenes.)

4. When people talk about movies, television, and influence, they often focus on children—on the way popular culture prompts feelings and behaviors in developing lives. But what about adults? Using your own experiences and observations, explain how popular entertainment may influence healthy and fully mature adults.

5. Do you think Americans are more able to resist the allure of popular entertainment than they were in previous eras? Why or why not?

Stefan Babich
The Fall of the Female Protagonist in Kids' Movies

Stefan Babich is a blogger for *Persephone Magazine*, which describes itself as "a daily blog focused on topics of interest for modern, intelligent, clever women." The blog's goal is to "give a voice to more women from a variety of backgrounds and with diverse interests." In the following post, Babich considers the role of female protagonists in animated children's films.

There was a time, not too long ago, when two-dimensional, hand-drawn animation and computer-generated cartoons existed side-by-side. Every fall, sometime around Thanksgiving, Pixar and Disney would collaborate and release a family comedy featuring anthropomorphic creatures or objects rendered with state-of-the-art computer graphics. Every summer, Disney would come out with another one of its more traditional pieces, an animated musical based on some hopelessly depressing classic story made kid-friendly by the addition of rousing songs and sidekicks with attention deficit hyperactivity disorder. It seemed a perfect arrangement, one built to last. The two types of films were different enough that there was room for both—the classic adventure/dramas that earned Disney its name, and the edgier, more tongue-in-cheek Pixar films that were designed to amuse adults as well as kids.

The alliance was not to last. Slowly but inexorably, the new, computer-animated films drove their hand-drawn cousins aside, until now, hand-drawn children's films are (at least in America) a relic of the past. All the major animated films of this year so far (*Rango, Rio, Gnomeo and Juliet*) have been made with computers.

It's not entirely clear what killed the hand-drawn animated movie. Maybe it was Disney's decision to abandon the musical format in its latest summer releases (*Atlantis* and *Lilo and Stitch* featured no songs, and *Tarzan,* while containing a fair number of songs, did not have any singing characters). Maybe it was the box-office triumphs of computer-animated films like *Shrek* and *Monsters, Inc.* over their hand-drawn counterparts (*Monsters, Inc.* trounced *Atlantis, The Lost Empire* in box offices worldwide). In any case, it soon became clear that the battle between the two forms of animation was over, and the victor clear.

In any battle, there are casualties, and the "animation war" was no exception. One of the most unfortunate (and surprising) side effects of the triumph of computer-generated animation was the death of the female protagonist in children's movies.

Think of all the female protagonists in Disney musicals. There are quite 5 a number, almost as many as there are males—Cinderella, Belle, Ariel, Pocahontas, Mulan . . . the list goes on. Now think of female protagonists in Pixar movies.

There aren't any. Not a single one.

In Dreamworks, the story isn't quite as bad. But it still took them until 2009 to release their first movie starring a female character in a leading role (*Monsters v. Aliens*).

In 2012, Pixar, maybe having noticed the troubling discrepancy in its numbers, is aiming to change its game by releasing its first female-centric film, titled *Brave*. One has to wonder what took them so long.

It's easy to cut Pixar a break. After all, they've made a lot of critically-acclaimed movies, the most recent of which (*Up* and *Toy Story 3*) were nominated for Best Picture at the Academy Awards. They've combined state-of-the-art technology with skillful and emotionally resonant storytelling. And, despite the shortage of female protagonists, they have had a number of strong, memorable female characters. Characters like Elastigirl from *The Incredibles,* and Eve, from *Wall-E*. Fernanda Diaz of FlavorWire argues: "For Pixar to have a gender 'problem,' it would have to systematically place women in subservient roles and make the male superior—something which none of the films actually do." But is this really the only definition of sexism? Arguably, Pixar—and other similar companies—do show male superiority by showing, time and again, that the most important figures in a story are always male.

10   The most confusing part is that most of the stories in these animated movies would work just as well with a female protagonist. Is there any reason the rat in *Ratatouille* couldn't have been a lady? Is there any reason *Wall-E* couldn't have been the story of a female-voiced robot who encounters a male-voiced love interest named ADAM? It's not as though the gender of these characters is their most important feature, or indeed, very relevant at all to their personalities or the stories they are a part of. As Linda Holmes writes for NPR:

> Russell, in *Up,* is Asian-American, right? And that's not a big plot point; presumably, he just is because there's no particular reason he shouldn't be. You don't need him to be, but you don't need him not to be, either. It's not politics; it's just seeing the whole big world. Well, the whole big world has a lot of little girls in it, too.

Just as it's easy to defend Pixar, it is fairly easy to criticize Disney films for being sexist. And to be fair, there's a lot about Disney's past portrayals of women that's deserving of criticism, beyond the fact that almost all its female characters happen to be princesses. A disturbingly large percentage of their female leads end up getting saved by a man at some point, usually the climax. Ariel is rescued from the villainess by heroic prince Eric; Jasmine is rescued from the villain by Aladdin. Furthermore, a pretty big percentage of the female leads in Disney musicals seem to have only one goal—to get the guy. Their desire to obtain a man seems to be the most important motivating force in their lives, and the drama of the films often revolve around that desire. There is Ariel, in *The Little Mermaid,* who gives away her voice in order to obtain the love of Prince Eric. There is Cinderella, whose escape from her family lies in getting the prince to fall in love with her. Is Disney portraying women as weak, dependent people dependent on a man's love for their happiness and well-being?

Well, Disney might not be quite as sexist as it first appears. After all, when it comes to the focus on finding romance above all else, it's pretty much the same deal with the male protagonists. Though the girls seem to be driven by a desire to get the guy, the guys also seem unable to find happiness unless they get the girl. A lot of the male-centric story lines mirror the female-centric ones in key respects. In place of Cinderella, we have Aladdin, who pretends to be a prince to get the princess just as she disguises herself in order to get the prince. We have Hercules, who gives up his godhood to be with a woman, just as Ariel gives up her kingdom under the sea to be with Eric. Tarzan is only really happy when he gets to be with Jane. Often, when we see a Disney princess pining over a man, it's not really sexism on display—it's just the romantic nature of Disney movies. The men are just as single-mindedly obsessed with romance as are the women.

Admittedly, this defense doesn't address the fact that so many females in Disney movies need rescuing during the big action scenes. Yes, Disney has a justified reputation for sexism. But it was improving with the times. Mulan and Pocahontas were certainly more proactive characters than Belle and Ariel, just as these characters were stronger than Cinderella and Sleeping Beauty. And the fact is that Disney had a much higher percentage of female protagonists than Hollywood as a whole. That has to count for something.

It's not that hard to argue Disney is no more sexist than Pixar or Dreamworks. After all, if little girls fifteen years ago were left with somewhat stereotypical princesses as their role models, girls today have to come to grips with the fact that the male character is almost always the center of attention.

Surely such a striking trend has to be due to more than coincidence. 15 So, what exactly, killed the female animated protagonist?

The answer may lie in the few female protagonists there have been since the rise of Pixar and Dreamworks. Susan Murphy of *Monsters vs. Aliens,*

Rapunzel of *Tangled,* and Mérida of the upcoming *Brave* all share a striking characteristic—they are human.

Whereas most of the Disney movies of the '80s and '90s focused on human characters taken from classic fairytales and from history (people like Tarzan, Pocahontas, Quasimodo and of course, the Little Mermaid), the vast majority of computer animated films these days tend to revolve around anthropomorphic animals and objects ranging from toys to penguins to cars. Maybe it's because humans are harder to animate realistically with computers than cute talking critters; maybe it's because early CGI animated films like *Toy Story* and *A Bug's Life* set a trend that later movies just happened to follow. But it's odd that when female protagonists do show up in modern animated films, it's almost always in the ones starring actual people. There are exceptions, like Mala in the somewhat lesser known *Battle for Terra.* But the statistics are still pretty striking—and pretty intriguing.

Why is it that anthropomorphic creatures are far more likely to be male? It seems to suggest that our conception of the heroine is somehow linked to the physical. Why is it so important that a heroine have an attractive human body, while a male hero can be a rat, penguin, or robot?

Though we'd all like to think we've taken strides forward in terms of sexism in children's movies, it seems filmmakers are having difficulty separating the concept of "heroine" from the concept of "sexiness." But if most kids' movies are going to be about animals and objects, rather than human beings, that's what needs to happen if the female protagonist is to finally be revived.

Analyze

1. In some passages, Babich defends Disney and Pixar for their sluggish progress on female protagonists. Explain how those passages function. What do they help Babich to do? How do they help to develop the main idea?

2. According to Babich, what particular ideas, forces, or trends are behind the lack of female protagonists in kids' movies?

3. In the middle of this article, Babich quotes Linda Holmes from NPR. Explain how the quotation functions. How does it support or develop Babich's main idea?

4. Babich's article was published in *Persephone Magazine*—"a daily blog for bookish and clever women." How does the publication influence your understanding of the specific claims or support used throughout the article?

5. Explain how Babich's article deals with or points to cultural change.

Explore

1. Babich explains that "In 2012, Pixar, maybe having noticed the troubling discrepancy in its numbers, is aiming to change its game by releasing its first female-centric film, titled *Brave*. One has to wonder what took them so long." What do you think took Pixar so long?

2. Read Amanda Marcotte's article, "The Shocking Radicalism of *Brave*" (in this chapter). Does Marcotte offer any answers to the previous question?

3. Consider the following questions from Babich's article: "Why is it that anthropomorphic creatures are far more likely to be male?" "Why is it so important that a heroine have an attractive human body, while a male hero can be a rat, penguin, or robot?" What answers can you provide?

4. Consider other recent mainstream movies that feature female protagonists. Explain how those characters, or a particular character, upholds or challenges the trend in kids' movies. Are the lead women sexy and strong? Are any simply strong, intelligent, or savvy?

5. Consider the following online comment to Babich's blog: "The thing with Disney is that generally they just re-hash old fairy tales, which did contain princess characters that needed rescuing etc. That's not Disney's fault, it's just how the story goes. It *is* their fault however that they end up bland and soul-less after being 'Disneyfied.'" The commenter, Martin, makes a fairly common charge about Disney's shallow or uncomplicated movies. How do you think Martin's charge relates to Babich's concern about gender? How might the two points overlap?

Amanda Marcotte
The Shocking Radicalism of *Brave*

A feminist writer, Amanda Marcotte offers a witty perspective on contemporary political issues. She is a blogger and the author of the books *It's a Jungle Out There: The Feminist Survival Guide to Politically Inhospitable Environments* (2007) and *Get Opinionated: A Progressive's Guide to Finding Your Voice (and Taking a Little Action)* (2010). In the following article, Marcotte analyzes Pixar's film *Brave* (2012) through a feminist lens.

The marketing for Pixar's new girl-centric film, *Brave,* suggests it is a movie in which a wild-haired heroine single-handedly conquers the monarchy, the patriarchy, and the myth that there are no attractive flat-heeled shoes. Feminists as much as anyone imagined that this would be the story, since so much of today's media aimed at girls is about "empowering" young women (as if the main obstacle to women's equality throughout most of history has been a lack of spunk, instead of eons of direct and indirect oppression based on the notion that women exist to be the trophies and helpmeets of men). Small wonder then that so many critics have emerged from the theater a bit befuddled by what they saw: the story of a young princess and her mother trying to understand each other despite their radically different approaches to life as a woman in medieval society.

Tom Carson, while praising the movie's effectiveness, argued that the filmmakers "seem to be playing by rules that don't interest them very much and not making an especially bright job of it." Jacyln Friedman also loved the movie but asked, "If the sparkling minds at Pixar can't imagine their way out of the princess paradigm, how can we expect girls to?" It's hard to blame these critics for feeling a bit let down. The movie fails to present any alternatives to stifling gender roles; the lead character, Merida, is all rebellion, but she never offers any ideas for how to fix things other than a speech denouncing arranged marriages.

Still, there's a danger in letting this disappointment blind us. For all its faults, *Brave* is shockingly radical for a mainstream movie. As with *Wall-E* before it, *Brave* is an example of what happens when Pixar gets political. We don't get much in the way of imaginative alternatives to our current problems, but we do get a scathing satire that doesn't hold back despite being in a children's movie. *Wall-E* turned its satirical eye on the problem of mass consumerism and environmental destruction; the laziness and greed of the human race allows our planet to become a landfill while we become formless blobs without any goals higher than being fed more sugary sodas. In the end, no real path to prevent this dystopia is suggested. *Wall-E* seems satisfied to go no further than biting commentary.

Brave turns that same satirical eye toward the patriarchy. In the imaginary medieval Scotland of Merida's world, unquestioned male dominance lets men be buffoons. They spend all their time puffing out their chests and bragging about how tough they are. These men know so little outside of violent competition that the smallest upset—Merida's unwillingness to be traded in marriage like a baseball card—nearly dissolves the kingdom in war. As in real life, men in *Brave* often tune out women telling them things they don't want to hear, and Merida's father's reluctance to listen to his daughter almost causes him to accidentally kill his beloved wife.

Even more interesting, the filmmakers take a critical look at the way 5 women function under male dominance. Many patriarchal societies leave the stressful job of forcing girls to comply with degrading social norms to women, especially mothers. Unlike other movies such as *Real Women Have Curves,* where sexism-enforcing mothers are painted as villains, Merida's mother, Elinor, pushes her daughter to perform femininity out of love. As with mothers throughout history who have done everything from put young girls on diets to hold them down to have their clitorises removed at puberty, they are acting not out of hatred but out of a love that leads them to protect their daughters from the price of rebellion. In real life, that price is often exile; in this movie, it's war. With stakes this high, it's hard not to feel for a mother in such a bind.

In this grim world of male dominance, the fantasy of a single individual changing everything with a grand gesture of empowerment starts to look silly indeed. A lesser film would have made Merida's plot to out-man the men at archery the end of the story, but this more realistic portrayal shows how individual action can make the situation worse. Only when the female characters start to work together—to take the collective action so beloved by progressive organizers—does actual change occur. In the end, *Brave* doesn't have much to do with girl-power fantasies that imagine girls doing it for themselves without offering a real challenge to male privilege. But it tells a story that feels awfully familiar to those doing feminist work in the maddeningly complex real world.

Analyze

1. For Marcotte, *Brave* represents a significant cultural shift—at least in terms of entertainment. In your own words, explain that shift.

2. In Marcotte's introductory paragraph, she puts quotes around "empowering." Why? What is she suggesting? What idea or subtle debate might the quotation marks signal or suggest?

3. Explain the function of Marcotte's second paragraph. What purpose does it serve? How do the Carson and Friedman critiques of *Brave* help to support Marcotte's main idea?

4. Explain how Marcotte's title relates to her main idea.

5. Carefully examine Marcotte's concluding paragraph. Explain how the distinction between individual and collective action figures into Marcotte's point about *Brave*.

6. Consider Stefan Babich's argument in "The Fall of the Female Protagonist in Kids' Movies" in this chapter. What particular ideas or beliefs do you think Marcotte shares with Babich?

Explore

1. *Brave* is about cultural change in a medieval society. What other movies take on big cultural shifts related to gender, race, or sexuality?

2. Why do you think so many movies focus on princesses? What's the appeal?

3. What is "the patriarchy"? Look up the term online. How are you part of it? How are you outside it?

4. Marcotte argues that *Brave* is more sophisticated than a girl-power fantasy. Can you think of another movie that could be labeled a boy- or girl-power fantasy? What specific elements of the movie (such as the characters, storyline, setting) make you think that it deserves the label?

5. How does a movie like *Brave* support or undermine a sense of community?

Steve Yates
The Sound of Capitalism

Steve Yates is a writer for the British publication *Prospect*, which defines itself as "an entertaining, informative and open-minded magazine that mixes compelling argument and clear headed analysis with elegance and vitality in design." In the following article, Yates considers the cultural value of hip hop. (Note British spelling conventions throughout.)

The latest album by the twin titans of hip hop has been a record-breaking success. On its release, Jay-Z and Kanye West's *Watch the Throne* had the highest ever first week sales on iTunes of any new album. A total of 290,000 copies were downloaded that week, and when CDs are taken into account, the album's sales approached the 450,000 mark. Hip hop is big business.

Watch The Throne is symbolic of the status that hip hop, or rap, has now reached. Originating in the South Bronx in New York City in the late 1970s, when performers began rapping over looped beats taken from soul and funk records, hip hop has since journeyed right into the heart of mainstream culture.

Jay-Z is married to Beyoncé Knowles, queen of R&B, and together they form the most influential power couple in global music. His wealth is estimated by *Forbes* at around $450m, and he has had 12 U.S. number one albums (only the Beatles, with 19, have had more). Kanye West's fortune is around $70m. *Watch the Throne* is thick with references to wealth—even the sleeve is designed by Givenchy's Riccardo Tisci: "Luxury rap, the Hermès of verses," raps Kanye, giving the brand its French pronunciation, lest anyone should think he was mistaking the high-end goods manufacturer for a mythic Greek messenger.

But for its detractors, this materialism is one of rap's three deadly sins, along with its violence and misogyny. Casual fans of hip hop often see its materialistic side as something either to be played down or embraced "ironically." Some commentators judge it more harshly. When the riots broke out across Britain this summer, many saw hip hop's celebration of materialism as one of the key causes. Paul Routledge, writing in the *Mirror,* summarised this view when he said, "I blame the pernicious culture of hatred around rap music, which glorifies violence and loathing of authority . . . [and] exalts trashy materialism."

Routledge is not *entirely* wrong. The story of hip hop's journey into the cultural mainstream is the story of its love affair with materialism, or, more accurately, capitalism. Its lead exponents, like Jay-Z and Kanye West, are brilliant entrepreneurs with vast fortunes (even if their music advocates a profligacy that is anathema to the savvy business operator). Hip hop's rise has been, at root, a straightforward process of free-market enterprise: an excellent product has been pushed with great skill and new markets opened up with real dynamism and flair.

Unsurprisingly, corporate brands have been keen to get involved. Darren Wright, creative director of the Nike account at advertising agency

Wieden+Kennedy explains the appeal: "With hip hop you're buying more than music. It isn't a genre—it's a lifestyle, encompassing fashion, break dancing, the clothes or the jewels you wear. . . . The lifestyle is worth its weight in gold because it's not just about one rap song, it's so much more."

The view of hip hop as a genre concerned only with the basest forms of materialism is a serious oversimplification. It misunderstands the way that rap's relationship with capitalism has fed its creativity and led to both its commercial and artistic success.

While modern hip hop is unashamedly materialistic, its ancestors were different. As far back as the 1960s, artists such as *The Last Poets* and Gil Scott-Heron combined African-American music with spoken word poetry. But Scott-Heron, like others of that generation, was critical of the passive materialism that he saw working its way into black culture. As he intoned on "The Revolution Will Not Be Televised": "The revolution will not go better with Coke/The revolution will not fight the germs that may cause bad breath/The revolution will put you in the driver's seat." This political consciousness was taken up in the 1980s by the extraordinary Public Enemy, a New York group that mixed incendiary politics with apocalyptic music, militaristic dress and cartoon humour. Gentler, but still political, takes on "Afrocentricity" were advanced by the brilliant Native Tongues collective including groups like De La Soul, A Tribe Called Quest and the Jungle Brothers.

But by the early 1990s, this "conscious" streak was being eclipsed by the giddy thrills of gangsta rap. Its motivation was pithily summarised by NWA (Niggaz With Attitude), the group who named and codified the subgenre, on their track "Gangsta Gangsta"—"life ain't nothin' but bitches and money." Despite this apparent nihilism, NWA embraced the American dream with relish. They set down the unapologetic "money-is-all" credo of the low-level street hustler, in which drug dealing, guns and the police swirl about in a ferocious urban storm. Like other popular representations of American gangsterism—*The Godfather, Scarface*—it was a vision of unfettered free market enterprise.

10   Slowly, the early political message was replaced by this focus on accumulation, both in the lyrics and also the business practice of those who were running the scene. One of hip hop's key entrepreneurs was Percy "Master P" Miller, who grew his No Limit empire from an L.A. record shop into a record label and then into a conglomerate. Miller spearheaded a new wave of hip hop business by entering into joint ventures with music companies.

He chose Priority, which was independent of the major record labels, and which had made a packet out of NWA and other leading artists. His deal brought all the benefits of working for major labels, such as distribution and marketing muscle, without the drawbacks—Master P was able to retain copyright control over the music and release records to his own schedule.

But not content with music, he diversified wildly: clothing, property, Master P dolls—even telephone sex lines. His debut film, the low-budget, straight-to-video *I'm Bout It* (1997) raked in sales that would have satisfied major studios. In 1998, Miller's companies grossed $160m.

In New York, the business interests of Sean "Puff Daddy" Combs developed along parallel lines: music, restaurants, a magazine, the inevitable clothing line, all name-stamped in a manner that led the consumer back to the man himself. Dan Charnas, in his masterful book *The Big Payback: The History Of The Business Of Hip Hop,* describes Miller and Combs as "the embodiment of the superpowered artist, two one-man brands, the fulfilment of [the] vision of self-determination and ownership—not just for hip hop artists, not just for black artists, but for all American artists." Having turned their art into business, they turned their business back into art. According to Charnas, their success "would mark the beginning of an unprecedented spike in black American entrepreneurship."

So while hip hop started off as an underground, and often political movement, it has for many years pursued an increasingly intimate relationship with business. Hip hop now has a materialist, acquisitive streak hardwired into its identity. It is this embrace of capitalism that has taken hip hop from outsider status right to America's core. This ascent was neatly symbolised when Barack Obama, on the nomination campaign trail in 2008, dismissed criticisms from the Clinton camp by mimicking Jay-Z's famous "dirt off my shoulder" gesture. Asked which rappers were on his iPod, there was only one candidate.

British variants of rap music have been growing in success, too. Yet the contrast with America is marked. Maybe the conflicting attitudes are born of economic realism: the market is much smaller, and British hip hop has a limited international audience. That was perhaps why British rap's flirtation with outlandish "bling" materialism was comparatively short-lived. In the early 2000s, the south London group So Solid Crew emerged at the forefront of the "garage" scene. Its members imitated the flow, though not the accents, of American rap superstars over electronic dance rhythms that successfully merged influences ranging from American house and hip hop, to Jamaican dancehall and British drum 'n' bass. Instantly, they became the sound of young black London. "Proper [rap] songs started with So Solid," says Elijah Butterz, a 24-year-old DJ and label owner, over a pint of Guinness in a Walthamstow pub. "When they hit, *eeeeveryone* was into them. If you listened to garage you were cool. If you didn't you weren't."

15   So Solid, along with other British garage acts, brought American-style bling culture to Britain's clubs. Smart dress, diamonds and champagne became dancefloor staples. But this quickly generated a backlash. Wretch 32 is a 26-year-old from Tottenham who found fame this year with two number one singles and a top five album. He feels that the norms of American hip hop do not always translate well in Britain: "I think because of our culture, people don't go for stuff like that—someone making them feel like they're less of a person for having less money."

In response, east London rapidly developed its own sound, called grime—a rap-dominated genre with a harsh, electronic edge, and lyrics that sounded like a fight in a fried chicken shop. Chantelle Fiddy, 30, a journalist and label consultant, agrees: "Grime was the middle finger to [garage]. It was for those people who were either not old enough or didn't have the money to go to the [garage] raves. Someone like me, who came up through jungle and just danced like a dick in trainers, I never felt comfortable with garage."

Grime has had its triumphs. Dizzee Rascal scored a significant success with his 2003 debut *Boy In Da Corner*. Others, such as Tinchy Stryder, Tinie Tempah and now Wretch 32 have followed in Dizzee's wake, increasingly adapting the sound for the mainstream. But inflated claims of riches don't really fly. "In grime you can't really lie about it," says Sian Anderson, a 20-year-old writer, label consultant, PR and DJ for the influential radio station Rinse FM. "If you're talking about popping champagne and then you go out on [the] road and you haven't got an amazing car and you don't look that great, then everyone knows you're a liar and your music's not real, so you're back to square one."

Road rap is south London's counterpart to the east end's grime. Slower and meaner than grime, and with a closer resemblance to U.S. gangsta rap, it's shown little interest in winning mainstream acceptability. Its biggest name, Giggs, has served time on weapons charges—he started in the music business when he got out. But his career has been dogged by police interference. His shows have frequently been cancelled and contract talks with a major record company were curtailed, reputedly after a call to the label from Operation Trident, the unit in the Metropolitan Police dealing with black-on-black gun crime. Then came Form 696, a risk-assessment form requiring London promoters to submit extensive details about themselves, their performers and even, in the original version, the probable ethnic make-up of the audience. After this, grime and road rap often struggled to get live bookings. Although the Met denied racial profiling, senior music industry figures complained to the Equality and Human Rights Commission about this stringent requirement.

Denied a live platform, they've found a new one online, notably on SBTV, now confidently billed as Britain's biggest youth media channel. But not everyone cares about chasing the music mainstream anyway. "I don't want to be part of it," says Elijah Butterz. "Apart from Rinse, there's nothing there doing what I want to do. Everyone expects you to dig into the music industry, but as long as I can make money from bookings and merchandising, I'll continue doing what I'm doing." For Elijah, that means running the eponymous Butterz label, one of very few to still release vinyl records, Djing (for free) on Rinse and living off his DJ club bookings.

This quiet determination seems a long way from the hardheaded ambitions of American hip hop, whose outlook has always been more expansive. "There's no protocol to the things I'm selling because I'm selling my culture," Jay-Z's partner Damon Dash, told me in 2003. Dash was the driving force behind the growth of Roc-A-Fella, their jointly-owned music business, whose name is an explicit reference to the capitalist heights they sought to scale. 20

The relationship between American hip hop and leading brands has always been strong. Adidas sales spiked after Run-DMC's 1986 track "My Adidas"; Tommy Hilfiger went from obscurity to being the highest-traded clothing company on Wall Street in 1996 after steady name-dropping by hip hop artists from 1992. Courvoisier reportedly received a 30 percent sales boost in the U.S. after Busta Rhymes released "Pass The Courvoisier"—the largest single rise since Napoleon III named it the official cognac of the imperial court. Its rival, Hennessy, the most popular brandy in hip hop, estimates that the majority of its customers are young black males.

British rappers are learning this lesson. Dizzee Rascal has had two Nike trainers of his own—an invaluable tie-in—and now owns his own label, Dirtee Stank. Tinie Tempah has a clothing range with Disturbing London, while Tinchy Stryder's Star In The Hood line looks a more durable bet than his records.

· ✦ ·

But this is still a far cry from the U.S., where rappers get to hobnob with the president. On *Watch The Throne*'s emblematic "Murder To Excellence," Kanye and Jay-Z contrast the black-on-black murder of American ghettoes with their lives of luxury. "Black tie, black Maybachs/Black excellence, opulence, decadence/Tuxes next to the President, I'm present," raps Jay-Z, before bemoaning how few black faces he sees at the pinnacle and calling on more to join him.

When critics zero in on hip hop's materialism, as they did this summer, they see just a fraction of the story—the fraction that talks about money, cars and glamour. But fixating on this element of hip hop ignores its limited appeal in Britain, where rappers have largely ditched the "bling" posturing of the early 2000s. When Wiley, the most influential man in grime after Dizzee Rascal, called his recent album *100% Publishing*, he was celebrating his bargaining power. It's a similar sentiment expressed by Margate rapper Mic Righteous, who, contrasting his homeless past with his present, raps, "I used to cherish every pound I got, now I cherish every pound I earn."

25   In the past 30-or-so years, hip hop has tried politics and it has tried gangsterism. But in the end it settled for capitalism, which energized it and brought it to a position of global dominance. American rappers like Puff Daddy and Master P, men who fought their way into the big time, did so by selling a vision of independence, empowerment and material success. That vision is also found, if less vividly, in Britain's rap music. And though hip hop retains unpleasant features, the core message, that people can have better lives, is incontestably a good one.

Analyze

1. How is this a pro-hip hop article?
2. Early in the article, Yates mentions hip hop's materialism. What does he mean by materialism?
3. Yates gives a brief history of hip hop in America and Britain. How does that history help to support his point about "the sound of capitalism"?
4. Toward the end of his article, Yates describes a relationship between cognac and a Busta Rhymes album. Explain how this passage relates to Yates's main idea.

5. How is this article about cultural change and resistance to change? If hip hop has become normal, a substantial phenomenon at the center of society, how did it happen? How does Yates's article help to make sense of the process?

Explore

1. Yates says that "Hip hop now has a materialist, acquisitive streak hard-wired into its identity." Give some examples that you know of to support or challenge this statement.

2. Yates explains, "In the past 30-or-so years, hip hop has tried politics and it has tried gangsterism. But in the end it settled for capitalism." How are politics and gangsterism fundamentally different from capitalism? Or how are they not different?

3. Yates discusses the relationship between American and British hip hop artists almost interchangeably. What does this say about the relationship between the U.S. and British cultures?

4. How do you think hip hop represents late 20th-century America? What particular values or beliefs does the musical style embody?

5. Make a case that Yates's article should have appeared in Chapter 2, "Consumerism: How We Spend." In other words, explain why his ideas are more related to how we consume than what we do to entertain ourselves.

Forging Connections

1. Consider the ways nature gets used to sell products and services. For example, in car commercials, vast desert landscapes often surround a family sedan, rushing mountain streams are used to market beer, and forest canopies help to sell sleeping pills. Write an essay that examines the America's relationship with nature through advertisement. What do our ads suggest about the purpose of the natural world? What do they suggest about its role in human life or our role in the world around us? What kinds of attitudes and beliefs about nature do our most common ads reinforce? Borrow insights from Robert Moor, "Mother Nature's Sons" (Chapter 7) and Freddie deBoer, "The Resentment Machine" (Chapter 2).

2. Examine the language of your favorite movie or television program. Study the characters' vocabulary, use, formality, and dialect. What

particular phrases get repeated or promoted? What do those phrases suggest about the shared values? Write an analytical essay—or what is sometimes called an *ethnography*—about the language and the way it shapes the community of characters. Before writing, consider the strategies of writers in Chapter 3, "Language: What We Mean," specifically Blake Gopnik ("Revolution in a Can"), Robert Lane Greene ("OMG, ETC"), and Autumn Whitefield-Madrano ("Thoughts on a Word: Fine"). Although these writers have different purposes, they explore language and its influence on communities. As you develop your essay, integrate specific quotations and phrases from the movie or program.

Looking Further

1. Whether we like or not, television programs have messages. They suggest politics, tension between genders, age groups, races, classes, and religious traditions. Even the absence of people reinforces a way of thinking. For example, until the 2009 appearance of Susan Boyle on *Britain's Got Talent,* such programs consistently reinforced the idea that superstar singers are, or should be, young and sexy. This wasn't an overt message, but it was suggested by a range of judgments, storylines, camera angles, and audience responses. Take on a specific television program and examine the social or political messages it suggests. Write an analytical essay that focuses on one of those messages. Explain how the program whispers, implies, and quietly reinforces the message. Integrate quotations, images, and scene descriptions—anything to help illustrate your point.

2. What is your favorite genre of music? Examine its role as an economic force. As Yates does with rap music ("The Sound of Capitalism"), explore the way another genre has become part of the broader culture of commerce. What particular artists, albums, or technological advances helped the genre to become a viable part of the economy? What musical qualities or marketing strategies (or both) developed the genre into something that generates revenue and sustains the art form? Develop an essay that explains its emergence and role in people's lives. Rather than making a case for or against the genre, try to analyze it. Try to uncover why it has thrived—or barely survived—in the marketplace.

Nature: How We Share the Planet

7

Americans have always had a complex relationship with the wild. As quickly as possible, early colonists drove back the forests and the uncertainties they contained. Through the eighteenth and nineteenth centuries, settlers turned the hardwood forests that blanketed much of the continent into vast agricultural zones. And the industrial revolution turned lakes and rivers into shipping highways. But through those years, Americans also preserved much open country from their own commercial needs. They called for, and even mandated, restraint so that segments of a once vast wilderness would live on.

Today, some politicians call for remaining wild places to be charted out for drilling and mining. Others argue for increased preservation. Some Americans want at least part of the country to remain wild whereas others want to extract as many resources as possible. For some, the untouched land is, itself, a resource. For others, it is wasteland unless mined. But most Americans, despite their political positions, take refuge in the natural places within our borders: the Grand Canyon, the Everglades, the Painted Desert, the Great Lakes, or the thousands of rivers that run through the country. People take their families to the mountains, to the beaches, or even to the small parks in their hometowns. And many hard-working, city-dwelling Americans dream of retiring on a small plot of land surrounded by woods and wilderness. In short, American culture is unsure about nature—what it's for, what it can do, what it should do, and what we should do for or within it.

Just as the lawn, trees, and bushes around a home say something about the people inside, the waterways, shorelines, and forests around a country say something about a culture's reflexes. We can learn something about America, then, by looking at the way it treats the natural world. We can understand some tensions, yearnings, and dynamics at work. The writers in this chapter all assume, to some degree, a deep relationship between nature and culture. They all share a reverence—or at least respect—for the natural world beyond human engineering. But they also understand, as Michael Shellenberger and Ted Nordhaus argue, that a complex human civilization need not be the antithesis of nature. Ongoing modernization, and the culture it creates, might be veering closer, not further, from the wild.

Jerry Dennis
Smoke Gets in Your Eyes

A nature writer and conservationist, Jerry Dennis seeks the poetry inherent in nature. He was named the Michigan Author of the Year by the Michigan Library Association in 1999 and a global "Action Figure" for his environmental activism by the independent news organization Circle of Blue in 2012. The author of numerous nature books, Dennis has published several essays and short stories in such publications as *Audubon*, *Epoch*, *Michigan Quarterly Review*, the *New York Times*, *Orion*, and *Smithsonian*. In the following excerpt from his book *From a Wooden Canoe* (1999), Dennis examines the role of fire in human culture.

A campfire is only as good as the wood it is built with, an easy truth learned the hard way by many a camper hunched hungry and cold over a smoking pile of basswood. If you appreciate a good campfire—better yet, if you appreciate the difference between a good campfire and a great campfire—you're probably a connoisseur of wood and a fastidious builder of woodpiles. Our breed could live by the credo "Not Just Any Stick Will Do."

Camping manuals often recommend packing those dinky folding camp saws, some of which have nothing more than a length of serrated wire for a blade. The implication is that cutting wood on a camping trip is no big deal and you might not want to bother bringing a saw at all. Sure, you can break enough wood over your knee to get by, if all you want from a fire is enough heat to warm your Spam and maybe smoke-dry a pair of socks. But if you're after more than mere utility you flat-out need a decent saw and an ax.

Substandard woodcutting implements are not only frustrating, they're dangerous. One of the first things you learn in Boy Scouts is that if you must use a hatchet, never swing it freely to chop wood. Instead, cut a mallet—a two-foot length of branch the diameter of a rolling pin or baseball bat—and use the mallet to drive the head of the hatchet like a splitting wedge. Better yet, use an ax. An ax can have a shortened handle for convenient transport, but it should be hefty enough to prevent it from glancing off a chunk of firewood—the most common cause of ax and hatchet accidents. Likewise, don't waste your money on a flimsy camp saw. Spend the extra ten or twenty bucks for a good one like the Schmidt Packsaw, which is made in Maine of red oak, folds into a compact, safe package, and can cut logs up to a foot in diameter. Thus armed, you can get on with the important business of cutting and stacking wood.

I like building woodpiles, enjoy their suggestion of industry and readiness and the aura of permanence they lend to a campsite. When I make camp, even a quick camp I know will last only until the next morning, the first thing I do after putting up the tent is get to work on the woodpile. Thoreau's famous dictum that his fire warmed him twice suggests the great holistic truth of open fires. The pleasure is much greater than the flame itself. It starts with the cutting, carrying, splitting, and stacking of the wood, and it continues through every stage of building, lighting, and feeding the fire. It doesn't end until the last orange coal winks out in its bed of ashes.

5   The reason thousands of homeowners prefer real fireplaces to gas imitations should be obvious. An open fire appeals to all the senses. The crack of
exploding resin, the enthusiastic whoop of flame sucking oxygen, the
thump of a log settling into coals are sounds we learn to associate with con-
tentment and well-being. A fire sounds good and looks good. It also smells
good. If I didn't come home surrounded by a nimbus of campfire scent, I'd
think the weekend had been wasted. Woodsmoke flushes tear ducts and
perfumes a body with the aroma of the woods. Anyone with a fairly good
nose learns the differences among those aromas. You can recognize the
bright fragrance of mesquite, the subtle sweetness of
cherry, the cloying thickness of balsam and spruce
and red cedar.

"The reason
thousands of
homeowners prefer
real fireplaces to gas
imitations should be
obvious."

Everyone seems to have their favorite firewood. Thoreau liked "hard green wood just cut"
because it burned long enough to be waiting in
his cabin when he came home after walking for
hours. Sigurd Olson gathered old pine knots that
had lain for years under pine needles, preserved by
the heavy resin impregnated in their grains, and considered burning them
a spiritual event. Edward Abbey gathered desert juniper for his "squaw" fire
and declared it "the sweetest fragrance on the face of the earth. . . . I doubt
if all the smoking censers of Dante's paradise could equal it."

Aldo Leopold insisted that mesquite, that ubiquitous shrub of the
Southwest, was the best of fragrant fuels. "Brittle with a hundred frosts
and floods," he wrote in *A Sand County Almanac,* "baked by a thousand
suns, the gnarled imperishable bones of these ancient trees lie ready-to-
hand at every camp, ready to slant blue smoke across the twilight, sing a
song of teapots, bake a loaf, brown a kettle of quail, and warm the shins of
man and beast."

In the upland forests of the Great Lakes region, our campfire wood of
choice is dead maple, air-dried on the stump. We look for saplings a few
inches in diameter that died young in the battle for sunlight and space,
crowded out by bigger, more robust trees. They're found in every stand of
hardwoods, in the shade of every grandfather maple, sometimes dying in
thickets dense as cane brakes. Long after they lose their leaves, branches,
and bark, the dead saplings remain upright, bone dry, brittle, and clean, like
ancient lances. They can be brought down with a push, dragged to camp,
and sawed into lengths. They split easily into kindling, or, burned in the

round, roar with flame and heat, creating a fire that burns for hours, sends a trail of fragrant smoke wisping through the woods, and builds a bed of coals that lasts the night. Those small logs of maple can be stacked so neatly that there's a tendency to construct woodpiles that will live on long after you've left a camp.

· ❖ ·

There's an art to building a fire, and those who get good at it tend to become intolerant of techniques other than their own. The first time Kelly Galloup and I camped together, on a stretch of trout river in Michigan, we circled each other warily, each certain the other would put together a less-than-perfect fire. It was raining—had been all day—and the fire demanded special attention. We went in opposite directions looking for wood. Both of us sought old pine, the remnant stumps of white and red pines cleared in the turn-of-the-century logging frenzy that decimated the old forests of Michigan. Kelly got back to camp before me and whittled the wet wood away from the dry, resin-soaked heart of the pine and placed it at the center of a teepee of maple and cedar. I was relieved to see that he knew what he was doing.

The secret is patience and oxygen. The more adverse the conditions—the wetter the woods and the scarcer the fuel—the more important it is to take your time. Kindling must be dry and abundant, larger wood stacked at hand and ready to apply one stick at a time. The foundation of a fire is built on a carefully assembled structure of dry tinder. It must be solid enough to resist falling apart but spacious enough to allow air to circulate to the flames. A hundred camp manuals suggest a hundred techniques, but nothing teaches better than trial and error.

When there's fire, of course, there's smoke. When we were children my friends and I were convinced that saying the phrase "I hate rabbits" would cause pesky smoke to shift away from us. The habit stuck. We're adults now, too often distracted by adult problems, but when we sit around a campfire together, sipping drinks, eating, talking, we still squint and lean back as the smoke turns in our direction, and, without thinking, say, "Rabbits."

The fire is the heart of a camp. It connects us with a hundred generations of fire watchers, making us part of a tradition so ancient and elemental it has no name. A fire initiates conversation, breaks social ice, gives comfort and satisfaction. It's especially satisfying when you can watch it change your old friends into kids again.

Analyze

1. How does the reference to Henry David Thoreau (in paragraph 4) support Dennis's main idea?
2. How does Dennis's description of maple saplings relate to his main idea?
3. What does the description of different wood types do for the reader? How do these passages affect you and your understanding of fire?
4. For Dennis, fire is more than flame and smoke—more than combustion and heat. In your own words, explain the role of fire for firewatchers like Dennis.
5. Based on this essay, what do you think Dennis would say about humans' relationship to nature?

Explore

1. Are you a firewatcher? If so, what does an open fire do for you—or to you? If you're not a firewatcher, why not?
2. Why do most adults in our culture move away from nature? Why do they associate camping, fishing, and fire building exclusively with childhood?
3. What do you think Dennis's essay says about our culture at this point in time? What does it suggest about the people—our beliefs, our hopes, and our abilities?
4. In the concluding chapter of his book *The Living Great Lakes,* Dennis makes the following statement. How does it make you rethink the essay printed here? What does it suggest about fire, wood, smoke, and fire building?

> The world overflows with bounty. It's rich and diverse and nearly inexhaustible. But here's the dilemma: The things of the earth are fascinating, amazing, bizarre, wonderful—and insufficient. We need more. We've always been driven to explore not only the physical world but our responses to it. Bracketed by mysteries, adrift, alone, despairing of our ignorance, we turn to the physical because there, at least, we can know a thing or two for certain. But we're creatures of spirit, too. It's our spirit that makes us encounter the wonders of the world and know that they are wonders.

Stephanie Mills
Some Words for the Wild

A nature writer and ecological activist, Stephanie Mills explores human relationships with the natural world. Named one of the world's leading visionaries by *Utne Reader* in 1996, she is the author of numerous books, including *Tough Little Beauties* (2007), from which the following essay is excerpted. Here, Mills examines the impact of human culture on natural environments.

Thirty years ago, when I was a youthful hothead, we decried the callous absurdity of a society that was knee-deep in garbage, firing rockets at the moon.

Today we're in the midst of the sixth great extinction crisis. The climate is changing even faster than scientists first warned. 1.1 billion human beings lack access to potable water, and the United States, or rather the ruling cabal of the United States, insists on building a missile defense system to protect us from some yet-to-be-named enemy.

About that extinction crisis: technology and globalization have, over the last half-millennium, done for the planet's biodiversity what the asteroid that hit the earth and put paid to the dinosaurs did. Given the imminent consequences of global warming for nature and humanity, it seems fair at this point to call anything that promotes increased consumption of fossil fuels heinous. Transoceanic and transcontinental trade, trucking, and mass travel by conventional means—the delivery systems of globalization—all come under this heading. The synergy of technology and globalization is ending the evolution of whole lineages of life and even threatens whole biomes.

The engines of destruction have been gaining momentum since 1692, when, legend has it, a Dutch sailor shipwrecked on an islet off Mauritius saw and, perhaps, ate the last dodo bird. It was an inadvertent thing, just a side effect of the navigation of the Indian Ocean in a quest for resources, markets, and territory. The sailing vessel was the technology of globalization that happened to end the dodo's evolutionary journey and enrich the idioms for deadness.

5   Today, according to the International Union for the Conservation of Nature's Red List of Threatened Species, one in four mammal species and one in eight bird species face a high risk of extinction. In the last 500 years human activity has forced 816 species to extinction or extinction in the wild. The rate of extinctions now is fifty times what it would be without benefit of modern economics and technology. "Fifty times" is an aggregated number, but the reality consists of distinct lives and traits and talents—the wonders of nature and the basis of life.

Today, like Thoreau, I wish to speak a word for nature, because nature's flourishing—which means our own—is under devastating assault. So I'm going to talk about some of those lives and traits and talents, to flesh in some of the details of what's going on out there beyond the human community.

Why do you suppose that Thoreau, that great American pencil-maker and sage, tax resister and bean planter, declared that "in wildness is the preservation of the world"?

It's because evolution is wild. This 4.5 billion year old planet has been, for all but the tiniest fraction of its history, wild. Of its own self-will, Earth has brought forth marvels: bowerbirds, coral reefs, compass plants, jellyfish, white pines, snow fleas, lammergaier vultures, root fungi, monarch butterfly migrations, 290,000 species of beetles, rainforests, prairies, sperm whales, wallabies, strangler figs, sturgeon, purple lady slippers and *Homo sapiens*. Natural barriers like oceans and mountain ranges promoted this wild variety of life forms, this natural diversity and cultural diversity and its fruit. The adaptations to place and circumstance and the vast web of relationships amongst all these creatures are astonishing, but mostly disregarded.

Consider the yucca and the yucca moth. This is a story of seed for seeds. Most insects pollinate flowers incidentally, on their way to the nectar. In some species of Chihuahuan yucca and yucca moths, though, the female moths have specialized mouthparts with which they collect pollen from the yucca flowers. They gather pollen and stuff a big ball of it into the yucca flower's stigma, the part that leads to its ovary, which holds the future yucca seeds and is also the place where the moth deposits her eggs. Thus a portion of the fertile seeds will feed the larvae, the future yucca moths. Insect pollination as deliberate as this is quite unusual. The moths and the yucca depend on each other. When the moths are absent, the yuccas don't set seed and soon die out. And when the yuccas are absent there are no yucca moth nurseries. Such vital partnerships are everywhere in the wild and generally

overlooked when CEOs and their henchpeople in lab coats try to stream-
line nature for profit.

Although Thoreau undoubtedly never saw a Chihuahuan yucca, he was 10
a keen observer of the forestry practices of his neighbors the squirrels and
jays, and understood their collaboration with oaks and pines. All the free
self-willed phenomena he saw during his sauntering around Concord must
indeed have declared to Thoreau that in wildness is the preservation of the
world. Wildness tells us that everything is hitched to everything else. But
the extinction crisis is rapidly uncoupling myriad vital relationships and
fraying the fabric of life on earth.

We may take from Thoreau that we should hearken to our own deepest
experience. As a species, human beings have more experience being wild,
living as semi-nomadic subsistence peoples embedded in healthy ecosystems, than in any other lifeway. For about ninety thousand years, wild
was us. Agriculture has been going on a mere ten thousand years; reliance
on fossil fuels a hundred and fifty years, and only in the last thirty years
has human life come under the influence of computer-based technology.
Subsistence is given by the whole web of life. But in the accelerating drive
to subjugate nature to profit—the narrowest of human purposes—
technologies that are blundering in the extreme and global in their effects
are unleashed.

In the manufacture of paper, plastics, pesticides, and refrigerants, the
chemical industry has managed to pervade the tissues of most higher animals on the planet with persistent organic pollutants (POPs). Many of
these chemicals mimic hormones. They interfere with the reproduction
and development processes of many vertebrates. Such hormone disrupters
have induced subtle damaging changes in the behavior and intelligence of
children born to mothers whose diet included fish with such POPs concentrated in their flesh. In some places, alligators, cormorants, and gulls have
hatched with deformed gonads. Are learning-disabled kids and impotent
wildlife a reasonable price to pay for profit, or even progress?

Nobody knew or thought to ask whether propellants like freon would
eat ozone. But they do, and extra ultraviolet radiation exposure is a consequence. Increased UV exposure seems to be among the reasons that frog
populations around the world are crashing. Nobody even knows where
trifluoromethyl sulfur pentafluoride, a greenhouse gas 18,000 times more
potent than CO_2, comes from, but it's in the atmosphere doing its warming
work now.

Meanwhile, the trade geniuses are arguing against the precautionary principle. That is the sensible idea that new chemistries, technologies, and other tampering with evolution should be presumed hazardous until proven innocent. Economic activities like long-wall coal mining, gold extraction by cyanide leaching, clearcut forestry, petroleum exploration, drilling, and transport do their visible, immediate damage locally, but in sum they also accelerate a planetary extinction crisis. Unbridled profiteering at the expense of the wild has been effecting ecosystem-scale damage for centuries. The world trade in furs did a job on the North American landscape by decimating its beavers, of which there were an estimated 60 million in 1492. With their appropriate-scale, low-tech dam-building talents, beavers renewed the landscape. Their pond-making, water filtration, and meadow creation led to a rich patchwork of habitats. Tough luck for the beavers that in the 18th century beaver hats were all the rage. In just one year, 1743, just two shipments of furs to France included over 150,000 beaver skins between them.

15   The modern era, then, with its relatively crude technologies like rifles, steel leg-hold traps, double-bitted axes, two-man saws, ox-drawn sleds, canoes, railroads and steamers, spurred the extinction crisis. Wildlife and wild habitats in the "New World" were already depleted and fragmented going into our era of megatechnology and globalization. Today's technologies of mass commercial transportation—jets, cargo ships, tankers, superhighways, and trucking, even electrical transmission lines and towers—are intrinsically destructive of ecosystems. For instance, a conservative estimate finds that each year 80 million birds die due to collision when power lines and towers impede their natural migratory cues. Larger birds are simply electrocuted. Several of the newly released California condors, fetched back from the jaws of extinction by a captive breeding program, met their doom in exactly this way.

No wonder there are Luddites still among us!

In a famous article in the April 2000 issue of *Wired* magazine, Bill Joy, a cybergenius who describes himself as "an architect of complex systems," published "Why the Future Doesn't Need Us," which created a serious buzz. In it, Joy worried aloud about the imminent advances in, and synergy of, robotics, genetically engineered organisms, and nanotechnology. These technologies share, he said, "a dangerous amplifying factor: they can self-replicate."

Thus we may have to confront a technology that is not just *autonomous,* to use Langdon Winner's formulation, but *autopoetic.* Joy feared that certain applications of these technologies might be capable of reducing life on the planet to "gray goo," if, say, a rogue nanobot with a mind of its own and a bad attitude flew the coop.

We have good historical grounds for expecting bad things to result from the introduction of alien organisms to innocent environments. In addition to being the vehicles for extracting resources from the New World, the sailing vessels that launched the modern colonial era were vectors for a biological invasion of the new world.

Local extinctions are a common result of biological invasion. And "local" can be as large as Lake Michigan. Here's a for-instance. The Great Lakes basin's aquatic fauna was revolutionized by commerce and transportation in little more than a century. First over-fishing stressed the system, and then the construction of the Erie and third Welland canals allowed the sea lamprey to enter the Lakes and dine heavily on the native lake trout, which were top predators. Too bad, because the lake trout could have come in handy to eat up some of the millions of invasive alewives. The alewife is an oceanic fish that entered and naturalized in the lakes, but with limited success. Occasionally at spawning time, the alewives, poorly adapted for life in fresh water, will die by the millions, leaving Lake Michigan's shores piled with drifts of rotting fish. Meanwhile, the sea lamprey were beat back with poisons and spawning barriers, and Pacific salmon were introduced to fill the niche of the lake trout. The salmon aren't reproducing naturally in the lakes, but the sport fishers like to catch them, so Michigan continues to stock the lakes with hatchery fish. Hatcheries, which are basically aquatic feedlots, are themselves problematic because they produce nutrient-laden effluents that degrade water quality. That tragicomedy of ecological errors gets us from the mid-nineteenth to the mid-twentieth century in the Great Lakes.

Late in the twentieth century, just 13 years ago, came zebra mussels, lurking in the ballast waters of some vessel that passed through the Caspian Sea. These little mollusks are so enormously prolific that they smother and out-compete native mussels and hamper their reproduction. Zebra mussels gum up the works of lakeside cities by encrusting and clogging water intake pipes. They are so numerous that their filter feeding is making the water too clear, which may be causing blooms of blue-green algae. These algae blooms make life difficult for still other old-time residents of the lakes.

It seems only fair to ask whether, with regard to technology and globalization, we know what we are doing. The sorry state of the Great Lakes ecosystem is just one piece of evidence arguing that the answer to that question is no and hell no. Bear in mind that all of those biological upsets were accomplished without benefit of NAFTA, GMOs and nanotechnology.

The commodities, conveniences, and consumer goods whose mass production is the justification for much of this technical innovation and trade liberalization are marketed now on an unprecedented scale. There are six billion of us. Whereas, just at the turn of the last millennium, there were a paltry 275 million human beings, and most of the world had yet to suffer the onslaught of what the West was pleased to call civilization. So the sheer magnitude of the human population accounts, in part, for the magnitude of the effects that the planet is experiencing.

Notice the two opposing patterns: globalization leads to simplification and instability, not to mention ugliness and misery; evolution leads to diversity, dynamic equilibrium, life, and beauty. Structural alternatives like relocalization can favor life's flourishing. Locales have always outlasted empires. And the collapse of empires is the rule, not the exception.

The vision and power and will to resist corporate imperialism and its technological tyrannies, and to implement diverse alternatives, desperately need to be kindled. Most large-scale human interventions in the planet's biology have worked like giving a Swiss watch a tuneup with a sledge hammer. People are beginning to understand this, but assume as given that you can't stop progress.

• ❖ •

25   As he pondered the Promethean technologies he saw emerging, Joy looked to the reflections of Freeman Dyson, a theoretical physicist, on the development and use of the atom bomb, certainly one of the most horrific manifestations to date of what Dyson himself termed "technical arrogance."

The race to mutually assured destruction began with the bomb. Dyson said that "the reason that it was dropped was just that nobody had the courage or foresight to say no."

Nevertheless, at the end of his article, Bill Joy comes to the conclusion that "the only realistic alternative"—to gray goo, I guess—is to have the courage to say no. Joy proposes *relinquishment:* to limit development of the technologies that are too dangerous by limiting our pursuit of certain kinds of knowledge.

Is it too late to direct those inquiring minds back to the task of learning the plants? Or too late to promote the idea that it is not knowledge that's scarce, but wisdom and the wildness that engenders the flourishing of human, and more than human life?

Analyze

1. Explain how Mills's allusion to the dodo bird (in paragraph 4) relates to her main idea.
2. What is Mills's purpose? She explains that she is, on one level, speaking for nature. But what else is she up to? Is she informing, persuading, entertaining, solving, or something else? Be as specific as possible in your response.
3. How does Mills's claim that "evolution is wild" relate to her main idea? And how does it relate to her purpose?
4. If you have not already read and studied Henry David Thoreau, look him up. Read a bit about his life and writing, and then explain why Mills relies on Thoreau—why she puts him at the center of her own writing.
5. Mills explains that "for about ninety thousand years, wild was us." What does she mean? Why is this a critical point in her essay?

Explore

1. Unlike some other writers in this chapter, Mills openly and directly condemns specific practices and people who seek to exploit the natural world. What passage do you think is most condemning?
2. How is Mills's essay about the tension between tradition and change? What type of change is she suggesting? What forms of tradition are in the way?
3. Are you caught up in the "technological tyranny" that Mills describes? Why or why not?
4. Mills argues, "Most large-scale human interventions in the planet's biology have worked like giving a Swiss watch a tuneup with a sledgehammer." Explain at least one "large-scale human intervention" and how it worked, as Mills says, like a sledgehammer on a watch.
5. Mills says that the "collapse of empires is the rule, not the exception." How does this rule figure into your life—or manage not to? What is your relationship with the inevitable collapse of our culture? How do you consider or avoid the idea?

Hugh Pennington
Bug-Affairs

Hugh Pennington is a bacteriologist who explores the history and politics of public health, disease, and food-borne illness. He is the author of numerous articles and books, including the 2005 book *Food Poisoning, Policy and Politics: Corned Beef and Typhoid in Britain in the 1960s*. In the following journal article, Pennington examines our cultural relationship with bedbugs over time.

Bedbugs never went away. DDT gave them a hard time in the 1940s and for years afterwards, until Rachel Carson's campaigns outlawed it, but resistant strains survived. Other insecticides—synthetic organophosphates and pyrethroids—have come and gone, but none has been a challenge for the bugs' versatile genomes. Blood is their only food. The bug explores the skin of its victim with its antennae. It grips the skin with its legs for leverage, raises its beak, and plunges it into the tissues. It probes vigorously, tiny teeth at the tip of the beak tearing the tissues to forge a path until it finds a suitable blood vessel. A full meal takes 10 to 15 minutes. A hungry bug is squat and flat like a lentil. When replete, its distension shapes it like a long berry. A bug will feed weekly from any host that is handy.

Bedbugs do not spread disease. Their presence has been taken as an indicator of poor home hygiene, and they can be a precipitant of entomophobia, but beyond that they haven't had much significance for public health. Nobody counts them or keeps national records of infestation rates. There are hardly any 20th-century baseline measures that might enable us to assess the accuracy of claims that there has been an upsurge in the 21st. Anecdote has driven the perception that the bugs have gone on the rampage, and epidemiologists are reluctant to put much weight on stories. But the recent ones have been very persuasive. In New York in 2010 bedbugs turned up in the Empire State Building, a theatre in the Lincoln Center, and at the Metropolitan Opera House. It is said that they were in attendance at the 2005 Labour Party Conference in Brighton, and in 2006 they were found in a guest room at the five-star Mandarin Oriental Hyde Park Hotel in Knightsbridge. Analyses show that the number of bedbug calls to pest controllers in London and Australia has increased significantly since 2000.

Why the resurgence? The bugs' resistance to insecticides has been blamed, along with the increase in international travel and in the sale of second-hand furniture. Genetic fingerprinting of the bugs might shed light on the comparative importance of movement from city to city, travel across national boundaries and purely local spread; but such studies have only just started. In truth our understanding of how bedbugs get about has changed little since 1730, when John Southall published his *Treatise of Buggs:*

> By Shipping they were doubtless first brought to *England,* so are they now daily brought. This to me is apparent, because not one Sea-Port in *England* is free; whereas in Inland-Towns, Buggs are hardly known ... If you have occasion to change Servants, let their Boxes, Trunks, &c. be well examin'd before carried into your Rooms, lest their coming from infected Houses should prove dangerous to yours ... Upholsterers are often blamed in Bugg-Affairs; the only Fault I can lay to their Charge, is their Folly, or rather Inadvertency, in suffering old Furniture, when they have taken it down, because it was buggy, to be brought into their Shops or Houses, among new and free Furniture, to infect them.

Southall's worries about the role of ships in transporting bedbugs persisted. Robert Usinger, the author of the monumental *Monograph of Cimicidae* (the family to which the bedbug belongs), saw a thriving colony of the tropical bedbug, *Cimex hemipterus,* on a liner sailing from Hong Kong to San Francisco. But local transport is just as much of a problem. In 1944, Usinger was bitten by the common bug, *Cimex lectularius,* on a bus in Atlanta, Georgia. And in the summer of 1947 a number of ladies in Dundee were referred to the local dermatologist because they had developed a red band studded with blisters, some described as being "as big as a pigeon's egg," on the backs of their calves. All of them had travelled on the lower deck of a tram on the same route. Investigation showed that only one tram was infested. The bugs had settled in a groove in a wooden slat that held a seat in place. They sat in a row on the edge of the wood, the dermatologist said, "extracting nourishment from the legs of unsuspecting lady passengers. Men were never affected, their stouter nether garments providing sufficient protection. The tram was disinfected, the grooves were planed out ... the epidemic came to an end."

In 2008, bugs were found on the New York subway, on wooden benches on station platforms at Hoyt-Schermerhorn in Brooklyn, Union Square in Manhattan and Fordham Road in the Bronx, and in 2010 in a booth at Ninth Street Station on the D Line. "If you put out your Linnen to wash," 5

Southall said, "let no Washer-woman's Basket be brought into your houses; for they often prove as dangerous to those that have no Buggs." The Australian Quarantine and Inspection Service has found bedbugs at airports in woven cane baskets and woven straw bags—as well as on roses from Kenya, in baggage from Europe, and on an airport inspection bench.

So it is clear that bedbugs can hitch-hike long distances and ride about town. But how good they are at very local travel remains undetermined. Urban myths have been around for a long time. "Bedbugs are popularly credited with an amazing amount of intelligence," observed the British Ministry of Health's "Report on the Bedbug" in 1934. "It is stated that they will travel long distances, 50 yards or more, in search of food, will unerringly choose the direction in which their food is to be found, will go by way of windows, eaves and gutters if unable to get through the party wall, and will drop from the ceiling onto their victims. We are not prepared to say how much of this may be due to popular superstition." The report was produced because "the infestation of new council houses has become a matter of concern to Local Authorities who are responsible for their maintenance and management." Whether bugs became common in these council houses is not clear; it is certain, however, that the current upsurge in bedbug numbers cannot be blamed on an increase in social housing stock.

Hundreds of scientific papers have been published on bugs, though funding for bug research has never been easy to get because of their medical unimportance. Surveys of prevalence are expensive and are hardly ever done. But bugs are easy to keep in the laboratory. Some investigators have allowed bugs to feed on them for convenience, and to save money. Much attention has been paid to their method of reproduction. Males mate preferentially with recently fed females. The male sexual organ, called the paramere, has a sharp point, which the male bug uses to penetrate the abdominal wall of the female. Sperm are injected into the abdominal cavity. This process is sometimes lethal; repeated matings reduce the female lifespan. This sexual conflict of interests has been of great interest to evolutionary biologists.

Males attempt to mate with any moving object the size of a fed female, including juvenile bugs and males who have sucked blood. But in these cases they dismount quickly—good news both for the male, who doesn't waste his sperm, and for the mountee, since penetration would quite likely have perforated his guts to mortal effect. The males back off because inappropriate partners produce chemical deterrents—alarm pheromones. Their smell is easily detected by humans. It has been described as an "obnoxious sweetness," and is characteristic of a bedroom with a heavy infestation. It is highly likely that these pheromones are what the bedbug-sniffer dog detects. Two firms in Florida train them, usually using animals rescued from shelters. One firm prefers beagle mixes, the other labrador retriever mixes. Bold claims are made for their success. New York City is hiring two, and Lola, a Jack Russell bitch, has been imported into the UK.

Bedbugs avoid the light and are thigmotactic: they love contact with rough surfaces. They seek cracks and crevices, preferably in wood or paper, in which they establish refugia to digest their meals and breed, among an accumulation of faeces, egg shells and cast-off skins. Bugs in refugia are hard to reach with pesticides. Drastic measures have been used. A note in the *Journal of the Royal Army Medical Corps* in 1926 entitled "Disinfestation of Barracks" records that the British Army of the Rhine had been contacted by the representative of a firm in Frankfurt am Main who wanted to explain the use of a substance with the trade name Zyklon "B." He described it as "siliceous earth impregnated with hydrogen cyanide, to which is added a tear gas," and noted that it was extensively used by the German government. A large advertisement inside the front cover of the standard German work on bedbugs published in 1936 says: "Zyklon and T-Gas exterminates bugs ... without damaging the furnishings."

The current upsurge has been good news for pest controllers. Booksellers have benefited too: a copy of Southall's 44-page treatise was auctioned by Bonhams at Oxford in October 2010, and despite being disbound, lacking a frontispiece and having numerous ink annotations, went for £132 inclusive of the buyer's premium. And bugs have brought business to lawyers. The landmark case this century has been Mathias v. Accor Economy Lodging Inc. The plaintiffs, Burl and Desiree Mathias, were bitten by bugs while staying at a Motel 6 in downtown Chicago. They claimed that in allowing guests to be attacked by bedbugs in rooms costing upwards of $100 a day, the defendant was guilty of willful and wanton conduct. The jury awarded each plaintiff $5000 in compensatory damages and $186,000 in punitive damages. The defendant appealed, complaining primarily about the level of the punitive damages, but the appeal court judge, Richard Posner, dismissed the appeal. His decision was bold: a Supreme Court statement had been made not long before that "few awards exceeding a single-digit ratio between punitive and compensatory damages, to a significant degree, will satisfy due process." Posner noted that bedbugs had been discovered at the motel in 1998 by EcoLab, an extermination service. They recommended that every room be sprayed, at a cost of $500. The motel refused. Bugs were found again in 1999. The motel tried without success to get an exterminator to sweep the building free of charge. In the spring of 2000 the motel manager told her superior that guests were being bitten and were demanding, and receiving, refunds, and recommended that the motel be closed while every room was sprayed. Her boss refused. On one occasion a guest was moved from a room after being bitten, only to discover insects in the second room; then, within 18 minutes of being moved to a third, he found them there as well. "Odd that at that point he didn't flee the motel," Posner comments. He was unimpressed by the instruction given to desk clerks by the motel management that bedbugs should be called ticks, "apparently on the theory that customers would be less alarmed, though in fact ticks are more dangerous than bedbugs because they spread Lyme Disease and Rocky Mountain Spotted Fever." This is the bedbug paradox. For most individuals their bites have only nuisance value. Yet they arouse much more disgust than many other insects whose bites transmit potentially lethal infections.

The bugs in the Empire State Building, Lincoln Center Theater and the Met were found in the basement employee changing room, a dressing-room, and back of house. The likelihood of being bitten in a public place without beds is remote. And if the New York subway had the London Tube's metal seats rather than wooden ones there would be no bug refugia. Alleviation here would be easy. But it is unlikely that the public will come to terms with bugs. They will continue to turn to lawyers. Posner's judgment and its financial consequences are on record.

The bedbugs' lifestyle makes it unlikely that they will go away soon. The contrast with the body louse is instructive. Their refugia and breeding places are the seams of human clothing. Body heat is necessary for egg hatching, so those who take their underclothes off at night and change their garments more than once a month will never be very lousy even if they consort with those who are. The natural habitat of the bedbug is the home. In Europe and North America the only one left for the body louse is the homeless.

Analyze

1. What is Pennington's purpose? Do you think this article is attempting to inform, persuade, entertain, solve a problem, or something else? In short, what is Pennington up to?

2. Explain Pennington's introductory strategy. How does the description of a bedbug's feeding process fit into his overall purpose?
3. Pennington uses sources from decades and even centuries ago. Why? What do these texts from the past help to show?
4. How does Pennington's description of bedbug reproduction help to support or relate to his main idea?
5. This article was published in a British journal. How, then, is it about American culture?

Explore

1. Why do you think bedbugs create such alarm and disgust among people?
2. If you found bedbugs in your home, what steps would you take?
3. What does the resurgence of bedbugs in major U.S. cities say about us—about our culture, our relationship to nature, or our progress?
4. Pennington says that the American public will likely not "come to terms" with bedbugs and will, instead, "turn to lawyers." First, what do you think he means by "come to terms"? Second, do you agree?
5. Consider Rob Dunn's essay "Fly on Wall Sees Things It Wishes It Hadn't" in this chapter. How do Pennington and Dunn's points overlap? What assumptions or beliefs (about bugs or people or American culture) do they share?

Robert Moor
Mother Nature's Sons

A New York–based freelance writer and environmental journalist, Robert Moor examines environmental issues through a pop culture lens. His articles have appeared in such publications as *n+1* magazine, *New York* magazine, the *New York Observer,* and *OnEarth* magazine. In the following magazine article, Moor considers the gender implications of our culture's fascination with the great outdoors.

For the last few years I've been seeing woodsmen on my city's streets. They wear long beards and long hair, or long beards and no hair. They favor beat-up leather boots and wool beanies and jobs involving wood. At Best Made Co., a downtown boutique, they purchase hand-painted axes and canvas portage packs. At French atelier APC, they try on pieces by Carhartt, a manufacturer of blue-collar outdoor wear, that have been recut for slimmer legs and thicker wallets. Until recently, they were able to hone their bow-hunting skills in the basement archery range of clothier/ barbershop Freeman's Sporting Club. These urban dwellers seem to be getting ready for a long camping trip that never takes place; their flannel grows tatty and their boots scuffed, but they are never stained with real dirt.

Actual lumberjacks, of course, no longer wear flannel. They wear polyester fleeces and CAT boots and wraparound sunglasses and XXL T-shirts. Professional explorers (mountaineers, polar researchers) now wear outfits— often puffy down or synthetic loft in a breathable waterproof shell—that resemble spacesuits. Turn on the Discovery Channel or NatGeo, and you'll see both types of outdoorsman within two hours: the blue-collar workers emptying our forests of trees, our oceans of crabs, and our rivers of gold; and the explorers, Gore-Tex clad, embarking on extravagant, high-risk vacations. But in order to find Brooklyn's *noveaux voyageurs,* you'll need to flip over to FashionTV, because they do not exist in the wild.

In any era since the invention of polyester fleece, flannel is a patently absurd choice for outdoor work: when woven from wool it is too heavy; when woven from cotton it fails to retain heat once wet. But the fashion industry, in its ongoing campaign to dust off bygone archetypes of masculinity, has revived the fabric. Along with waxed canvas and leather, flannel plays an important role in repackaging the sex appeal of the vintage outdoorsman while sidestepping both the flimsy artificiality of petroleum-spun fabrics and also the earnestness of organic cloth, which carries with it a whiff of environmentalism—a supposedly emasculating ethos that prudishly promotes the suppression of desire.

Basic physics dictate that, in order to become more sustainable, technology must become ever lighter, quieter, and less hungry. Is it merely a coincidence that these engineering constraints also mirror our favored model of femininity? In a recent study, pollsters found that 82 percent of respondents felt that going green is "more feminine than masculine." The risk of feminine contamination, the researchers concluded, "holds men back from visible green behavior like using reusable grocery bags or carrying around reusable water bottles." Add to that the reproachful tone that environmentalists often resort to in their attempts to spread the gospel of Deep Ecology—which stresses the rights of the ecosystem over those of man—and you glimpse how environmentalists came to be miscast as sanctimonious nags.

To expiate their green guilt, tough guys go to extreme lengths: they live   5
in unheated houses, fuel their trucks with rancid cooking oil, subsist on other people's trash. The tension emerges most clearly with regards to food. Many progressives would like to eat local and organic but don't want to be seen as either pampering or depriving themselves (or both pampering *and* depriving themselves, like the diners in *Portlandia* who must personally visit a chicken on its farm before they can feel sure of its free-range pedigree). In an attempt to live more naturally, a few dozen men in New York City, along with one woman, have reportedly committed themselves to a so-called caveman diet. The diet's strictures allow them to eat only meat and vegetables—no grains, sugar, dairy, or oil—and requires days of fasting between meals. "I didn't want to do some faddish diet that my sister would do," one of the dieters told the *New York Times*.

Like many Americans, the cave people seem distrustful, even contemptuous, of vegan asceticism. Abstaining from animal byproducts is considered difficult, but not tough: your kid sister might gladly survive on barbecued seitan and cartons of Rice Dream. Even as progressive men renounce the traditional notion of subordinated femininity, many still harbor conflicted notions about manhood. They want to feel individually reckless, but not socially irresponsible. They want to minimize carbon emissions, but not to scold, scrimp, or carry tote bags. They want to be pure of deed but wild at heart. So they dig ever deeper into the past, searching for a way of life that existed before "real" men and their ecological consciences parted ways.

Five years ago—roughly when the ultra-rustic trend in men's fashion began—the Discovery Channel began broadcasting a reality series called *Man vs. Wild*. The man in question is a boyish, cocksure Brit named Bear Grylls, a professional adventurer who honed his survival skills as a trooper and a medic in the British Special Forces. In each episode, Grylls is dropped from a helicopter in various remote locations and is forced to find his way back to civilization on foot while eating slimy things and fending off the occasional predator. In the very first episode, raves the DVD jacket, Grylls "encounters a grizzly bear, jumps off a 70-foot cliff and floats nearly 12 miles in treacherous and freezing white water, all on a diet of rattlesnake, raw fish and worms." The show fascinated me, in part because Grylls appeared to resolve the problem of eco-masculinity: by adding radical self-sufficiency and the heightened possibility of death to the conservationist norm, he managed to look both principled and macho. Bear (real name Edward) is both a wild man and a man who worships the wild.

The show quickly attracted a loyal following among armchair outdoorsmen who watch basic cable, averaging over 1.6 million viewers in its first year. (At its peak—an episode guest-starring a bumbling, mock-terrified Will Ferrell—the show grabbed 4 million viewers, as many as last year's Stanley Cup finals.) But in 2006, allegations arose that Grylls had misled his viewers about the extent of his risk-taking. Among the outrages: after feigning sleep for few minutes in a crude shelter, Grylls was often spirited to a hotel; certain "wild" animals were in fact domesticated creatures brought in as props; and one memorable scene, in which Grylls leaped over a steaming volcanic fissure in Hawaii, was "enhanced" using hot coals and smoke machines to make the cool lava appear molten.

Grylls eventually apologized to his fans in interviews with BBC News and *Outside* magazine. Amazingly, his ratings rebounded; unlike readers of salacious memoirs, Grylls's viewers didn't seem to mind if their reality TV lacked a firm foundation in reality. The Discovery Channel attempted to sidestep the *Man vs. Wild* controversy by tacking on an awkward disclaimer to each episode warning that certain situations are "presented" to Grylls in order to "show the viewer how to survive." The wording is ironic, because the sharpest criticism leveled at the show was not that it was theatrical, but that it was dangerously misinformative.

10   In the years since, the Discovery Channel has doubled down on the Grylls model of survivalism, adding highly produced, minimally perilous fare like *Man, Woman, Wild* (which pits a survival expert and his lovely, weak-stomached wife against the elements) and *Dual Survival* (an *Odd Couple*–style pairing of barefoot hippie and military tough guy). Whenever I watch these shows, I catch myself wondering: why do they continue to feel so urgent, even when we know that the hosts are in no real danger?

Survival shows succeed in part because they grant us a false sense of ecological detente. At each episode's conclusion, when the professional survivalist emerges from the wilderness, his beard coated in hoarfrost or soil or dried blood, it allows us the comforting thought that we, too, if so imperiled, would pull through. To be successful entertainment, survival shows must be embellished, because if they showed the hardship unvarnished—like Les

Stroud's bleak, shivery *Survivorman*—or worse, if they were to end in death, that fantasy would be shattered.

When I was 10 years old, my parents dropped me off at Pine Island, a summer camp on a fishhook-shaped piece of land in the middle of a lake in Maine. For six weeks each summer, a few dozen other boys and I learned to live like 19th century woodsmen: we bathed in chilly lake water, read by the light of kerosene lanterns, slept in canvas tents, chopped wood, built fires, constructed hemlock shelters, fished, shot bolt-action .22s, hiked, canoed, and shat in holes dug in the ground. One year, on the third day of camp, a propane tank in the kitchen exploded and the camp burned down, but for some reason no one went home. While the camp was getting rebuilt, we bunked on cots in giant Army tents, wore clothes from the Salvation Army, and went on a lot of hiking trips in the nearby Appalachians. Occasionally I would sneak off to pick through the mounds of ash that used to be the dining hall or the library for souvenirs. It was like excavating relics of a lost civilization: spoons melted into dull tin blobs, charred photographs of children in strange costumes, rusty nails, lengths of rope, a Styrofoam buoy blackened but otherwise weirdly unscathed. During our lessons in shelter building or knife sharpening, I found myself listening with new interest, because the possibility of being stranded alone in the woods suddenly didn't seem so far-fetched.

I returned home with dirt caked so deep in the pores of my neck that my mother had to scrub for an hour with a washcloth to make me presentable. Over the fall and winter, I devoured Gary Paulsen's *Hatchet* series of survivalist YA novels, learned archery, had a brief flirtation with pyromania. I prowled my backyard, hunting Coke cans and the occasional squirrel with a BB gun. I returned to Pine Island the next summer, and the one after that. But in the years that followed, my jones for survivalism was worn down by the pumice of adolescence. In the preppy Chicago suburbs, starting fires and killing squirrels was behavior reserved for psychopaths.

I gradually forgot the small joys of rusticity—though I always missed, with a dull itch, the satisfying *thu-chunk* an axe makes when it splits a piece of wood. So in my freshman year of college, finding myself without a summer job, I applied for a position teaching woodcraft back at Pine Island. "Do you remember how to sharpen a knife? Triangulate your location on a topo map? Build a wet-wood fire?" the camp's director asked me. I didn't; the closest I'd come to building a fire in the last decade was remote-igniting the gas fireplace in my family's living room. "It's all right," he reassured me. "It's like riding a bike."

15   That summer, I spent my days watching tiny hands fumble around with sharp objects and spent my nights studying up to avoid looking incompetent in the eyes of 12-year-olds. I began obsessively reading survival guides—the authoritative *Wilderness Survival* by Gregory Davenport, the folksy *Primitive Living and Survival Skills* by John and Geri McPherson, the factually outdated but cleverly packaged *How to Stay Alive in the Woods* by Bradford Angiers, which came bound in stippled rubber, like a ping pong paddle. In an attempt to boost woodcraft class's notoriously poor attendance, I coined the catchphrase, "Woodcraft is wilderness survival. And wilderness survival is—cool." It was moronic, but for some reason it clicked with the kids. By the end of the summer, attendance had doubled.

Though we Pine Islanders defined ourselves primarily in opposition to other nearby camps—the snobs at Camp Kieve, the hippies at Chewonki, the Jewish water-skiers at Camp Modin—we were all inheritors of the same turn-of-the-century anxieties: fears of masculine degeneration, military frailty, urban sprawl, shrinking wilderness, and teenage ruffianism. America's first summer camp was founded in 1861 by an abolitionist named Frederick Gunn, who began taking boys on long hikes through the Connecticut foothills to recreate the living conditions of Union soldiers. Backpacking was—and to some extent, remains—a kind of de-weaponized marching. The original Boy Scouts of America uniforms were just miniaturized versions of U.S. Army fatigues. Over the years, the design underwent a series of makeovers, including an overhaul by Oscar De La Renta in 1980 to downplay the organization's martial overtones. When none other than Bear Grylls was dubbed the Chief Scout (or "king of the Scouts") in 2009, he posed for press photos in a hoodie, polo shirt, and khaki hiking pants. His sole gesture to the original uniform was a red-white-and-blue neckerchief cinched around his throat with a woven brass slide. Similarly, many of the movement's founding principles have been edited out over time—though not the neckerchiefs, aggressive patriotism, misappropriation of American Indian traditions, or the belief that teaching wilderness skills helps young boys mature into well-tempered adults.

But does exposure to wilderness turn boys into men? Much of the time, it seems the opposite: the woods are a place that men go to revert back to boyhood, to forget about the complex entanglements of love and career. What became clear to me in the course of teaching woodcraft is that survivalist gestures are a pantomime of the kind of self-reliance that adulthood is said to entail. The kids' hemlock shelters were always rickety and porous, their traps never caught any actual animals, and starting a fire in heavy rain—without resorting to chemical accelerants like white gas or Purell—was damn near impossible. What wilderness survival teachers ultimately impart is not knowledge, but sentiment: how it feels to flourish in a menacingly vast and alien environment. This is a good thing. Roughing it in the woods remains one of the few activities in American life where children can act out their transition into adulthood without resorting to the violent initiation rites of gang or military warfare.

Sometimes, after waking up, firing up my laptop, and scrolling through a newsfeed choked with stories about deforestation and strip mining and bottom-trawl fishing and toxified Chinese rivers and bleached coral reefs and ecosystems petrified into barren canyons of stucco and vinyl and brick, I stop reading and begin fantasizing about pressing a planetary reset button. I am not alone. For those of us who believe that the globe's ecosystem is inching toward a catastrophic tipping point, both in terms of population growth and the earth's ability to absorb anthropogenic waste, there are few foreseeable solutions. Techno-utopians hope that future scientific breakthroughs will let our growth and consumption continue to balloon; eco-moralists advocate indoctrinating young people in an ethos of sustainability; economists (and a handful of impervious Congress people) propose forcing polluters to "internalize the externalities" of their business activities through taxes, carbon credits and public shame. But as time goes on, these options—each valid in its own right—sound less like pragmatic possibilities.

If all else fails, there is another option that doesn't require of us any major shifts in paradigm or industry—only the resourcefulness to surf the wave of civilization as it crashes. Reversion is typically considered a fringe position, a campaign led by militant environmentalists and anarcho-primitivists. But its supposed extremism is belied by the popular interest in survivalists like Bear Grylls and the continued growth of institutions like the Boulder Outdoor Survival School, whose popular twenty-eight day survival field course costs nearly $4,000. Our culture's commitment to radical reversion as a fallback plan runs deeper than most people care to admit.

Like survivalism, the Reversion Option is an adolescent obsession held mainly by first-world males. The people who successfully lived (and continue to live) off the land, from Paleolithic Africa to modern Papua New Guinea, did so (and do so) with centuries of inherited cultural knowledge as well the benefits of a tight knit community and a lifetime of physical

20

conditioning. We have no such advantages—and subsequent generations will have even fewer.

Should the twilight of the Anthropocene come, the retro-woodsmen fashionistos would likely be among the first to die off. But some others—hardcore survivalists, off-the-gridders, those country boys that can still skin a buck and run a trout line—might survive. And as they comb through the storefronts of downtown Manhattan for supplies, one imagines that beneath the piles of moth-eaten flannel and sun-cracked leather they might uncover an axe—beautifully crafted, with a handle of Appalachian hickory and a gleaming head of 5160 high carbon steel—and finally put it to its intended use.

Analyze

1. Moor explains that environmentalists are often seen as "sanctimonious nags." How does this admission fit into his main idea?
2. According to Moor, what is the "problem of eco-masculinity?"
3. How does the reference and explanation of *Man vs. Wild* support Moor's main idea?
4. Consider Sameer Pandya's essay, "The Picture for Men: Superhero or Slacker" (Chapter 5). What beliefs about men, identity, gender, or popular media do Pandya and Moor share?
5. Moor argues that "Our culture's commitment to radical reversion as a fallback plan runs deeper than most people care to admit." What is he suggesting about our culture? What flawed thinking is he pointing out?

Explore

1. Why do you think people associate environmental awareness with femininity?
2. Why aren't women featured in survivalism programs as often as men?
3. Why do men veer toward flannel and other "outdoorsy" clothing—when it's actually impractical for outdoor activity?
4. What does the popularity of shows like *Man vs. Wild* or *Dual Survival* say about our culture at this point in time?
5. Why is survivalism attractive to people in one of the most stable and advanced civilizations in the world?

Rob Dunn
Fly on Wall Sees Things It Wishes It Hadn't

A biology professor at North Carolina State University, Rob Dunn seeks meaning in the messy and baffling natural world. In describing his research, he explains, "Central to all of this work is the sense that much of what we assume someone else knows (such as which species live around us in cities) is totally unknown." Dunn is the author of numerous magazine articles and two books, including *The Wild Life of Our Bodies: Predators, Parasites (2011), and Partners That Shape Who We Are Today*. In the following blog post, Dunn considers what the common housefly reveals about human culture and endurance.

Each day, in each country, a housefly is born. Lots of houseflies really. Houseflies have been being born around us for thousands of years. They are born of what everyone else abandons, corpses, cakes, and excrement. Yet their story is inescapably a version of our story. They spread early out of Africa, bound to us. You find them wrapped in mummies, their bodies held tight against the bodies of pharaohs [1]. You find them in ancient latrines, as larvae, tunneling through what we would rather be done with. At picnics they sit on hot dogs. In bedrooms, they look down from walls. In war and tragedy, they mouth what we cannot countenance. They brushed upon Gandhi, Mother Theresa and Caesar, but also Mussolini and you. And before they brushed upon you (or Mussolini) they brushed upon, well, you don't want to know.

> "Where there are humans, you'll find flies, and Buddhas."
> —Kobayashi Issa

Actually, you might want to know. Or at least some scientists think you might want to know. So it is that there is now a large book worth of scientific studies of just what can be found living on flies. All of these studies are interesting, some are a bit disgusting, and one study from a pig farm in North Carolina is the kind of thing that might just change how you live your life.

Although we have seen houseflies for millennia, complained about them in a thousand languages using a hundred thousand adjectives, in some ways they are still among the least known guests at the table. No one knows for sure where they come from (only that they had already found us as of five thousand years ago). No one knows what they did before they found us (though one imagines it involved decay). What we do know about house-flies is that they gather a little bit of life from everything they touch and redistribute it, a sort of Robin Hood of germs.

Some of the bacteria living on houseflies are their partners. Housefly eggs and larvae depend on beneficial bacteria (such as the species Klebsiella oxytoca) bestowed upon them by their mothers. These bacteria produce compounds that kill fungi and, in doing so, help hungry young flies outcompete those same fungi for their otherwise rapidly decaying food [2]. Others though are hangers on, gathered by accident as the flies bump around the world. When a fly lands, its sticky hairs become covered in bacteria, which can then be trans-ferred to whatever the flies land on next. Flies also store bacteria (gathered from their food) in their alimentary tract. These germs are brought to new places in fly poop, but also—as one treatise on flies delicately puts it—"in small droplets of regurgitated matter which have been called vomit spots."

5   Just where do houseflies pick up these other bacteria, the ones they give back to us in vomit spots, feces and footsteps? Well, they find them in what we have abandoned, the remains on which they can survive. Once, house-flies emerged from horseshit by the billions. When that ran out (thanks to the invention of cars), they turned to our garbage and so we collected it more frequently and took it far away. When the garbage became rare (some places, though not everywhere), they found the dog waste we left behind in cities. Now that New Yorkers, for instance, in their fancy shoes and dark clothes, gather the dog poop in bags, the flies have found those places we have taken our waste to hide it (both from them and from ourselves). At garbage dumps flies flock in dense halos. They are born too out of the rough parts of towns—smoke signals of neglect. They have even found the places we have moved our animals, the modern mangers of chickens and pigs where waste is dumped into vast pools. Here, their naked children eclose as writhing maggots only to be born again later to their, hairy, winged forms.

It is among these last flies that my friend Coby Schal recently decided to spend some of his days [3]. Coby has studied insects at pig farms for a while. There are probably worse places to study insects, though I can't think of them right now. At pig farms pigs accumulate, so, in great ponds, does pig waste. Coby has looked at the movement of roaches from one pig farm to another, but what he wanted to study with the flies was something differ-ent. Along with colleagues at Kansas State University, Coby wanted to know just what was being carried aloft as those flies rose. Flies, incidentally, take care in their rise. They bend their legs a little and, ever so gingerly, bounce, while flapping their wings.

Coby and his colleagues found fecal bacteria in 93.7% of the flies at the pig farm (The aptly named Enterococcus faecalis was the most common species). This came as no surprise. Houseflies the world over carry fecal bacteria. The surprise was many of those bacteria were resistant to antibiotics, such as tetracycline and erythromycin, antibiotics used to treat human bacterial diseases [4]. Such resistant forms, so-called superbugs, can kill, and while finding them on flies near pig farms does not guarantee they are making their way from the farms to our bodies via flies, it certainly suggests the possibility.

But why would the flies in pig farms tend to have antibiotic resistant bacteria? Herein lies the secret you might not have heard. Most pigs in the U.S., as well as most farm animals more generally, are fed antibiotics. By some estimates, eighty percent of antibiotics produced in the U.S. are used on animals. The antibiotics are not used to treat infections. Instead they serve solely to promote rapid growth, to make your bacon or burger cheaper and faster. As an evolutionary side effect when pigs are fed those antibiotics their weak bacteria—those susceptible to the antibiotics being used—die. Those most likely to survive are the lineages resistant to antibiotics, the tough mothers. If isolated on pig farms, all of this is imprudent but not tragic in as much as it seems isolated, faraway from our daily lives. Then the flies enter the story.

Houseflies can fly and they can do so more effectively than you might imagine. They fly with the wind, but even against it. Individual houseflies have been recorded having traveled more than ten miles [5]. Consider the geography of farms. Imagine the flies rising up from them and flying toward you. Whatever new resistant strains of bacteria they bear may be closer than you think. They might be tapping at your window now or, as Chekhov said of them, "brushing against the ceiling," their bodies bouncing along as they leave their bacteria behind.

Humans tend to dislike successful animals. We scorn the murders of crows, the flocks of starlings and the even the ants that boil up around and into our houses. Their bodies seem vulgar. The flies though, we conclude, are not just loathsome but dirty and even, in the context of Coby Schal's new study, potentially deadly. This is one lesson to take from the flies, but the wrong one. The real truth they offer, if we pay attention, is more about the nature of humans than it is the nature of flies. Anopheles mosquitoes are vectors of malaria, but houseflies, well, they are vectors of what we leave behind, carrying it back to us, as though to say, "Over here! You forgot something ..." They are the messenger nobody asked for, bearing the messages nobody wants, whether about the overuse of antibiotics or some other of our failings. So go ahead and kill the messenger, but heed the message. Meanwhile, billions of fly eggs are ready to hatch out of whatever we leave behind.

Notes

1 Panagiotakopulu E, Buckland PC, Kemp BJ (2010) "Underneath Ranefer's Floors—Urban Environments on The Desert Edge." *J Archaeol Sci*, 37:474–481.

2 Zvereva EL (1986b) "Peculiarities of Competitive Interaction Between Larvae of The House Fly Musca Domestica and Microscopic Fungi." *Zoologicheskii Zhurnal* 65:1517–1525, Lam K, Thu K, Tsang M, Moore M, Gries G. 2009. "Bacteria on Housefly Eggs, Musca Domestica, Suppress Fungal Growth in Chicken Manure Through Nutrient Depletion or Antifungal Metabolites." *Naturwissenschaften*, 96:1127–1132.

3 Well, and to send his students, postdocs and technicians, to spend theirs.

4 Ahmad A., A. Ghosh, C. Schal, and L. Zurek. 2011. "Insects In Confined Swine Operations Carry a Large Antibiotic Resistant and Potentially Virulent Enterococcal Community." *BMC Microbiology*, 11:23.

5 Chakrabarti S, Kambhaampati Zurek L. 2010. "Assessment of House Fly Dispersal between Rural and Urban Habitats in Kansas, USA." *J Kans Entomol Soc*, 83:172–188.

Analyze

1. This article begins with flies, moves to feces, then to bacteria, and then to human behavior. Given that progression, what, in your understanding, is the main idea?

2. *Scientific American* articles are written for a general audience—people who haven't spent years studying bacteria, feces, or houseflies. Identify the passages in which you learn something new. Explain, if you can, how Dunn condenses background knowledge for a general audience.

3. Explain the role of questions in Dunn's article. Point to at least two specific questions and describe how they serve a particular purpose.

4. Scientists often refer to one another's work—to the studies they've done, to the theories and conclusions they've generated. In this article Dunn refers to Coby Schal and introduces him as "my friend." How does this personalization affect you and how you read the article?

5. *Euphemism* is a language practice that conceals the uncomfortable side of things. For instance, people say "slept together" instead of "had sex" or "I have to use the restroom" instead of "I have to urinate." Identify a euphemism in Dunn's article and an instance in which he uses less polite phrasing. Explain the difference between the passages. Why might Dunn have chosen a euphemism in one passage and something less euphemistic in another?

Explore

1. In his conclusion, Dunn explains that flies offer a "real truth" about human behavior. In your own words, explain that truth.

2. How are houseflies "vectors of what we leave behind?"

3. Flush toilets and modern sewer systems allow us to ignore a part of our everyday lives. In other words, we have a *system* for ignoring the stuff we flush away every day. What other topics have we managed to ignore? And how does our society's infrastructure help us to forget, not consider, or blatantly ignore it?

4. In his conclusion, Dunn admits that people "overuse antibiotics," but he also mentions other "failings." What other failings does Dunn suggest in his article?

5. Dunn says that "humans tend to dislike successful animals." What evidence in your own life supports or refutes this claim?

David P. Barash
Two Cheers for Nature

An evolutionary biologist and psychology professor at the University of Washington, David P. Barash is an expert on evolutionary psychology, sociobiology, and peace studies. A blogger for the *Chronicle of Higher Education,* he is the author of numerous books, including *Homo Mysterious: Evolutionary Puzzles of Human Nature (2012).* In the following *Chronicle* article, Barash considers the meaning of the term *natural.*

Remember the BP oil spill, and the lessons we were supposed to learn from it? For months last summer, we were riveted by daily updates from the Gulf of Mexico, as pundits galore offered up advice, not least that it is often dangerous and even downright despicable to fool with Mother Nature.

But as the conversation turns (alas, almost exclusively) to compensation for damages in the region, we need to look back at what was—and was not—discussed. There is this surprising and provocative fact: Oil itself, that yucky, death-dealing substance, is altogether natural (mostly compressed diatoms and other plankton). Here, accordingly, is a lesson from the Gulf, not so much about oil as about our shared attitudes and often unstated assumptions: Although we don't always like to admit it, nature isn't very nice.

For many, myself included, criticizing nature doesn't come, well, naturally. My own preferred recreational activities—hiking, climbing, running, snorkeling, riding horses—embed me in nature. I have surrounded myself with animals of all sorts, and I try to avoid consuming pesticides, herbicides, and the antibiotics and hormones to which industrial agriculture has become addicted. I was delighted when a natural-foods supermarket recently opened within a mile of our home, and I patronize it almost exclusively.

Nonetheless, in resisting many things that I view as "unnatural"—nuclear weapons, global warming, chemical pollution, habitat destruction—while also honoring, respecting, defending, admiring, and nearly worshiping many things that are natural (sometimes just *because* they are natural), it is all too easy to get carried away, to forget that much in the world of nature is unpleasant, indeed odious. Consider typhoid, cholera, polio, plague, and HIV: What can be more natural than viruses or bacteria, composed as they are of proteins, nucleic acids, carbohydrates, and the like? Do you object to vaccination? You'd probably object even more to smallpox.

5   I recall returning soaking wet, cold, and miserable, more than half hypothermic after a backpacking trip in the gloriously natural Canadian Rockies, during which fog and mist had alternated with rain, hail, and snow (in August!), and then encountering this bit of wisdom from the 19th-century English writer and art critic John Ruskin: "There is no such thing as bad weather, only different kinds of good weather." One may conclude that Mr. Ruskin hadn't spent much time in the mountains. Similarly, I suspect that those well-intentioned people who admire "natural" raw milk have never experienced the ravages of *Campylobacter,* pathogenic *E. coli,* or bovine tuberculosis, each spread by the unpasteurized McCoy.

Even in sports, with its cult of the drug-free "natural athlete," devotees strive to move beyond nature's gifts to what is beautiful, elegant, or impressive, fully recognizing that it takes time and work. Hence: spring training, exhibition games, coaches, trainers, and interminable "practice." Dressage, the classical form of horsemanship, seeks to help a horse move with a mounted rider as beautifully as it would solo, in nature. To do so takes at least a decade of effort, pushing horse and rider to work hard and in unnatural ways, in order to achieve harmony and beauty. It is natural for horses to stand around in fields, eating and pooping and swatting flies. It is not natural for them to dance to music.

In short, what is natural is often good, but not always. It may be natural to be a couch potato, to punch someone in the nose if he has angered you, for people to get sick, or for a child to resist toilet training. And of course, bacterial infections, lousy weather, and troublesome behavioral inclinations aren't the only regrettable entities out there in the oh-so-natural world. Don't forget hurricanes, tsunamis, earthquakes, droughts, the devastation wrought by volcanoes, lightning storms, sandstorms, and blizzards. Oh, yes, also by oil.

In his *A Treatise of Human Nature,* in the 18th century, David Hume presented, and criticized, what has come to be known as the "is-ought problem"—the notion that we can derive what ought to be from an examination of what is. Is there any way, he asked, that we can legitimately connect how the world "is" (which, by extension, I believe, includes our own behavioral inclinations) with how it "ought" to be (including how we ought to behave)? Simply by raising the question, he so conclusively severed "is" from "ought" that the distinction—between the descriptive and the prescriptive, between facts and values—is called "Hume's Guillotine." His insight that it is fallacious to derive "ought" from "is" has become known as the "naturalistic fallacy," a term coined by the British philosopher G.E. Moore in his 1903 book, *Principia Ethica.*

In 1710, three decades before Hume sliced into the issue, the philosopher and mathematician Gottfried Leibniz struggled with the problem of theodicy, the theological effort to reconcile the existence of evil and suffering in a world supposedly governed by a god all powerful and wholly benevolent. It was—and still is—a tall order. Leibniz concluded that since God is necessarily good (by Judeo-Christian-Islamic definition, at least), as well as omnipotent, and since the deity evidently chose to make the world as it is, then this must be "the best of all possible worlds." That famous phrase proved easy to satirize, most notably by Voltaire in Candide, the picaresque adventures of Mr. Pangloss (a Leibniz caricature) and his student, who experience no end of terrible events but always interpret them through a cheerful lens.

Voltaire was especially outraged by a devastating natural disaster, the Lisbon earthquake of 1755, estimated to have killed tens of thousands of people. But he wasn't shy about depicting the cruel but equally "natural" behavior of murderers, rapists, and torturers. It's a theme that continued to resonate: In the 19th century, John Stuart Mill argued that "nature cannot be a proper model for us to imitate. Either it is right that we should kill because nature kills; torture because nature tortures; ruin and devastate because nature does the like; or we ought not to consider what nature does, but what it is good to do."

So philosophy has long taught us, or at least tried to. What does modern evolutionary biology have to offer? "Nature," acting through natural selection, whispers in our ears—cajoling, seducing, imploring, sometimes threatening or demanding—and undoubtedly inclining us in one direction or another. Those inclinations are derived from a remarkably simple process: the automatic reward that comes from biological success. If a given behavior leads to greater eventual reproductive success for the behaver (or, more crucially, for the genes that predispose us toward that behavior), then selection will promote those genes, and thus the behavior. It will seem—and be—natural.

Natural selection (the very term reverberates) has a very efficient way of getting animals and people to do things that are "good" for the organism, or at least for the genes involved. Call it pleasure. Living things find it pleasurable to eat when hungry, drink when thirsty, sleep when tired, obtain sexual satisfaction when aroused. The evolutionary benefit to genes for, say, self-nourishment would not be well served if those genes induced us to refrain from eating. But whether, in Mill's terms, such things are necessarily "good to do," in the sense of ethics and morality, is another matter entirely.

Should we refrain from cleaning the house, since the Second Law of Thermodynamics, a fundamental natural law, dictates that disorder necessarily increases within any closed system—in which case it follows that entropy is good and struggling against it is wrong? Is it unethical to exceed the speed of light, or simply impossible? Similar absurdities arise if one attempts to "naturalize" ethics from chemistry, geology, astronomy, mathematics, and so forth. When it comes to biology, however, many people seem to feel otherwise.

Isn't there something good—maybe even magnificent—in the song of a nightingale, the majesty of a bull elephant trumpeting? If nothing else, they bring pleasure, even delight, to people. And isn't it downright estimable for a mother robin to feed her nestlings? It's certainly good for the baby robins, and thus for the evolutionary success of the adults—or, more precisely, for any genes that predispose adult birds to feed their offspring. It is easy to assume that the working of biological nature—as distinct, perhaps, from physical nature, or chemical nature, or geological nature—is not only admirable, but also ethically instructive.

The result, however, can be disquieting. Take advances in reproductive   15 technology. Contraception has long been opposed by those—especially, but not solely, in the Roman Catholic Church—who claim that to interfere with the "natural" act of reproduction is, *ipso facto,* wrong. Ditto for much of the objection to cloning and stem-cell research. Consider, as well, in vitro fertilization: For decades the developers of that immensely beneficial medical option were vilified for "playing God" by promoting unnatural "test-tube babies." (The 2010 Nobel Prize in Physiology or Medicine was awarded to Robert G. Edwards, who, with the late Patrick Steptoe, pioneered the technology, undaunted by the criticism that it violated the presumption that only the natural is good.)

Any dispassionate look at the natural world should confirm just how fallacious the naturalistic fallacy really is, along with its implied and oft-assumed inverse: What is unnatural is bad. It simply does not follow that biological nature is necessarily good for giving us insight into morality or ethics. To an extent that should trouble any "natural ethicist," the living world is a zero-sum game, in which benefit for one organism often comes at the expense of others, and where no sign of overarching ethical restraint, no independent claim to goodness, can be discerned.

After all, many carnivorous animals devour their prey alive. The usual method seems to be to subdue the victim by downing or grasping it so it can't flee. Snakes eat everything whole, often dislocating their own jaws as they stuff their prey—sometimes alive—into their mouths. Ants don't even have to catch their quarry: In the spring they swarm over newly hatched, featherless birds in the nest and eat them tiny bite by bite.

Annie Dillard's marvelous meditation on nature, *Pilgrim at Tinker Creek,* contains an unforgettable account of her encounter with a "very small frog with wide, dull eyes," whom she watches being devoured by a huge water bug. Dillard notes with understatement that "it's rough out there, and chancy," that "every live thing is a survivor on a kind of extended emergency bivouac," and that "cruelty is a mystery," along with "the waste of pain." We must, she concludes, "somehow take a wider view, look at the whole landscape, really see it, and describe what's going on here. Then we can at least wail the right question into the swaddling band of darkness, or, if it comes to that, choir the proper praise."

Rereading that section of the book, I must confess that I am not at all sure what is the right question, or indeed, whether given the myriad unknowns that intervene between our human consciousness and the rest of the natural world, there are any inquiries that could support the designation "right" or "wrong." (As for choiring the "proper praise," my atheist self declines that, right off the top.)

20   Nonetheless, I think I know what Dillard means, at least insofar as there is a profound and desperate need, a deeply human responsibility, to wail or choir, or in some other way to impel an urgent inquiry into what it means to take a wider view, and not just describe what's going on in this gorgeous but deeply troubling landscape of which we are a part; to figure out what our rightful place is, and how to occupy it.

Some especially devout Jains hire sweepers to walk before them, brandishing large fans to displace any tiny invertebrates, lest they be stepped upon. But even Jains and Western vegans must eat. To survive—never mind, to prosper—is to perpetuate a grim tragedy, one that goes beyond simple ethics, be they Kantian, utilitarian, situational, deontological, consequential, theological, or whatever. As beautiful as it is bountiful and awe-inspiring, life proceeds via the taking of life, and is therefore no less likely to be ugly, amoral, and awful. And we are stuck in it, up to our necks . . . and more. Indeed, our immersion in the natural world goes further and deeper than that of any other life form, insofar as we are masters at manipulating, distorting, and restructuring it, all the while knowing—or at least bearing responsibility—for what we are doing.

In Stephen Sondheim's dark musical *Sweeney Todd,* we learn that "the history of the world, my sweet, is who gets eaten and who gets to eat." In the nonfiction world we all inhabit, there is pleasure and pain, suffering and delight, eaten and eater, life and death, growth and decay, luscious Louisiana salt marshes teeming with innumerable, natural, glorious lives and horrendous pollution and destruction wrought by noxious eruptions of equally natural petroleum. One could argue that nothing on this planet can ever be unnatural—including our own actions, since everything (not least our own DNA and neurons) is necessarily composed of the elements of the periodic table.

And yet just a moment's reflection tells us that it is precisely because some things are wholly natural, and also wholly loathsome, that they had best be left alone, Pandora's boxes that should never be opened. If folly and avarice (acting, for example, via hunger for petroleum) do so nonetheless, those things must be struggled against with all the strength and determination, natural or not, that we possess.

Analyze

1. What idea is Barash attempting to counter? What basic assumption about nature is he trying to change or complicate?
2. How does his allusion to the BP oil spill help to support his main idea?
3. Explain how Barash's reference to Annie Dillard supports his main idea.
4. According to Barash, how are humans fundamentally different from other life forms on the planet?
5. Ultimately, Barash wants people to think differently. What particular (but fairly complex) idea does he want readers to accept?

Explore

1. In your understanding, what is the dividing line between natural and unnatural? Give specific examples to illustrate the distinction.
2. Barash borrows from Annie Dillard to argue that "it's rough out there, and chancy." How does this statement relate to your life? How does (or doesn't) it figure into your thinking, experience, or behavior?
3. Barash invites readers to "take a wider view, and not just describe what's going on in this gorgeous but deeply troubling landscape of which we are a part." In your own words, explain this "wider view." What does it mean? How is it possible?
4. Look up the following ethical positions: utilitarian, situational, and deontological. Which seems most reasonable or attractive to you? Why?
5. Barash suggests (but doesn't necessarily support) the idea that everything on the planet is, in some way, natural. Do you accept this position? Or do you think that some products or inventions are, in fact, unnatural?

Michael Shellenberger and Ted Nordhaus
Evolve: A Case for Modernization as the Road to Salvation

Michael Shellenberger and Ted Nordhaus are environmental writers whose work focuses on policy change. They are the cofounders of the Breakthrough Institute, which aims "to accelerate the transition to a future where all the world's inhabitants can enjoy secure, free, prosperous, and fulfilling lives on an ecologically vibrant planet." Shellenberger and Nordhaus coauthored numerous articles and two books, including the 2011 book *Love Your Monsters: Postenvironmentalism and the Anthropocene.* In the following magazine article, they examine the role of technology in cultural evolution.

Sometime around 2014, Italy will complete construction of seventy-eight mobile floodgates aimed at protecting Venice's three inlets from the rising tides of the Adriatic Sea. The massive doors—twenty meters by thirty meters, and five meters thick—will, most of the time, lie flat on the sandy seabed between the lagoon and the sea. But when a high tide is predicted, the doors will empty themselves of water and fill with compressed air, rising up on hinges to keep the Adriatic out of the city. Three locks will allow ships to move in and out of the lagoon while the gates are up.

Nowhere else in the world have humans so constantly had to create and re-create their infrastructure in response to a changing natural environment than in Venice. The idea for the gates dates back to the 1966 flood, which inundated 100 percent of the city. Still, it took from 1970 to 2002 for the hydrologist Robert Frassetto and others to convince their fellow Italians to build them. Not everyone sees the oscillating and buoyant floodgates as Venice's salvation. After the project was approved, the head of World Wildlife Fund Italy said, "Today the city's destiny rests on a pretentious, costly, and environmentally harmful technological gamble."

In truth, the grandeur that is Venice has always rested—quite literally—on a series of pretentious, costly, and environmentally harmful technological gambles. Her buildings rest upon pylons made of ancient larch and oak trees ripped from inland forests a thousand years ago. Over time, the pylons were petrified by the saltwater, infill was added, and cathedrals were constructed. Little by little, technology helped transform a town of humble fisherfolk into the city we know today. Saving Venice has meant creating Venice, not once, but many times since its founding. And that is why her rescue from the rising seas serves as an apt metaphor for solving this century's formidable environmental problems. Each new act of salvation will result in new unintended consequences, positive and negative, which will in turn require new acts of salvation. What we call "saving the Earth" will, in practice, require creating and re-creating it again and again for as long as humans inhabit it.

Many environmentally concerned people today view technology as an affront to the sacredness of nature, but our technologies have always been perfectly natural. Our animal skins, our fire, our farms, our windmills, our nuclear plants, and our solar panels—all 100 percent natural, drawn, as they are, from the raw materials of the Earth.

Furthermore, over the course of human history, those technologies have not only been created by us, but have also helped create us. Recent archaeological evidence suggests that the reason for our modern hands, with their opposable thumbs and shorter fingers, is that they were better adapted for tool use. Ape hands are great for climbing trees but not, it turns out, for striking flint or making arrowheads. Those prehumans whose hands could best use tools gained an enormous advantage over those whose hands could not.

As our hands and wrists changed, we increasingly walked upright, hunted, ate meat, and evolved. Our upright posture allowed us to chase down animals we had wounded with our weapons. Our long-distance running was aided by sweat glands replacing fur. The use of fire to cook meat allowed us to consume much larger amounts of protein, which allowed our heads to grow so large that some prehumans began delivering bigger-brained babies prematurely. Those babies, in turn, were able to survive because we were able to fashion still more tools, made from animal bladders and skins, to strap the helpless infants to their mothers' chests. Technology, in short, made us human.

Of course, as our bodies, our brains, and our tools evolved, so too did our ability to radically modify our environment. We hunted mammoths and other species to extinction. We torched whole forests and savannas in order to flush prey and clear land for agriculture. And long before human emissions began to affect the climate, we had already shifted the albedo of the Earth by replacing many of the world's forests with cultivated agriculture. While our capabilities to alter our environment have, over the last century, expanded substantially, the trend is long-standing. The Earth of one hundred or two hundred or three hundred years ago was one that had already been profoundly shaped by human endeavor.

None of this changes the reality and risks of the ecological crises humans have created. Global warming, deforestation, overfishing, and other human activities—if they don't threaten our very existence—certainly offer the possibility of misery for many hundreds of millions, if not billions, of humans and are rapidly transforming nonhuman nature at a pace not seen for many hundreds of millions of years. But the difference between the new ecological crises and the ways in which humans and even prehumans have shaped nonhuman nature for tens of thousands of years is one of scope and scale, not kind.

Humans have long been cocreators of the environment they inhabit. Any proposal to fix environmental problems by turning away from technology risks worsening them, by attempting to deny the ongoing coevolution of humans and nature.

10   Nevertheless, elites in the West—who rely more heavily on technology than anyone else on the planet—insist that development and technology are the causes of ecological problems but not their solution. They claim that economic sacrifice is the answer, while living amid historic levels of affluence and abundance. They consume resources on a vast scale, overwhelming whatever meager conservations they may partake in through living in dense (and often fashionable) urban enclaves, driving fuel-efficient automobiles, and purchasing locally grown produce. Indeed, the most visible and common expressions of faith in ecological salvation are new forms of consumption. Green products and services—the Toyota Prius, the efficient washer/dryer, the LEED-certified office building—are consciously identified by consumers as things they do to express their higher moral status.

The same is true at the political level, as world leaders, to the cheers of the left-leaning postmaterial constituencies that increasingly hold the balance of political power in many developed economies, offer promise after promise to address climate change, species extinction, deforestation, and global poverty, all while studiously avoiding any action that might impose real cost or sacrifice upon their constituents. While it has been convenient for many sympathetic observers to chalk up the failure of such efforts to corporate greed, corruption, and political cowardice, the reality is that the entire postmaterial project is, confoundingly, built upon a foundation of affluence and material consumption that would be considerably threatened by any serious effort to address the ecological crises through substantially downscaling economic activity.

It's not too difficult to understand how this hypocrisy has come to infiltrate such a seemingly well-meaning swath of our culture. As large populations in the developed North achieved unprecedented economic security, affluence, and freedom, the project that had centrally occupied humanity for thousands of years—emancipating ourselves from nature, tribalism, peonage, and poverty—was subsumed by the need to manage the unintended consequences of modernization itself, from local pollution to nuclear proliferation to global warming.

Increasingly skeptical of capitalist meritocracy and economic criteria as the implicit standards of success at the individual level and the defining measure of progress at the societal level, the post–World War II generations have redefined normative notions of well-being and quality of life in developed societies. Humanitarianism and environmentalism have become the dominant social movements, bringing environmental protection, preservation of quality of life, and other "life-political" issues, in the words of British sociologist Anthony Giddens, to the fore.

The rise of the knowledge economy—encompassing medicine, law, finance, media, real estate, marketing, and the nonprofit sector—has further accelerated the West's growing disenchantment with modern life, especially among the educated elite. Knowledge workers are more alienated from the products of their labor than any other class in history, unable to claim some role in producing food, shelter, or even basic consumer products. And yet they can afford to spend time in beautiful places—in their gardens, in the countryside, on beaches, and near old-growth forests. As they survey these landscapes, they tell themselves that the best things in life are free, even though they have consumed mightily to travel to places where they feel peaceful, calm, and far from the worries of the modern world.

These postmaterial values have given rise to a secular and largely inchoate ecotheology, complete with apocalyptic fears of ecological collapse, disenchanting notions of living in a fallen world, and the growing conviction that some kind of collective sacrifice is needed to avoid the end of the world. Alongside those dark incantations shine nostalgic visions of a transcendent future in which humans might, once again, live in harmony with nature through a return to small-scale agriculture, or even to hunter-gatherer life.

The contradictions between the world as it is—filled with the unintended consequences of our actions—and the world as so many of us would like it to be result in a pseudorejection of modernity, a kind of postmaterialist nihilism. Empty gestures are the defining sacraments of this ecotheology. The belief that we must radically curtail our consumption in order to survive as a civilization is no impediment to elites paying for private university educations, frequent jet travel, and iPads.

Thus, ecotheology, like all dominant religious narratives, serves the dominant forms of social and economic organization in which it is embedded. Catholicism valorized poverty, social hierarchy, and agrarianism for the masses in feudal societies that lived and worked the land. Protestantism valorized industriousness, capital accumulation, and individuation among the rising merchant classes of early capitalist societies and would define the social norms of modernizing industrial societies. Today's secular ecotheology values creativity, imagination, and leisure over the work ethic, productivity, and efficiency in societies that increasingly prosper from their knowledge economies while outsourcing crude, industrial production of goods to developing societies. Living amid unprecedented levels of wealth and security, ecological elites reject economic growth as a measure of well-being, tell cautionary tales about modernity and technology, and warn of overpopulation abroad now that the societies in which they live are wealthy and their populations are no longer growing.

Such hypocrisy has rarely been a hindrance to religion and, indeed, contributes to its power. One of the most enduring characteristics of human civilization is the way ruling elites espouse beliefs radically at odds with their own behaviors. The ancient Greeks recited the cautionary tales of Prometheus and Icarus while using fire, dreaming of flight, and pursuing technological frontiers. Early agriculturalists told the story of the fall from Eden as a cautionary tale against the very agriculture they practiced. European Christians espoused poverty and peacemaking while accumulating wealth and waging war.

In preaching antimodernity while living as moderns, ecological elites affirm their status at the top of the postindustrial knowledge hierarchy. Affluent developed-world elites offer both their less well-to-do countrymen and the global poor a laundry list of don'ts—don't develop like we developed, don't drive tacky SUVs, don't overconsume—that engender resentment, not emulation, from fellow citizens at home and abroad. That the ecological elites hold themselves to a different standard while insisting that all are equal is yet another demonstration of their higher status, for they are thus unaccountable even to reality.

Though it poses as a solution, today's nihilistic ecotheology is actually a significant obstacle to dealing with ecological problems created by modernization—one that must be replaced by a new, creative, and life-affirming worldview. After all, human development, wealth, and technology liberated us from hunger, deprivation, and insecurity; now they must be considered essential to overcoming ecological risks.

There's no question that humans are radically remaking the Earth, but fears of ecological apocalypse—of condemning this world to fiery destruction—are unsupported by the sciences. Global warming may bring worsening disasters and disruptions to rainfall, snowmelts, and agriculture, but there is little evidence to suggest it will deliver the end of modernization. Even the most catastrophic United Nations scenarios predict rising economic growth. While wealthy environmentalists claim to be especially worried about the impact of global warming on the poor, it is rapid, not retarded, development that is most likely to protect the poor against natural disasters and agricultural losses.

What modernization may threaten most is not human civilization, but the survival of those nonhuman species and environments we care about. While global warming dominates ecological discourse, the greatest threats to nonhumans remain our direct changes to the land and the seas. The world's great, diverse, and ancient forests are being converted to tree plantations, farms, and ranches. Humans are causing massive, unprecedented extinctions on Earth due to habitat destruction. We are on the verge of losing primates in the wild. We have so overfished the oceans that most of the big fish are gone.

The apocalyptic vision of ecotheology warns that degrading nonhuman natures will undermine the basis for human civilization, but history has shown the opposite: the degradation of nonhuman environments has made us rich. We have become rather adept at transferring the wealth and diversity of nonhuman environments into human ones. The solution to the unintended consequences of modernity is, and has always been, more modernity—just as the solution to the unintended consequences of our technologies has always been more technology. The Y2K computer bug was fixed by better computer programming, not by going back to typewriters. The ozone-hole crisis was averted not by an end to air conditioning but rather by more advanced, less environmentally harmful technologies.

The question for humanity, then, is not whether humans and our civilizations will survive, but rather what kind of a planet we will inhabit. Would we like a planet with wild primates, old-growth forests, a living ocean, and modest rather than extreme temperature increases? Of course we would—virtually everybody would. Only continued modernization and technological innovation can make such a world possible.

25   Putting faith in modernization will require a new secular theology consistent with the reality of human creation and life on Earth, not with some imagined dystopia or utopia. It will require a worldview that sees technology as humane and sacred, rather than inhumane and profane. It will require replacing the antiquated notion that human development is antithetical to the preservation of nature with the view that modernization is the key to saving it. Let's call this "modernization theology."

Where ecotheology imagines that our ecological problems are the consequence of human violations of a separate "nature," modernization theology views environmental problems as an inevitable part of life on Earth. Where the last generation of ecologists saw a natural harmony in Creation, the new ecologists see constant change. Where ecotheologians suggest that the unintended consequences of human development might be avoidable, proponents of modernization view them as inevitable, and positive as often as negative. And where the ecological elites see the powers of humankind as the enemy of Creation, the modernists acknowledge them as central to its salvation.

Modernization theology should thus be grounded in a sense of profound gratitude to Creation—human and nonhuman. It should celebrate, not desecrate, the technologies that led our prehuman ancestors to evolve. Our experience of transcendence in the outdoors should translate into the desire for all humans to benefit from the fruits of modernization and be able to experience similar transcendence. Our valorization of creativity should lead us to care for our cocreation of the planet.

The risks now faced by humanity are increasingly ones of our own making—and ones over which we have only partial, tentative, and temporary control. Various kinds of liberation—from hard agricultural labor and high infant mortality rates to tuberculosis and oppressive traditional values—bring all kinds of new problems, from global warming and obesity to alienation and depression. These new problems will largely be better than the old ones, in the way that obesity is a better problem than hunger, and living in a hotter world is a better problem than living in one without electricity. But they are serious problems nonetheless.

The good news is that we already have many nascent, promising technologies to overcome ecological problems. Stabilizing greenhouse gas emissions will require a new generation of nuclear power plants to cheaply replace coal plants as well as, perhaps, to pull carbon dioxide out of the atmosphere and power desalination plants to irrigate and grow forests in today's deserts. Pulling frontier agriculture back from forests will require massively increasing agricultural yields through genetic engineering. Replacing environmentally degrading cattle ranching may require growing meat in laboratories, which will gradually be viewed as less repulsive than today's cruel and deadly methods of meat production. And the solution to the species extinction problem will involve creating new habitats and new organisms, perhaps from the DNA of previously extinct ones.

In attempting to solve these problems, we will inevitably create new   30
ones. One common objection to technology and development is that they will bring unintended consequences, but life on Earth has always been a story of unintended consequences. The Venice floodgates offer a pointed illustration. Concerns raised by the environmental community that the floodgates would impact marine life have been borne out—only not in the way they had feared. Though the gates are still under construction, marine biologists have announced that they have already become host to many coral and fish species, some of which used to be found only in the southern Mediterranean or Red Sea.

Other critics of the gates have questioned what will happen if global warming should raise sea levels higher than the tops of the gates. If this should become inevitable, it is unlikely that Venetians would abandon their city. Instead, they may attempt to raise it. One sweetly ironic proposal would levitate the city by blowing carbon dioxide emissions two thousand feet below the lagoon floor. Some may call such strong faith in the technological fix an instance of hubris, but others will simply call it compassion.

The French anthropologist Bruno Latour has some interesting thoughts on the matter. According to Latour, Mary Shelley's *Frankenstein* is not a cautionary tale against hubris, but rather a cautionary tale against irrational fears of imperfection. Dr. Frankenstein is an antihero not because he created life, but rather because he fled in horror when he mistook his creation for a monster—a self-fulfilling prophecy. The moral of the story, where saving the planet is concerned, is that we should treat our technological creations as we would treat our children, with care and love, lest our abandonment of them turn them into monsters.

"The sin is not to wish to have dominion over nature," Latour writes, "but to believe that this dominion means emancipation and not attachment." In other words, the term "ecological hubris" should not be used to describe the human desire to remake the world, but rather the faith that we can end the cycle of creation and destruction.

Analyze

1. What do Shellenberger and Nordhaus mean by the "coevolution of humans and nature"?
2. Explain what the authors mean by "postmaterial constituencies." Who are these people, generally, and what do Shellenberger and Nordhaus say about them?
3. Explain the authors' take on global warming. How will it impact civilization?
4. Explain Latour's understanding of Mary Shelley's *Frankenstein*. How does his reading support Shellenberger and Nordhaus's main idea?
5. Compare this article with "Two Cheers for Nature" by David P. Barash (in this chapter). How are the articles similar? What beliefs or assumptions seem to overlap? How are they different? What are the points of friction?

Explore

1. Would you call Shellenberger and Nordhaus environmentalists? Why or why not?
2. Shellenberger and Nordhaus argue that saving Venice from the sea "serves as an apt metaphor for solving this century's formidable environmental problems." Explain what they mean. How is saving Venice a metaphor? How does it represent broader environmental problems?
3. The authors argue that technology helped humans to evolve. How is this assertion contrary to or different from other positions on evolution or technology?
4. Toward the end of their article, the authors admit that technology always brings unintended consequences. How do you think people should deal with this fact?

5. Shellenberger and Nordhaus argue that ongoing modernization, not a return to the past, will preserve nature. Do you agree? Why or why not?

Forging Connections

1. Consider the ways nature gets used to sell products and services. For example, in car commercials, desert landscapes often surround a family sedan, rushing mountain streams are used to market beer, and forest canopies help to sell sleeping pills. Write an essay that examines America's relationship with nature through advertisement. What do our ads suggest about the purpose of the natural world? What do they suggest about its role in human life or our role in the world around us? What kinds of attitudes and beliefs about nature do our most common ads reinforce? Borrow insights from Robert Moor ("Mother Nature's Sons," this chapter) and Fredrik deBoer ("The Resentment Machine," Chapter 2).

2. Consider your favorite television programs or movies. How do they characterize nature beyond human infrastructure? Is the natural world a theme park, an escape, an academic subject, a spiritual zone, or something else? Or maybe the natural world is simply background? With these questions in mind, develop an essay that forges a connection between entertainment and nature. Use your favorite programs or movies to focus your exploration, but also borrow insights from writers in this chapter as well as Chapter 2, "Consumerism: How We Spend."

Looking Further

1. Stephanie Mills refers to an "extinction crisis" in her essay "Some Words for the Wild." Research this concept. Find out what biologists, research organizations, and other scholars have said about the current wave of extinction. Develop an essay that reports on the most common results related to an extinction crisis—the number of species involved, the timeline, and the most affected global regions. Consider not only the current facts and projections but also the implications for American culture. What does an ongoing extinction crisis suggest for shared

beliefs, fears, and hopes? Integrate images, charts, or graphs to help illustrate the ideas you discover.

2. Michael Shellenberger and Ted Nordhaus argue that modernization is not nature's enemy. In fact, they call for a new kind of faith: ecotheology. Research this concept. Find out how others characterize the belief system. Develop an essay that explains its emergence and role in people's lives. Rather than making a case for or against the belief system, try to analyze it. Try to uncover why it has come about, why it appeals to people, and how it relates to mainstream American culture.

8 Politics: How We Govern

Politics is a cultural drama. In no other arena can we more directly witness the tensions of a culture—the friction between the past and future, hopes and fears, values and needs, and even reality and imagination. In a televised representative democracy like the United States, we get to watch these frictions performed. We get to see questions grow into issues, debates, and drawn-out battles. In short, we get to witness a civilization arguing with and sometimes screaming at itself.

In literal terms, politics is about the *polis* (Greek for *city* or *gathering place*). In practical terms, politics is the implementation of laws that govern all realms public and private life: commerce, work, education, language, entertainment, consumption, even sex and procreation. It's no wonder, then, that politics garners so many emotions and that people demonize their opponents so openly. Everything about people's lives, at some point, comes down to political decisions. From preschool to nursing homes, from birth to burial, from inheritance to estate planning, our entire lives are governed by decisions that other people make on our behalf. If you are a citizen, an immigrant, or even a fetus, you are a political entity. Even if you are not interested in politics, they are interested in you—and to a large degree, they govern your daily and nightly behavior.

The readings in this chapter focus on a range of political issues. Jeremy Brecher, David Korten, and Deanna Isaacs take on economic inequalities. Starhawk and David R. Dow deal with issues of health care. Janice Brewer and Katelyn Langdale explore the problems of immigration policy. As in other chapters, the authors do not necessarily take opposing views. In fact, they do not necessarily take on the same point of contention. For example, Janice Brewer argues about the problems of illegal immigration across the Mexican border while Katelyn Langdale explains the struggle of people trying to gain legal entry through the formal bureaucracy. As you read, then, try not to get caught up in contrary opinions about each topic. Avoid falling into the typical either/or political positions. Instead, read to better understand how your culture is managing these complex topics.

Jeremy Brecher
The 99 Percent Organize Themselves

A historian, social activist, and documentarian, Jeremy Brecher studies the human drives behind major cultural shifts. Focusing his work on issues related to labor, globalization, and social change, Brecher is the author of numerous articles and books, including the 2012 book *Save the Humans? Common Preservation in Action.* In the following magazine article, Brecher considers the cultural significance of the Occupy movement.

In mid-October I spent two days and a night with Occupy Wall Street in Zuccotti Park. Since then I've read a barrage of advice for what OWS and its companion movements around the world should be doing. But I've been haunted by another question: What should those of us who are sympathetic to OWS (according to polls, roughly two-thirds of Americans are), but are not going to relocate to a downtown park, be doing to advance the well-being of the 99 percent?

I got one part of my answer as I groggily logged on to the web at 5:30 the morning after I returned home from Zuccotti Park. When I left the park, its private owner Brookfield Properties had announced it would clear the park "for cleaning" and enforce rules preventing tarps, sleeping bags and lying down. Mayor Bloomberg said the NYPD would enforce those rules, effectively ending the encampment.

But a funny thing happened on the way to the eviction. When OWS put out a call for support, thousands of people began to converge on the park for nonviolent resistance to eviction. Unions called on their members to protect the encampment. The president of the AFL-CIO's Central Labor Council lobbied the city to cancel the crackdown. Lawyers prepared to bring suit to protect the occupiers' First Amendment rights. City council members and other New York politicians lobbied the mayor to halt the eviction. Against all expectation, Mayor Bloomberg announced that Brookfield was abandoning the "cleanup" plan and the company announced it would try to reach an accommodation with the occupiers. The mobilization of supporters had forced the mayor and the park owners to back down. I had my first answer to what the rest of the 99 percent can do: protect the occupations.

Since then, there have been similar mobilizations to protect occupations in cities from Atlanta to Oakland. Many have involved a similar combination of public officials, trade unions and rank-and-file 99 percenters just showing up to defend their rights. In one extraordinary case, law enforcement officials themselves were responsible for saving the Occupy Albany encampment in Academy Park across from the State Capitol and City Hall. As protests grew, Police Chief Steven Krokoff issued an internal memo stating, "I have no intention of assigning officers to monitor, watch, videotape or influence any behavior that is conducted by our citizens peacefully demonstrating in Academy Park" and that the department would respond "in the same manner that we do on a daily basis" to any reported crime.

According to the Albany *Times-Union,* Albany Mayor Jerry Jennings, 5 under pressure from the administration of Governor Andrew Cuomo, thereupon directed city police to arrest several hundred Occupy Albany protesters. The police refused. The *Times-Union* reported that "State Police supported the defiant posture of Albany police leaders to hold off making arrests for the low-level offense of trespassing, in part because of concern it could incite a riot or draw thousands of protesters in a backlash that could endanger police and the public." According to the official, "The bottom line is the police know policing, not the governor and not the mayor." Meanwhile, Albany County District Attorney David Soares informed the mayor and police officials that, "Unless there is property damage or injuries to law enforcement we don't prosecute people for protesting."

A 99 Percent Movement?

I remember well how the movement against the Vietnam War, so powerful among the youth on America's campuses in the 1960s, was largely isolated from the rest of the country. Something very different is happening right now, however: the Occupy movements have been building alliances through direct action mutual aid. And 99 percenters are connecting with them and utilizing their spirit and methods to contest their own injustices. The result is that OWS, instead of becoming isolated, is morphing before our eyes into what some are calling the 99 Percent Movement.

When Rose Gudiel received an eviction notice for her modest home in La Puente, a working-class suburb of Los Angeles, she announced, "We're not leaving." She and her family hunkered down while dozens of friends and supporters camped in their yard, determined to resist. When thousands started to gather outside Los Angeles City Hall to launch Occupy LA, Rose Gudiel went down and told her story to one of its first General Assemblies. A group from Occupy LA joined the vigil at her home and some stayed to camp out. Next Rose Gudiel and an Occupy LA delegation protested in front of the $26 million dollar Bel Air mansion of Steve Mnuchin, CEO of OneWest, which serviced her mortgage. The next day they held a sit-in at the Pasadena regional office of Fannie Mae, where Rose Gudiel's 63-year-old disabled mother made an impassioned plea to save her home and nine protesters were arrested—all broadcast that night on the TV news. The next day Rose Gudiel received a letter from the bank saying her eviction had been called off and soon she had a deal for a renegotiated mortgage. Housing advocates are now considering a campaign called "Let a thousand Roses bloom." MSNBC commented that Rose Gudiel provides "an example of how the sprawling 'Occupy' movement—often criticized for its lack of focus—can lend muscle to specific goals pursued by organizations and individuals."

An alliance has been developing between the occupations around the country and many different layers of organized labor. In New York a group from OWS joined a march of 500 to a Verizon store held to support the contract campaign of Verizon workers. "We're all in this together," 53-year-old Steven Jackman, a Verizon worker from Long Island, said about Occupy Wall Street. In Albany, New York, Occupy Albany joined a protest outside the State Capitol featuring a roasted pig wearing a gold top hat, sporting a gold chain and chomping on a cigar. The adoption of OWS themes and language was apparent. A local union official said, "The corporate pig's been out there, taking a bite out of America, out of the 99 percent, for years and I'm inviting all of the 99 percent of America to come on down today and take a bite out of the corporate pig."

The collaboration of OWS and labor can take some unusual forms. To support art handlers of the Teamsters' union, activists from OWS started showing up at Sotheby's auctions, masquerading as clients. They would suddenly stand up and, instead of offering a bid, disrupt the proceedings with loud denunciations of the company's labor practices. OWS activists likewise went to a Manhattan restaurant owned by a prominent Sotheby's board member, clinked on glasses for silence, and then denounced the company as a union-buster. Jason Ide, president of the Teamsters local that represents the art handlers, told the *Washington Post* that the Occupy tactics surprised and inspired him and his members—so much so that the workers have become regulars at OWS. "Now is this rare opportunity for labor unions, and especially the union leadership, to take some pointers," for example by considering the civil-disobedience approach taken by Occupy demonstrations.

Meanwhile, a close working relationship has developed between climate 10 and environmental activists and the Occupy movement. A number of environmental activists, including Bill McKibben and Naomi Klein, were early endorses of the Occupy movement, and a delegation from Occupy DC marched to join a rally against the Keystone XL pipeline. Next a group of students and climate activists organized an "#OccupyStateDept" action and occupied the area outside the Ronald Reagan Building overnight to protest the Keystone XL pipeline—and to secure admission to a hearing on the pipeline the next day. Ethan Nuss, who had stood in line for fourteen hours, told the hearing, "Every day I wake up and work for a vision in this country of a 100 percent clean energy economy that will create jobs for my generation when my generation is facing the largest unemployment since the Great Depression." Bill McKibben urged pipeline opponents to join the Occupy DC encampment and invited Occupy DC to join the upcoming anti-pipeline action at the White House.

Bringing It All Back Home

Just as workers, community residents, students, and even housewives in the 1930s adopted the "sit-down strike" to address their grievances, so the robust but nonviolent direct action of the Occupy movements is being adopted by diverse communities and constituencies to address their own concerns. For example, a hundred students and teachers recently occupied a New York Board of Education meeting to protest budget cutbacks, layoffs, large class sizes and overemphasis on standardized testing. After the city school chancellor and school board members fled the meeting, the crowd held an impromptu "general assembly." Her voice amplified by the echo of the "people's microphone," an elementary school student named Indigo told the assembly,

> "Mic check. I'm Indigo, and I am an 8-year-old third grader, and I'm sad Ms. Cunningham is doing work for free. I don't think it's fair that teachers are getting laid off. The thing that would help me learn more would be if we had smaller classes. My teacher, Ms. Lamar, has to shout to be heard."

99 percenters are also bringing the OWS message back into their own communities. For example, OWSers joined a protest in Harlem against "stop and frisk" racial profiling by law enforcement officials. Soon, activists began holding Occupy Harlem General Assemblies. And civil rights and labor groups, including the Coalition of Black Trade Unionists, the A. Philip Randolph Institute, the Labor Council for Latin American Advancement, the Asian Pacific American Labor Alliance, the National Action Network and the New York State and New York City chapters of the NAACP organized their own rally in City Hall Park and marched to the Zuccotti Park to show their support for the OWS movement.

Occupy College provides another example of how 99 percenters are taking the Occupy message—and mode of self-organization—into other arenas. It is organized both to support the occupations around the country and around the world, and to address the specific issues affecting college students like the cost of education and the burden of college debt that have been important themes of the Occupy movements. Occupy College has established a website and is initiating national solidarity teach-ins in early November at colleges around the country.

While there has been a lot of debate in recent years about face-to-face vs. Internet organizing, in fact the Occupy and 99-percenter movements have brilliantly combined the two. While many Occupy groups and General Assemblies have been highly local, there is also widespread self-organization occurring on the web by groups such "Knitters for Occupy Wall St" and "Knitters for the 99 Percent" linking people all over the country who are making warm clothes for the occupiers. Here are some ways 99 percenters might want to think about organizing with their own real and virtual communities:

- Bring a speaker from your local Occupy group to a meeting in your living room or to whatever organizations you belong to.
- Organize a General Assembly in your neighborhood to discuss the issues of the 99 percent. Discuss what is upsetting people and decide on some concrete action to address it.
- If your PTA supports teachers' jobs and programs for low-income students, get them to visit their political representatives and also do a joint action with your local Occupy group.
- If your church's food pantry or homeless shelter needs money, hold an action at your local bank offices demanding that they feed the homeless in "their" community. If they won't, ask your elected officials to take a look at the benefits they receive from "their" community. (Remember, according to Mayor Bloomberg it was the threat of city council officials to look into benefits received by the owners of Zuccotti Park that led them to back off their efforts to shut down OWS.)
- Create a Facebook page for your own equivalent of "Knitters for the 99 Percent."
- Create a group to monitor local media and to protest when they favor the concerns of the 1 percent over those of the 99 percent.
- Organize public hearings in your town about what's really happening to the 99 percent and how the 1 percent's power is affecting them.
- Create your own temporary occupations in your own milieu addressing concerns about housing, jobs, media or whatever else concerns you and your fellow 99 percenters.

While the connections that have developed with unions are of great importance, we need to remember that the great majority of 99 percenters don't have unions. Self-organization of non-union workers is a crucial next step. Take some of your co-workers down to visit your local occupation. Invite someone from your local Occupy group to meet with people from your workplace. Discuss what support you can give each other and the 99 Percent movement.

The Power of the Powerless

There is clearly a bigger movement growing out of the Occupy movement. But how will it develop? Some expect it to become like the Tea Party, a pressure group within the political party system. Others imagine something like the Tahrir Square demonstrations that toppled the Mubarak regime in one concentrated upheaval.

Neither of these visions takes enough account of the role of "secondary institutions"—schools, religious congregations, workplaces, communities, ethnic groups, and subcultures—in American society. The cooperation and acquiescence of these institutions provide the "pillars of support" on which both the government and the corporations depend—and through which their power can be humbled. And they provide arenas in which people can make change that will genuinely affect their lives long before they are powerful enough to defeat corporate control of national politics.

> "In our top-down, corporate-controlled political system, even our political parties and local governments can be considered secondary institutions."

In our top-down, corporate-controlled political system, even our political parties and local governments can be considered secondary institutions. Those who are active in political parties and organizations can play a role supporting the Occupy movements and addressing the needs of the 99 percent. You can invite a speaker from your local Occupation group; support them in the street; and insist your organization's leaders and the politicians it supports take a pro-Occupation stand. You can identify ways in which your organization and those it supports acquiesce in the interests of the 1 percent and demand that they stop.

The same is true of local governments. In Los Angeles, for example, the city council unanimously passed a resolution supporting "the continuation of the peaceful and vibrant exercise in First Amendment Rights" of the Occupy LA. 20

Beyond that, local governments and political parties can start pursuing the interests of the 99 percent and stop supporting those of the one percent. In Los Angeles, for example, the same night the city council voted to endorse Occupy LA, it also reaffirmed its support for a "Responsible Banking Initiative," which would leverage the city's over $25 billion in pension and cash investments to pressure banks to invest in the city. Moving city funds to nonprofit development banks is also being discussed.

In Brooklyn, Assemblyman Vito J. Lopez proposed a millionaire's tax to raise $4 billion to prevent the cutting of vital social services. Absent such a tax, he proposed a $4 billion fund to be voluntarily contributed by 400 companies in the financial sector each contributing $5 million to $10 million for three years to create jobs, fix infrastructure and build affordable housing. He did not say how the companies would be persuaded to contribute, but his proposal was made at the start of a march from the Brooklyn Borough Hall across the Brooklyn Bridge to Wall Street.

I remember when, during the Vietnam War millions of people joined the monthly demonstrations and "work breaks" known as the Vietnam Moratorium—only to have the national leadership shut it down and move into electoral politics. Although some politicians and labor leaders have called for OWSers to campaign for Obama or the Democratic Party, such a shift is unlikely to happen to the Occupy movement. For those who want that to happen, their best strategy will be to make Obama and the Democratic Party something the Occupy movement (and the rest of the 99 percent) believe is worth supporting. Start freezing foreclosures, taxing the rich, creating new public works jobs and housing the homeless. Build an alternative to corporate greed and they will come.

Winter Soldiers

The occupations have been incredibly successful. But nothing can fail like success. Z magazine founder Michael Albert, just returned from conversations with protest veterans in Greece, Turkey, London, Dublin and Spain, reports he was told that their massive assemblies and occupations at first were invigorating and uplifting. "We were creating a new community. We were making new friends. We were hearing from new people." But as days and weeks passed, "it got too familiar. And it wasn't obvious what more they could do."

25   Besides boredom (rarely a problem so far), winter is coming. I can testify just from sleeping out on one rainy night in October that, whatever the occupiers' determination, it's going to be tough. Some will need to create sturdier encampments better protected against the elements. Some will need to come inside.

When a threatened army successfully repositions itself it is a victory, not a defeat. What matters is that the social forces that have made OWS and its kin continue their feisty, imaginative, nonviolent reclaiming of public space by marches, occupations and other forms of direct action without getting pinned down in positions they can't sustain. That way they can continue their crucial role in inspiring the rest of us 99 percenters to organize ourselves.

For that, they need help right now from the rest of us 99 percenters. In New York, there is now a campaign to let the protesters stay and set up tents. Elsewhere possibilities for using indoor spaces where occupiers can "come in from the cold" (with or without official permission) are being explored. Occupiers need both material aid and political pressure from unions, religious groups and ordinary 99 percenters to make the transition to the next phase.

In 1932 at the pit of the Great Depression, labor journalist Charles R. Walker visited "Hoovervilles" and unemployed workers' organizations around the country. He predicted:

> There will be increasing outbursts of employed and unemployed alike—a kind of spontaneous democracy expressing itself in organized demonstrations by large masses of people. They will "march or meet in order, elect their own spokesmen and committees, and work out in detail their demands for work or relief. They will present their formulated needs to factory superintendents, relief commissions, and city councils, and to the government at Washington."

What Walker called a "rough and ready democracy" is what OWS and its progeny around the country are creating today.

30   The unemployed councils Walker described lasted only a few years, but from them sprang the Workers Alliance, a hybrid of a trade union for workers on government public works projects and a welfare rights organization. It in turn was a crucial springboard for the industrial union movement that would transform the U.S. economic and political system.

The Occupy movement is not unlikely to last forever, nor would it be a good thing if it did. It could be forgotten like so many movements of the past. But it instead it could be remembered as the progenitor of the 99 Percent Movement. That depends on the rest of us 99 percenters.

Analyze

1. Explain how Brecher's allusions to the Vietnam War help to support his main idea.
2. Subheadings help writers to organize ideas, but they also help to create subtlety and dimension in an essay. Examine Brecher's subheadings and explain how they add subtlety or dimension to his main idea.
3. How does the paragraph about Rose Gudiel (paragraph 7) support Brecher's main idea?
4. Brecher admits that "nothing can fail like success." Explain what he means by this and how it relates to the success of the 99 Percent Movement.
5. How is Brecher's argument about culture—about a process through which things become normal?

Explore

1. People in the top 1 percent earn nearly $400,000 per year. Chances are, you're in the 99 percent. What does this mean to you? How does it impact your decisions about college, loans, work, or voting?
2. Have you or do you know someone who has directly participated in an Occupy movement? How does your answer influence your thinking about the movement?
3. When should American citizens protest? What kinds of issues, systems, or events should prompt people to take to the streets (or parks) and be heard?
4. Brecher explains that police departments have had a complex and evolving response to the Occupy movement. Consider the role of police departments in protests. What should they do? To whom should they listen? What are the gray areas? What are the questions or complexities they have to consider?
5. According to a range of studies, the United States ranks far behind European countries in upward mobility (the ability to keep earning more throughout one's life). In other words, moving from working

class to middle class—and from middle class to upper middle class—
is more difficult in the United States than many other places in
the world. Why is this? What forces or beliefs or systems might be
involved?

David Korten
When Bankers Rule the World

David Korten is a writer and speaker who is deeply involved in the efforts of
public interest citizen action groups. After working for many years to transform political structures in Southeast Asia, he realized that to achieve "a
positive human future, the United States must change." He is the author of
numerous articles and books, including the 2010 book *Agenda for a New
Economy: From Phantom Wealth to Real Wealth*. In the following magazine
article, Korten examines the cultural impact of Wall Street.

The tell-all defection of Greg Smith, a former Goldman Sachs executive,
provided an insider's view of the moral corruption of the Wall Street
banks that control of much of America's economy and politics. Smith confirms what insightful observers have known for years: the business purpose
of Wall Street bankers is to maximize their personal financial take without
regard to the consequences for others.

Wall Street's World of Illusion

Why has the public for so long tolerated Wall Street's reckless abuses
of power and accepted the resulting devastation? The answer lies in
a cultural trance induced by deceptive language and misleading indicators
backed by flawed economic theory and accounting sleight-of-hand. To
shatter the trance we need to recognize that the deception that Wall
Street promotes through its well-funded PR machine rests on three false
premises.

1. We best fulfill our individual moral obligation to society by maximizing our personal financial gain.
2. Money is wealth and making money increases the wealth of the society.
3. Making money is the proper purpose of the individual enterprise and is the proper measure of prosperity and economic performance.

Wall Street aggressively promotes these fallacies as guiding moral principles. Their embrace by Wall Street insiders helps to explain how they are able to reward themselves with obscene bonuses for their successful use of deception, fraud, speculation, and usury to steal wealth they have had no part in creating and yet still believe, as Goldman CEO Lloyd Blankfein famously proclaimed, that they are "doing God's work."

The devastation created by Wall Street's failure affirms three truths that are the foundation on which millions of people are at work building a New Economy:

1. Our individual and collective well-being depends on acting with concern for the well-being of others. We all do better when we look out for one another.
2. Money is not wealth. It is just numbers. Sacrificing the health and happiness of billions of people to grow numbers on computer hard drives to improve one's score on the Forbes Magazine list of the world's richest people is immoral. Managing a society's economy to facilitate this immoral competition at the expense of people and nature is an act of collective insanity.
3. The proper purpose of the economy and the enterprises that comprise it is to provide good jobs and quality goods and services beneficial to the health and happiness of people, community and nature. A modest financial profit is essential to a firm's viability, but is not its proper purpose.

The critical distinction between making money and creating wealth is the key to seeing through Wall Street's illusions. 5

Ends/Means Confusion

Real wealth includes healthful food, fertile land, pure water, clean air, caring relationships, quality education and health care, fulfilling opportunities for service, healthy and happy children, peace, time for meditation and spiritual reflection. These are among the many forms of real wealth to which we properly expect a sound economy to contribute.

Wall Street has so corrupted our language, however, that it is difficult even to express the crucial distinction between money (a facilitator of economic activity), and real wealth (the purpose of economic activity).

Financial commentators routinely use terms like wealth, capital, resources, and assets when referring to phantom wealth financial assets, which makes them sound like something real and substantial—whether or not they are backed by anything of real value. Similarly, they identify folks engaged in market speculation and manipulation as investors, thus glossing over the distinction between those who game the system to expropriate wealth and those who contribute to its creation.

The same confusion plays out in the use of financial indicators, particularly stock price indices, to evaluate economic performance. The daily rise and fall of stock prices tells us only how fast the current stock bubble is inflating or deflating and thus how Wall Street speculators are doing relative to the rest of us.

10   Once we are conditioned to embrace measures of Wall Street success as measures of our own well-being, we are easily recruited as foot soldiers in Wall Street's relentless campaign to advance policies that support its control of money and thus its hold on nearly every aspect of our lives.

Modern Enslavement

In a modern society in which our access to most essentials of life from food and water to shelter and health care depends on money, control of money is the ultimate instrument of social control.

Fortunately, with the help of Occupy Wall Street, Americans are waking up to an important truth. It is a very, very bad idea to yield control of the issuance and allocation of credit (money) to Wall Street banks run by con artists who operate beyond the reach of public accountability and who Greg Smith tells us in his *New York Times* op-ed view the rest of us as simple-minded marks ripe for the exploiting.

By going along with its deceptions, we the people empowered Wall Street to convert America from a middle class society of entrepreneurs, investors, and skilled workers into a nation of debt slaves. Buying into Wall

Street lies and illusions, Americans have been lured into accepting, even aggressively promoting, "tax relief" for the very rich and the "regulatory relief" and "free trade" agreements for corporations that allowed Wall Street to suppress wages and benefits for working people through union busting, automation, and outsourcing jobs to foreign sweatshops.

Once working people were unable to make ends meet with current income, Wall Street lured them into making up the difference by taking on credit card and mortgage debt they had no means to repay. They were soon borrowing to pay not only for current consumption, but as well to pay the interest on prior unpaid debt.

This is the classic downward spiral of debt slavery that assures an ever-growing divide between the power and luxury of a creditor class and the powerless desperation of a debtor class.

Bust the Trusts, Liberate America

Before Wall Street dismantled it, America had a system of transparent, well-regulated, community-based, locally owned, Main Street financial institutions empowered to put local savings to work investing in building real community wealth through the creation and allocation of credit to finance local home buyers and entrepreneurs.

Although dismissed by Wall Street players as small, quaint, provincial, and inefficient, this locally rooted financial system created the credit that financed our victory in World War II, the Main Street economies that unleashed America's entrepreneurial talents, the investments that made us the world leader in manufacturing and technology, and the family-wage jobs that built the American middle class. It is a proven model with important lessons relevant for current efforts to restore financial integrity and build an economy that serves all Americans.

Two recent reports from the New Economy Working Group—*How to Liberate America from Wall Street Rule* and *Jobs: A Main Street Fix for Wall Street's Failure*—draw on these lessons to outline a practical program to shift power from Wall Street to Main Street, focus economic policy on real wealth creation, create a true ownership society, unleash Main Street's entrepreneurial potential, bring ourselves into balance with the biosphere, meet the needs of all, and strengthen democracy in the process.

15

For far too long, we have allowed Wall Street to play us as marks in a confidence scam of audacious proportion. Then we wonder at our seeming powerlessness to deal with job loss, depressed wages, mortgage foreclosures, political corruption and the plight of our children as they graduate into debt bondage.

20   Let us be clear. We will no longer play the sucker for Wall Street con artists and we will no longer tolerate public bailouts to save failed Wall Street banks.

Henceforth, when a Wall Street financial institution fails to maintain adequate equity reserves to withstand a major financial shock or is found guilty of systematic violation of the law and/or defrauding the public, we must demand that federal authorities take it over and break it up into strictly regulated, community-accountable, cooperative member-owned financial services institutions.

Occupy Wall Street has focused national and global attention on the source of the problem. Now it's time for action to bust the Wall Street banking trusts, replace the current Wall Street banking system with a Main Street banking system, and take back America from rule by Wall Street bankers.

Analyze

1. According to Korten, how has Wall Street (and the illusion it has perpetuated) threatened democracy?

2. Korten argues, "By going along with its deceptions, we the people empowered Wall Street to convert America from a middle class society of entrepreneurs, investors, and skilled workers into a nation of debt slaves." How does this statement support or relate to his main idea?

3. Korten also argues, "Real wealth includes healthful food, fertile land, pure water, clean air, caring relationships, quality education and health care, fulfilling opportunities for service, healthy and happy children, peace, time for meditation and spiritual reflection." How does this definitional statement support his main idea?

4. Explain what values or beliefs Korten shares with Jeremy Brecher ("The 99 Percent Organize Themselves").

5. How is Korten's article an examination of culture? In other words, beyond the economic issues, what is Korten pointing to and arguing about?

Explore

1. Korten explains that Americans are in a "cultural trance" when it comes to financial matters. What have you seen that supports or challenges this idea?

2. Korten uses the term "Wall Street" to suggest a broader system of banks, companies, and stock portfolios. He contrasts this to "Main Street." What do you think the latter refers to or includes? Who or what makes up "Main Street"?

3. Because of retirement policies and tax laws, most working Americans are now directly connected to Wall Street. Why should or shouldn't people be concerned about this?

4. What does the phrase "community-accountable" mean? What organizations or companies should be community-accountable?

5. Consider the next essay in this chapter, Deanna Isaacs's "The Transnational Economy," and explain how a "transnational economy" might be related to Korten's concerns or hopes.

Deanna Isaacs
The Transnational Economy

The culture columnist for the *Chicago Reader,* Deanna Isaacs writes on issues related to art and architecture, urban culture, education, and politics. In the following article, she examines the phenomenon of global capitalism, and what it means for our work and well-being.

Amid all the blather about V-shaped and U-shaped economic recoveries, it's become pretty clear that we don't have any recovery at all. And that there's none on the near horizon. It looks, in fact, like we're screwed. What's less clear is exactly what happened.

A housing bubble and bust? Sure, but DeVry University history professor Jerry Harris says that's only one piece of a much bigger picture. According to Harris, we're undergoing a change so profound it portends the decline not only of America, but of the nation-state as an institution.

This startling development is the rise of global capitalism, complete with a transnational ruling elite that operates through nondemocratic bodies like the World Trade Organization, the G-20, the IMF, and the World Bank, Harris said in an Open University of the Left lecture at the Lincoln Park branch of the Chicago Public Library last month. In other words, the escape of big money from its historic national anchors and the social obligations that went with them.

The enabler is our friend technology. Both the *Chicago Tribune* and *The New York Times* carried stories this week about how technological innovation is taking jobs away rather than increasing them, as many experts expected. But that's not news to Harris, who began studying the economy after he was laid off from U.S. Steel's South Works plant in 1982.

5   "We lost a lot of jobs to technology before we lost them to other countries," Harris says. At U.S. Steel, where he started out in the blast furnace and then became a machine-shop apprentice, he recalls that the skilled workers he was training with "came in one day and found computer boards attached to their machines." During that decade, in factories across America, skilled labor was replaced by microchips, middle management was eliminated, and productivity skyrocketed. "By 1988," Harris notes in his 2008 book, *Dialectics of Globalization: Economic and Political Conflict in a Transnational World,* "the U.S. required only 40 percent of its blue-collar labor force to produce an amount of manufactured goods equal to that produced in 1977."

And then, IT advances made it practical to manage production anywhere in the world, and—whoosh.

Democracy and capitalism had grown up together, rooted in the French and American revolutions and bound by a socioeconomic contract that balanced property rights with personal rights, Harris says. "For many decades we had a nation-centric economy," with companies that identified themselves as loyal corporate citizens. Remember the slogan 'What's good for General Motors is good for the country'? At that time, the majority of General Motors' employment, sales, and assets were all inside the United States. Now the reverse is true: a majority of their employment, sales, and assets are outside their home country. And that's the case for all the major corporations around the world."

This should not be confused with that quaint old thing we once knew as the "international economy," Harris cautions. That was based on the export of products made in one country and sold in another. "Today, companies produce, invest, and employ everywhere, so what you have is a transnational corporation and a global assembly line. And in that scenario, he adds, as production moves to whatever country offers the cheapest sweatshop, "we're seeing the economic and social contract ripped up."

Harris says he doesn't "want to overstate the case" (i.e., nations aren't dead yet), "but transnational corporations and those who run them have less and less invested in any one particular country. They can make money anywhere, and the logic of capitalism itself drives them to lower their cost of production and increase their efficiency. If they don't do that, they become less competitive. They're driven to globalize, and as they do, they're less invested, for example, in the education system at home. They don't need as many engineers and scientists coming out of the United States when they can use Chinese, Indian, and Brazilian graduates at lower cost. The same logic drives their tax strategies. There are more corporate headquarters in the Cayman Islands than there are people there."

Meanwhile, we have a shrinking middle class here and growing poverty. 10 "That has political implications that we're seeing, for example, in the Occupy protests," Harris says. "There's a feeling of alienation, a sense that the national government is controlled by corporations. We gave billions to the banks (including foreign-owned banks), which they used to increase their own bonuses. What if that money went into infrastructure development, hiring people to build bridges, sewer systems, roads?

"We're not in the same situation as the southern European countries, but when you see the inability of the Obama administration to get the jobs bill through, and the whole discussion at the congressional level goes toward debt rather than stimulus, I think that's totally ass-backwards. About 76 percent of the people in polls say, yeah, raise the taxes on the wealthy and superrich, and yet not one Republican will do it. So where's the democracy in that?"

Analyze

1. What is the difference between an international and a transnational economy?
2. Why is a transnational economy a potential problem for or challenge to democracy?
3. Isaacs explains that "Democracy and capitalism had grown up together, rooted in the French and American revolutions and bound by a socioeconomic contract that balanced property rights with personal rights." How is this point related to her main idea?
4. Explain how Isaacs's parenthetical statement "nations aren't dead yet" functions in her overall argument.

5. Like David Korten ("When Bankers Rule the World"), Isaacs is arguing about more than economic issues. Explain how she is dealing with the culture—with broader processes surrounding any particular regulation or policy.

Explore

1. Why is a "shrinking middle class" a concern for so many economists?
2. What is the profound change that Isaacs references in her opening paragraphs? Have you seen evidence of it in your life?
3. Isaacs argues that the U.S. economy experienced no recovery, but most analysts have concluded the opposite: that the United States has been, since the recession of 2007, gaining momentum. So is Isaacs simply wrong? Or is she arguing about something bigger than the current situation?
4. This article was published at the end of 2011. Do you think anything significant has changed since then? Has anything happened to slow or shift the trend that Isaacs describes?
5. One commenter, "Pelham," to Isaacs's article on the *Chicago Reader* website suggested a proposal: "Mandate that all Fortune 500 companies' charters be put up for nationwide vote every four years. Let's all have a hand in deciding whether companies that offshore and outsource American jobs and technology should continue to function under their current management or be handed over to their workers or nationalized. This would also have the ancillary effect of establishing, for the first time in human history, truly representative democracy." Respond to Pelham's suggestions.

Starhawk
A Pagan Response to the Affordable Care Act

A social activist and religious leader, Starhawk (www.starhawk.org) examines political issues from a Neo-Pagan perspective, which emphasizes a feminine, earth-based spirituality. Named an *Utne Reader* Visionary in 1995, she is a blogger, a contributor to the *Washington Post,* and the author of numerous books of nonfiction, fiction, and children's literature. In the following blog post, Starhawk considers the spiritual and political dimensions of health care.

Jason Pitzi-Waters, of the Pagan Newswire Collective, asked a few of us to respond to the Supreme Court's decision that the Affordable Care Act is constitutional. Here's mine:

A Pagan response—or rather, this Pagan's response for there is no universal agreement among Pagans on any issue—to the upholding of the Affordable Care Act has two aspects: is it good for us, individually and as a community, and is it in concert with our Pagan values.

While the Act is not as good for me, individually or many of us as a single-payer system would be, it is definitely an improvement over the callous and greed-ridden system we've got. Like many other Pagan writers and teachers, I'm self-employed and have been pretty much all my adult life. I've had health insurance since my mother brow-beat me into getting it in my twenties, with the same company. While I'm pretty healthy for my age, I've seen my premiums go up and up every year, to the point that they were costing me more than my mortgage, more than my food budget, more than anything else. Now, if I were being taxed for a single-payer system, when my income went down my payments would go down. But with private insurance, the price just keeps going up and up and up! When it finally reached over $1200 a month, I started looking for other options. I tried switching companies, but I'm now over sixty, overweight (not alone among Pagans in being so!) and with minor but irritating health problems that somehow drove my projected premiums up even higher! So I switched to a lower-cost plan that has a $6000 deductible. That would keep me from losing my house should I get a serious illness, and having lost five friends in the last five months, mostly to cancer, I can't ignore that possibility. I'm still trying to save up the $6000 to have ready in the bank should I need it suddenly—because if I do get sick, I won't be able to travel and teach which provides the bulk of my income.

Meanwhile, I encountered the dreaded Socialized Medicine when I was in England and needed a new asthma inhaler. I was able to get an appointment at the local clinic in Totnes—the same day I asked for one. I saw a doctor, who gave me a new prescription. He very apologetically informed me that I would have to pay for it, he was so sorry, because I'm not on National Health. I said that was okay, as an American, I was used to it. The clinic had a pharmacy on the premises, and the pharmacist filled the prescription, also expressing regret and embarrassment that I had to pay. He then charged me just over 5 English pounds—less than $10, for two inhalers, each of which costs me about $35 in the US!

I left, infuriated—not at the National Health, but at our own rip-off 5 system. Why should we pay two, four, seven times as much if not to enrich somebody at our expense? Since I shifted my insurance, and since my own trusted doctor retired, I haven't been to see a doctor since, except for a couple of weeks ago when I had a serious bout with asthma after camping out in the desert. I went to the clinic at the University of California. I had to fill out a form before I saw anyone, stating my financial qualifications to be seen. The form informed me that the visit would like cost something in the neighborhood of $450! But they couldn't tell me how much, ahead of time. No one tells you what any specific treatment costs, before you have it—yet you are expected to pay. I know there are many preventive things I should be doing, at my age—like keeping a watch on my blood sugar levels, but when money is short, as it often is, I hesitate to make an appointment or sign up for tests that might break the budget. And I think many others, Pagans and not-Pagans, are in the same situation.

So for me personally, the ACA will help. The insurance exchanges may allow me to get a better policy at lower cost. Some of the provisions of the act assure more justice and fairness for everyone. And while it's not the National Health or Canada's public insurance, I believe we are in a better position to push for more when we build on success than we would be if we had to recover from failure.

I didn't mean to write quite this much. Do I have feelings about this? Evidently I do!

Now, as for the ethics. Our traditions tell us that we Witches were the village healers, the wise women and cunning men who offered herbs and treatment and magic to the sick, especially to the poor. As such we have a special interest in assuring access to health care for all.

I believe the core value in Pagan ethics is the understanding that we are interconnected and interdependent. On that basis, health care is an important right and everyone should have access to it. My personal health is not separate from your well-being. Health is partly a matter of personal responsibility, but all of us are subject to forces beyond our control. If we suffer illness or injury or sheer bad luck, we shouldn't be left alone to suffer the consequences unaided. We live in a more and more toxic environment, and the constant assaults on our health from pollutants and radiation and the degradation of our food supply are our collective responsibility. No one should be left alone to bear the consequences of our collective failure to protect the life-support systems around us. Rather, it is to all of our benefit to share a public responsibility for our mutual well being, because every single one of us, at some point in life, will need that help. No one gets through life unscathed, and in the end we die. If we truly accept death as part of life, with its attendant break-downs of the body and the many sorts of mischance that befall us along the way, then we do well to offer one another solidarity and succor.

To sum up, universal access to health care is consonant with our core   10 Pagan values of interconnection and interdependence. The Affordable Care Act is a small step toward that end, flawed but better than no change at all. As Michael Moore has said, it should spur us to keep working for a better, more equitable system. But I believe we'll do better building on a small success than we would have trying to recover from an abject failure. I hope as Pagans we can help to lead the way.

Analyze

1. How is Starhawk's Paganism central to her position?
2. Starhawk says, "No one gets through life unscathed, and in the end we die." How does this point relate to her main idea? Explain the intellectual steps required to go from this bold and general statement to her point about health care.
3. Explain how Starhawk's experience in England supports her main idea.
4. How is Starhawk's position related to Katelyn Langdale's essay "The Illogical World of U.S. Immigration"? Despite the topics and specific policy positions, what beliefs or assumptions might they share?
5. How does Starhawk's post show or dramatize the tension between tradition and cultural change?

Explore

1. You might be accustomed to hearing politicians and news channel pundits explain their views on health care policy. How has this text, written by a tax-paying citizen and Pagan, impacted your thinking?
2. Where did you derive your opinions about health care? From what people, channels, programs, or texts?
3. What principle or concept should be at the center of health care policy? Profit? Individual responsibility? Public responsibility? Unity? Something else?
4. It's a well-published fact that U.S. citizens pay dramatically more than most European countries for health care. What do you think is the cause? What causes have you heard or read about?
5. Why do you think positions on health care policy are often dependent on people's loyalty to the Republican and Democratic parties?

David R. Dow
We Stop the Next Aurora Not with Gun Control but with Better Mental Health Treatment

A professor at the University of Houston Law Center and Rice University, David R. Dow is a death penalty lawyer whose work focuses on capital punishment, justice, and jurisprudence. He is the author of numerous articles and books, including the forthcoming book *Things I've Learned from Dying* (2014). In the following *Daily Beast* article, Dow considers the phenomenon of mass shootings as a mental health issue.

I've been a gun-control advocate for thirty years, but when I received two e-mails Friday afternoon advocating gun control while the bodies in Aurora, Colo. were still warm, the solicitations left me cold. It's not just because the exploitation of a tragedy to achieve a political objective is obscene; it's because we've had this argument before, we know it by heart, and it doesn't matter a whit.

Gun-control advocates say if we had more rigorous laws, Columbine and Virginia Tech, and now Aurora, would not have happened. The NRA says if more people at the scene of the tragedy had been packing heat, they could have taken the shooter down.

Both arguments are equally absurd. If reports are accurate, James Holmes, the accused shooter in Aurora, was wearing body armor head to toe. Nobody carrying a .38 or a .45 was going to stop him. If ten people had been carrying guns with 10 rounds each, another hundred people would have been wounded, some probably mortally.

More important, what these mass slaughters have in common has less to do with the ease of getting weapons than with our society's reaction to monstrous acts perpetrated by those with mental illness. The key word is reaction; we do not do anything until it is too late.

5   In his magisterial book about Columbine, Dave Cullen exposes the broken brains of Eric Harris and Dylan Klebold, and the portrait that emerges, in my view, is one that strict gun laws could not have altered. I suspect we'll learn the same of Jared Lee Loughner, who shot Rep. Gabrielle Giffords and killed six others, if he ever goes on trial. All three are

psychological siblings of Anders Breivik, the diseased Norwegian who murdered 77 men and women last year. And Breivik in turn is the psychological cousin of our own Timothy McVeigh, who murdered 168 people without any guns at all. (Norway, by the way, has a higher rate of gun ownership than any other country in Western Europe, but gun-control advocates in America would be thrilled for even a watered-down version of the country's restrictions.)

Some people are talking about mental illness today who were not talking about it Thursday, and that's good, but most people are talking about gun control and capital punishment. A friend asked me on my Facebook page whether Aurora is a good reason for the death penalty.

If you are talking about the death penalty now, you are talking about closing the barn door after the mare is a mile down the road, and if you are talking about gun control, you're bringing a knife to a gun fight. The problem we have in America is a deep cultural denial that there are thousands of damaged human beings whom we ignore until they explode, and who get worse while—and because—we ignore them.

Here's what we should have learned by now: You do not mend broken people by trying to close off their access to guns, because they will get them online or use homemade bombs instead, and you do not deter other broken people by killing the ones who crack. If you were to ask Jared Loughner or James Holmes about Timothy McVeigh, your answer would probably be a blank stare.

Gun control is good for a lot of things. It will keep kids from killing themselves with their dads' unsecured guns. It will make it harder for drug dealers to kill each other, and it will save lives in ordinary robberies. It might even prevent wildfires in the West. But it will not stop the mentally ill from reaping carnage because the proximate cause of their carnage is disease, not hardware.

If you say that a ten-round clip would have limited the damage in Aurora, you might be right. But you also might be wrong, because Holmes might have walked in instead with a bomb. Either way, here we are arguing about how to limit the damage broken people do rather than talking about how to mend broken people.

Of course nobody needs an AK-47 or a twenty-round clip, and the Supreme Court ruling making it more difficult for communities to restrict access to guns was deeply unsound. But before we get sidetracked for the umpteenth time talking about limiting access to certain calibers, or muzzle velocities, or clip size, we should perhaps start talking about how we can identify broken people—not just when they walk into a gun store to purchase a weapon (although certainly there as well), but also when they apply to college, or for a driver's license, or do anything else that might call them to the attention of people who are trained to look.

Prisons, homeless shelters, and highway underpasses are teeming with mentally ill human beings because our society thinks harsh punishment will solve most of the problem, and restrictions to the implements of crime will solve the rest. Wrong and wrong again. Nobody is responsible for the unspeakable tragedy James Holmes unleashed besides James Holmes. But all of us share responsibility for ignoring the James Holmeses of our world until they force us to learn their infamous names.

Analyze

1. Dow calls the two most common policy positions on mass shootings "equally absurd." In your own words, explain those two positions and Dow's criticism of each.
2. Explain the function of Dow's references to other mass shootings. How do they serve his main idea?
3. Dow says, "If you are talking about the death penalty now, you are talking about closing the barn door after the mare is a mile down the road." Articulate his point without the interesting metaphor. Explain why he thinks the death penalty is an irrelevant issue when it comes to mass shootings.
4. In his conclusion, Dow argues that "all of us share responsibility for ignoring the James Holmses of the world." Explain how this point relates to his main idea.
5. Explain how Dow's argument relates to culture. (How is his main idea related to the way people grapple with or resist change?)

Explore

1. This article was written before the December 2012 mass shooting of schoolchildren in Newtown, CT. How do you think Dow's argument might change with news of that shooting, which took the lives of 20 children, several of their teachers, and the gunman's mother?
2. Consider Starhawk's blog post in this chapter about the Affordable Care Act ("A Pagan's Response to the Affordable Healthcare Act").

How is her point related to Dow's? What is the relationship between health care policy and homicidal behavior?

3. Some people argue that mass shootings are a natural, or at least inevitable, consequence of living in a free society. What do you think?

4. One commenter, "robwriter," responded to Dow's article with the following point about mental illness. How would you respond to robwriter?

> I have no argument against the premise of this piece; it seems clear that the problem is mental illness, not weaponry per se. However, we've had this conversation before too and it turns out that advocating for the mentally ill is a long row to hoe. As a healthcare worker who has had occasional to frequent contacts with the mentally ill I can assure you that as a group they are not very sympathetic. In short, they are mostly difficult to relate to at best, a pain in the ass generally, extremely dangerous at worst. AIDS and breast cancer have their nationally recognized ribbons. People with degenerative neurological diseases like Lou Gehrig's are objects of pity. People with Down's Syndrome are typically open and affectionate. The mentally ill, not so much. So basically, the mentally ill aren't getting a ribbon any time soon.
>
> The U.S. has quietly divested itself of the responsibility to care for the mentally ill. The national wave of state hospital closures in decades past was an abdication excused with the specious argument that the severely incompetent would be managed as outpatients. Instead they ended up off their meds, sleeping in doorways, rummaging for food in dumpsters, mumbling to themselves as they wander the streets, covered in filth and stinking to high heaven for lack of bathing. In a word, no one we want to cuddle with.
>
> America will massively incarcerate pot smokers in for-profit prisons, but not drunk drivers who commit vehicular homicide. America will pursue corporate welfare schemes like Romneycare, but won't commit to any form of a single payer system that might extend basic healthcare to all its citizens at sustainable cost. Apology in advance to Mr. Dow, but the notion that the U.S. will get serious about mental health just because some sicko guns down a few score people every six months or so is nearly delusional.

Janice Brewer
Letter from Governor Janice Brewer to President Barack Obama

A member of the Republican Party, Janice Brewer is Arizona's 22nd governor. In the wake of her anti-illegal immigration measures as governor, Brewer has been at the center of national debate about immigration law, reform, and rights. She is the author of the 2011 book *Scorpions for Breakfast: My Fight Against Special Interests, Liberal Media, and Cynical Politicos to Secure America's Border*. In 2010, Brewer corresponded with President Obama about the problem of illegal immigration in Arizona. The following letter was part of the exchange between the White House and the governor's office.

STATE OF ARIZONA

JANICE K. BREWER   EXECUTIVE OFFICE
GOVERNOR   JUNE 23, 2010

The Honorable Barack Obama
The President of the United States
The White House
1600 Pennsylvania Avenue
Washington, DC 20500

Dear Mr. President:

Thank you for the opportunity to visit with you in person during my recent trip to Washington, D.C. As you know, the issue of border security is foremost in the thoughts of many Arizonans and Americans alike, and I appreciated the chance to personally relate to you my concerns and outline my proposed solutions.

Mr. President, the need for action to secure Arizona's border could not be clearer. Recently, my office received a number of calls from constituents concerned at reports of new sign postings in interior counties of Arizona warning residents not to access federal lands due to criminal activity associated with the border. These warnings signal to some that we have handed over portions of our border areas to illegal immigrants and drug traffickers. This is unacceptable. Instead of warning Americans to stay out of parts of our own country, we ought to be warning international lawbreakers that they will be detained and prosecuted to the fullest extent of the law. We ought to be establishing measures to ensure that illegal traffic of any sort is kept to an absolute minimum, and that Americans are safe and secure within our own borders.

When we visited, you committed to present details, within two weeks of our meeting, regarding your plans to commit National Guard troops to the Arizona border and expend $500 million in additional funds on border security matters. You also discussed sending members of your senior staff to Arizona to discuss your plans. While I am pleased the 28th has been set for a meeting time and we have reviewed a copy of the Department of Homeland Security's "Southwest Border Next Steps" press release, I am still awaiting details on National Guard deployments and how the proposed additional border security funding will specifically affect Arizona (and the other Border States). As I mentioned to you on June 3rd, it is very difficult to have much of a dialogue without specific details regarding your proposals. I strongly urge you to request your staff provide us with missing details of your proposals prior to the meeting on the 28th.

While we await the specific details of your border security plans, I wanted to take the time to reemphasize some of what I shared with you and respond further to some of what we discussed. In essence, I have proposed a four-point Border Surge strategy, as outlined in my recent letter to Senator Charles Schumer, summarized as follows:

1. National Guard Personnel and Aviation

I believe a significant number of troops operating with a legitimate mission set is an essential part of any strategy to secure the border. I appreciate your commitment of 1,200 troops and the promise that Arizona would receive the largest contingent. I am concerned, however, that more is required, such as the deployment of 6,000 personnel proposed by Senators Jon Kyl and John McCain for the entire southwestern border.

In addition, I want to make sure that these troops have legitimate missions that:

- Support federal, state and local law enforcement—all three!
- Serve as a blocking force to stop illegal crossing activities.
- Employ the troops in a way that speaks loudly to all—both north and south of the border—that the U.S. is serious about this matter.

As part of your commitment, I also hope that you order a significant increase in aviation resources supporting border security operations on the ground. After meeting and talking to various experts, I am persuaded that aviation support is critical to the effort on the ground. Any effort will fail absent the ability to coordinate ground assets from the air, particularly given the nature of much of Arizona's border region terrain. I respectfully ask that you give serious consideration to my May 20, 2010 correspondence, which makes a very reasonable request for a reallocation of National Guard OH-58 helicopter assets in order to make a Border Surge effective. Your support of this request can make a significant difference between a winning effort versus a losing effort.

2. Border Fence

In short Mr. President, we need to complete, reinforce and then maintain the border fence. In my April 6, 2010 letter to you I proposed inmate labor and other methods (i.e., purchasing instead of leasing equipment) as a means to bring down construction/maintenance costs. I certainly support efficient and effective Ports of Entry where both American and Mexican border officials can allow legal traffic and crossings. Everywhere else along the border, though, I strongly believe we must have fencing and barriers that are both substantial and monitored if the illegal crossings are to be minimized.

3. Enforce Federal Law and Appropriately Fund the Effort

The United States must be prepared to detain, prosecute and then incarcerate convicted violators of United States laws. The current "no consequences policy" has resulted in a border security failure. I appreciate your general proposal to commit additional resources, but it is very difficult for me to comment without any details. It is without doubt, though, that the current border policy will continue to fail the State of Arizona without additional resources committed to the Border Patrol, Immigration and Customs Enforcement (ICE) personnel and detention facilities; prosecution; public defense; and federal prisons.

4. Reimburse States for the Additional Burden of Illegal Immigration

As I mentioned the very first time we met last year, I must continue the calls for Arizona to be reimbursed for expenses we are forced to carry because of our porous southern border. Arizona and a few other states are at a terrible disadvantage in good times, and an even worse position during bad times, because of the additional costs of illegal immigration. Just in terms of state prison costs, we estimate ongoing expenses at approximately $150 million to incarcerate criminal aliens. While substantial on its own, this figure does not include law enforcement, prosecution and defense costs, or the enormous societal costs of the criminal behavior of those who are not even legally entitled to be here.

We are hundreds of millions of dollars short of what we should receive to relieve the disproportionate law enforcement/jail/prison, health care and education burdens we face due to our porous southern border and rampant illegal immigration. It is simply unfair for the federal government to force Border State taxpayers to carry these burdens.

Immigration Reform

You shared with me your thoughts about the matter of immigration reform and I am grateful you listened to mine. As I mentioned in our meeting, the phrase "comprehensive immigration reform" is code for "amnesty" to many in Arizona and elsewhere in our Nation. Many Americans are still waiting for the reforms that were promised by the federal government in the 1980s when amnesty was granted to thousands of illegal immigrants. Until we establish a secure border, and reestablish trust with the public that our international borders are meaningful and important, and enforcement of federal immigration law is not an idle threat, any discussion of "comprehensive reform" is premature.

Let's first block illegal entry into the United States and enforce current law, and then other discussions, including immigration reform, might then, and only then, make sense to the public. I am committed to a serious discussion of legitimate reform—but not any false front for amnesty—when the federal government halts the free flow of illegal immigrants and illegal drugs across the southwestern border.

Arizona's Law

You also shared some concerns about a "patchwork" approach to policy. This makes sense to me, but the failure of the federal government has driven frustration levels to the point that tolerating the status quo is no longer acceptable for Arizona. From my perspective, the single most significant factor behind the passage this year of SB 1070 and HB 2162 (the follow-up bill with amendments to SB 1070) was the frustration of Arizona elected officials, and the public we serve, regarding the failure of the federal government over the years to effectively address the problem of illegal immigration.

The growing concerns over spillover violence, the increased awareness of kidnappings, the spread of drop houses in neighborhoods throughout metropolitan areas, the scourge of the drug trade and the oppressive financial burdens posed by illegal immigration—burdens even more difficult to shoulder in this economic downturn—all contributed to accelerating the public's frustration.

I am 100% committed to fair and just enforcement of the new Arizona law. I have made it clear that civil rights will not be compromised. The first step has been educating and training law enforcement, as well as the public, on the details of the law—a step I have already ordered in Arizona.

Instead of any discussion about suing Arizona and not cooperating with the efforts of local Arizona law enforcement to address illegal immigration, the federal government should reassure Arizona (and other states) that securing the border and enforcing federal immigration laws are duties to which the federal government will make a renewed and sincere commitment.

When the public sees consistent evidence of federal commitment, I am convinced the demand for state actions will wane. State and local governments have plenty to do and will be happy to stay out of border security and immigration law enforcement—along with the expenses of such work—if the federal government takes a firm and effective grip on the problem.

Conclusion

In closing, I want to assure you that I am looking to develop a solution, not have a standoff, with you and the federal government. Illegal immigration is a serious problem and I am sincerely committed to seeing something done to curb it. The real challenges at hand are about violent crime, huge taxpayer burdens, the rule of law and ensuring that our southern border does not become an open door for radical terrorists. Commerce with other countries is important to me and Arizonans— I truly want a vibrant and positive relationship with Sonora, other Mexican States and the rest of the world. Federal immigration law, however, must be honored and enforced, and our border must represent an effective means to help ensure our sovereignty and security.

I remain eager to receive the specific details of your proposals and to have the follow-up meeting with your senior staff. It is disappointing that we are such a short time away from the meeting and Arizona and the other Border States still are awaiting the specific details of what you are proposing. There is still time, however, to ensure the meeting next week is productive.

Finally, I want to re-extend the invitation I made to you to come to Arizona yourself, visit with families living along the southwestern border and see the situation firsthand. My prior visits to the border and the air survey of the Cochise County region have been very important to shaping my perspectives and thinking. Governor Richardson joined me for one trip and I believe you would also benefit from such an experience.

And when you do come, lunch is on me!

Yours in service to the great state of Arizona,

Janice K. Brewer
Governor

Analyze

1. Identify passages in which Brewer is deferential or conciliatory to President Obama. How do these passages function in her argument? What do they accomplish or help to establish?
2. Brewer refers several times to her visit with President Obama. Why? What do these references do for her argument?
3. In her section on Immigration Reform, Brewer explains that "comprehensive immigration reform" is code for "amnesty." What does she mean here? What is her subtle argument?
4. Explain how Brewer addresses concerns about racial profiling.
5. How is Brewer's letter about the tension between state government and federal government? What passages most dramatize that tension?

Explore

1. Should the National Guard protect the border between Arizona and Mexico? Why or why not?
2. Should the federal government reimburse Arizona (and other border states) for the costs incurred from border protection, incarceration, and health care related to illegal immigration? Why or why not?
3. Why do Mexican citizens continue immigrating to the United States despite the perils?
4. Where do you place illegal immigration as a national priority? Consider other national issues such as education, economic stimulus, environmental protection, banking regulation, and terrorism. Where is illegal immigration? Why would you give it high or low priority?
5. Consider Katelyn Langdale's argument in this chapter ("The Illogical World of U.S. Immigration") about immigrating to the United States. How does her argument relate to Brewer's? How does it complicate the immigration issue?

Katelyn Langdale
The Illogical World of U.S. Immigration

Katelyn Langdale is pursuing a degree in computer science. In the following essay, developed for a first-semester writing course, she questions the effectiveness of U.S. immigration policy in promoting cultural diversity. She relies on personal testimony and several outside sources to make her case.

I was minutes away from talking to the man or woman who was about to change my life. For the past thirty minutes, I had been sitting on hold, waiting to speak to a Global Visas representative about the possibility of moving to the United States and starting a new life. I envisioned myself working, enjoying all the sights and sounds that the country had to offer, and finally being able to live with my boyfriend. My heart leapt into my throat as I heard the call being transferred through, and found myself shocked by the gruff, abrupt man on the other end. "Yeah, hello. Global Visas." I stated my case and heard an audible sigh at the other end. "Are you a doctor or a highly trained professional? Do you have immediate relatives in the United States? Are you wealthy?" My answer to all of his questions was a big, resounding "no." The representative did not sound enthused and simply told me, "You won't get in. Move to Canada, they let all sorts of people live in their country. Goodbye."

The world of immigration is an interesting one, with the policies being so perplexing and mind-bending that many seek the help of immigration lawyers. With a lawyer's assistance, I discovered that I had two choices: The first was to apply for a fiancé visa and marry my boyfriend within three months of arriving in the United States, and the second was to obtain a student visa and go to school. The first would have been easier, but I didn't want to be forced into a rushed marriage. Because of such restrictive immigration laws, it looked as though school was my only chance to enter the country for an extended period of time.

Immigration debates stir up emotions. Plenty of politicians and organizations link immigration to population control and unemployment. One such organization, FAIR (The Federation for American Immigration Reform), claims that "Immigration is directly responsible for over sixty percent of population growth in America" (7) and that "An estimated

1,880,000 American workers are displaced from their jobs every year by immigration" (7). With the U.S. population standing at a projected 314,913,484 as of December 2012 (United States Census Bureau), it seems unreasonable and maybe a little far-fetched for FAIR to make such a bold claim in regards to the role of immigrants in population increase. In terms of employment, while FAIR'S evidence against immigrants is damning, *New York Times* writer Eduardo Porter suggests otherwise:

> The most recent empirical studies conclude that the impact is slight: they confirm earlier findings that immigration on the whole has not led to fewer jobs for American workers. More significantly, they suggest that immigrants have had, at most, a small negative impact on the wages of Americans who compete with them most directly, those with a high school degree or less.

In "Immigration's Impact on U.S. Workers," writer Steven Camarota comments that "the overall impact of immigration is almost certainly very small," and he states that "arguments for or against immigration are as much political and moral as they are economic." In addition to these facts, jobs have technically been lost due to talented, skilled international students having their next round of visas denied. Snapdeal.com founder Kunal Bahl is an Ivy League–educated student who found himself unable to stay in the United States after his visa application was rejected. Back in his home country of India, Bahl's online-based business flourished, to the point where he had to hire 300 employees in order to cope with the massive workload. If his visa application to stay in the United States had been accepted, Bahl would have hired U.S. citizens to fill these roles ("Strict U.S.").

As an international student, I feel as though my days are numbered   5 unless I choose to get married within the next two years. But even if this is the case, I will still find myself stuck in the visa war. I viewed the United States as a free, welcoming country, but now I live in fear that one mistake at school will cost me my newfound American life. Failing a subject results in a violation of my visa terms and I will be told to leave the country. I can work, but only on-campus for a maximum of 20 hours. I pay almost three times as much for tuition as a regular in-state student and I do not get offered any kind of payment plan. Once I am finished with my education, I don't get to stay here and put my skills into practice in the United States.

Some people may argue that I should just accept the visa the way it is, and I honestly do. When my student visa got approved, I knew exactly what to expect in terms of employment limitations, the costs involved and the strict academic requirements. However, as someone who loves this country, and as someone who wants to start a family here, I find it nonsensical that literally no other options exist for individuals like me. Of course, there is the controversial Diversity Visa Lottery Program to take into consideration, but the chance of me "winning" an immigration visa is few and far between.

For the uninitiated, the Diversity Visa Lottery Program is a United States Government-based initiative that encourages diversity by handing out 50,000 immigration visas each year to anyone from an "underrepresented" country who enters their name (Krikorian). 50,000 visas sounds like a generous amount, but take into consideration the millions of people who submit their name every year. Since its conception, the program's rules and guidelines have no doubt become more refined and strict, but the number of entries is still immense.

Some would argue that this is diversity at its finest, but how can the United States even justify this program when so many individuals have been genuinely battling the immigration system for years? As if the whole idea of the lottery isn't ridiculous enough, past visa winners have even been involved in terrorist activity, which brings the program's integrity and filtering methods into question. According to Mark Krikorian, executive director of the Center for Immigration Services, there is one man in particular who was able to take complete advantage of the lottery system:

> The most notorious lottery winner is Hesham Mohamed Ali Hedayet, the Egyptian immigrant who went to Los Angeles International Airport to kill Jews on July 4, 2002. Hedayet came to this country on a temporary visa, became illegal when he overstayed his welcome, then applied for asylum, was denied, again becoming an illegal alien, and finally got a green card when his wife won the lottery.

While I oppose FAIR's stance on completely slashing immigration numbers, I do agree with the organization's wish to have the lottery abolished. Such a warped system is an insult to anyone who has been, or is currently, tied up in the legalities of the immigration system. In some cases, the whole immigration and citizenship process can take up to 28 years for an individual (Flynn and Dalmia 33). How can this be justified?

So, let me break it down: The United States upholds the strictest of im-   10
migration policies in order to keep the country safe, yet it allows thousands
of relatively unchecked, unfiltered, potentially dangerous people into the
country each year with the childlike belief that it creates diversity. This
leads me to believe that the immigration process is flawed. And it is infuri-
ating to think that the path to citizenship can be as hard as waiting 28 years
or as easy as submitting a name to the lottery and winning.

I want nothing more than to prove myself to the people of the United
States. I promise that I will be a good, valuable citizen. I want to work hard,
help support the economy and eventually start a family, and so do many
others stuck in the immigration system. Unfortunately though, a promise
alone is not enough to satisfy the United States government and its policies.
In a country so concerned with the safety, security, and livelihood of its
citizens, I can understand why many may still oppose immigration—even
the idea—but Edwin Yohnka, the chair of the ABA Pro Bono Immigration
Project makes a plea: "If we're concerned about protecting our way of life,
we have to start by respecting it. Part of that is recognizing that we welcome
people to come here" (qtd. in Tebo 47).

Works Cited

Camarota, Steven A. "Immigration's Impact on U.S. Workers."
    Center for Immigration Studies, 19 Nov. 2009. Web. 4
    Dec. 2012.

Flynn, Mike, and Shikha Dalmia. "What Part of Legal Immigra-
    tion Don't You Understand?" *Reason.org* Reason Foundation,
    Oct. 2008. Web. 19 Nov. 2012.

Federation for American Immigration Reform. "Immigration 101:
    A Primer on Immigration and the Need for Reform." *FAIR.*
    Federation for American Immigration Reform, 2000. Web.
    4 Dec. 2012.

Krikorian, Mark. "Gambling with Visas." *The American Enterprise*
    15.3: 52–56. *Academic OneFile.* Web. 4 Dec. 2012.

Porter, Eduardo. "Immigration and American Jobs." *The New York
    Times*, 19 Oct. 2012. Web. 4 Dec. 2012.

"Strict U.S. immigration policies contribute to high unemploy-
    ment." *RT.* Autonomous Non-Profit Organisation (ANO)
    "TV-Novosti," 4 Aug. 2012. Web. 4 Dec. 2012.

Tebo, Margaret Graham "The Closing Door: U.S. Policies Leave Immigrants Separate and Unequal." *ABA Journal* 88.9: 43–47. Web. 19 Nov. 2012.

United States Census Bureau, Dec. 2012. Web. 9 Dec. 2012.

Analyze

1. What is Langdale's point about immigration policy?
2. Explain how Langdale's personal testimony functions in this essay. What specific idea does it help to flesh out or support?
3. How does the allusion to Hedayet, the Egyptian immigrant arrested in Los Angeles, help to support Langdale's argument?
4. In her conclusion, Langdale appeals directly to the people of the United States. What is the effect? How does this support her main idea?
5. What assumptions or beliefs do you think Langdale shares with Governor Janice Brewer ("Letter from Governor Janice Brewer to President Barack Obama")?

Explore

1. What do you think of the Diversity Visa Lottery Program? Should the United States continue the program? Why or why not?
2. What is the inherent value of diversity to a civilization like the United States of America? What does ethnic and racial diversity do for the culture?
3. Beyond the two options available to immigrants like Langdale (get married or attend school), what else can you imagine? If immigrants want to move here through all the legal channels, what else could they do on the road to full citizenship?
4. When did your family emigrate to the United States? Under what conditions? What country did they leave behind? What were they hoping for?
5. How will racial and ethnic diversity figure into your future professional life? For example, in what capacity will you interact with people of different racial backgrounds? What languages will help you to thrive in your work?

Forging Connections

1. Are you in the 99 percent? The top 5 percent? The bottom 50 percent? How has your socioeconomic class impacted your decisions as a college student? Did you consider, for instance, applying to the Ivy League, a local community college, or a state school in your region? Even if you didn't consciously weigh your own or your parents' income level, how might it have played a role in your present situation? Write a reflective essay that explores answers to these questions. Borrow insights from Jeremy Brecher ("The 99 Percent Organize Themselves") or David Korten ("When Bankers Rule the World"), or authors in Chapter 1, "Work: What We Do" such as Mike Rose ("Blue-Collar Brilliance"), Christian Williams ("This, That, and the American Dream"), or Jason Storms ("In the Valley of the Shadow of Debt").

2. How is entertainment or consumerism related to politics? More specifically, how have television programs like *The Daily Show, The Colbert Report,* and *The O'Reilly Factor* impacted political views in this country? Research one of these shows and explore its demographic. Examine how the viewing audience tends to vote or what political positions it champions. Or you might take a less direct path. Consider, for example, how football and advertisements surrounding it have suggested a kind of worldview or a certain set of values. Or imagine how prime time sitcoms have prompted a way of thinking about socioeconomic class. Write an analytical essay that makes connections between a particular program (or type of program) and some broader political trend. Borrow insights from writers such as Fredrik deBoer ("The Resentment Machine," Chapter 2), James Gleick ("What Defines a Meme?," Chapter 4), or Sameer Pandya ("The Picture for Men: Superhero or Slacker," Chapter 5).

Looking Further

1. Research the Affordable Care Act and examine, specifically, how the new health care laws within it affect you as a college student. Write an analytical essay that traces specific provisions to your living situation. In addition to financial issues, explore the indirect impact on your decisions. For example, one provision allows college students to remain on their parent or legal guardian's health care plan without taking a full

load of courses. Students can take six or eight credit hours and still retain health care. How might this provision, or others, impact your life?

2. What kind of political creature are you? Are you socially liberal and fiscally conservative or the opposite? Are you moderate in all things or do you veer dramatically to the left or right? Are you a secular humanist who seeks further separation of church and state or a neo-conservative pushing for prayer in public schools? Before answering, research some political party platforms: the Republican, Democratic, Libertarian, Socialist, and Green. Try to understand some of the common tensions and positions on issues related to taxes, education, the environment, immigration, and women's rights. In a personal essay, describe which principles from these parties seem most appealing to you. If you do not subscribe to one party entirely, make up your own. Give it a name, a motto, and even a symbol. Integrate images to help express the nature of your political party platform.

9 War: How We Fight

War can be seen as the end of culture—its apex, ultimate conclusion, and most direct expression. In this perspective, war and culture are bound together. The soldiers, bombs, and machinery are natural extensions of shared beliefs. The whole society, in fact, culminates in military force. Serving as a signof this union, the national flag announces no difference between the soldier and an elementary school student, between a tank and a church back home, or between a bomb dropped on an enemy and the town where the bomb was made. In this perspective, citizens have duties: to sacrifice their children's lives, to pay taxes, or even to protest policies that seem out of line with shared beliefs. But war can also be seenas separate from culture, as a necessary reflex to keep culture alive. In this perspective, war is the sacrificial lamb. As Donald

Rumsfeld argued after the administration of President George W. Bush invaded Iraq in 2003, "We fight them over there so we don't have to fight them here."

These two perspectives are always in conflict. A country at war can never maintain one exclusively. When we hear monstrous stories (soldiers urinating on dead bodies, shooting a roomful of children, or raping a young woman), the connection between war and mainstream culture seems impossible. But we also elect, celebrate, and cling to the soldiers who fight in our name. Even if the front lines are halfway around the world, we know the people on those lines. Some are our children, spouses, parents, and dear friends. And maybe their return best dramatizes our ongoing inability to reconcile culture and war: in our communities, towns, and national policies, we always seem ill-equipped to help veterans come all the way home. The writers in this chapter wrestle with the relationship between war and culture. Doug Stanton begins with a meditation on the distance of war and its quiet invasion of his hometown. Benjamin Busch argues that war is the opposite of culture. Chris Hedges, Nick Turse, and Tom Malinowski, Sarah Holewinski, and Tammy Schultz suggest a close relationship. They point out subtle and explicit overlap between U.S. institutions and its military force. And Emily Chertoff reminds us that war, sometimes, happens within our own borders.

Doug Stanton
What the Water Dragged In

Doug Stanton is a political, travel, and adventure writer whose work focuses on war and insurgency. The author of two books, he has written numerous articles for magazines such as *Esquire*, *Men's Journal*, *Outside*, and *Sports Afield*. In the following *New York Times* article, Stanton considers the local effects of global crises.

I t's strange having your own oil spill.

What we have, of course, is a blip compared to the one in the Gulf of Mexico, which this week formally broke all records for offshore spills. But after watching the gulf catastrophe unfold from afar, the news that oil was gushing from a pipeline just three hours south of here into a small creek that flows into the Kalamazoo River and, eventually, into Lake Michigan, came as a surprise.

Until last week, I wasn't aware that a pipeline even existed, though I must have driven over or past it hundreds of times. The leak is now under control, but a good storm could still blow some of the estimated one million gallons of spilled oil into the lake, and maybe even north along its sandy coast, past numerous resort towns and into the Grand Traverse Bay, to a place called Clinch Park, where I've been swimming most mornings from June to October since I was a kid.

It's hard enough to try to capture oil floating in an ocean. But oil moving downstream in a swift river? Forget about it. As the pre-Socratic philosopher Heraclitus said, you can't step into the same river twice.

But despite the danger to the lake, many people here, busy enjoying their 5 summer vacations, haven't paid much attention to the spill. After all, Lake Michigan has lived through worse. It may be near the center of the continent, but it's not immune to the outside world, as we've learned over and over.

First there were the invasive Asian carp, swimming around the Chicago River a mere six miles from the mouth of the lake. These voracious eaters get excited by the sound of boat motors and can leap by the hundreds into the air all at once, in some hellish version of a water ballet. An oil spill seems almost benign in comparison.

We've also had to contend with an invasion of gobies—small, bug-eyed fish you're supposed to kill if you catch. They disrupt the food chain that normally supports native lake trout, perch and bass. They entered the lake in the ballast water of international shipping traffic, along with zebra mussels, which filter micro-organisms—also food for native fish—out of the water.

As a result of the zebra mussel infestation, the lake, several summers ago, was often as clear as a Bahamian bay. When I swam, I could see 50 feet in any direction. This extra sunlight fed more algae at deeper depths, which created algal blooms that floated up on the beach in smelly heaps. Now that the mussels have died off, the lake has returned to something like normal.

So for now, I swim. Winters are so long in northern Michigan, nearly nine months of gray skies and deep snow, that summer comes as a fresh burst. Amnesia sets in—you forget that winter will ever return. Friends from other parts of the country descend. The days ripen perfectly, the air no warmer or colder than your skin so that the edges of your body seem to extend beyond you, up and down the tree-lined streets.

10   Traverse City sits halfway between the North Pole and the Equator, and our summer days are long. The light seems to take forever to vanish from the sky and, when it does, it goes out like someone folding a white sheet in the dark. A flare on the horizon. Then a rustle: Goodnight.

"No zebra mussels, no carp, no oil spill headed my way. No politicians, no bloggers."

I swim in the midst of bad news to stay sane. I crawl over the sand bottom in six feet of water, which is cold and green, and nothing has changed in my life—I'm a kid again. No zebra mussels, no carp, no oil spill headed my way. No politicians, no bloggers. Every day I step refreshed and clean from the water, and go up to the bookstore, Horizon's, and order a coffee and stand on the street in flip-flops in the chill air, feeling the hot cup in my hand, the fine texture of its paper, feeling as if I've just come awake from a dream.

And what I carry around in my head is this, the image of the water, of looking around 20 feet in any direction, and beyond my periphery the lake darkening to the color of light in a storm. Sometimes I see fish slicing around my field of vision—silver missiles headed to deeper water. The work day is about to begin; traffic pours past on the four-lane parkway. I wonder what the people driving by think of me, when I'm swimming out there along the buoys; and in a time when there is too much news to think about, I hope they think nothing at all.

When the oil spill in Michigan began, I heard about a memorial service for Paul Miller, a 22-year-old Marine corporal from the nearby village of Lake Ann, who was killed on July 19 in Afghanistan. Later in the week, I stood in the funeral home, not far from the beach where I swim, and stared at Corporal Miller's flag-draped coffin.

I thought this: that the world's troubles can be nearer to us than we think, flowing in our direction, flowing toward *home*.

15   And while it's true that we used to live in Lake Ann, and our son may have played summer baseball with Corporal Miller years earlier, I don't remember meeting him. Maybe I passed him on the street, a tyke headed

over to the ice cream shop with his parents, where we were standing in line, too, with our children, all of us oblivious to the news to come, the depth and coldness of the water ahead.

Analyze

1. How are an oil spill, invasive species, and the death of a soldier related?
2. What single sentence do you think embodies Stanton's main idea?
3. Explain the role of swimming in this essay. How is it related to Stanton's main idea?
4. How are the small towns (Traverse City and Lake Ann) important to Stanton's main idea?
5. Compare Stanton's article to "Throwing the Last Stone" by Benjamin Busch (in this chapter). What beliefs or assumptions do you think they might share?

Explore

1. Explain how a national or global problem manifests in your everyday life.
2. How do you forget about the troubles of the world beyond your own town?
3. Stanton's essay was published during the BP oil spill in the Gulf of Mexico in 2010. How did this crisis reach into your community?
4. How has the war in Afghanistan reached into or influenced your community? Explain the degree to which people discuss, ignore, or avoid the issue.

Benjamin Busch
Throwing the Last Stone

Benjamin Busch is a writer, filmmaker, actor, photographer, and illustrator. As a U.S. Marine Corps infantry officer, he served two combat tours in Iraq and was awarded the Bronze Star. In his memoir *Dust to Dust,* Busch tells of a rambunctious and often reckless boyhood that seemed inevitably "drawn to conflict." In the following *Daily Beast* article, published in March 2012 after a U.S. soldier gunned down sixteen Afghan civilians, Busch examines our collective responsibilities related to war.

Sixteen Afghan civilians have been killed, in their homes, under our protection. One man acting alone we are quick to say. And it's probably true. An Army of one. But that one man is one of us.

There will be official statements, medical conjecture, military analysis, political showmanship, and protest. We will learn the facts over time, everyone hurrying to rule out abject senselessness with a justification of one kind or another. Posttraumatic stress and brain injury will be broadly blamed and we will hope that it is only something as terrible as that. We will become procedural in order to avoid being emotional. This will happen because this is how we respond to world events, but what is important now is what this one stunning occurrence means to our national soul.

The Taliban, our enemies, the group that justified our invasion of Afghanistan by harboring Bin Laden and al Qaeda, have vowed revenge. The very men who have a brutal record of torture, barbarous treatment of women, murder, and terrorism have found in this massacre of families a way to claim righteous indignation. It is here where we have no defense. Our moral character is built on the emphatic claim that we defend the innocent, that we and our allies are just. We have tried with tremendous sacrifice to prove it: 1,787 Americans brought home from the valleys of Afghanistan to be buried, 15,460 wounded there . . . and now this.

In a land where trust is hard won, this betrayal will echo. Our president and commanders have apologized. The military necessarily speaks with humble resignation when civilians are killed because it knows that when villages are battlefields, collateral casualties are unavoidable. Afghans have simply come to expect tragedy. But these fatalities were not the result of an official operation, not an accident justified by the presence of an enemy. President Obama has said that "This incident does not represent the exceptional character of our military," which is true except that our military *is* represented by this incident. The killer wore an American flag on his shoulder, a soldier of the rank and file, and by that symbol our military is colored by his act, and so are we. We cannot distance ourselves from him because we sent him there.

5   These Afghan children, the oldest being 12, were born into uncertainty and had lived their whole lives in a war we brought upon them, killed finally by a soldier we sent to protect them. This man, an American, was able to seek them in their sleep, shoot and stab them, and burn them in their blankets. Children the age of his own. Murderers exist without war, but because this act took place in war it makes him a war criminal, and it

indicts the nation he serves. We know who threw the first stone, but history will judge us by how we throw the last one.

I commanded Marines in Iraq and I was responsible for every bullet my unit fired. The war was fought in villages, on farmland, in cities, and through homes. We endangered ourselves by how carefully we tried to avoid causing harm to noncombatants, but they lived in the crossfire and I have seen people cry for sorrows I had a hand in delivering. I cannot restore the dead, and I will not forget them.

Our wars have long haunted veterans who have survived their survival. I was born in the year of the Tet offensive, my parents protestors, but we have learned few lessons from that conflict. Civilian casualties were staggering. 700,000 men were drafted, most sent against their will to fight in the jungles, returning home to be vilified for serving the nation that sent them. Many have taken their own lives in part because of the lives they've taken and for those they've seen lost. The conflict is now known as a taxing lost cause, a mistake, the sufferings of our soldiers pointless, our view of the enemy never sensible. It was a war made by the generation that prides itself on its clean moral victory over fascism in World War II, but that war was ended by dropping atomic bombs on families.

We seem not to notice how linear our world perspective is. What we call the Vietnam War the Vietnamese call the American War. Veterans of Vietnam see all the same signs in Afghanistan and have long been vocal opponents of our deepening involvement. We would do well to ask them how we should feel right now.

In their oath of vengeance, the Taliban called us "sick-minded American savages." We will be afraid to call our soldier mad, to admit that he lost his mind in war. This allows for the possibility that any one of us could go insane at any time, and that every veteran poisoned by their combat experience could be on edge for life. And some will be. The mind keeps our morality in balance, reminds us of learned social consequences, keeps rage and other primal instincts civilized. In many ways our ethical stability is preserved by our sense of community, security, and home. War takes all of those elements away, immerses the military in danger, and makes its members vulnerable to an involuntary loss of self-control. What is truly surprising is how rarely these acts of madness occur and how powerfully most veterans preserve their humanity.

Experts will try to find a cause to blame: fatigue, injury, disassociation, 10
derangement, leadership, agreeing finally that all leave the act inexcusable,

but we have to believe that we are in some way responsible, and feel regret. The cause may be our mission in Afghanistan and we might ask if that is a noble cause, something we believe in enough to invest so much life and produce so much death. What happens in the lives of others has yet to upset us where we live, and that has made these wars something that somehow does not include us here. Therein lies the danger in national disinterest. Do we have an honest collective emotional reaction to efforts that do not reach deep into our days and take something from us? Distant events stir little public empathy and we are a people known more and more for our selfish distractions than for our awareness. We will want to say that war estranged this soldier from our society, but there is much evidence that our society is completely disconnected from his war. This rampage far from us is part of what should be a much larger discussion about who we are now and what our wars mean. This act of one man is not allowed the convenience of being isolated, unrepresentative of our "deep respect for the people of Afghanistan." President Karzai stated, "When Afghan people are killed deliberately by U.S. forces this action is murder and terror and an unforgivable action." He is careful not to mention *accidental* deaths which have been tolerated as inevitable. We might consider this as we think about why we keep sending service members into situations in which they cannot be forgiven for what could occur.

We will put our children to sleep in our homes tonight, safe from wars, free to dream. We might take a moment to imagine what it would be like to lose our entire family, tonight, to a policeman, and wonder aloud what apologies would be worth.

Analyze

1. Explain Busch's opening strategy. How does he use the Army's motto?
2. How does Busch not allow himself or readers (us) to dismiss the shooting in Afghanistan as an isolated incident? Identify specific passages and explain how they work to this end.
3. How does Busch's own role as a Marine function in the article?
4. In paragraph 7, Busch alludes to the Vietnam War. Why? What does the allusion accomplish? How does it relate to the main idea?
5. How is this an argumentative article? What particular point is Busch arguing? What idea or claim do you think he is arguing against?

Explore

1. Busch says, "In many ways our ethical stability is preserved by our sense of community, security, and home." How does this statement resonate with your experience?

2. What is America's right to wage war throughout the world? Why does the United States, more than any other country, engage in military operations so widely?

3. Why is the Taliban our enemy? What have you heard, read, or experienced to help you answer this question?

4. How much should veterans' claims about war figure into national military policy? Explain your reasoning.

5. In early 2013, President Obama announced an acceleration of the military withdrawal from Afghanistan. Do you remember this announcement? What do you remember about the situation in early 2013? What were people saying?

Emily Chertoff
Occupy Wounded Knee: A 71-Day Siege and a Forgotten Civil Rights Movement

Emily Chertoff is a writer and producer for *The Atlantic*, which "is dedicated to equipping opinion leaders with breakthrough ideas and original insights." In her work, she explores issues related to national and international politics, education, and technology. Here, Chertoff reflects on a historical case of war at home.

On February 27, 1973, a team of 200 Oglala Lakota (Sioux) activists and members of the American Indian Movement (AIM) seized control of a tiny town with a loaded history—Wounded Knee, South Dakota. They arrived in town at night, in a caravan of cars and trucks, took the town's residents hostage, and demanded that the U.S. government make good on treaties from the 19th and early 20th centuries. Within hours, police had surrounded Wounded Knee, forming a cordon to prevent protesters from exiting and sympathizers from entering. This marked the beginning of a 71-day siege and armed conflict.

Russell Means, one of AIM's leaders, died yesterday. Means was a controversial figure within the movement and outside of it; as his *New York Times* obituary put it, "critics, including many Indians, called him a tireless self-promoter who capitalized on his angry-rebel notoriety." After getting his start in activism in the 1970s, Means went on to run for the Libertarian presidential nomination in 1987, and for governor of New Mexico in 2002. He also acted in scores of films, most famously in a lead role in the 1992 version of *The Last of the Mohicans*.

For all the contradictions of his life, he was no less controversial than AIM itself. The Wounded Knee siege was both an inspiration to indigenous people and left-wing activists around the country and—according to the U.S. Marshals Service, which besieged the town along with FBI and National Guard—the longest-lasting "civil disorder" in 200 years of U.S. history. Two native activists lost their lives in the conflict, and a federal agent was shot and paralyzed. Like the Black Panthers or MEChA, AIM was a militant civil rights and identity movement that sprung from the political and social crisis of the late 1960s, but today it is more obscure than the latter two groups.

The Pine Ridge reservation, where Wounded Knee was located, had been in turmoil for years. To many in the area the siege was no surprise. The Oglala Lakota who lived on the reservation faced racism beyond its boundaries and a poorly managed tribal government within them. In particular, they sought the removal of tribal chairman Dick Wilson, whom many Oglala living on the reservation thought corrupt. Oglala Lakota interviewed by PBS for a documentary said Wilson seemed to favor mixed-race, assimilated Lakota like himself—and especially his own family members—over reservation residents with more traditional lifestyles. Efforts to remove Wilson by impeaching him had failed, and so Oglala Lakota tribal leaders turned to AIM for help in removing him by force. Their answer was to occupy Wounded Knee.

5   Federal marshals and National Guard traded heavy fire daily with the native activists. To break the siege, they cut off electricity and water to the town, and attempted to prevent food and ammunition from being passed to the occupiers. Bill Zimmerman, a sympathetic activist and pilot from Boston, agreed to carry out a 2,000-pound food drop on the 50th day of

the siege. When the occupiers ran out of the buildings where they had been sheltering to grab the supplies, agents opened fire on them. The first member of the occupation to die, a Cherokee, was shot by a bullet that flew through the wall of a church.

To many observers, the standoff resembled the Wounded Knee Massacre of 1890 itself—when a U.S. cavalry detachment slaughtered a group of Lakota warriors who refused to disarm. Some of the protesters also had a more current conflict in mind. As one former member of AIM told PBS, "They were shooting machine gun fire at us, tracers coming at us at nighttime just like a war zone. We had some Vietnam vets with us, and they said, 'Man, this is just like Vietnam.'" When PBS interviewed federal officials later, they said that the first death in the conflict inspired them to work harder to bring it to a close. For the Oglala Lakota, the death of tribe member Buddy Lamont on April 26 was the critical moment. While members of AIM fought to keep the occupation going, the Oglala overruled them, and, from that point, negotiations between federal officials and the protesters began in earnest. The militants officially surrendered on May 8, and a number of members of AIM managed to escape the town before being arrested. (Those who were arrested, including Means, were almost all acquitted because key evidence was mishandled.) Even after the siege officially ended, a quiet war between Dick Wilson and the traditional, pro-AIM faction of Oglala Lakota continued on the reservation—this despite Wilson's re-election to the tribal presidency in 1974. In the three years following the stand-off, Pine Ridge had the highest per capita murder rate in the country. Two FBI agents were among the dead. The Oglala blamed the federal government for failing to remove Wilson as tribal chairman; the U.S. retorted that it would be illegal for them to do so, somewhat ironically citing reasons of tribal self-determination.

Today, the Pine Ridge reservation is the largest community in what may be the poorest county in the entire United States. (Per capita income in 2010 was lower in Shannon County, South Dakota, where Pine Ridge is located, than in any other U.S. county.) Reports have the adult unemployment rate on the reservation somewhere between 70 and 80 percent. AIM—and Means—drew a lot of attention to the treatment of indigenous people in the U.S. But perhaps more than any other civil rights movement, its work remains unfinished.

Analyze

1. A eulogy is a speech or text that honors the memory of someone who has passed away. How is this article a eulogy? What other genre is at work?

2. Chertoff's title borrows a phrase from more recent civil disturbances. How does the title support or relate to her main idea about Means?

3. How is this article about cultural change, tradition, or resistance to change? In your answer, consider the role of eulogy and the particular memory of Russell Means.

4. What is the most detailed or graphic passage in the article? How does it support or relate to the main idea?

5. How does Chertoff collapse the difference between war and civil disorder?

Explore

1. When we think of war, at least in the United States, we might imagine military operations in other countries—places far beyond our own borders. We use phrases like "civic unrest" or "civil disorder" to characterize a country at war with itself. How would you describe the events at Wounded Knee? As war, civil unrest, or something else?

2. Research the Wounded Knee Massacre. How does it fit into U.S. history? What do you think it means in the story of American culture?

3. Find out more about the Pine Ridge reservation. What do you think its presence—and its particular economic condition—means to American culture? How does it fit into a description of the United States?

4. American Indian reservations are technically sovereign countries. They are, literally, countries within a country. How does this impact your understanding of the Wounded Knee siege and standoff?

5. Explain how Chertoff's article relates to Chris Hedges's essay in this chapter, "War Is Betrayal."

Nick Turse
A Six-Point Plan for Global War

A journalist and historian, Nick Turse studies the cultural effects of our propensity for war. The author of numerous articles and three books, he is the
managing editor for *TomDispatch,* a website that considers itself "a regular
antidote to the mainstream media." In the following blog post, Turse examines the intersection between war and culture.

It looked like a scene out of a Hollywood movie. In the inky darkness, men
in full combat gear, armed with automatic weapons and wearing night-
vision goggles, grabbed hold of a thick, woven cable hanging from a MH-47
Chinook helicopter. Then, in a flash, each "fast-roped" down onto a ship
below. Afterward, "Mike," a Navy SEAL who would not give his last name,
bragged to an Army public affairs sergeant that, when they were on their
game, the SEALs could put 15 men on a ship this way in 30 seconds or less.

Once on the aft deck, the special ops troops broke into squads and method-
ically searched the ship as it bobbed in Jinhae Harbor, South Korea. Below deck
and on the bridge, the commandos located several men and trained their weapons on them, but nobody fired a shot. It was, after all, a training exercise.

All of those ship-searchers were SEALs, but not all of them were American.
Some were from Naval Special Warfare Group 1 out of Coronado, California;
others hailed from South Korea's Naval Special Brigade. The drill was part of
Foal Eagle 2012, a multinational, joint-service exercise. It was also a model
for—and one small part of—a much publicized U.S. military "pivot" from
the Greater Middle East to Asia, a move that includes sending an initial contingent of 250 Marines to Darwin, Australia, basing littoral combat ships in
Singapore, strengthening military ties with Vietnam and India, staging war
games in the Philippines (as well as a drone strike there), and shifting the
majority of the Navy's ships to the Pacific by the end of the decade.

That modest training exercise also reflected another kind of pivot. The
face of American-style war-fighting is once again changing. Forget full-scale
invasions and large-footprint occupations on the Eurasian mainland;
instead, think: special operations forces working on their own but also
training or fighting beside allied militaries (if not outright proxy armies) in

hot spots around the world. And along with those special ops advisors, trainers, and commandos expect ever more funds and efforts to flow into the militarization of spying and intelligence, the use of drone aircraft, the launching of cyber-attacks, and joint Pentagon operations with increasingly militarized "civilian" government agencies.

5   Much of this has been noted in the media, but how it all fits together into what could be called the new global face of empire has escaped attention. And yet this represents nothing short of a new Obama doctrine, a six-point program for 21st-century war, American-style, that the administration is now carefully developing and honing. Its global scope is already breathtaking, if little recognized, and like Donald Rumsfeld's military lite and David Petraeus's counterinsurgency operations, it is evidently going to have its day in the sun—and like them, it will undoubtedly disappoint in ways that will surprise its creators.

The Blur-ness

For many years, the U.S. military has been talking up and promoting the concept of "jointness." An Army helicopter landing Navy SEALs on a Korean ship catches some of this ethos at the tactical level. But the future, it seems, has something else in store. Think of it as "blur-ness," a kind of organizational version of war-fighting in which a dominant Pentagon fuses its forces with other government agencies—especially the CIA, the State Department, and the Drug Enforcement Administration—in complex, overlapping missions around the globe.

In 2001, Secretary of Defense Donald Rumsfeld began his "revolution in military affairs," steering the Pentagon toward a military-lite model of high-tech, agile forces. The concept came to a grim end in Iraq's embattled cities. A decade later, the last vestiges of its many failures continue to play out in a stalemated war in Afghanistan against a rag-tag minority insurgency that can't be beaten. In the years since, two secretaries of defense and a new president have presided over another transformation—this one geared toward avoiding ruinous, large-scale land wars which the U.S. has consistently proven unable to win.

Under President Obama, the U.S. has expanded or launched numerous military campaigns—most of them utilizing a mix of the six elements of 21st-century American war. Take the American war in Pakistan—a poster-child for what might now be called the Obama formula, if not doctrine.

Beginning as a highly-circumscribed drone assassination campaign backed by limited cross-border commando raids under the Bush administration, U.S. operations in Pakistan have expanded into something close to a full-scale robotic air war, complemented by cross-border helicopter attacks, CIA-funded "kill teams" of Afghan proxy forces, as well as boots-on-the-ground missions by elite special operations forces, including the SEAL raid that killed Osama bin Laden.

The CIA has conducted clandestine intelligence and surveillance missions in Pakistan, too, though its role may, in the future, be less important, thanks to Pentagon mission creep. In April, in fact, Secretary of Defense Leon Panetta announced the creation of a new CIA-like espionage agency within the Pentagon called the Defense Clandestine Service. According to the *Washington Post,* its aim is to expand "the military's espionage efforts beyond war zones."

Over the last decade, the very notion of war zones has become remark- 10 ably muddled, mirroring the blurring of the missions and activities of the CIA and Pentagon. Analyzing the new agency and the "broader convergence trend" between Department of Defense and CIA missions, the *Post* noted that the "blurring is also evident in the organizations' upper ranks. Panetta previously served as CIA director, and that post is currently held by retired four-star Army Gen. David H. Petraeus."

Not to be outdone, last year the State Department, once the seat of diplomacy, continued on its long march to militarization (and marginalization) when it agreed to pool some of its resources with the Pentagon to create the Global Security Contingency Fund. That program will allow the Defense Department even greater say in how aid from Washington will flow to proxy forces in places like Yemen and the Horn of Africa.

One thing is certain: American war-making (along with its spies and its diplomats) is heading ever deeper into "the shadows." Expect yet more clandestine operations in ever more places with, of course, ever more potential for blowback in the years ahead.

Shedding Light on "the Dark Continent"

One locale likely to see an influx of Pentagon spies in the coming years is Africa. Under President Obama, operations on the continent have accelerated far beyond the more limited interventions of the Bush years. Last year's war in Libya; a regional drone campaign with missions run out of airports and bases in Djibouti, Ethiopia, and the Indian Ocean archipelago nation of Seychelles; a flotilla of 30 ships in that ocean supporting regional operations; a multi-pronged military and CIA campaign against militants in Somalia, including intelligence operations, training for Somali agents, a secret prison, helicopter attacks, and U.S. commando raids; a massive influx of cash for counterterrorism operations across East Africa; a possible old-fashioned air war, carried out on the sly in the region using manned aircraft; tens of millions of dollars in arms for allied mercenaries and African troops; and a special ops expeditionary force (bolstered by State Department experts) dispatched to help capture or kill Lord's Resistance Army leader Joseph Kony and his senior commanders, operating in Uganda, South Sudan, the Democratic Republic of the Congo, and the Central African Republic (where U.S. Special Forces now have a new base) only begins to scratch the surface of Washington's fast-expanding plans and activities in the region.

Even less well known are other U.S. military efforts designed to train African forces for operations now considered integral to American interests on the continent. These include, for example, a mission by elite Force Recon Marines from the Special Purpose Marine Air Ground Task Force 12 (SPMAGTF-12) to train soldiers from the Uganda People's Defense Force, which supplies the majority of troops to the African Union Mission in Somalia.

15 Earlier this year, Marines from SPMAGTF-12 also trained soldiers from the Burundi National Defense Force, the second-largest contingent in Somalia; sent trainers into Djibouti (where the U.S. already maintains a major Horn of Africa base at Camp Lemonier); and traveled to Liberia where they focused on teaching riot-control techniques to Liberia's military as part of an otherwise State Department spearheaded effort to rebuild that force.

The U.S. is also conducting counterterrorism training and equipping militaries in Algeria, Burkina Faso, Chad, Mauritania, Niger, and Tunisia. In addition, U.S. Africa Command (Africom) has 14 major joint-training exercises planned for 2012, including operations in Morocco, Cameroon, Gabon, Botswana, South Africa, Lesotho, Senegal, and what may become the Pakistan of Africa, Nigeria.

Even this, however, doesn't encompass the full breadth of U.S. training and advising missions in Africa. To take an example not on Africom's list, this spring the U.S. brought together 11 nations, including Cote d'Ivoire, The Gambia, Liberia, Mauritania, and Sierra Leone to take part in a maritime training exercise code-named Saharan Express 2012.

Photo Gallery 2

The timeline of American history is often marked by politics—by the people who've led the government, who've overseen the military, and who've executed wars. Consider some common historical phrases: *antebellum South, the Cold War era, the postwar boomers, the Vietnam era, postcolonial decades.* Such language shows how we mark our collective experience, even how we know ourselves as a civilization. Our museums are full of paintings that recall our leaders and military victories: generals, forts, battlefields, airplanes, pilots, great vessels and machinery that say something of that era's industry.

This gallery focuses on war and politics, so it parallels a historical tradition. It does, after all, mark an era when the United States was engaged in persistent military conflict—especially in the Middle East. But this gallery also veers away from tradition. Consider, for instance, how a small Iraqi girl with a rainbow duster speaks about our war—how it says something different than an image of a great battleship or general. Imagine how the image of a stunt woman above the American flag says something about our politics and entertainment—or how we communicate patriotism to ourselves. More broadly, consider how the whole gallery poses questions: What is the relationship between war and the culture behind it? What kind of culture goes to war? How does that culture interact with the people— the children, the citizens—of other countries?

Several of these photographs, taken in Iraq, speak directly to articles in Chapter 9, "War: How We Fight"—to Busch, Nick Turse, Neal Whitman, and Chris Hedges. Beyond those direct connections, consider how the images might facilitate relationships among articles. For example, how might a photograph of a Marine in Ramadi forge a connection between war and work—between the military and dirty jobs, blue-collar life, office work, or even the American dream? As a photographer, Busch says that photography grants him "the right to assign longevity to impermanent observations." If that is the case, then the meaning and suggestions of these images resonate beyond particular moments and situations around them. If there is longevity here, it is tied up in the meaning we assign.

Flag Lady

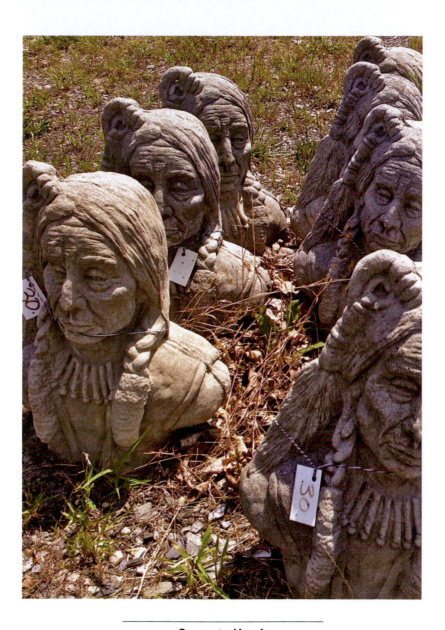

Concrete Heads

Defaced

Girl with Flowered Dress

Ramidi (Marine by Trash Fire)

Blood Trail

Cross

Back in the Backyard

Since its founding, the United States has often meddled close to home, treating the Caribbean as its private lake and intervening at will throughout Latin America. During the Bush years, with some notable exceptions, Washington's interest in America's "backyard" took a backseat to wars farther from home. Recently, however, the Obama administration has been ramping up operations south of the border using its new formula. This has meant Pentagon drone missions deep inside Mexico to aid that country's battle against the drug cartels, while CIA agents and civilian operatives from the Department of Defense were dispatched to Mexican military bases to take part in the country's drug war.

In 2012, the Pentagon has also ramped up its anti-drug operations in Honduras. Working out of Forward Operating Base Mocoron and other remote camps there, the U.S. military is supporting Honduran operations by way of the methods it honed in Iraq and Afghanistan. In addition, U.S. forces have taken part in joint operations with Honduran troops as part of a training mission dubbed Beyond the Horizon 2012; Green Berets have been assisting Honduran Special Operations forces in anti-smuggling operations; and a Drug Enforcement Administration Foreign-deployed Advisory Support Team, originally created to disrupt the poppy trade in Afghanistan, has joined forces with Honduras's Tactical Response Team, that country's most elite counternarcotics unit. A glimpse of these operations made the news recently when DEA agents, flying in an American helicopter, were involved in an aerial attack on civilians that killed two men and two pregnant women in the remote Mosquito Coast region.

Less visible have been U.S. efforts in Guyana, where Special Operations Forces have been training local troops in heliborne air assault techniques. "This is the first time we have had this type of exercise involving Special Operations Forces of the United States on such a grand scale," Colonel Bruce Lovell of the Guyana Defense Force told a U.S. public affairs official earlier this year. "It gives us a chance to validate ourselves and see where we are, what are our shortcomings."

The U.S. military has been similarly active elsewhere in Latin America, concluding training exercises in Guatemala, sponsoring "partnership-building" missions in the Dominican Republic, El Salvador, Peru, and Panama, and reaching an agreement to carry out 19 "activities" with the Colombian army over the next year, including joint military exercises.

Still in the Middle of the Middle East

Despite the end of the Iraq and Libyan wars, a coming drawdown of forces in Afghanistan, and copious public announcements about its national security pivot toward Asia, Washington is by no means withdrawing from the Greater Middle East. In addition to continuing operations in Afghanistan, the U.S. has consistently been at work training allied troops, building up military bases, and brokering weapons sales and arms transfers to despots in the region from Bahrain to Yemen.

In fact, Yemen, like its neighbor, Somalia, across the Gulf of Aden, has become a laboratory for Obama's wars. There, the U.S. is carrying out its signature new brand of warfare with "black ops" troops like the SEALs and the Army's Delta Force undoubtedly conducting kill/capture missions, while "white" forces like the Green Berets and Rangers are training indigenous troops, and robot planes hunt and kill members of al-Qaeda and its affiliates, possibly assisted by an even more secret contingent of manned aircraft.

The Middle East has also become the somewhat unlikely poster-region for another emerging facet of the Obama doctrine: cyberwar efforts. In a category-blurring speaking engagement, Secretary of State Hillary Clinton surfaced at the recent Special Operations Forces Industry Conference in Florida where she gave a speech talking up her department's eagerness to join in the new American way of war. "We need Special Operations Forces who are as comfortable drinking tea with tribal leaders as raiding a terrorist compound," she told the crowd. "We also need diplomats and development experts who are up to the job of being your partners."

Clinton then took the opportunity to tout her agency's online efforts, aimed at websites used by al-Qaeda's affiliate in Yemen. When al-Qaeda recruitment messages appeared on the latter, she said, "our team plastered the same sites with altered versions . . . that showed the toll al-Qaeda attacks have taken on the Yemeni people." She further noted that this information-warfare mission was carried out by experts at State's Center for Strategic Counterterrorism Communications with assistance, not surprisingly, from the military and the U.S. Intelligence Community.

These modest online efforts join more potent methods of cyberwar being employed by the Pentagon and the CIA, including the recently revealed "Olympic Games," a program of sophisticated attacks on computers in Iran's nuclear enrichment facilities engineered and unleashed by the National Security Agency (NSA) and Unit 8200, Israeli's equivalent of the NSA. As with other facets of the new way of war, these efforts were begun under the Bush administration but significantly accelerated under the current president, who became the first American commander-in-chief to order sustained cyberattacks designed to cripple another country's infrastructure.

From Brushfires to Wildfires

Across the globe from Central and South America to Africa, the Middle East, and Asia, the Obama administration is working out its formula for a new American way of war. In its pursuit, the Pentagon and its increasingly militarized government partners are drawing on everything from classic precepts of colonial warfare to the latest technologies.

The United States is an imperial power chastened by more than 10 years of failed, heavy-footprint wars. It is hobbled by a hollowing-out economy, and inundated with hundreds of thousands of recent veterans—a staggering 45% of the troops who fought in Afghanistan and Iraq—suffering from service-related disabilities who will require ever more expensive care. No wonder the current combination of special ops, drones, spy games, civilian soldiers, cyberwarfare, and proxy fighters sounds like a safer, saner brand of war-fighting. At first blush, it may even look like a panacea for America's national security ills. In reality, it may be anything but.

The new light-footprint Obama doctrine actually seems to be making war an ever more attractive and seemingly easy option—a point emphasized recently by former Chairman of the Joint Chiefs of Staff General Peter Pace. "I worry about speed making it too easy to employ force," said Pace when asked about recent efforts to make it simpler to deploy Special Operations Forces abroad. "I worry about speed making it too easy to take the easy answer—let's go whack them with special operations—as opposed to perhaps a more laborious answer for perhaps a better long-term solution."

As a result, the new American way of war holds great potential for unforeseen entanglements and serial blowback. Starting or fanning brushfire wars on several continents could lead to raging wildfires that spread unpredictably and prove difficult, if not impossible, to quench. 30

By their very nature, small military engagements tend to get larger, and wars tend to spread beyond borders. By definition, military action tends to have unforeseen consequences. Those who doubt this need only look back to 2001, when three low-tech attacks on a single day set in motion a decade-plus of war that has spread across the globe. The response to that one day began with a war in Afghanistan, that spread to Pakistan, detoured to Iraq, popped up in Somalia and Yemen, and so on. Today, veterans of those Ur-interventions find themselves trying to replicate their dubious successes in places like Mexico and Honduras, the Central African Republic and the Congo.

History demonstrates that the U.S. is not very good at winning wars, having gone without victory in any major conflict since 1945. Smaller interventions have been a mixed bag with modest victories in places like Panama and Grenada and ignominious outcomes in Lebanon (in the 1980s) and Somalia (in the 1990s), to name a few.

The trouble is, it's hard to tell what an intervention will grow up to be—until it's too late. While they followed different paths, Vietnam, Afghanistan, and Iraq all began relatively small, before growing large and ruinous. Already, the outlook for the new Obama doctrine seems far from rosy, despite the good press it's getting inside Washington's Beltway.

What looks today like a formula for easy power projection that will further U.S. imperial interests on the cheap could soon prove to be an unmitigated disaster—one that likely won't be apparent until it's too late.

Analyze

1. This article chronicles change in military culture. In your own words, describe that change.
2. What does Turse mean by the "blurring" of military operations?
3. Turse explains that military operations will become "more clandestine," or more secretive in coming years. He also says that we should expect "ever more potential for blowback." What do you think he means? And why is a more secretive military apt to generate more blowback?
4. Turse says that President Obama was "the first American commander-in-chief to order sustained cyberattacks designed to cripple another country's infrastructure." Explain how this point supports Turse's main idea.
5. In Turse's understanding, why might cyberwar be an especially dangerous turn?

Explore

1. Turse argues that America has primarily been losing small-scale wars for the past sixty years. Why, then, do you think we continue to launch or maintain military operations?

2. What does Turse's point about newer and more agile military operations make you think about the future of war?
3. What is the relationship between a country's culture and its war making? Are they opposite? Do they overlap? Is one the cause of the other?
4. Reread Turse's final paragraph. What do you think he's predicting— or at least suggesting?
5. Compare Turse's article to Neal Whitman's ("'Kinetic' Connections"). How do they overlap?

Neal Whitman
"Kinetic" Connections

Neal Whitman is a linguist who studies the impact of words on our daily lives. A columnist for *Visual Thesaurus* magazine, he writes scripts for the *Grammar Girl* podcast and blogs for *Literal-Minded*. In the following magazine article, Whitman dissects the word *kinetic* in the context of war.

I stayed up late on the night of May 1 to hear President Obama's stunning announcement: A special-forces mission, which could have gone humiliatingly wrong, had instead succeeded in killing Osama bin Laden, the man behind the worst terrorist attack on American soil. I watched until the news reporters ran out of things to say, when they began to fill airtime by repeating things and asking the opinions of people in the streets while waiting for something else to happen.

I had to wait until the next morning to read more about how U.S. forces had actually managed to achieve this victory, when I read this article in the *National Journal* online. The team of Navy SEALs that carried out the mission, I learned, were part of a special group of special-missions units and task forces known as the Joint Special Operations Command. The article went on to explain some more about JSOC, saying:

> Recently, JSOC built a new Targeting and Analysis Center in Rosslyn, Va. Where the National Counterterrorism Center tends to focus on threats to the homeland, TAAC, whose existence was

first disclosed by the Associated Press, focuses outward, on active "kinetic"—or lethal—counterterrorism missions abroad.

The definition of *kinetic* caught my eye. It was in quotation marks, followed by a gloss to explain its meaning. Apparently the author, Mark Ambinder, didn't expect his readers to be familiar with this specialized meaning of *kinetic*. But people have been getting familiar with it for several months now. My introduction to it was during the annual meeting of the American Dialect Society in January, when the term *kinetic event* won the "Most Euphemistic" category in the ADS's 2010 Word of the Year vote. A kinetic event is "a violent action in the field of battle," according to the definition Ben Zimmer is writing in the "Among the New Words" column in next month's issue of *American Speech,* the journal of the ADS. The term had been in the news from Afghanistan in reports like this one from September (to appear in Ben's entry):

> The coalition is reporting . . . that in August, just last month, there were more than 4,900 kinetic events. That's an attack, mortars, rockets, small arms, IEDs.

In March, the public awareness of this new sense of *kinetic* was raised further by the phrase *kinetic military action,* the widely ridiculed term used by Ben Rhodes, the Deputy National Security Advisor in describing the United States' role in the ongoing conflict in Libya. Jonathan Allen wrote an article on *Politico.com:*

> Police action, conflict, hostilities and now "kinetic military action." They're all euphemisms for that word that this White House and many before it have been so careful not to say: War.

> Administration officials told congressional aides in a closed briefing earlier this week that the United States is not at war with Libya, and Deputy National Security Adviser Ben Rhodes danced around the question in a Wednesday exchange with reporters aboard Air Force One.

> "I think what we are doing is enforcing a resolution that has a very clear set of goals, which is protecting the Libyan people, averting a

humanitarian crisis, and setting up a no-fly zone," Rhodes said. "Obviously that involves kinetic military action, particularly on the front end. But again, the nature of our commitment is that we are not getting into an open-ended war, a land invasion in Libya."

Although the military sense of *kinetic* seeped into public consciousness   5 in 2010 and 2011, as with many seemingly new words, it turns out to have spent a number of years paying its dues before getting its big break.

The euphemistic feel of *kinetic* comes from its association with scientific inquiry. Unless you're a teacher (who deals with visual, auditory, and kinesthetic learning styles) or an artist (who might create kinetic sculptures), the word *kinetic* probably brings to mind high-school physics class, and lectures about potential and kinetic energy. In fact, in its first uses relating to the military or national defense, *kinetic* did mean "relating to kinetic energy." In the 1978 edition of the *Code Name Handbook: Aerospace Defense Technology* the acronym *SKEW* is defined as a "shoulder-fired kinetic energy weapon." A kinetic-energy weapon, as opposed to a chemical-energy weapon, is one that does its damage with the simple kinetic energy of the projectiles it fires. A gun with ordinary, non-exploding bullets would be one example of a kinetic energy weapon.

Alternatively, a kinetic energy weapon could be a missile or other heavy object hurled from space, as long as it isn't equipped with, say, a nuclear warhead. A 1983 article in the *Boston Globe* quotes a brochure for a weapons conference as mentioning missiles as kinetic energy weapons. One part of Ronald Reagan's proposed Strategic Defense Initiative/"Star Wars" missile-defense system was the "kinetic kill vehicle" (KKV). The term starts appearing in news reports from 1985, and continues to do so even now, though these days the focus is more on destroying Chinese rather than Russian missiles or satellites.

A year after the proposal of SDI, the phrase *kinetic energy penetrator* as a synonym/euphemism for *bullet* was in circulation, and five years after that, it got a real workout during Operation Desert Storm, when U.S. tanks were equipped with kinetic energy penetrators made of depleted uranium—a good conveyor of kinetic energy because of its high density. (I have to say, though, that using DU as a weapon by turning it into a really heavy piece of ammunition is like using a barometer to determine the height of a building by throwing it over the edge and timing how long it takes to hit the ground.)

These uses of *kinetic* seem to have paved the way toward its broader meaning of military attacks, which had become well-established by the time of the September 11 terrorist attacks. In a 2002 article in *Slate*, Timothy Noah introduces his readers to the term *kinetic warfare:* "Retronym" is a word coined by Frank Mankiewicz, George McGovern's campaign director, to delineate previously unnecessary distinctions. Examples include "acoustic guitar," "analog watch," "natural turf," "two-parent family," and "offline publication." Bob Woodward's new book, *Bush at War,* introduces a new Washington retronym: "kinetic" warfare.

10   Noah then quotes from page 150 of *Bush at War,* in which President Bush and his advisors talk about "going kinetic" against al Qaeda after 9/11. Noah continues:

> In common usage, "kinetic" is an adjective used to describe motion, but the Washington meaning derives from its secondary definition, "active, as opposed to latent." Dropping bombs and shooting bullets—you know, killing people—is kinetic. But the 21st-century military is exploring less violent and more high-tech means of warfare, such as messing electronically with the enemy's communications equipment or wiping out its bank accounts. These are "non-kinetic." . . . Asked during a January [2002] talk at National Defense University whether "the transformed military of the future will shift emphasis somewhat from kinetic systems to cyber warfare," Donald Rumsfeld answered, "Yes!" (Rumsfeld uses the words "kinetic" and "non-kinetic" all the time.)

In addition to *kinetic warfare* and *kinetic systems,* there is a host of other 21st-century *kinetic* terms, including *kinetic operations, kinetic capability, kinetic engagements, kinetic strike, kinetic activity,* and *kinetic targeting,* i.e., bombing. These days the bombs don't have to be non-explosive; the opposite of kinetic targeting is *soft targeting:* dropping leaflets. Areas where fighting is going on are *kinetic areas. Kinetic* can be a predicate adjective, too, i.e., one that comes after a linking verb. An army unit might *go kinetic,* and an article from 2006 tells how British soldiers in Iraq believed their American counterparts were "too kinetic." (Kinetic Yankees, if you will.) There is even an adjective, *post-kinetic,* to describe reconstruction, or places where battles have taken place.

Commander Philip Thrash, an old high-school friend and former field artillery officer in the U.S. Army, served in Afghanistan in 2007 and 2008. He confirms that it isn't just the top brass who use *kinetic*. He started to hear it among his superiors in 2003 or 2004, and during his service, he and his peers and subordinates used it often. As he explained: You hear your superiors use it, and if you want to communicate effectively with them, you use the words they use, and then it just becomes part of your lexicon. *Kinetic* is useful because it can cover a lot of more specific verbs, such as *engage, acquire (a target), move to contact, destroy, neutralize.* Summing up, Philip used an unsettling but soberingly accurate turn of phrase that has been in print since at least the late 1970s, and that some veterans remember from the Vietnam War. Basically, he said, *kinetic* is "a polite way of saying 'kill people and break things.'"

Analyze

1. What does "kinetic" mean in terms of the military? Why do you think kinetic is used rather than some other terms?

2. What is Whitman's point? What subtle argument does he make about "kinetic" as a term for military operation?

3. How does Whitman's introduction function in the article? What mood or idea does it help to establish?

4. Whitman says, "I have to say, though, that using DU [depleted uranium] as a weapon by turning it into a really heavy piece of ammunition is like using a barometer to determine the height of a building by throwing it over the edge and timing how long it takes to hit the ground." What does he mean and what is he suggesting about depleted uranium?

5. How is Whitman's essay about culture? How does he draw out the process through which acts, words, or concepts become normal?

Explore

1. Whitman finds "kinetic" to be a *euphemism*. What other euphemisms are used in times of war?

2. What nonmilitary euphemisms do you use on daily basis? What unpleasant qualities or acts are you trying to conceal?

3. Why do you think the term *kinetic* is not widely used among nonmilitary personnel?
4. What is a retronym? How is it important to Whitman's article?
5. How would you say military culture and nonmilitary culture overlap? Are they the same? Does one promote or support the other?

Chris Hedges
War Is Betrayal

A Pulitzer Prize–winning journalist and cultural critic, Chris Hedges writes about cultural myths related to war, progress, and religion. Named Online Journalist of the Year by the Los Angeles Press Club in 2009 and 2011, he is the author of numerous books and a column for the news website Truthdig, which strives to "challenge conventional wisdom." In the following magazine article, Hedges considers the morality of war.

We condition the poor and the working class to go to war. We promise them honor, status, glory, and adventure. We promise boys they will become men. We hold these promises up against the dead-end jobs of small-town life, the financial dislocations, credit card debt, bad marriages, lack of health insurance, and dread of unemployment. The military is the call of the Sirens, the enticement that has for generations seduced young Americans working in fast food restaurants or behind the counters of Walmarts to fight and die for war profiteers and elites.

The poor embrace the military because every other cul-de-sac in their lives breaks their spirit and their dignity. Pick up Erich Maria Remarque's *All Quiet on the Western Front* or James Jones's *From Here to Eternity*. Read *Henry IV*. Turn to the *Iliad*. The allure of combat is a trap, a ploy, an old, dirty game of deception in which the powerful, who do not go to war, promise a mirage to those who do.

I saw this in my own family. At the age of ten I was given a scholarship to a top New England boarding school. I spent my adolescence in the schizophrenic embrace of the wealthy, on the playing fields and in the dorms and classrooms that condition boys and girls for privilege, and came back to my working-class relations in the depressed former mill towns in Maine. I traveled between two universes: one where everyone got chance after chance after chance, where connections and money and influence almost guaranteed that you would not fail; the other where no one ever got a second try. I learned at an early age that when the poor fall no one picks them up, while the rich stumble and trip their way to the top.

Those I knew in prep school did not seek out the military and were not sought by it. But in the impoverished enclaves of central Maine, where I had relatives living in trailers, nearly everyone was a veteran. My grandfather. My uncles. My cousins. My second cousins. They were all in the military. Some of them—including my Uncle Morris, who fought in the infantry in the South Pacific during World War II—were destroyed by the war. Uncle Morris drank himself to death in his trailer. He sold the hunting rifle my grandfather had given to me to buy booze.

He was not alone. After World War II, thousands of families struggled   5 with broken men who, because they could never read the approved lines from the patriotic script, had been discarded. They were not trotted out for red-white-and-blue love fests on the Fourth of July or Veterans Day.

The myth of war held fast, despite the deep bitterness of my grandmother— who acidly denounced what war had done to her only son—and of others like her. The myth held because it was all the soldiers and their families had. Even those who knew it to be a lie—and I think most did—were loath to give up the fleeting moments of recognition, the only times in their lives they were told they were worth something.

"For it's Tommy this, an' Tommy that, an' 'Chuck him out, the brute!'" Rudyard Kipling wrote. "But it's 'Saviour of 'is country' when the guns begin to shoot."

Any story of war is a story of elites preying on the weak, the gullible, the marginal, the poor. I do not know of a single member of my graduating prep school class who went into the military. You could not say this about the high school class that graduated the same year in Mechanic Falls, Maine.

Geoff Millard was born in Buffalo, New York, and lived in a predominately black neighborhood until he was eleven. His family then moved to Lockport, a nearby white suburb. He wrestled and played football in high school. He listened to punk rock.

10   "I didn't really do well in classes," he says. "But that didn't seem to matter much to my teachers."

At fifteen he was approached in school by a military recruiter.

"He sat down next to me at a lunch table," Millard says. "He was a Marine. I remember the uniform was crisp. All the medals were shiny. It was what I thought I wanted to be at the time.

"He knew my name," Millard adds. "He knew what classes I was taking. He knew more about me than I did. It was freaky, actually."

Two years later, as a senior, Millard faced graduation after having been rejected from the only college where he had applied.

15   "I looked at what jobs I could get," he says. "I wasn't really prepared to do any job. I wasn't prepared for college. I wasn't prepared for the workforce. So I started looking at the military. I wanted to go active duty Marine Corps, I thought. You know, they were the best. And that's what I was going to do.

"There were a lot of other reasons behind it, too," he says. "I mean, growing up in this culture you envy that, the soldier."

Any story of war is a story of elites preying on the weak, the gullible, the marginal, the poor.

His grandfather, in the Army Air Corps in World War II, had died when he was five. The military honor guard at the funeral had impressed him. As a teenager, he had watched the burial of his other grandfather, also with military honors. Millard carried the folded flag to his grandmother after receiving it from the honor guard.

The pageantry has always been alluring. "We marched a long time," Louis-Ferdinand Céline, who fought in World War I, writes in *Journey to the End of the Night*:

> There were streets and more streets, and they were all crowded with civilians and their wives, cheering us on, bombarding us with flowers from café terraces, railroad stations, crowded churches. You never saw so many patriots in all your life! And then there were fewer patriots. . . . It started to rain, and then there were still fewer and fewer, and not a single cheer, not one.

20   And nearly a century later it is the same.

When Millard told his mother he wanted to be a Marine, she pleaded with him to consider the National Guard. He agreed to meet with the

Guard recruiter, whose pitch was effective and simple: "If you come here, you get to blow shit up."

"I'm seventeen," Millard says. "I thought being in the military was the pinnacle of what coolness was. I was just like, oh, I get to blow up stuff! I signed up right then and there on the spot. But the interesting thing he didn't tell me was that the 'shit' that he referred to would be kids.

"They don't teach you when you're in land mine school that the overwhelming percentage of victims of land mines are little kids. Because, like, in the States, a little kid will chase a soccer ball in the streets. And overseas, a little kid will chase a soccer ball into a minefield. Whether, you know, it happens in Korea or Bosnia or Iraq, kids get killed all the time by land mines. They get maimed by them. And that's just a reality of our military industrial complex. We put out these mines. We have no concern for what they do."

Not that this reality intruded on his visions of life in the military when he began.

"I just thought of it like this stuff you see on TV where cars blow up and stuff like that," he says.   25

For Anthony Swofford—author of *Jarhead,* a memoir about being a Marine in the first Gulf War—the tipping point came when the recruiter, who assured him he would be "a fine killer," told him he could book a threesome for $40 in Olongapo in the Philippines. "I'd had sex three times and been the recipient of five blow jobs and fourteen hand jobs," he writes. "I was sold."

But sometimes there's no need for a recruiting pitch. The culture does enough to make war, combat, and soldiering appealing.

Ali Aoun was born in Rochester, New York. His father is Lebanese. His mother is from the Caribbean. He says he wanted to be a soldier from the age of nine. He was raised watching war films. But even antiwar films such as *Platoon* and *Full Metal Jacket* celebrate the power and seductiveness of violence. He wanted this experience as his own. He says no one pushed him into it.

"I enlisted," he explains. "It was something I always wanted to do, although I got more than I bargained for. You never really know a woman until you jump in bed with her. It's just like the Army: you never really know about it until you enlist. It's not about defending the country or serving our people. It's about working for some rich guy who has his interests."

30   At first Millard liked the National Guard. He was able to enroll in Niagara County Community College as a business major, where he signed up for an African American studies class thinking it would be an easy A. He read *The Autobiography of Malcolm X*. He read Howard Zinn's *A People's History of the United States*. He read Frederick Douglass.

"It was the first time I'd really started to read," he says.

He was in the African American studies class when the attacks of 9/11 occurred. His wrestling coach came into the room to tell him he had been activated. He went home. He packed his bags. He thought about combat.

"I was pissed," he says. "I was like, they attacked us. I was ready to go to war."

But he was confused from the start.

35   "I really wanted to go to war with somebody, because we were attacked," he says. "But the one question I couldn't answer was, who were we going to go to war with?"

At first he did military funerals. Then he was called up for Iraq. He was by then a sergeant and was assigned to work in the office of a general with the 42nd Infantry Division, Rear Operation Center. He became, in military slang, a REMF—a rear echelon motherfucker. He was based in Tikrit, where he watched the cynical and cold manipulation of human life.

"It's not about defending the country or serving our people. It's about working for some rich guy who has his interests."

He relates the story of a traffic-control mission gone awry when an eighteen-year-old soldier made a bad decision. He was sitting atop an armored Humvee monitoring a checkpoint. An Iraqi car approached, and the soldier, fearing it might be carrying a suicide bomber, pressed the butterfly trigger on his .50 caliber machine gun. He put two hundred rounds into the car in less than a minute, killing a mother, a father, a four-year-old boy, and a three-year-old girl.

"They briefed this to the general," Millard says. "They briefed it gruesome. I mean, they had pictures. And this colonel turns around to this full division staff and says: 'If these fucking Hadjis learned to drive, this shit wouldn't happen.'

40   "If you lift your rifle and you look through the sights and you see a person, you can't pull the trigger," Millard says. "But if you lift your rifle and you look through the sights and you see a fucking Hadji, then what's the difference.

"That's a lot of what I saw in Iraq," he says. "These officers, high-ranking officers, generals, colonels, you know, the complete disregard. They knew all the stuff that happened. They got all the briefings. They knew what happened. And they either didn't speak up, they didn't say anything about it or they openly condoned it. When Iraqis got killed, to them, it was one less fucking Hadji around."

Millard's thirteen months in Iraq turned him into a passionate antiwar activist. He is the cofounder of the Washington, D.C., chapter of Iraq Veterans Against the War and served as its president for three years. He has taken part in numerous antiwar demonstrations around the country, was one of the organizers of the Winter Soldier hearings, returned to Iraq on a humanitarian aid mission in 2011, and now directs a homeless veterans initiative.

The briefing that Millard and his superiors received after the checkpoint killing was one of many. Sergeant Perry Jeffries, who served in the Fourth Infantry Division in Iraq after being called out of retirement, said the killing of Iraqi civilians at checkpoints was routine.

"Alpha troop and Balad Ruz shot somebody at least once," he says, referring to a troop detachment and to the soldiers manning a checkpoint in a small Diyala Province village. "Somebody else on what we called the Burning Oil Checkpoint, they shot somebody with a .50 cal, shot a guy once, and then several times."

Killing becomes a job. You do it. Sometimes it unnerves you. But the 45 demons usually don't hit until you come home, when you are lying alone in bed and you don't dare to tell your wife or your girlfriend what you have become, what you saw, what you did, why you are drinking yourself into a stupor, why you so desperately want to forget your dreams.

The disillusionment comes swiftly. It is not the war of the movies. It is not the glory promised by the recruiters. The mythology fed to you by the church, the press, the school, the state, and the entertainment industry is exposed as a lie. We are not a virtuous nation. God has not blessed America. Victory is not assured. And we can be as evil, even more evil, than those we oppose. War is venal, noisy, frightening, and dirty. The military is a vast bureaucratic machine fueled by hyper-masculine fantasies and arcane and mind-numbing rules. War is always about betrayal—betrayal of the young by the old, of idealists by cynics, and of soldiers and Marines by politicians.

"The biggest misconception about the war is that the soldiers care about politics," Jeffries says. "The right thinks the soldiers want support. They want to feel good. They want everybody to fly their flag and have a bumper sticker and go, 'Rah! Rah! Rah! I support the troops. Yay, thank you! Thank you! Thank you!' The left thinks the soldiers all want to run off and get out of there, that they're dying in a living hell. I think that most of the soldiers are young people that are having a decent adventure."

But, he goes on, "They may be having a very hard time. They're frustrated about the amount of resources they have been provided—how many hours of sleep they get, how nice their day is, whether they get to play their PlayStation or read their book at night or whatever. Like any human, you'd like to have some more of that."

Yet, while soldiers don't want to be forgotten, the support-the-troops brigade only maintains the mythology of war on the home front by pretending that we're actually all in it together, when in fact it's overwhelmingly the poor, powerless, and adrift who suffer.

50   Jeffries has little time for lawn chair warriors: "I remember hearing that somebody said, 'Oh, we're going to have a barbecue to support the troops.' I heard about this when I was in Iraq. I said, how the hell is that going to support me? It's not doing anything. Don't drink beer. Send me the beer. It's not doing me any good to have you drink it. I still don't like the yellow ribbons."

It is no surprise that soldiers sometimes come to despise civilians who chant patriotic mantras. Those soldiers may not be fans of the remote and rarely seen senior officers who build their careers on the corpses of others, including comrades, either. But to oppose the machine and risk being cast out of the magic circle of comradeship can be fatal. Fellow soldiers are the only people who understand the psychological torment of killing and being shot at, of learning to not think at all and instead be led as a herd of animals. Those ostracized in war have a hard time surviving, mentally and physically, so most service members say and do nothing to impede the madness and the killing.

Jessica Goodell came to understand that torment only too well, as she relates in her 2011 memoir *Shade it Black: Death and After in Iraq*. Goodell wasn't poor. She grew up in a middle-class home near Chautauqua Lake in upstate New York. Her father was a lawyer, and her mother worked at home. But her "universe fractured" when she was sixteen and her parents divorced. She could barely continue "the motions of everyday existence."

She was accepted at Ithaca College her senior year, but just before gradua-tion a uniformed Marine came to her high school. He told her he had come to find "tough men."

"What about tough women?" she asked.

By that afternoon she was in the Marine recruiting office. She told the recruiter she wanted to be part of a tank crew but was informed that women were prohibited from operating tanks. She saw a picture of a Marine stand-ing next to a vehicle with a huge hydraulic arm and two smaller forklift arms. She signed up to be a heavy equipment mechanic, although she knew nothing about it.

Three years later, while stationed at the Marine Corps Air Ground 55 Combat Center in the desert town of Twentynine Palms, California, she volunteered to serve in the Marine Corps' first official Mortuary Affairs unit, at Al Taqaddum Airbase in Iraq. Her job, for eight months, was to "process" dead Marines—collect and catalog their bodies and personal effects. She put the remains in body bags and placed the bags in metal boxes. Before being shipped to Dover Air Force Base, the boxes were stored, often for days, in a refrigerated unit known as a "reefer."

Her unit processed six suicides. The suicide notes, she told me in an in-terview, almost always cited hazing. Marines who were overweight or unable to do the physical training were subjected to withering verbal and physical abuse. They were called "fat nasties" and "shit bags." They were as-signed to other Marines as slaves. Many were forced to run until they vom-ited or to bear-crawl—walk on all fours—the length of a football field and back. This would be followed by sets of monkey fuckers—bending down, grabbing the ankles, crouching like a baseball catcher, and then standing up again—and other exercises that went on until the Marines collapsed.

Goodell's unit was sent to collect the bodies of the Marines who killed themselves. They usually blew their faces off with assault rifles in port-a-johns or in the corners of abandoned bunkers or buildings. She and the other members of the Mortuary Affairs unit would have to scrape the flesh and brain tissue from the walls.

Goodell fell into depression when she returned home. She abused drugs and alcohol. And she watched the slow descent of her comrades as they too tried to blunt the pain with narcotics and self-destructive behavior. She details many of her experiences in *Shade It Black,* a term that refers to the missing body parts of dead Marines, which she colored black on diagrams of the corpses.

In a poignant passage, she talks about what it was like for her and a fellow Marine named Miguel to come home and see all those yellow ribbons:

> We'd frequently pass vehicles displaying the yellow ribbon "support-our-troops decal," but we never once mentioned it. We probably passed a hundred or more decals—two hundred if you count the multiple decals decorating the cars of the more patriotic motorists—and yet neither of us even once said, "Look, more support from the citizenry. Let's give the 'thumbs up' as we pass.'" . . . I knew that these people on their way to work or home or dinner had no idea what it was they were supporting. They did not have a clue as to what war was like, what it made people see, and what it made them do to each other. I felt as though I didn't deserve their support, or anyone's, for what I had done. . . . No one should ever support the people who do such things.

60   Stateside "support" not only reflects the myths of war, but it also forces Goodell and her comrades to suppress their own experiences:

> Here we were, leaving the ribbons behind us as we sped up on our way to Hell, probably, where we would pay for the sins these magnetic decals endorsed. There was an irony of sorts shaping the dynamic between our ribbon decal supporters and us. They were uninformed but good people, the kind whose respect we would welcome—if it were based upon something true. It was when we were around them that we had to hide the actual truth most consciously.

· ❖ ·

Those who return to speak this truth, like Goodell or Millard, are our contemporary prophets. They struggle, in a culture awash in lies, to tell what few have the fortitude to digest. The words these prophets speak are painful.

As a nation we prefer to listen to those who speak from the patriotic script. We prefer to hear ourselves exalted. If veterans speak of terrible wounds visible and invisible, of lies told to make them kill, of evil committed in our name, we fill our ears with wax. Not our boys and girls, we say, not them, bred in our homes, endowed with goodness and decency. For if it is easy for them to murder, what about us? It is simpler and more comfortable not to hear, to wish only that they would calm down, be reasonable, get some help, and go away. We brand our prophets as madmen. We cast them into the desert. This is why so many veterans are estranged and enraged. This is why so many succumb to suicide or addictions. Not long ago Goodell received a text message from a Marine she had worked with in Mortuary Affairs after he tried to commit suicide. "I've got $2,000 in the bank," the message read. "Let's meet in NYC and go out with a bang."

War comes wrapped in patriotic slogans; calls for sacrifice, honor, and heroism; and promises of glory. It comes wrapped in the claims of divine providence. It is what a grateful nation asks of its children. It is what is right and just. It is waged to make the nation and the world a better place, to cleanse evil. War is touted as the ultimate test of manhood, where the young can find out what they are made of. From a distance it seems noble. It gives us comrades and power and a chance to play a bit part in the great drama of history. It promises to give us identities as warriors, patriots, as long as we go along with the myth, the one the war-makers need to wage wars and the defense contractors need to increase their profits.

But up close war is a soulless void. War is about barbarity, perversion, and pain. Human decency and tenderness are crushed, and people become objects to use or kill. The noise, the stench, the fear, the scenes of eviscerated bodies and bloated corpses, the cries of the wounded all combine to spin those in combat into another universe. In this moral void, naïvely blessed by secular and religious institutions at home, the hypocrisy of our social conventions, our strict adherence to moral precepts, becomes stark. War, for all its horror, has the power to strip away the trivial and the banal, the empty chatter and foolish obsessions that fill our days. It might let us see, although the cost is tremendous.

Analyze

1. Look up "call of the Sirens" online. Try to find the mythological origin and then explain how the reference works in Hedges's introduction.
2. How is this article about socioeconomics?
3. Explain how Jessica Goodell's testimony supports Hedges's main idea.
4. Hedges says that in war, "the hypocrisy of our social conventions, our strict adherence to moral precepts, becomes stark." What does he mean? In your own words, explain this idea.
5. How is Hedges's article about American culture?

Explore

1. Hedges says, "War comes wrapped in patriotic slogans; calls for sacrifice, honor, and heroism; and promises of glory." List some specific and recent patriotic slogans that have been associated with war.

2. What do you think about the yellow ribbons in support of soldiers? How does Hedges's article—Goodell's words specifically—influence your thinking?

3. How does Hedges's article relate to "Throwing the Last Stone" by Benjamin Busch (in this chapter)? What specific claims, ideas, or values do the two writers share? Identify specific passages to support your answer.

4. Hedges argues that war is betrayal. How is war also a form of truth or honesty?

5. What's the connection between soldiers and politics?

Tom Malinowski, Sarah Holewinski, and Tammy Schultz
Post-Conflict Potter

Specializing in U.S. foreign policy and human rights policy, Tom Malinowski is the Washington director for Human Rights Watch. His articles have appeared in *Foreign Policy*, *The New Republic*, and the *Washington Post*. Sarah Holewinski is the executive director of the Campaign for Innocent Victims in Conflict (CIVIC), which seeks to "make warring parties more responsible to civilians before, during, and after armed conflict." Her articles have appeared in the *International Herald Tribune*, *USA Today*, and the *Washington Post*. Tammy Schultz is the director of national security and joint warfare at Marine Corps University. She writes for newspapers such as *Defense News*, the *Washington Post*, and the *Washington Times*. In the following *Foreign Policy* article, Malinowski, Holewinski, and Schultz use J. K. Rowling's fantasy world, and its terminology, as a lens for examining international policy.

At last, the long war against Voldemort and his army of Death Eaters has been brought to a responsible end. A short time ago, just a small band of brave witches and wizards at Hogwarts School stood between the dark forces and their ascension to power. Now their evil leader is dead, his armies are scattered, and the wizarding world can begin to recover from the terror they inflicted.

At such a moment of deliverance, it is natural to feel elation and closure— to allow ourselves the brief comfort of imagining that the drama, so meticulously documented by J.K. Rowling, is over. But if history teaches us anything (consider the bitter legacy still lingering from the 17th-century Goblin Wars or the recent experience of American Muggles in Iraq and Afghanistan), it is that the defeat of Voldemort by Harry Potter may have been the easy part. Indeed, one might even say it was child's play. The hard work of postwar stabilization still lies ahead.

Former U.S. Deputy Defense Secretary John Hamre and retired Gen. Gordon Sullivan have described four pillars of post-conflict reconstruction: security, governance and participation, urgent social and economic needs, and justice and reconciliation. Of these pillars, the magical world can currently afford to feel complacent about only one—social and economic needs. After all, with the proper application of scouring, mending, and engorgement charms, much of the physical damage wrought by the war can be repaired, and food can be multiplied to meet the needs of the population. But with respect to the other imperatives, critical challenges remain.

Surviving Death Eaters will have to be brought to justice or reintegrated into magical society. Long-standing rifts among magical communities that the war widened must be healed. Most of all, we must ensure that the values that triumphed in the final battle—tolerance, pluralism, and respect for the dignity of all magical and non-magical creatures alike—are reflected in the institutions and arrangements that emerge from the conflict. What ultimately matters is not just whether something evil was defeated, but whether something good is built in its place.

As experts on human rights, civilian protection, and national security, 5 we were recently asked by officials in the British Ministry of Magic to suggest lessons from the Muggle world that might apply to challenges facing post-Voldemort magical society. Our recommendations are summarized below.

Transitional Justice and Reconciliation

Thousands of Death Eaters fought with or provided material support to Voldemort, including prominent members of key magical institutions. It will be impossible to move forward unless we come to terms with the abuses they committed and meet legitimate demands for redress. In the magical world, after all, the ghosts of the past can literally haunt future generations.

Members of Voldemort's inner circle and others guilty of the worst crimes—the unforgivable curses of killing ("Avada Kedavra"), torture ("Crucio"), and mind control ("Imperio")—should be prosecuted before a court of law. We should reject calls by Order of the Phoenix hard-liners like Joe Lieberbottom, John "Mad Eye" McCain, and Lindsey Gramger to instead detain them without charge as "unlawful enemy spell-casters" for as long as the "war" against dark magic continues (though all three men deserve our thanks for their early warnings about the Dark Lord's return).

A more difficult dilemma arises with respect to the thousands of other wizards and witches who aided the Dark Lord's cause in less obvious ways. We cannot sweep their complicity under an invisibility cloak. At the same time, it would be impractical and unwise to prosecute all of them. For every wizard who willingly committed crimes for the Death Eaters, another was blackmailed, threatened, or coerced while under the Imperius Curse. Some actively participated in hostilities against other wizards and Muggles; others merely provided financing or shelter. A campaign to punish everyone would get out of hand, creating a climate of suspicion and score-settling in which innocents are snared. The last thing the wizarding world needs is a witch hunt.

A legitimate process must hold the victors to account as well. Remember, under the ruthless Barty Crouch, the Ministry of Magic's Department of Magical Law Enforcement was itself formally authorized to use unforgivable curses, including torture, against suspected Death Eaters, and innocent suspects were imprisoned after what were essentially show trials. When the ministry came under Voldemort's sway, how many of its employees went along with the abuses it committed? What about the controversial decisions made by those who are widely seen as heroes, like Hogwarts headmaster Albus Dumbledore—for, say, his use of child soldiers? What of Harry Potter himself, who once used the torture curse?

One way to address these challenges would be to establish a Truth and   10
Reconciliation Commission modeled on the experience of Muggle South
Africa. Rank-and-file Death Eaters and collaborators—as well as those
who fought against them—would be given the opportunity to testify about
their actions and be forgiven for those less serious offenses to which they
fully and honestly confessed. Such a process would not only be cathartic,
but would also help establish a more accurate and complete version of these
traumatic events and could, in turn, become part of Hogwarts's curriculum.
It would be important to ensure, however, that those who testify to such
a commission tell the truth voluntarily, and not under the influence of
Veritaserum.

Victims should also have their day in court. The Ministry of Magic
should provide amends, in the form of gold or perhaps a bottle of Felix
Felicis, to all those civilian wizards and witches harmed by either side
during the war. Meanwhile, a property claims commission should be established to gather unlawfully amassed assets and return them to their rightful owners. The goblins in charge of Gringotts Bank should be required to
question and report suspiciously large deposits of gold, especially by Politically Exposed Wizards. Some seized assets should be used to help wounded
and cursed warriors and loved ones of the fallen, like the Weasley family.
This year's Quidditch World Cup should be dedicated to their memory;
it will be a chance to heal.

Finally, true reconciliation in the magical world must involve its
nonhuman inhabitants as well. For complicated historical reasons, some
magical creatures such as giants, trolls, and spiders fought alongside the
Death Eaters during the final battle at Hogwarts. Given the anger felt
by the wizarding community toward those who aided Voldemort, some
might try to inflict collective punishment on these beings, as well as on
those, like centaurs and merpeople, whose loyalties were uncertain or
who remained neutral in the face of mass atrocities. In the short term,
the International Confederation of Wizards (a consortium of magical
lands, often meeting by a river in New York) should deploy a mission
of peacekeeping Aurors with a mandate to protect vulnerable communities of magical creatures from revenge attacks. In the longer term,
the International Confederation of Wizards should initiate a multi-
stakeholder dialogue with these creatures and negotiate a compact that
addresses the long-standing grievances that led them, tragically, to side
with the Dark Lord.

Governance Reform

In their aptly named essay, "Dealing with Demons," Michèle Flournoy and Michael Pan argue that the reconciliation pillar of post-conflict reconstruction requires more than just dealing with past abuses and grievances. It also calls for "(1) law enforcement instruments that are effective and respectful of human rights; (2) an impartial, open, and accountable judicial system; (3) a fair constitution and body of law; (4) mechanisms for monitoring and upholding human rights; [and] (5) a humane corrections system." The wizarding world will need to implement fundamental reforms in each of these areas.

Members of the anti-Voldemort Order of the Phoenix will presumably form the core of a transitional governing authority, which would then organize elections for a permanent government. As democratic forces in Muggle Egypt and Libya have recently discovered, the legitimacy of post-revolutionary but pre-election transitional governments can be tenuous. This problem could be minimized in the magical world by having the Hogwarts Sorting Hat assign ministerial positions in the transitional authority.

15   The new government should rapidly draw up and submit to a referendum a new legal framework establishing checks and balances on its powers, as well as a Charter on the Rights of Witches and Wizards. We would also recommend that the Wizengamot, the high council of Magical Great Britain, be split into separate legislative and judicial bodies. The wizards who conjure the laws should not be the ones who interpret them.

The use of any form of torture should be banned, whether by the infamous Cruciatus Curse or methods euphemistically known as "enhanced hexation." We welcome J.K. Rowling's report that soul-sucking dementors will be banished from the prison at Azkaban, but we do not think this measure goes far enough. The next Minister of Magic should close Azkaban on day one of his administration. It is a symbol of abuse and a recruiting tool for future Death Eaters. (We recognize the practical difficulties in closing Azkaban so quickly, but believe that the prisoners could initially be moved to penal facilities in enchanted caves or castles as secure as Azkaban, but without the baggage. A judicial panel could then review each prisoner's case to determine whether he should be given a new trial, transferred to another magical state, or allowed to disapparate. As U.S. President Barack Obama will surely confirm when his magical counterpart next drops into the Oval Office, delay could be fatal. All it will take is one more attempted Death Eater attack and scaremongers in the Wizengamot will start calling for the return of dementors, making the closure of Azkaban politically impossible.)

In parallel, legitimate law enforcement measures should be stepped up. Merchants should be required to report bulk sales of magical supplies that could be combined for dark purposes. Lawful surveillance of dark alleys and curse-tracing spells on wands should be permitted, with a judicial warrant. Full body and Polyjuice Potion scanners should also be installed for international travelers across the Floo Network.

One of the great weaknesses of magical institutions is that they function top down, with little input from ordinary wizards and witches. And yet the war against Voldemort was won almost entirely bottom up, by grassroots organizations such as Dumbledore's Army and the Order of the Phoenix. The legal and political reforms we advocate depend on the growth of civil society (we assume a charm can be developed to make magical civil society especially vibrant).

Another urgent priority should be media diversification. A single wizarding newspaper—the *Daily Prophet*—cannot maintain its independence and hold government officials accountable when it has no competition (especially given the rumor, first published in the tabloid the *Quibbler,* that the *Prophet* may soon be bought by dark wizard Rupert Murdoch). New media should also be promoted in the magical world. Right now, for example, wizards and witches stay in touch by sending letters of any length by the slow, reliable method of owl post. A new system could be developed employing faster, lighter sparrows, which could distribute shorter messages—say under 140 characters—to larger numbers of people.

Finally, the Ministry of Magic must become more transparent to the public and press. Fewer documents should be protected by the Fidelius Charm, and the budget of the Department of Mysteries should be declassified. Too much secrecy will only invite more WizenLeaks scandals. [20]

International Magical Security

The great question remaining now is whether Voldemort's death means that the threat posed by dark magic has passed. Some might be tempted to believe so. After all, for ages many witches and wizards have let themselves believe that if they ignore the phenomenon entirely, if they lock it in the restricted section of the library or refrain from uttering the names of dark wizards, it will somehow go away. But as renowned defense-against-the-dark-arts expert Marc Sageman argued in his incisive book, *Leaderless Maleficium,* most dark wizards, while originally inspired by Voldemort, have over time transitioned to membership in an amorphous "social movement" organized into small cells and networked through Legilimency, a system likely to survive the demise of its leader and of "Death Eater Central." This view may be exaggerated (see Bruce Hoffman's response to Sageman, "The Myth of Grass-Roots Dark Magic"). But it would be unrealistic to assume that Voldemort's death will mark the end of magical extremism or that no other leader will emerge to unite his followers. For one thing, the House of Slytherin still remains.

The overall reform of states that already have strong institutions, such as Magical Great Britain, would help prevent the resurgence of new security threats and enshrine the values for which Voldemort's opponents fought. Resuming international events like the Triwizard Tournament could help spread those values and forge bonds among the established states. But none of this will suffice so long as dark wizards can find refuge in failed magical states where lawlessness reigns, as Voldemort did in Albania for over a dozen years. Far deeper international magical cooperation will be needed to deal with these ungoverned spaces.

For a start, new standards must be agreed upon. We suggest that the International Confederation of Wizards negotiate a Comprehensive Curse Ban Treaty, forbidding use or testing of certain forms of dark magic anywhere on the planet. The treaty should be enforced by deploying a ground-based network of sensors, or Sneakoscopes, throughout the world to detect unlawful spells.

Each sovereign magical state should be seen as having a responsibility to protect its citizens from dark magic. But if they fail to meet their responsibility, it should be the duty of the international magical community to step in. And when that community does act to pacify an unstable area, it should not try to do so on the cheap, by targeting dark wizards (or unruly trolls, giants, or dragons) with stunning spells deployed from unmanned aerial brooms. Stabilization Aurors will need to deploy to these places, employing a "clear, hold, and conjure" strategy designed to win hearts, minds, and souls.

We trust that these preliminary recommendations will be helpful to all 25
magical persons as they recover from their recent conflict. If we have been
of service to the community of witches and wizards, we humbly hope they
might render us Muggles a service or two in return. For starters, we would
very much appreciate it if they could lift the Petrificus Totalus curse someone has clearly placed on the U.S. Congress.

Analyze

1. In this article, the world of Harry Potter is used as an extended metaphor
   to help make sense of modern military policy. What is the main idea?
   What point do the authors make?
2. In the world of Harry Potter, Muggles are everyday, nonmagical
   humans. In this extended metaphor, explain who the Muggles are.
3. Who are "all magical persons"?
4. The authors assert, "The legal and political reforms we advocate depend
   on the growth of civil society (we assume a charm can be developed to
   make magical civil society especially vibrant)." Explain this point.
   What are they saying about legal and governmental institutions in the
   United States?
5. This article describes a major shift in international policy. Explain how
   it describes a change in culture.

Explore

1. What is postconflict reconstruction? See what others have said about it.
2. Why is a free media—one not owned by major political figures or
   parties—a vital part of democracy?
3. The authors argue, "The wizards who conjure the laws should not be
   the ones who interpret them." How does this point translate into
   modern U.S. institutions?
4. The authors reference a dark wizard at work in Albania. Who was this
   person?
5. The article calls for international collaboration to bring down evil dictators and to balance out bad international policy. What body or group
   in our world offers such collaboration?

Forging Connections

1. How does warfare get used to sell products and services in mainstream culture? Even beyond video games such as *Medal of Honor,* how has military conflict and armed battle become part of marketing? What are some terms, phrases, references, or even images that marketers now rely on to create a message? Focus on specific ads or ad campaigns. What do these ads suggest about war? What do they suggest about the relationship between war and everyday life? What kinds of attitudes and beliefs about war or patriotism do the ads reinforce? Borrow insights from Dan Heath and Chip Heath ("How to Pick the Perfect Brand Name," Chapter 2), Juliette Kayyem ("Never Say 'Never Again,'" Chapter 3), and James Gleick ("What Defines a Meme?," Chapter 4).

2. Explore the relationship between film and war. Focus on a specific film such as *The Deer Hunter, Full Metal Jacket, The Hurt Locker, Inglourious Basterds,* or a miniseries such as *Generation Kill.* Write an essay that explains how specific features (such as plot, character development, direction, or cinematography) make a point about war. For instance, what does the focus on Robert DeNiro's character in *The Deer Hunter* say about the relationship between the battlefield and home? What does the plot of *Inglourious Basterds* say about the way we learn about the history of war? What do the characters in *Generation Kill* say about the generation of U.S. soldiers that served after 9/11?

Looking Further

1. How will warfare change in the future? Consider the claims and descriptions made in this chapter and write an essay that describes a detailed future. Focus your ideas by narrowing on a specific branch of the military or a specific defense policy. Finally, consider the implications for American culture. What does this future suggest about mainstream culture? What will Americans tolerate, accept, or support? What kinds of conflict or loss will they accept? Integrate images, charts, or graphs to help illustrate your vision of the future.

2. Hedges claims that the military appeals to poor and working-class young people—those with few options in life. Research this claim. Try to find the average income of new recruits or their families. Seek out information about military recruiting strategies—the schools, colleges, and neighborhoods they designate as prime locations. Explain your findings in a thorough explanatory essay.

appendix

Researching and Writing About Culture
Barbara Rockenbach and Aaron Ritzenberg[1]

Research-based writing lies at the heart of the mission of higher education: to discover, transform, and share ideas. And it is through writing and research that you will become an active participant in an intellectual community. Doing research in college involves not only searching for information but also digesting, analyzing, and synthesizing what you find to create new knowledge. Your most successful efforts as a college writer will report on the latest and most important ideas in a field as well as make new arguments and offer fresh insights.

It might seem daunting to be asked to contribute new ideas to a field in which you are a novice. After all, creating new knowledge seems to be the realm of experts. In this guide, we offer strategies that demystify the research and writing process, breaking down some of the fundamental steps that scholars take when they do research and make arguments. You'll see that contributing to scholarship involves strategies that can be learned and practiced.

Throughout this guide we imagine doing research and writing as engaging in a scholarly conversation. When you read academic writing, you'll see that scholars reference the studies that came before them and allude to the studies that will grow out of their research. When you think of research as engaging in a conversation, you quickly realize that scholarship always has a social

---

1. Barbara Rockenbach, Director of Humanities & History Libraries, Columbia University; Aaron Ritzenberg, Associate Director of First-Year Writing, Columbia University.

aspect. Even if you like to find books in the darkest corners of the library, even if you like to draft your essays in deep solitude, you will always be awake to the voices that helped you form your ideas and to the audience who will receive your ideas. As if in a conversation at a party, scholars mingle: They listen to others and share their most recent ideas, learning and teaching at the same time. Strong scholars, like good conversationalists, will listen and speak with an open mind, letting their own thoughts evolve as they encounter new ideas.

You may be wondering, "What does it mean to have an open mind when I'm doing research? After all, aren't I supposed to find evidence that supports my thesis?" We'll be returning to this question soon, but the quick answer is: To have an open mind when you're doing research means that you'll be involved in the research process well before you have a thesis. We realize this may be a big change from the way you think about research. The fact is, though, that scholars do research well before they know any of the arguments they'll be making in their papers. Indeed, scholars do research even before they know what specific topic they'll be addressing and what questions they'll be asking.

When scholars do research they may not know exactly what they are hunting for, but they have techniques that help them define projects, identify strong interlocutors, and ask important questions. This guide will help you move through the various kinds of research that you'll need at the different stages of your project. If writing a paper involves orchestrating a conversation within a scholarly community, there are a number of important questions you'll need to answer: How do I choose what to write about? How do I find a scholarly community? How do I orchestrate a conversation that involves this community? Whose voices should be most prominent? How do I enter the conversation? How do I use evidence to make a persuasive claim? How do I make sure that my claim is not just interesting but important?

GETTING STARTED

You have been asked to write a research paper. This might be your first research paper at the college level. Where do you start? The important thing when embarking on any kind of writing project that involves research is to find something that you are interested in learning more about. Writing and research is easier if you care about your topic. Your instructor might have given you a topic, but you can make that topic your own by finding something that appeals to you within the scope of the assignment.

Academic writing begins from a place of deep inquiry. When you are sincerely interested in a problem, researching can be a pleasure, as it will satisfy your own intellectual curiosity. More important, the intellectual problems that seem most difficult—the questions that appear to resist obvious answers—are the very problems that will often yield the most surprising and most rewarding results.

Presearching to Generate Ideas

When faced with a research project, your first instinct might be to go to Google or Wikipedia, or even to a social media site. This is not a bad instinct. In fact, Google, Wikipedia, and social media can be great places to start. Using Google, Wikipedia, and social media to help you discover a topic is what we call *presearch*—it is what you do to warm up before the more rigorous work of academic research. Academic research and writing will require you to go beyond these sites to find resources that will make the work of researching and writing both easier and more appropriate to an academic context.

Google   Let's start with Google. You use Google because you know you are going to find a simple search interface and that your search will produce many results. These results might not be completely relevant to your topic, but Google helps in the discovery phase of your work. For instance, you are asked to write about the impact of social media on relationships.

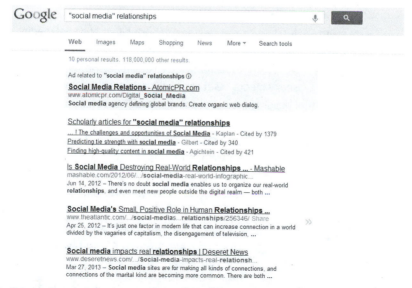

Google Results of a Google search for "social media" and relationships.

A Google search will produce articles from many diverse sources—magazines, government sites, and corporate reports among them. It's not a bad start. Use these results to begin to hone in on a topic you are interested in pursuing. A quick look through these results might yield a more focused topic such as how social media is impacting the ways people relate in school or the workplace, or how the nature of friendship is evolving because of tools like Facebook and Twitter.

Wikipedia   A Wikipedia search on social networking services and relationships will lead you to several articles that address both concepts. The great thing about Wikipedia is that it is an easy way to gain access to a wealth of information about thousands of topics. However, it is crucial to realize that Wikipedia itself is not an authoritative source in a scholarly context. Even though you may see Wikipedia cited in mainstream newspapers and

References

1. ^ Ahlqvist, Toni; Bäck, A.; Halonen, M.; Heinonen, S (2008). "Social media road maps exploring the futures triggered by social media". *VTT Tiedotteita - Valtion Teknillinen Tutkimuskeskus* (2454): 13.

2. ^ Kaplan Andreas M., Haenlein Michael, (2010), Users of the world, unite! The challenges and opportunities of social media, Business Horizons, Vol. 53, Issue 1 (page 61)

3. ^ *a b c d e f g h i j* H. Kietzmann, Jan; Kristopher Hermkens (2011). "Social media? Get serious! Understanding the functional building blocks of social media". *Business Horizons* **54**: 241–251.

4. ^ *a b* Agichtein, Eugene; Carlos Castillo. Debora Donato, Aristides Gionis, Gilad Mishne (2008). "Finding high-quality content in social media". *WSDM'08 - Proceedings of the 2008 International Conference on Web Search and Data Mining:* 183–193.

5. ^ *a b c d e f g h* Nigel Morgan; Graham Jones; Ant Hodges. "Social Media" 🔊. *The Complete Guide to Social Media From The Social Media Guys*. Retrieved 12 December 2012.

Wikipedia List of references from a Wikipedia search on social media. Use these links to further your research.

popular magazines, academic researchers do not consider Wikipedia a reliable source and do not consult or cite it in their own research. Wikipedia itself says that "Wikipedia is not considered a credible source. . . . This is especially true considering that anyone can edit the information given at any time." For research papers in college, you should use Wikipedia only to find basic information about your topic and to point you toward scholarly sources. Wikipedia might be a great starting point for presearch, but it is not an adequate ending point for research. Use the References section at the bottom of the Wikipedia article to find other, more substantive and authoritative resources about your topic.

Using Social Media   Social media such as Facebook and Twitter can be useful in the presearch phase of your project, but you must start thinking about these tools in new ways. You may have a Facebook or Twitter account and use it to keep in touch with friends, family, and colleagues. These social networks are valuable, and you might already use them to gather information to help you make decisions in your personal life and your workplace. Although social media is not generally useful to your academic research, both Facebook and Twitter have powerful search functions that can lead you to resources and help you refine your ideas.

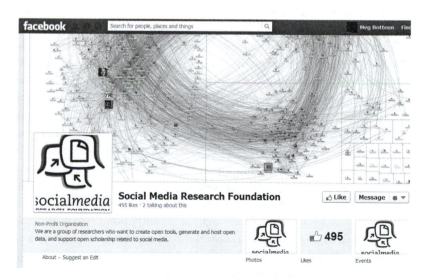

Facebook Facebook page for the Social Media Research Foundation.

After you log in to Facebook, use the "Search for people, places, and things" bar at the top of the page to begin. When you type search terms into this bar, Facebook will first search your own social network. To extend beyond your own network, try adding the word "research" after your search terms. For instance, a search on Facebook for "social media research" will lead you to a Facebook page for the Social Media Research Foundation. The posts on the page link to current news stories on social media, links to other similar research centers, and topics of interest in the field of social media research. You can use these search results as a way to see part of the conversation about a particular topic. This is not necessarily the scholarly conversation we referred to at the start of this guide, but it is a social conversation that can still be useful in helping you determine what you want to focus on in the research process.

Twitter is an information network where users can post short messages (or "tweets"). Although many people use Twitter simply to update their friends ("I'm going to the mall" or "Can't believe it's snowing!"), more and more individuals and organizations use Twitter to comment on noteworthy events or link to interesting articles. You can use Twitter as a presearch tool because it aggregates links to sites, people in a field of research, and noteworthy sources. Communities, sometimes even scholarly communities, form around topics on Twitter. Users group posts together by using hashtags—words or phrases that follow the "#" sign. Users can respond to other users by using the @ sign followed by a user's Twitter name. When searching for specific individuals or organizations on Twitter, you search using their handle (such as @barackobama or @whitehouse). You will retrieve tweets that were created either by the person or organization, or tweets that mention the person or organization. When searching for a topic to find discussions, you search using the hashtag symbol, #. For instance, a search on #globalization will take you to tweets and threaded discussions on the topic of globalization.

There are two ways to search Twitter. You can use the search book in the upper right hand corner and enter either a @ or # search as described above. Once you retrieve results, you can search again by clicking on any words that are hyperlinked within your results such as #antiglobalization.

If you consider a hashtag (the # sign) as an entry point into a community, you will begin to discover a conversation around topics. For instance, a search on Twitter for #socialmedia leads you to Social Media Today (@socialmedia2day), a community that explores new developments and emerging technologies in social media and how it is used in government, education, business, advertising, and other areas. Major news sources from around the world are also active on Twitter, so articles, video, interviews, and other resources from the news media will be retrieved in a search. Evaluating information and sources found in social media is similar to how you evaluate any information you encounter during the research process. And, as with Wikipedia and Google searches, this is just a starting point to help you get a sense of the spectrum of topics. This is no substitute for using library resources. Do not cite Facebook, Twitter, or Wikipedia in a research paper; use them to find more credible, authoritative sources. We'll talk about evaluating sources in the sections that follow.

Create a Concept Map

Once you have settled on a topic that you find exciting and interesting, the next step is to generate search terms, or keywords, for effective searching. Keywords are the crucial terms or phrases that signal the content of any given source. Keywords are the building blocks of your search for information. We have already seen a few basic keywords such as "social media" and "relationships." One way to generate keywords is to tell a friend or classmate what you are interested in. What words are you using to describe your research project? You might not have a fully formed idea or claim, but you have a vague sense of your interest. A concept map exercise can help you generate more keywords and in many cases, narrow your topic to make it more manageable.

A concept map is a way to visualize the relationship between concepts or ideas. You can create a concept map on paper, or there are many free programs online that can help you do this (see, for instance, http://vue.tufts.edu/, http://www.wisemapping.org, or http://freeplane.sourceforge.net). There are many concept mapping applications available for mobile devices; the concept map here was created using the app SimpleMind.

Here is how you use a concept map. First, begin with a term like "social media." Put that term in the first box. Then think of synonyms or related words to describe social media such as "relationships," "Web 2.0," "friendship," "communication," "alienation," and "loneliness." This brainstorming process will help you develop keywords for searching. Notice that keywords can also be short phrases.

After some practice, you'll discover that some phrases make for excellent keywords and others make for less effective search tools. The best keywords are precise enough to narrow your topic so that all of your results are

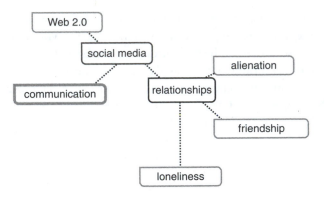

Concept map A concept map about social media and relationships.

relevant, but are not so specific that you might miss helpful results. Concept maps created using apps such as SimpleMind allow you to use templates, embed hyperlinks, and attach notes, among other useful functions.

Keyword Search

One of the hardest parts of writing is coming up with something to write about. Too often, we make the mistake of waiting until we have a fully formed idea before we start writing. The process of writing can actually help you discover what your idea is, and most important, what is interesting about your idea.

Keyword searches are most effective at the beginning stages of your research. They generally produce the most results and can help you determine how much has been written on your topic. You want to use keyword searches to help you achieve a manageable number of results. What is manageable? This is a key question when beginning research. Our keyword search in Google on "social media and relationships" produced almost 3 million results. The same search in JSTOR.org produces almost 200 results. These are not manageable results sets. Let's see how we can narrow our search.

Keyword searches, in library resources or on Google, are most effective if you employ a few search strategies that will focus your results.

1. Use quotation marks around a phrase, and use AND when you are combining multiple keywords. We have used this search construction previously:

"social media" AND relationships

The AND ensures that all your results will contain both the term "social media" and relationships. Many search engines and databases will assume an AND search, meaning if you type

"social media" language

the search will automatically look for all terms. However, in some cases the AND will not be assumed and "social media language" will be treated as a phrase. Worse yet, sometimes the search automatically assumes an OR. That would mean that all your results would come back with either social or media or language. This will produce a large and mostly irrelevant set of results. Therefore, use AND whenever you want two or more words to appear in a result.

2. Using OR can be very effective when you want to use several terms to describe a concept such as:

relationships OR friendships OR communication

A search on social media and relationships can be broadened to include particular kinds of relationships between people. The following search casts a broader net because results will come back with social media and either relationships, friendship, or communication:

"social media" AND (relationships OR friendship OR communication)

Not all of these words will appear in each record. Note also that the parentheses set off the OR search indicating that "social media" must appear in each record and then either relationships, friendship, or communication needs to appear along with globalization.

3. Use quotation marks when looking for a phrase. For instance, if you are looking for information on social media and communication in multinational corporations you can ensure that the search results will include all of these concepts and increase the relevance by using the following search construction:

"social media" AND communication AND "multinational corporations"

This phrasing will return results that contain both the word globalization and the phrase "multinational corporation."

4. Use NOT to exclude terms that will make your search less relevant. You might find that a term keeps appearing in your search that is not useful. Try this:

"social media" NOT technology

If you are interested in the relational side of this debate, getting a lot of results that discuss the technological details of social media might be distracting. By excluding the keyword technology, you will retrieve far fewer sources, and hopefully more relevant results.

Researchable Question

In a college research paper, it is important that you make an argument, not just offer a report. In high school you might have found some success by merely listing or cataloging the data and information you found; you might have offered a series of findings to show your teacher that you investigated your topic. In college, however, your readers will not be interested in data or information merely for its own sake; your readers will want to know what you make of these data and why they should care.

To satisfy the requirements of a college paper, you'll need to distinguish between a topic and a research question. You will likely begin with a topic, but it is only when you move from a topic to a question that your research will begin to feel motivated and purposeful. A topic refers only to the general subject area that you'll be investigating. A researchable question, on the other hand, points toward a specific problem in the subject area that you'll be attempting to answer by making a claim about the evidence you examine.

"Social media and relationships" is a topic, but not a researchable question. It is important that you ask yourself, "What aspect of the topic is most interesting to me?" It is even more important that you ask, "What aspect of the topic is it most important that I illuminate for my audience?" Ideally, your presearch phase of the project will yield questions about social media and relationships that you'd like to investigate.

A strong researchable question will not lead to an easy answer, but rather will lead you into a scholarly conversation in which there are many competing claims. For instance, the question, "What are the official languages of the United Nations?" is not a strong research question, because there is only one correct answer and thus there is no scholarly debate surrounding the topic. It is an interesting question (the answer is: Arabic, Chinese, English, French, Russian, and Spanish), but it will not lead you into a scholarly conversation.

When you are interested in finding a scholarly debate, try using the words "why" and "how" rather than "what." Instead of leading to a definitive answer, the words "why" and "how" will often lead to complex, nuanced answers for which you'll need to marshal evidence to be convincing. "Why did Arabic become an official language of the UN in 1973?" is a question that has a number of complex and competing answers that might draw from a number of different disciplines (political science, history, economics, linguistics, and geography, among others). If you can imagine scholars having an interesting debate about your researchable question, it is likely that you've picked a good one.

Once you have come up with an interesting researchable question, your first task as a researcher is to figure out how scholars are discussing your question. Many novice writers think that the first thing they should do when beginning a research project is to articulate an argument, then find sources that confirm their argument. This is not how experienced scholars work. Instead, strong writers know that they cannot possibly come up with a strong central argument until they have done sufficient research. So, instead of looking for sources that confirm a preliminary claim you might want to make, look for the scholarly conversation.

Looking at the scholarly conversation is a strong way to figure out if you've found a research question that is suitable in scope for the kind of paper you're writing. Put another way, reading the scholarly conversation can tell you if your research question is too broad or too narrow. Most novice writers begin with research questions that are overly broad. If your question is so broad that there are thousands of books and articles participating in the scholarly conversation, it's a good idea for you to focus your question so that you are asking something more specific. If, on the other hand, you are asking a research question that is so obscure that you cannot find a corresponding scholarly conversation, you will want to broaden the scope of your project by asking a slightly less specific question.

Keep in mind the metaphor of a conversation. If you walk into a room and people are talking about globalization and language, it would be out of place for you to begin immediately by making a huge, vague claim, like, "New technology affects the way that people speak to each other around the world." It would be equally out of place for you to begin immediately by making an overly specific claim, like, "social media usage in Doha is a strong indicator of Facebook's growing strength in Qatar." Rather, you would gauge the scope of the conversation and figure out what seems like a reasonable contribution.

Your contribution to the conversation, at this point, will likely be a focused research question. This is the question you take with you to the library. In the next section, we discuss how best to make use of the library. Later, we explore how to turn your research question into an argument for your essay.

Your Campus Library

You have probably used libraries all your life, checking out books from your local public library and studying in your high school library. The difference between your previous library experiences and your college library experience is one of scale. Your college library has more stuff. It might be real stuff like books, journals, and videos, or it could be virtual stuff, like online articles, e-books, and streaming video. Your library pays a lot of money every year to buy or license content for you to use for your research. By extension, your tuition dollars are buying a lot of really good research material. Resorting to Google and Wikipedia means you are not getting all you can out of your college experience.

Not only will your college library have a much larger collection, but it will have a more up-to-date and relevant collection than your high school or community public library. Academic librarians spend considerable time acquiring research materials based on classes being taught at your institution. You might not know it, but librarians carefully monitor what courses are being taught each year and are constantly trying to find research materials appropriate to those courses and your professor's research interests. In many cases, you will find that the librarians will know about your assignment and will already have ideas about the types of sources that will make you most successful.

Get To Know Your Librarians! The most important thing to know during the research process is that there are people to help you. Although you might not yet be in the habit of going to the library, there are still many ways in which librarians and library staff can be helpful. Most libraries now have an e-mail or chat service set up so you can ask questions without even setting foot in a library. No question is too basic or too specific. It's a librarian's job to help you find answers, and all questions are welcome. The librarian can even help you discover the right question to ask given the task you are trying to complete.

Help can also come in the form of consultations. Librarians will often make appointments to meet one-on-one with students to offer in-depth help on a research paper or project. Chances are you will find a link on your library website for scheduling a consultation.

Among the many questions fielded by reference librarians, three stand out as the most often asked. Because librarians hear these questions with such regularity, we suggest that students ask these questions when they begin their research. You can go to the library and ask these questions in person, or you can ask vie e-mail or online chat.

How Do I Find a Book Relevant to My Topic?

The answer to this question will vary from place to place, but the thing to remember is that finding a book can be either a physical process or a virtual process. Your library will have books on shelves somewhere, and the complexity of how those shelves are organized and accessed depends on factors of size, number of libraries, and the system of organization your library uses. You will find books by using your library's online catalog and carefully noting the call number and location of a book.

Your library is also increasingly likely to offer electronic books or e-books. These books are discoverable in your library's online catalog as well. When looking at the location of a book you will frequently see a link for e-book versions. You will not find an e-book in every search, but when you do the advantage is that e-book content is searchable, making your job of finding relevant material in the book easier.

If you find one book on your topic, use it as a jumping-off point for finding more books or articles on that topic. Most books will have bibliographies either at the end of each chapter or the end of the book in which the author has compiled all the sources used. Consult these bibliographies to find other materials on your topic. You can also return to the book's listing in your library's online catalog. Once you find the listing, look carefully at the record for links to subjects, topics, or similar sources. For instance, in the Northwestern Michigan College library catalog, individual listings include the following links: "Find more by this author," "Find more on this topic," and "Nearby items on shelf."

What Sources Can I Use as Evidence in My Paper?

There are many types of resources out there to use as you orchestrate a scholarly conversation and support your paper's argument. Books, which we discussed earlier, are great sources if you can find them on your topic, but often your research question will be something that is either too new or too specific for a book to cover.

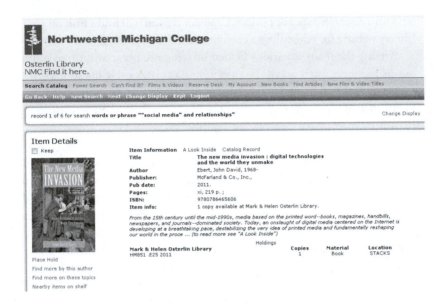

Online catalog Library catalog search for books about social media.

Books are very good for historical questions and overviews of large topics. For current topics, you will want to explore articles from magazines, journals, and newspapers.

Magazines or periodicals (you will hear these terms interchangeably) are published on a weekly or monthly schedule and contain articles of popular interest. These sources can cover broad topics like the news in magazines such as *Harper's, Time,* and *U.S. News and World Report.* They can also be more focused for particular groups like farmers (e.g., *Dairy Farmer*) or photographers (e.g., *Creative Photography*). Articles in magazines or periodicals are by professional writers who might or might not be experts. Magazines typically are not considered scholarly and generally do not contain articles with bibliographies, endnotes, or footnotes. This does not mean they are not good sources for your research. In fact, there could be very good reasons to use a magazine article to help support your argument. Magazines capture the point of view of a particular group on a subject, like how farmers feel about increased globalization of food production. This point of view might offer support for your claim or an opposing viewpoint to counter. Additionally, magazines can also highlight aspects of a topic at a particular point in time. Comparing a *Harper's* article from 1989 on Japan and globalization to an article on the same topic in 2009 allows you to draw conclusions about the changing relationship between the United States and Japan over that 20-year period.

Journals are intended for a scholarly audience of researchers, specialists, or students of a particular field. Journals such as *Globalization and Health, Modern Language Journal,* or *Anthropological Linguistics* are all examples of scholarly journals focused on a particular field or research topic. You might hear the term "peer-reviewed" or "referred" in reference to scholarly journals. This means that the articles contained in a journal have been reviewed by a group of scholars in the same field before the article is published in the journal. This ensures that that the research has been vetted by a group of peers before it is published. Articles from scholarly journals can help provide some authority to your argument. By citing experts in a field you are bolstering your argument and entering into the scholarly conversation we talked about at the beginning of this guide.

Newspaper articles are found in newspapers that are generally published daily. There is a broad range of content in newspapers ranging from articles written by staff reporters, to editorials written by scholars, experts, and general readers, to reviews and commentary written by experts. Newspapers are published more frequently and locally than magazines or journals, making them excellent sources for very recent topics and events as well as those with regional significance. Newspaper articles can provide you with a point of view from a particular part of the country or world (e.g., how do Americans feel about social media vs. the Chinese), or a strong opinion on a topic from an expert (e.g., a school psychologist writing an editorial on the effects of Facebook bullying on adolescents).

A good argument uses evidence from a variety of sources. Do not assume you have done a good job if your paper only cites newspaper articles. You need a broad range of sources to fill out your argument. Your instructor will provide you with guidelines about the number of sources you need, but it will be up to you to find a variety of sources. Finding two to three sources in each of these categories will help you begin to build a strong argument.

Where Should I Look for Articles on My Topic?   The best way to locate journal, magazine, or newspaper articles is to use a database. A database is an online resource that organizes research material of a particular type or content area. For example, PsycINFO is a psychology database where you would look for journal articles (as well as other kinds of sources) in the discipline of psychology. Your library licenses or subscribes to databases on your behalf. Finding the right database for your topic will depend on what is available at your college or university because every institution has a different set of resources. Many libraries will provide subject or research guides that can help you determine what database would be best for your topic. Look for these guides on your library website, which will have a way to search databases. Look for a section of the library website on databases, and look for a search box in that section. For instance, if you type "language" in a database search box, you might find that your library licenses a database called *MLA International Bibliography* (Modern Language Association). A search for "history" in the database search box might yield *American History and Life* or *Historical Abstracts*. In most instances, your best bet is to ask a librarian which database or databases are most relevant to your research.

When using these databases that your library provides for you, you will know that you are starting to sufficiently narrow or broaden your topic when you begin to retrieve 30 to 50 sources during a search. This kind of narrow result field will rarely occur in Google, which is one of the reasons why using library databases is preferable to Google when doing academic research. Databases will help you determine when you have begun to ask a manageable question.

When you have gotten down to between 30 and 50 sources in your result list, begin to look through those results to see what aspects of your topic is being written about. Are there lots of articles on social media, bullying, and adolescents? If so, that might be a topic worth investigating because there is a lot of information for you to read. This is where you begin to discover where your voice might add to the ongoing conversation on the topic.

Using Evidence

The quality of evidence and how you deploy the evidence is ultimately what will make your claims persuasive. You might think of evidence as that which will help prove your claim. But if you look at any scholarly book or article you'll see that evidence can be used in a number of different ways. Evidence can be used to provide readers with crucial background information. It can be used to tell readers what scholars have commonly thought about a topic (although you might disagree). It can offer a theory that you use as a lens. It can offer a methodology or an approach that you would like to use. And finally, evidence can be used to back up the claim that you'll be making in your paper.

Novice researchers begin with a thesis and try to find all the evidence that will prove that their claim is valid or true. What if you come across evidence that doesn't help with the validity of your claim? A novice researcher might decide not to take this complicating evidence into account. Indeed, when you come across complicating evidence, you might be tempted to pretend you never saw it! But rather than sweeping imperfect evidence under the rug, you should figure out how to use this evidence to complicate your own ideas.

The best scholarly conversations take into account a wide array of evidence, carefully considering all sides of a topic. As you probably know, often the most fruitful and productive conversations occur not just when you are talking to people who already agree with you, but when you are fully engaging with the people who might disagree with you.

Coming across unexpected, surprising, and contradictory evidence, then, is a good thing! It will force you to make a complex, nuanced argument and will ultimately allow you to write a more persuasive paper.

Other Forms of Evidence

We've talked about finding evidence in books, magazines, journals, and newspapers. Here are a few other kinds of evidence you might want to use.

Interviews   Interviews can be a powerful form of evidence, especially if the person you are interviewing is an expert in the field that you're investigating. Interviewing can be intimidating, but it might help to know that many people (even experts!) will feel flattered when you ask them for an interview. Most scholars are deeply interested in spreading knowledge, so you should feel comfortable asking a scholar for his or her ideas. Even if the scholar doesn't know the specific answer to your question, he or she might be able to point you in the right direction.

Remember, of course, to be as courteous as possible when you are planning to interview someone. This means sending a polite e-mail that fully introduces yourself and your project before you begin asking questions. E-mail interviews might be convenient, but an in-person interview is best, because this allows for you and the interviewee to engage in a conversation that might take surprising and helpful turns.

It's a good idea to write down a number of questions before the interview. Make sure not just to get facts (which you can likely get somewhere else). Ask the interviewee to speculate about your topic. Remember that "why" and "how" questions often yield more interesting answers than "what" questions.

If you do conduct an in-person interview, act professionally. Be on time, dress respectfully, and show sincere interest and gratitude. Bring something to record the interview. Many reporters still use pens and a pad, as these feel unobtrusive and are very portable.

Write down the interviewee's name, the date, and the location of the interview, and have your list of questions ready. Don't be afraid, of course, to veer from your questions. The best questions might be the follow-up questions that couldn't have occurred to you before the conversation began. You're likely to get the interviewee to talk freely and openly if you show real intellectual curiosity. If you're not a fast writer, it's certainly OK to ask the interviewee to pause for a moment while you take notes. Some people like to record their interviews. Just make sure that you ask permission if you choose to do this. It's always nice to send a brief thank-you note or e-mail after the interview. This would be a good time to ask any brief follow-up questions.

Images   Because we live in a visual age, we tend to take images for granted. We see them in magazines, on TV, and on the Internet. We don't often think about them as critically as we think about words on a page. Yet, a critical look at an image can uncover helpful evidence for a claim. Use a Google Image search or flickr.com to find images using the same keywords you used to find books and articles. Ask your instructor for guidance on how to properly cite and acknowledge the source of any images you wish to use. If you want to present your research outside of a classroom project (e.g., publish it on a blog or share it at a community event), ask a research librarian for guidance on avoiding any potential copyright violations.

Multimedia   Like images, multimedia such as video, audio, and animations are increasingly easy to find on the Internet and can strengthen your claim. For instance, if you are working on globalization and language you could find audio or video news clips illustrating the effects of globalization on local languages. There are several audio and video search engines available such as Vimeo (vimeo.com) or Blinkx (blinkx.com), a search engine featuring audio and video from the BBC, Reuters, and the Associated

Press, among others. As with images, ask your instructor for guidance on how to properly cite and acknowledge the source of any multimedia you wish to use. If you want to present your research outside of a classroom project (e.g., publish it on a blog or share it at a community event), ask a research librarian for guidance on avoiding any potential copyright violations.

Evaluating Sources   A common problem in research isn't a lack of sources, but an overload of information. Information is more accessible than ever. How many times have you done an online search and asked yourself the question, "How do I know what is good information?" Librarians can help. Evaluating online sources is more challenging than traditional sources because it is harder to make distinctions between good and bad online information than with print sources. It is easy to tell that *Time* magazine is not as scholarly as an academic journal, but online everything might look the same. There are markers of credibility and authoritativeness when it comes to online information, and you can start to recognize them. We'll provide a few tips here, but be sure to ask a librarian or your professor for more guidance whenever you're uncertain about the reliability of a source.

1. **Domain** The "domain" of a site is the last part of its URL. The domain indicates the type of website. Noting the web address can tell you a lot. A .edu site indicates that an educational organization created that content. This is no guarantee that the information is accurate, but it does suggest less bias than a .com site, which will be commercial in nature with a motive to sell you something, including ideas.

2. **Date** Most websites include a date somewhere on the page. This date could indicate a copyright date, the date something was posted, or the date the site was last updated. These dates tell you when the content on the site was last changed or reviewed. Older sites might be outdated or contain information that is no longer relevant.

3. **Author or editor** Does the online content indicate an author or editor? Like print materials, authority comes from the creator of the content. It is now easier than ever to investigate an author's credentials. A general Google search might lead you to a Wikipedia entry on the author, a LinkedIn page, or even an online resume. If an author is affiliated with an educational institution, try visiting the institution's website for more information.

Managing Sources

Now that you've found sources, you need to think about how you are going to keep track of the sources and prepare the bibliography that will accompany your paper. Managing your sources is called "bibliographic citation management," and you will sometimes see references to bibliographic citation management on your library's website. Don't let this complicated phrase deter you—managing your citations from the start of your research will make your life much easier during the research process and especially the night before your paper is due when you are compiling your bibliography.

EndNote and RefWorks   Chances are your college library provides software, such as *EndNote* or *RefWorks,* to help you manage citations. These are two commercially available citation management software packages that are not freely available to you unless your library has paid for a license. *EndNote* or *RefWorks* enable you to organize your sources in personal libraries. These libraries help you manage your sources and create bibliographies. Both *EndNote* and *RefWorks* also enable you to insert endnotes and footnotes directly into a Microsoft Word document.

Zotero   If your library does not provide *EndNote* or *RefWorks,* a freely available software called *Zotero* (Zotero.org) will help you manage your sources. *Zotero* helps you collect, organize, cite, and share your sources and it lives right in your web browser where you do your research. As you are searching *Google,* your library catalog, or library database, *Zotero* enables you to add a book, article, or website to a personal library with one click. As you add items to your library, *Zotero* collects both the information you need for your bibliography and any full-text content. This means that the content of journal articles and e-books will be available to you right from your *Zotero* library.

To create a bibliography, simply select the items from your *Zotero* library you want to include, right-click and select Create Bibliography from Selected Items . . . , and choose the citation style your instructor has asked you to use for the paper. To get started, go to Zotero.org and download *Zotero* for the browser of your choice.

Taking Notes   It is crucial that you take good, careful notes while you are doing your research. Not only is careful note taking necessary to avoid plagiarism, but it can also help you think through your project while you are doing research.

Many researchers used to take notes on index cards, but most people now use computers. If you're using your computer, open a new document for each source that you're considering using. The first step in taking notes is to make sure that you gather all the information you might need in your bibliography or works cited. If you're taking notes from a book, for instance, you'll need the author, the title, the place of publication, the publisher, and the year. Be sure to check the style guide assigned by your instructor to make sure you're gathering all the necessary information.

After you've recorded the bibliographic information, add one or two keywords that can help you sort this source. Next, write a one- or two-sentence summary of the source. Finally, have a section in your document that is reserved for specific places in the text that you might want to work with. When you write down a quote, remember to be extra careful that you are capturing the quote exactly as it is written—and that you enclose the quote in quotation marks. Do not use abbreviations or change the punctuation. Remember, too, to write down the exact page numbers from the source you are quoting. Being careful with small details at the beginning of your project can save you a lot of time in the long run.

WRITING ABOUT CULTURE

In your writing, as in your conversations, you should always be thinking about your audience. Although your most obvious audience is the instructor, most college instructors will want you to write a paper that will be interesting and illuminating for other beginning scholars in the field. Many students are unsure of what kind of knowledge they can presume of their audience. A good rule of thumb is to write not only for your instructor but also for other students in your class and for other students in classes similar to yours. You can assume a reasonably informed audience that is curious but also skeptical.

Of course it is crucial that you keep your instructor in mind. After all, your instructor will be giving you feedback and evaluating your paper. The best way to keep your instructor in mind while you are writing is to periodically reread the assignment while you are writing. Are you answering the assignment's prompt? Are you adhering to the assignment's guidelines? Are you fulfilling the assignment's purpose? If your answer to any of these questions is uncertain, it's a good idea to ask the instructor.

From Research Question to Thesis Statement

Many students like to begin the writing process by writing an introduction. Novice writers often use an early draft of their introduction to guide the shape of their paper. Experienced scholars, however, continually return to their introduction, reshaping it and revising it as their thoughts evolve. After all, because writing is thinking, it is impossible to anticipate the full thoughts of your paper before you have written it. Many writers, in fact, only realize the actual argument they are making after they have written a draft or two of the paper. Make sure not to let your introduction trap your thinking. Think of your introduction as a guide that will help your readers down the path of discovery—a path you can only fully know after you have written your paper.

A strong introduction will welcome readers to the scholarly conversation. You'll introduce your central interlocutors and pose the question or problem that you are all interested in resolving. Most introductions contain a thesis statement, which is a sentence or two that clearly states the main argument. Some introductions, you'll notice, do not contain the argument, but merely contain the promise of a resolution to the intellectual problem.

Is Your Thesis an Argument?

So far, we've discussed a number of steps for you to take when you begin to write a research paper. We started by strategizing about ways to use presearch to find a topic and ask a researchable question, then we looked at ways to find a scholarly conversation by using your library's resources. Now we discuss a crucial step in the writing process: coming up with a thesis.

Your thesis is the central claim of your paper—the main point that you'd like to argue. You could make a number of claims throughout the paper; when you make a claim, you are offering a small argument, usually about a piece of evidence that you've found. Your thesis is your governing claim, the central argument of the whole paper. Sometimes it is difficult to know if you have written a proper thesis. Ask yourself, "Can a reasonable person disagree with my thesis statement?" If the answer is no, then you likely you have written an observation rather than an argument. For instance, the statement, "There are six official languages of the UN" is not a thesis, because this is a true fact. A reasonable person cannot disagree with this fact, so it is not an argument. The statement, "Arabic became an official language of the UN for economic reasons" is a thesis, because it is a debatable point. A reasonable person might disagree (by arguing, for instance, that "Arabic became an official language of the UN for political reasons"). Remember to keep returning to your thesis statement while you are writing. Not only will you be thus able to make sure that your writing remains on a clear path, but you'll also be able to keep refining your thesis so that it becomes clearer and more precise.

Make sure, too, that your thesis is a point of persuasion rather than one of belief or taste. "Chinese food tastes delicious" is certainly an argument you could make to your friend, but it is not an adequate thesis for an academic paper, because there is no evidence that you could provide that might persuade a reader who doesn't already agree with you.

Organization

For your paper to feel organized, readers should know where they are headed and have a reasonable idea of how they are going to get there. An introduction will offer a strong sense of organization if it:

- introduces your central intellectual problem and explains why it is important.
- suggests who will be involved in the scholarly conversation.
- indicates what kind of evidence you'll be investigating.
- offers a precise central argument.

Some readers describe well-organized papers as having a sense of flow. When readers praise a sense of flow, they mean that the argument moves easily from one sentence to the next and from one paragraph to the next. This allows your reader to follow your thoughts easily. When you begin writing a sentence, try using an idea, keyword, or phrase from the end of the previous sentence. The next sentence, then, will appear to have emerged smoothly from the previous sentence. This tip is especially important when you move between paragraphs. The beginning of a paragraph should feel like it has a clear relationship to the end of the previous paragraph.

Keep in mind, too, a sense of wholeness. A strong paragraph has a sense of flow and a sense of wholeness: not only will you allow your reader to trace your thoughts smoothly, but you will ensure that your reader understands how all your thoughts are connected to a large, central idea. Ask yourself this question as you write a paragraph: What does this paragraph have to do with the central intellectual problem that I am investigating? If the relationship isn't clear to you, then your readers will likely be confused.

Novice writers often use the form of a five-paragraph essay. In this form, each paragraph offers an example that proves the validity of the central claim. The five-paragraph essay might have worked in high school, as it meets the minimum requirement for making an argument with evidence. You'll quickly notice, though, that experienced writers do not use the five-paragraph essay. Indeed, your college instructors will expect you to move beyond the five-paragraph essay. This is because a five-paragraph essay relies on static examples rather than fully engaging new evidence. A strong essay will grow in complexity and nuance as the writer brings in new evidence. Rather than thinking of an essay as something that offers many examples to back up the same static idea, think of an essay as the evolution of an idea that grows ever more complex and rich as the writer engages with scholars who view the idea from various angles.

Integrating Your Research

As we have seen, doing research involves finding an intellectual community by looking for scholars who are thinking through similar problems and might be in conversation with one another. When you write your paper, you will not merely be reporting what you found; you will be orchestrating the conversation that your research has uncovered. To orchestrate a conversation involves asking a few key questions: Whose voices should be most prominent? What is the relationship between one scholar's ideas and another scholar's ideas? How do these ideas contribute to the argument that your own paper is making? Is it important that your readers hear the exact words of the conversation, or can you give them the main ideas and important points of the conversation in your own words? Your answers to these questions will determine how you go about integrating your research into your paper.

Using evidence is a way of gaining authority. Even though you might not have known much about your topic before you started researching, the way you use evidence in your paper will allow you to establish a voice that is authoritative and trustworthy. You have three basic choices to decide how best you'd like to present the information from a source: summarize, paraphrase, or quote. Let's discuss each one briefly.

Summary   You should summarize a source when the source provides helpful background information for your research. Summaries do not make strong evidence, but they can be helpful if you need to chart the intellectual terrain of your project. Summaries can be an efficient way of capturing the main ideas of a source. Remember, when you are summarizing, to be fully sympathetic to the writer's point of view. Put yourself in the scholar's shoes.

If you later disagree with the scholar's methods or conclusions, your disagreement will be convincing because your reader will know that you have given the scholar a fair hearing. A summary that is clearly biased is not only inaccurate and ethically suspect; it will make your writing less convincing because readers will be suspicious of your rigor.

Let's say you come across the following quote that you'd like to summarize. Here's an excerpt from *The Language Wars: A History of Proper English*, by Henry Hitchings:

> No language has spread as widely as English, and it continues to spread. Internationally the desire to learn it is insatiable. In the twenty-first century the world is becoming more urban and more middle class, and the adoption of English is a symptom of this, for increasingly English serves as the lingua franca of business and popular culture. It is dominant or at least very prominent in other areas such as shipping, diplomacy, computing, medicine and education. (300)

Consider this summary:

> In *The Language Wars*, Hitchings says that everyone wants to learn English because it is the best language in the world (300). I agree that English is the best.

If you compare this summary to what Hitchings actually said, you will see that this summary is a biased, distorted version of the actual quote. Hitchings did not make a universal claim about whether English is better or worse than other languages. Rather, he made a claim about why English is becoming so widespread in an increasingly connected world.

Now let's look at another summary:

> According to Hitchings, English has become the go-to choice for global communications and has spread quickly as the language of commerce and ideas (300).

This is a much stronger summary than the previous example. The writer shortens Hitchings's original language, but she is fair to the writer's original meaning and intent.

Paraphrase Paraphrasing involves putting a source's ideas into your own words. It's a good idea to paraphrase if you think you can state the idea more clearly or more directly than the original source does. Remember that if you paraphrase you need to put the entire idea into your own words. It is not enough for you to change one or two words. Indeed, if you only change a few words, you could put yourself at risk of plagiarizing.

Let's look at how we might paraphrase the Hitchings quote that we've been discussing. Consider this paraphrase:

> Internationally the desire to learn English is insatiable. In today's society, the world is becoming wealthier and more urban, and the use of English is a symptom of this (Hitchings 300).

You will notice that the writer simply replaced some of Hitchings's original language with synonyms. Even with the parenthetical citation, this is unacceptable paraphrasing. Indeed, this is a form of plagiarism, because the writer suggests that the language is his or her own, when it is in fact an only slightly modified version of Hitchings's own phrasing.

Let's see how we might paraphrase Hitchings in an academically honest way.

> Because English is used so frequently in global communications, many people around the world want to learn English as they become members of the middle class (Hitchings 300).

Here the writer has taken Hitchings's message but has used his or her own language to describe what Hitchings originally wrote. The writer offers Hitchings's ideas with fresh syntax and new vocabulary, and the writer is sure to give Hitchings credit for the idea in a parenthetical citation.

Quotation The best way to show that you are in conversation with scholars is to quote them. Quoting involves capturing the exact wording and punctuation of a passage. Quotations make for powerful evidence, especially in humanities papers. If you come across evidence that you think will be helpful in your project, you should quote it. You might be tempted to quote only those passages that seem to agree with the claim that you are working with. But remember to write down the quotes of scholars who might not seem to agree with you. These are precisely the thoughts that will help you build a powerful scholarly conversation. Working with fresh ideas that you might not agree with can help you revise your claim to make it even more persuasive, as it will force you to take into account potential counterarguments. When your readers see that you are grappling with an intellectual problem from all sides and that you are giving all interlocutors a fair voice, they are more likely to be persuaded by your argument.

To make sure that you are properly integrating your sources into your paper, remember the acronym ICE: introduce, cite, and explain. Let's imagine that you've found an idea that you'd like to incorporate into your paper. We'll use a quote from David Harvey's *A Brief History of Neoliberalism* as an example. On page 7, you find the following quote that you'd like to use: "The assumption that individual freedoms are guaranteed by freedom of the market and of trade is a cardinal feature of neoliberal thinking, and it has long dominated the U.S. stance towards the rest of the world."

1. The first thing you need to do is **introduce** the quote ("introduce" gives us the "I" in ICE). To introduce a quote, provide context so that your readers know where it is coming from, and you must integrate the quote into your own sentence. Here are some examples of how you might do this:

   > In his book *A Brief History of Neoliberalism*, David Harvey writes . . .
   > One expert on the relationship between economics and politics claims . . .
   > Professor of Anthropology David Harvey explains that . . .
   > In a recent book by Harvey, he contends . . .

   Notice that each of these introduces the quote in such a way that readers are likely to recognize it as an authoritative source.

2. The next step is to **cite** the quote (the C in ICE). Here is where you indicate the origin of the quotation so that your readers can easily look up the original source. Citing is a two-step process that varies slightly depending on the citation style that you're using. We offer an example using MLA style. The first step involves indicating the author and page number in the body of your essay. Here is an example of a parenthetical citation which gives the author and page number after the quote and before the period that ends the sentence:

> One expert on the relationship between economics and politics claims that neoliberal thinking has "long dominated the U.S. stance towards the rest of the world" (Harvey 7).

Note that if it is already clear to readers which author you're quoting, you need only to give the page number:

> In *A Brief History of Neoliberalism,* David Harvey contends that neoliberal thinking has "long dominated the U.S. stance towards the rest of the world" (7).

The second step of citing the quote is providing proper information in the works cited or bibliography of your paper. This list should include the complete bibliographical information of all the sources you have cited. An essay that includes the quote by David Harvey should also include the following entry in the Works Cited:

> Harvey, David. *A Brief History of Neoliberalism.* New York: Oxford UP, 2005. Print.

3. Finally, the most crucial part of integrating a quote is **explaining** it. The E in ICE is often overlooked, but a strong explanation is the most important step to involve yourself in the scholarly conversation. Here is where you will explain how you interpret the source you are citing, what aspect of the quote is most important for your readers to understand, and how the source pertains to your own project. For example:

> David Harvey writes, "The assumption that individual freedoms are guaranteed by freedom of the market and of trade is a cardinal feature of neoliberal thinking, and it has long dominated the U.S. stance towards the rest of the world" (7). As Harvey explains, neoliberalism suggests that free markets do not limit personal freedom but actually lead to free individuals.

Or:

> David Harvey writes, "The assumption that individual freedoms are guaranteed by freedom of the market and of trade is a cardinal feature of neoliberal thinking, and it has long dominated the U.S. stance towards the rest of

the world" (7). For Harvey, before we understand the role of the United States in global politics, we must first understand the philosophy that binds personal freedom with market freedom.

Novice writers are sometimes tempted to end a paragraph with a quote that they feel is especially compelling or clear. But remember that you should never leave a quote to speak for itself (even if you love it). After all, as the orchestrator of this scholarly conversation, you need to make sure that readers are receiving exactly what you'd like them to receive from each quote. Notice, in the preceding examples, that the first explanation suggests that the writer quoting Harvey is centrally concerned with neoliberal philosophy, whereas the second explanation suggests that the writer is centrally concerned with United States politics. The explanation, in other words, is the crucial link between your source and the main idea of your paper.

Avoiding Plagiarism

Scholarly conversations are what drive knowledge in the world. Scholars using each other's ideas in open, honest ways form the bedrock of our intellectual communities and ensure that our contributions to the world of thought are important. It is crucial, then, that all writers do their part in maintaining the integrity and trustworthiness of scholarly conversations. It is crucial that you never claim someone else's ideas as your own, and that you always are extra-careful to give the proper credit to someone else's thoughts. This is what we call responsible scholarship.

The best way to avoid plagiarism is to plan ahead and keep track with careful notes as you read your sources. Remember the advice (above) on *Zotero* and taking notes: Find the way that works best for you to keep track of what ideas are your own and what ideas come directly from the sources you are reading. Most acts of plagiarism are accidental. It is easy when you are drafting a paper to lose track of where a quote or idea came from; plan ahead and this won't happen. Here are a few tips for making sure that confusion doesn't happen to you.

1. Know what needs to be cited. You do not need to cite what is considered common knowledge such as facts (the day Lincoln was born), concepts (the earth orbits the sun), or events (the day Martin Luther King was shot). You do need to cite the ideas and words of others from the sources you are using in your paper.

2. Be conservative. If you are not sure if you should cite something, either ask your instructor or a librarian, or cite it. It is better to cite something you don't have to than not cite something you should.

3. Direct quotations from your sources need to be cited as well as anytime you paraphrase the ideas or words from your sources.

4. Finally, extensive citation not only helps you avoid plagiarism, but it also boosts your credibility and enables your reader to trace your scholarship.

Citation Styles

It is crucial that you adhere to the standards of a single citation style when you write your paper. The most common styles are MLA (Modern Language Association, generally used in the humanities), APA (American Psychological Association, generally used in the social sciences), and Chicago (*Chicago Manual of Style*). If you're not sure which style you should use, you must ask your instructor. Each style has its own guidelines regarding the format of the paper. Although proper formatting within a given style might seem arbitrary, there are important reasons behind the guidelines of each style. For instance, whereas MLA citations tend to emphasize author's names, APA citations tend to emphasize the date of publications. This distinction makes sense, especially given that MLA standards are usually followed by departments in the humanities and APA standards are usually followed by departments in the social sciences.

There are a number of helpful guidebooks that will tell you all the rules you need to know to follow the standards for various citation styles. If your instructor hasn't pointed you to a specific guidebook, try the following online resources:

Purdue Online Writing Lab: owl.english.purdue.edu/

Internet Public Library: www.ipl.org/div/farq/netciteFARQ.html

Modern Language Association (for MLA style): www.mla.org/style

American Psychological Association (for APA style): www.apastyle.org/

The Chicago Manual of Style Online: www.chicagomanualofstyle.org/tools_citationguide.html

For an example of a researched argument about the impact of social media on relationships that uses MLA citation style, see Steven Krause's essay "Living Within Social Networks" in Chapter 4.

credits

Chapter 1:
Page 2 from Newsweek, October 20, 2011, © 2011 The Newsweek/Daily Beast Company LLC. All rights reserved. Used by permission and protected by the copyright laws of the United States. The printing, copying, redistribution, or retransmission of this Content without express written permission is prohibited.

Page 6 from "Why Americans Won't Do Dirty Jobs" by Elizabeth Dwoskin, reprinted from the Nov. 9, 2011 issue of Bloomberg Businessweek by permission. Copyright © 2011 Bloomberg L.P.

Page 15 by Julie Hanus, originally published in the Utne Reader (March/April 2008).

Page 19 from "I Go On Running" by Patricia Ann Mcnair.

Page 24 from "In the Valley of the Shadow of Debt" by Jason Storms.

Page 28 from Ross Perlin.

Page 31 by Christian Williams, originally published in the Utne Reader (July/August 2012).

Page 34 reprinted from The American Scholar, Volume 78, No. 3, Summer 2009. Copyright © 2009 by the author.

Chapter 2:
Page 45 reprinted by permission of Sara Davis.

Page 49 from Center for Engagement and Community Development, Kansas State University.

Page 54 from Fast Company, January 3, 2011 © 2011 Mansueto Ventures LLC. Used by permission and protected by the copyright laws of the United States. The printing, copying, redistribution, or retransmission of this Content without express written permission is prohibited.

Page 58 from Foreign policy by CARNEGIE ENDOWMENT FOR INTERNATIONAL PEACE; NATIONAL AFFAIRS, INC Reproduced with permission of CARNEGIE ENDOWMENT FOR INTERNATIONAL PEACE, ETC.] in the format Republish in a book via Copyright Clearance Center.

Page 61 from Drew Harwell—Tampa Bay Times.

Page 67 from Newsweek, October 30, 2011, © 2011 The Newsweek/Daily Beast Company LLC. All rights reserved. Used by permission and protected by the copyright laws of the United States. The printing, copying, redistribution, or retransmission of this Content without express written permission is prohibited.

Page 79 from © Copyright Fredrik deBoer 2011. Originally published in The New Inquiry.

Page 87 from "Sparks Will Fly" by Damien Walter, first published at aeonmagazine.com. Reprinted by permission of the author.

Chapter 3:
Page 100 reprinted by permission of Julie Traves.

Page 108 from Copyright 2011 Smithsonian Institution. Reprinted with permission from Smithsonian Enterprises. All rights reserved. Reproduction in any medium is strictly prohibited without permission from Smithsonian Institution.

Page 113 from Foreign Policy by CARNEGIE ENDOWMENT FOR INTERNATIONAL PEACE; NATIONAL AFFAIRS, INC Reproduced with permission of CARNEGIE ENDOWMENT FOR INTERNATIONAL PEACE, ETC.] in the format Republish in a book via Copyright Clearance Center.

Page 116 from "Thoughts on a Word: Fine" by Autumn Whitefield-Madrano in The Beheld/The New Inquiry, 10/4/12.

Page 120 from Foreign Policy by CARNEGIE ENDOWMENT FOR INTERNATIONAL PEACE; NATIONAL AFFAIRS, INC Reproduced with permission of CARNEGIE ENDOWMENT FOR INTERNATIONAL PEACE, ETC.] in the format Republish in a book via Copyright Clearance Center.

Page 129 from © The Economist Newspaper Limited, London.

Page 135 from "Art and Buddhism: Looking for What's True" by Fleda Brown.

Chapter 4:
Page 143 reprinted by permission of the Harvard Business Review.

Page 146 from "Living Within Social Networks" by Steven D. Krause.

Page 151 from "Lying, Cheating, and Virtual Relationships" by Cynthia Jones, published in Global Virtue Ethics Review, Vol. 6, No. 1. Reprinted by permission.

Page 161 first appeared in The Morning News.

Photo Gallery I © Benjamin Busch.

Page 165 Material reprinted with the express permission of: National Post, a division of Postmedia Network Inc.

Page 169 reprinted with permission of Roger Scruton.

Page 183 from Copyright 2011 by James Gleick.

Chapter 5:
Page 198 from Pacific standard by Miller-McCune Center for Research, Media, and Public Policy Reproduced with permission of Miller-McCune Center for Research, Media and Public Policy in the format Republish in a book via Copyright Clearance Center.

Page 202 reprinted by permission of Cristina Black.

Page 205 from "Undocumented Immigrants" by Doug LaForest.

Page 210 from "Despite the Controversy, We're Glad We Asked" by S. Alan Ray from The Chronicle of Higher Education. Reprinted by permission of the author. Copyright © 2011 by S. Alan Ray.

Page 214 reprinted with permission.

Page 218 reprinted by permission of Leila Ahmed.

Chapter 6:
Page 226 from The New Republic, Oct. 30, 2012.

Page 229 from © 2011 The Atlantic Media Co., as first published in The Atlantic Magazine. All rights reserved. Distributed by Tribune Media Services.

Page 234 reprinted by permission of Stefan Babich.

Page 239 reprinted by permission of Amanda Marcotte.

Page 242 first appeared in the October 2011 issue of Prospect Magazine. www.prospect-magazine.co.uk.

Chapter 7:
Page 252 from FROM A WOODEN CANOE SUNDANCE © 1999 by Jerry Dennis. Reprinted by permission of St. Martin's Press. All Rights Reserved.

Page 257 reprinted by permission of Ice Cube Press.

Page 264 first appeared in The London Review of Books.

Page 269 from Copyright 2011, Robert Moor. Originally published in N + 1.

Page 277 from Copyright © 2011, 2013 by Rob Dunn. Originally published by Scientific American.

Page 281 from Copyright David P. Barash.

Page 288 reprinted by permission of the authors Michael Shellenberger and Ted Nordhaus.

Chapter 8:
Page 300 reprinted with permission from the November 4, 2011 issue of The Nation. For subscription information, call 1-800-333-8536. Portions of each week's Nation magazine can be accessed at http://www.thenation.com.

Page 310 from "When Bankers Rule the World" by David Korten, at http://www.yesmagazine.org/blogs/david-korten/when-bankers-rule-the-world.

Page 315 from Chicago Reader, January 11, 2011 © 2011 Sun-Times Media. All rights reserved. Used by permission and protected by the copyright laws of the United States. The printing, copying, redistribution, or retransmission of this Content without express written permission is prohibited.

Page 318 by Starhawk Copyright 2012.

Page 322 from Newsweek, July 24, 2012, © 2011 The Newsweek/Daily Beast Company LLC. All rights reserved. Used by permission and protected by the copyright laws of the United States. The printing, copying, redistribution, or retransmission of this Content without express written permission is prohibited.

Page 326 from "Letter from Governor Janice Brewer to President Barack Obama."

Page 332 from "The Illogical World of U.S. Immigration" by Katelyn Langdale.

index